Islamic Psychology Around the Globe

بسم الله الرحمن الرحيم

# ISLAMIC PSYCHOLOGY AROUND THE GLOBE

EDITED BY

Amber Haque and Abdallah Rothman

This book first published 2021
International Association of Islamic Psychology Publishing
Seattle, Washington, USA


All proceeds of this book go to the IAIP Fazal Haque Scholarship Fund. Reprint and translation of the text in any form will carry the same conditions.

DEDICATION

The first editor would like to dedicate this book to his deceased parents
Syed Fazal and Safia Haque
May the contribution of my efforts increase their ranks in Jannah!

•

Both editors dedicate this book to the loving memory of
Professor Dr. Malik Badri
The founder of modern Islamic Psychology

# Contents

# Foreword

THE THOUGHTFUL AND evidence-based integration of religion, spirituality, and psychology during the past century has been a rather bumpy ride. Although several of psychology's founding influencers were very interested and encouraging about this area of both research and clinical practice (e.g., William James) others were certainly not (e.g., John Watson, Albert Ellis, Sigmund Freud). Psychology has been mostly a proudly secular field with the majority of psychologists being generally dismissive of religion and spirituality and with too many perceiving these interests and engagement as a sign of psychopathology. Thankfully, a sizeable minority of psychologists, who are both skilled researchers and outstanding clinicians, have bucked this trend and have conducted high quality research and offered evidence based clinical practice approaches to the integration of religion, spirituality, and psychology. In fact, the division of the American Psychological Association that highlights these particular interests (i.e., Division 36, the Society for the Psychology of Religion and Spirituality) has about 1,000 diverse members from across the globe. They also offer a fast growing and prestigious peer reviewed professional journal, *Psychology of Religion and Spirituality*, published by the American Psychological Association. Other related professional journals published by the American Psychological Association, such as *Spirituality in Clinical Practice*, have also been expanding rapidly too.

While there is much good news to report on the explosion of interest in the integration of religion, spirituality, and psychology, we still have a very long way to go. One problem is that the majority of research and practice work thus far has highlighted some, but not all, of the major wisdom and faith traditions. Much research and practice guidelines have emerged from the Christian tradition and more specifically from the Protestant and evangelical branches of the Christian faith tradition. Certainly, research and practice has been offered from the other

Christian branches such as Roman Catholic and Mormon traditions, but the majority of work produced thus far is from the Christian, broadly defined, perspective. However, in most recent years, research and practice highlighting mindfulness (emerging from the Buddhist tradition) and yoga (from the Hindu traditions) have exploded. Mindfulness based stress reduction, and other mindfulness associated research and practice, have taken the research and clinical practice communities by storm.

While it is certainly good news to see more interest in these areas of integration and acceptance of religion, spirituality, and psychology, we need to be much more attentive to the religious and wisdom traditions that have not received the kind of attention that Christian, mindfulness, and yoga influences have enjoyed. This volume, *Islamic Psychology from Around the Globe,* is a huge and critically important contribution in that it provides a state-of-the-art, evidence based, and global perspective on the integration of Islam and psychology. This book is like a cool drink of water on a very hot day as it is much needed and much appreciated, especially now. While Christianity is the largest religion in the world, Islam is right behind it in terms of growing numbers of people across the planet who consider themselves Muslims. Not only do we need to hear from Islamic scholars and practitioners in psychology but we also need to collaboratively work closer together to find common areas of interest in research and clinical practice. The people of the world, who typically take their religious and spiritual identities, beliefs, and practices very seriously, need well-informed religiously minded psychologists, among related researchers and practitioners, to find smart ways to use the great insights and practices from these faith and wisdom traditions in order to understand and serve people better from across the globe. I, for one, am grateful for the contribution of this important edited book project and hope that it will get wide readership, use, and perhaps that it will also stimulate future research and practice in Islamic psychology as well as collaboration with others of good will and interest in this field. We are all greatly enriched by this work regardless of our religious affiliation or identity.

I am reminded of a popular book published in 2007 by the British scholar, Karen Armstrong, entitled, *The Great Transformation: The Beginning of our Religious Traditions.* In it, she traces the beginning and the development of the great faith and wisdom traditions that emerged during the Axial Age (i.e., Judaism, Christianity, Islam, Buddhism, and Hinduism). While she concludes that all of the traditions have had their moments of struggle and even atrocities they all, at their best, are seeking compassion and a world of peace. In our terribly troubled world that often feels hopeless and apocalyptic, our faith traditions have an opportunity to make the world better, more peaceful, compassionate, sacred, humane, and just. This book offers those of us in psychology hope that our Islamic brothers and sisters, who are outstanding scholars and practitioners in psychology, will add their important and much needed voices and expertise to this better world vision for everyone. May it be so... and soon.

THOMAS G. PLANTE, PHD, ABPP
Santa Clara University, Stanford University School of Medicine
Editor, *Spirituality in Clinical Practice*(APA Journal)
February 1, 2021

# Acknowledgments

THERE ARE A growing number of books on Islamic Psychology (IP) but none that cover the IP scenario internationally in one volume. This is what the book editors planned to do in early 2020 and got the writers from across the globe to contribute their chapters to the present volume. This book's funding came from the Fazal Haque Scholarship Fund created for IAIP in 2018 by the first editor in memory of his loving father. A limited amount of the profit from book sales will go back into the scholarship fund to cover copy editing and the publication charges.

The editors wish to acknowledge the enormous contributions of our deceased colleague and mentor, Professor Malik Badri, who guided many of us to think critically about psychology and helped bring us back into the fold of Islamic Psychology. May Allah (SWT) raise his status in Jannah in sha Allah.

We want to sincerely acknowledge each author's contributions to this volume starting from Australia to Western Continental Europe. The chapters in this book are listed alphabetically, so the author names appear based on the countries they represent. Hanan Dover (Australia), Aid Smajic and Selvira Draganovic (Bosnia and Herzegovina), Khalid Elzamzamy, Roaa Moustafa Ahmed, Walid Hassan and Mohamed El-Mahdi, (Egypt), Akbar Hussain (India), Diana Setiawati and Bagus Riyono (Indonesia), Hamid Rafiei Honar and Masood Azarbayejani (Iran), Saleh bin Ibrahim Al-Sanie (Kingdom of Saudi Arabia), Alizi Alias (Malaysia), Salisu Shehu (Nigeria), Tamkeen Saleem and Muhammad Tahir Khalily (Pakistan), Jibril I.M. Handuleh, Abdikani Askar and Abdilahi E. Momin (Somalia), Juraida Latif and Shaakirah D. Boda (South Africa), Ahmed Shannan (Sudan), Suleyman Derin and Taha B. Toprak (Turkey), Rasjid Skinner (UK), Carrie York Al Karam (USA), and Paul M. Kaplick, Amin Loucif, and Ibrahim Ruschoff (Western Europe).

Our special thanks to Thomas G. Plante, Professor at Santa Clara and Stanford University, and Editor of the APA Journal of Spirituality in Clinical Practice, for writing the very generous foreword. We also want to thank the book endorsers, Professor Emeritus Tan Sri Dato' Dzulkifli Abdul Razak, Rector of the International Islamic University Malaysia, and Professor Dr. Recep Senturk, President of the Ibn Haldun University, Istanbul, Turkey. Your endorsements mean a lot to us.

Finally, we acknowledge the works of Raabia Haque, editorial assistant and Abdallateef Whiteman, typsetter and the book cover designer. It is only the sincerity and hard work of everyone involved in this project and primarily the chapter authors that brought this work to fruition.

The editors are deeply grateful to all of you!

AMBER HAQUE AND ABDALLAH ROTHMAN
*Book Editors*

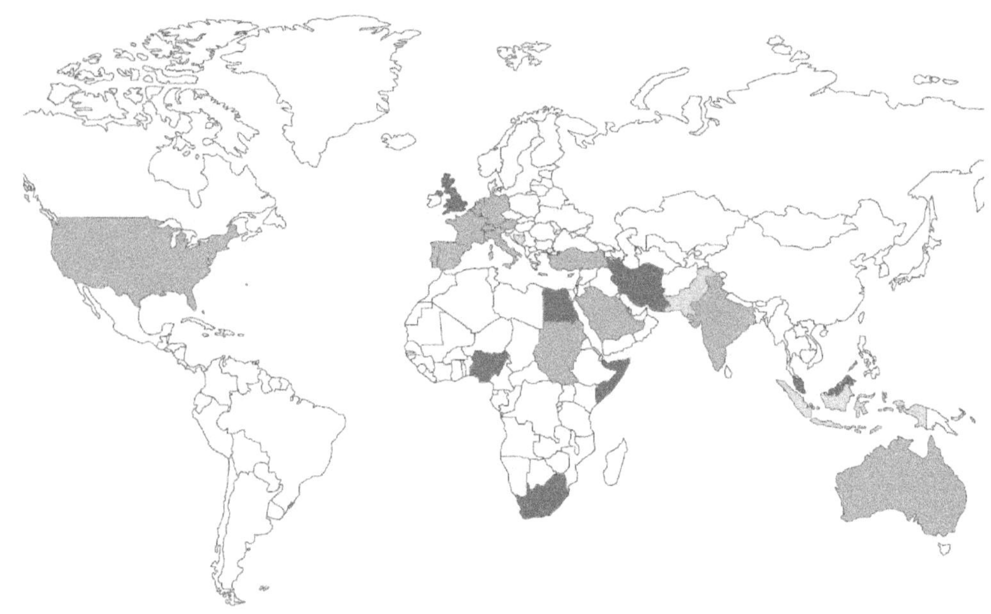

Islamic Psychology Around the Globe

# Introduction to Islamic Psychology Around the Globe

ABDALLAH ROTHMAN
AMBER HAQUE

ISLAMIC PSYCHOLOGY (IP) has become a popular topic among contemporary Muslims. The term has been used increasingly often in publications, lectures, conferences, and community forums. For many people, this term, and the area of inquiry that it references, is new and unfamiliar, as it has not been a widespread topic of discussion in mainstream Muslim communities until recently. This has led to the misconception that it is a new discipline arising out of intellectual discourse from Muslim academics and professionals in Western countries. As you will read in the chapters that follow in this book, the field of IP, which today is still considered an emerging field, had long been in development before it was recognized as a distinct discipline. This development has taken place, at times intentionally and systematically, and at times organically, across the globe as people have come to recognize the insights the Islamic tradition has to offer to our understanding of the human being.

The common question that arises when people are first introduced to the term 'Islamic psychology' is, "What is that?" For many, it is not obvious what is meant by the term, and indeed there is confusion, debate, and disagreement about what it is and what it is not. The primary confusion comes from the assumption of what is meant by the word 'psychology'. The word psychology has become synonymous with the academic and professional field as it is studied in universities, and as it is defined and practiced in Western institutions such as the American Psychological Association and the British Psychological Society. This field traces its inception back to 1854 in Leipzig, Germany, when Gustav Fechner developed the first theory of experimental discoveries of human behavior, and later in 1879, more formally, when Wilhelm Wundt established the first laboratory dedicated to psychological research. This historical narrative defines psychology as a science, and to this day the field is defined as "the scientific study of behavior and mental processes". However, the term psychology and what it previously referenced was considered a branch of philosophy, as the etymology of the Greek roots of the word means the 'study of the soul'.

Centuries before the designation of psychology as a science that studies human behavior and mental processes, philosophers understood it as the study of the soul, which was concerned with ontology, cosmology, and existential questions of the nature of the human being. Muslim scholars going back to the 9th century wrote about *ilm an nafs* (the study or science of the soul, in Arabic), which was informed by their knowledge and understanding of the Qur'an and Sunnah. There was no need to refer to *ilm an nafs islami* (IP) because it was implied that they were operating from within an Islamic perspective, or worldview, which informed their definition of the science and/or study of the soul. Thus, in the more recent advent of the term 'Islamic psychology', the addition of the word 'Islamic' before the word 'psychology' signifies the Islamic worldview within which the study of the soul is being approached. This is important because it distinguishes it from the way in which the term psychology has been used since the early 19th century, and the assumption that it refers to the experimental and scientific study of behavior, mental processes, and sometimes even the neuroscience of the brain, from a mostly secular perspective. Therefore, the term IP refers to the study and understanding of the soul (which includes the mind, heart, self, and spirit) as informed by the Qur'an, Sunnah, and works of early Muslim scholars. This is how the International Association of Islamic Psychology defines the term, and how we refer to it throughout this book.

An important distinction to make, which is often a point of confusion in reference to the term IP, is that it is expressly different to what is often termed 'Islamization of knowledge'. Again, while different meanings can be attached to this terminology, one strand of the Islamization of knowledge movement is seen as a retroactive attempt to reframe bodies of knowledge or academic disciplines using the perspective and terminology from the Islamic tradition. In the case of psychology, what this can amount to is the acceptance of the secular, scientific definition, and understanding of psychology as it has been used since the 19th century, and as is still to this day defined by the mainstream academic discipline, with Islamic concepts and terms adapted to, and mapped onto, this otherwise secular framework for understanding the human being. There is a line of research and practice like this within the field of psychology which had received much more attention and focus in the literature until recently.

This has culminated in what is often referred to as 'Muslim Mental Health', the application of mainstream behavioral health perspectives and services with Muslim-identifying populations. This is a useful and important movement and a welcome development, as it involves an effort to encourage Muslims to utilize much-needed mental health services where a majority of people in Muslim communities have historically been apprehensive about availing such services due to cultural stigma. The difference between IP and Muslim mental health or Muslim psychology is that IP starts from the assumptions about human nature and the soul as defined by an Islamic paradigm, versus approaches that start with the assumptions of psychology as defined by the Western scientific discipline.

The development of IP as a recognized field has been interwoven with the development of Muslim Mental Health and Muslim Psychology and, therefore, has inevitable overlaps and a shared history with these other developments. The fact that it is difficult to make clear delineations between these developments has a lot to do with the cultural complexities in the interface of the secular academy within the Muslim world. Whereas Muslims have a rich history of an Islamic intellectual heritage which has contributed to universally recognized discoveries in medicine, astronomy, philosophy, and many other fields, including psychology, contemporary Muslims in majority Muslim countries tend to value the ideas and perspectives imported from the West over their own Islamic heritage. Among other layers of circumstances which are the cause of this, the phenomenon is no doubt partly an effect of colonialism, since not only were Muslim lands conquered by the West, but also Muslim hearts and minds. The result of this has been a largely wholesale adoption of the secular Western point of view, particularly in terms of professionalism and the desire for people in majority Muslim countries to be seen as legitimate in the increasingly globalized, capitalist, and secular definitions of success and worth.

The point in history where it can be conceivably argued that IP began to emerge as a distinct field was a direct result of a backlash to this overarching tendency for Muslims to adopt Western, secular, colonized knowledge. This movement within the field of psychology was spearheaded by many individuals who recognized the need for a uniquely Islamic perspective of psychology, but who for the most part remained insular within their own language group, country, or region. Professor Dr. Malik Badri was the first psychologist to receive international attention for speaking out against the blind following of the secular paradigm of the study of the human being among Muslim academics and scientists. As a Sudanese, Arabic-speaking Muslim, who had trained within the Western academy of psychology, he recognized the problematic dichotomy between his own faith and worldview that his Islamic upbringing and education had taught him, and his professional career, which essentially required him to deny or reject the underlying philosophical assumptions of his religious beliefs. At the time, in the 1960s, in the early stages of his career, the field of psychology was dominated by Freudian theory, which had an inherently negative view of religion and essentially rejected the notion of God as a legitimate factor in the reality of the human psyche. Badri began to develop his ideas, not around the rejection of the Western paradigm of psychology, but the embracing of an inherently Islamic paradigm of psychology found in the Islamic tradition. As you will read in the following chapters of this book, there were other scholars around the same time, and before Dr. Badri, who developed similar ideas and who wrote extensively about IP in other languages, such as, Muhammad 'Uthman Nagati (1914–2000) and Muhammad Qutb (1919–2014), both from Egypt who wrote in Arabic, as well as others who wrote in Farsi, Malay, Turkish, Urdu, and so on. However, Dr. Badri's Western academic training in the UK, his ability to read and write in English, and his extensive travels and international career, allowed for his work to have a greater, widespread exposure throughout the world, which lead to his global impact and influence in developing the field.

In his first public lecture, at the University of Jordan in 1963, Dr. Badri addressed the problem of adopting a Western framework for Muslim patients and practitioners. The Muslim psychologists attending the lecture were outraged at his assertions and argued that psychology is a pure science and has no place for religion. He continued to be met with resistance and anger from his psychologist colleagues in the Muslim world, who were threatened by what they saw as a regression from the advances made by Muslims seen as legitimate and accepted academics in the idealized Western academy. Meanwhile, developments in the field of psychology in the West, with the decline of Freudian analysis and the advent of cognitive therapies, began to see a return to the acceptance of belief and philosophy in psychology. This paved the way for Dr. Badri's message for a unique paradigm of psychology from an Islamic perspective to begin to be appreciated, a full decade after his first lecture in Jordan. Ironically, it was in the West, in the United States, where his ideas were first embraced, when he gave a lecture titled "Muslim Psychologists in the Lizard's Hole" at the annual conference of the Association of Islamic Social Scientists in Indianapolis. The reception of that lecture prompted the expansion of the conference paper into the publication of the book *The Dilemma of Muslim Psychologists* in 1979. This was the real turning point for the development of IP as a field.

Since then, Dr. Badri's message began to find a receptive audience among Muslim psychologists, but it would not be for almost another 40 years from that late-1970s lecture in Indianapolis that IP would find a momentum among the American Muslim community. Much of the development from that point on took place primarily in the Muslim world, as Dr. Badri continued to write and teach on Islamic perspectives of psychology and psychotherapy. In the early 1990s, Professor Badri joined the International Islamic University in Malaysia (IIUM) and began teaching and developing courses on IP. At a conference held at IIUM in 1997, the Islam and psychology movement saw its next milestone, as there was an increased enthusiasm for the integration of Islam within the discipline of psychology. These advancements in Malaysia arose out of a growing movement in the Islamization of knowledge. Thus, while much advancement were made and progress was seen in the Muslim world in its adoption and acceptance of a view of religion within psychology, these advancements were primarily in the integration of Islamic principles within an otherwise secular paradigm of psychology, and not the overtly Islamic paradigm which Professor Badri had been calling for all along. During this time, the International Association of Muslim Psychologists (IAMP) was formed, with Professor Badri as its first president, and several conferences were held around the Muslim world, in Sudan, Indonesia, and Malaysia, among others. Most of this work focused on cultural adaptations of psychological practice in working with Muslim populations.

During the ensuing period, in the early 2000s, the field gradually leaned more towards the development of an Islamic paradigm of psychology, but the distinction between Muslim psychology or Islamized psychology and IP was still a gray area. An increasing number of papers, as well as books written in English, including some published outside of the United States, began to emerge, and the body of literature grew to a recognizable field in and of itself, in what Kaplick and Skinner (2017) called an "Islam and Psychology Movement". Haque etal.'s (2016) review article of research trends in the preceding decade reported five major themes in the literature on the integration of the Islamic tradition in modern psychology:(1) Unification of Western psychological models with Islamic beliefs and practices; (2) Research on historical accounts of IP and its rebirth in the modern era; (3) Development of theoretical models and frameworks within IP; (4) Development of interventions and techniques within IP; and (5) Development of assessment tools and scales normalized for use by Muslims. While the two areas found to have had the least development in the research were themes 3 and 4, what soon followed was an outpouring of literature from 2017 onwards. In the years that immediately followed Haque et al.'s (2016) article, several research articles emerged in the area of theme number 3 – the development of theoretical models and frameworks within IP (e.g., Keshavarzi& Khan, 2018; Rothman & Coyle, 2018), and in the last year up until the writing of this book, there has been more work done in the area of theme 4 –the development of interventions and techniques within IP (e.g., Keshavarzi et al., 2020; Rothman, 2021; Rothman & Coyle, 2020).

With the increase in research on IP, this recent surge in the awareness of, and interest in, the emerging field culminated in the forming of the International Association of Islamic Psychology (IAIP) in 2017. Dr. Badri founded the IAIP as the next step and final stage for Muslim psychologists, in what he termed "the stage of emancipation" (Badri, 1979). His vision for the IAIP was to finally stand firm on an Islamic paradigm and to build a comprehensive theory and practice for IP that is grounded in the ontological assumptions and lessons from the Qur'an and Sunnah. The association aims to be a platform for the development of that work, and a unifying vehicle for the global Islamic psychology movement, in order to galvanize and grow the field into a full-fledged discipline. This includes the development of research, the dissemination of publications, the training of practitioners, and the certification of practitioners and institutions. The focus internationally is important as it stands to provide a regulatory body for setting standards in the field to ensure that theory and practice are grounded in the knowledge and teachings from the Islamic tradition and involves the participation of the *ulama* (Islamic scholars) together with clinicians. As you will read in the chapters that follow, Professor Badri is referenced as the catalyst for the developments in several of the countries represented, even those he has never visited. His work has had an impact that has reverberated throughout the entire world and brought attention to the discourse on Islam and psychology, and which has seen numerous contributions from Muslim scholars from diverse countries and helped to give rise to the global development of IP.

## Personal Journeys of the Editors and How They Fit into the Development of IP

We want to share our stories about what brought us to this point of editing a book on IP around the globe. We were both trained in Western psychology and were both fortunate enough to work closely with Professor Malik Badri at different points in his career and in the development of the field of IP. What follows is a brief account from each of us giving context and background to where we came into the story of the global IP movement and what brought us each to that point.

### AMBER'S STORY

I did my undergraduate degree with a distinction in psychology in 1978 at Patna University (PU), India, and entered their master's program, but did not complete it because I migrated to the US in 1981. PU is the seventh oldest university in India and the third in establishing the psychology department in 1946 before the British left India. When the British arrived in India, they had a policy of funding only European-style education on its territories to produce a class of intelligentsia "who would be brown in color but English in their thinking" (Misra & Paranjpe, 2012). Academic psychology was transplanted in India from the West, and this happened in other countries as well. India always had its own brand of spiritual psychology that had influenced William James and his ideas of higher states of consciousness, leading him to write his book, *The Varieties of Religious Experience* (Taylor, 1988).

PU had some heavyweights in psychology, and almost allwere trained in the UK. Durganand Sinha, a graduate of PU, studied at Cambridge and was the first Indian psychologist to question the domination of Western concepts and theories. He published his article on paradigmatic limitations of mainstream psychology in the *Journal of Humanistic Psychology* (Sinha, 1965), was a founding member of the International Association of Cross-Cultural Psychology and established the *Journal of Psychology and Developing Societies*. After 1947, some psychologists from India migrated to Pakistan with their zeal for indigenous psychology, prominent among whom were Muhammad Ajmal and Syed Azhar Ali Rizvi. Ajmal linked mainstream psychology to spirituality in 1968, and Rizvi introduced the first Muslim psychology course in Government College, Lahore, in 1978.

I did not experience the indigenization of psychology movement back home because I had already left for the US and had joined the clinical psychology master's program at Eastern Michigan University. My professor, Dennis Delprato, called himself an inter-behaviorist and was not only opposed to the Freudian school of psychology, but also challenged behaviorism. Dennis believed in developmental history and field determinants of behavior, espoused by J.R. Kantor, who considered behaviorism reductionistic and simplistic and inseparable from mentalism.

Being in the clinical program, I was pulled between a psychoanalytic and behavioral approach and ended up in the latter camp for its objectivity over psychoanalysis. A year later, while doing my field internship in Detroit (1982), I came across Badri's book, *The Dilemma of Muslim Psychologists*, in a local Muslim bookstore. Having the germ of Eastern thinking and Islamic upbringing, I was drawn to Badri's thoughts. At about the same time, B.F. Skinner was invited to give a keynote address at the Applied Behavior Analysis Convention in Wisconsin (1983). I sought Dennis's assistance in writing to Skinner for a possible interview on both inter-behaviorism and ideas of religion in psychology.

Dennis prepared a few questions about inter-behavioral psychology, and I prepared questions on psychology and religion, and wrote to Skinner while he was at Harvard University. Skinner replied to say that he had eleven different commitments at the convention, but he would talk to me about my queries on both topics if he could find the time to do so. I met Skinner in Milwaukee, in his hotel room, and he answered all my questions that had lasting effects on me as a psychologist.

On the issue of dualism and mentalism, Skinner said,

> "The issue is not dualism; that was a great mistake. The question is whether behavior originates inside the individual or is retraceable to prior events and personal experiences. The question of the origination of behavior is parallel with Darwin's problem of the creation of the world and the version that somebody made it. The origin of behavior is parallel with the origination of species, and to account for behavior, one must look at what has happened to the individual. The behavior does not originate in anything."

Skinner's stance on religion was very clear when he said,

> "All cultures have *invented* Gods as someone usually as a father, a ruler, or a king. My wife and I have raised our children in a non-religious way, and as far as I know, they are highly moral people doing good in the world."

Skinner firmly believed that the Middle East conflict is a religious war and that religion does not serve peace.

The morning after my interview, Skinner arrived on the conference podium wearing a bishop's collar to give his keynote address. It made the audience laugh and while I was impressed by Skinner's politeness towards me during the interview, I was embarrassed by his gesture of mocking religion openly.

A few years later, I was a doctoral student at Western Michigan University, where we had the pioneers of Applied Behavior Analysis. My professors read Skinner's interview and one of the professors posted parts of Skinner's views on the bulletin board outside his office. Everyone was excited to read Skinner's views, but I was uncomfortable in an environment where religion had no place. At least, that was the way I felt it to be. I questioned my decision to study a discipline where religion is ridiculed but persisted in my studies to graduate from the program. I practiced behavior modification techniques with my clients in the institutions where I worked in the US, and the patients often asked me about spirituality. That was when I took a deeper interest in studying psychology and religion and moved to Malaysia in 1996 to teach psychology at the International Islamic University Malaysia (IIUM). Religion was then a taboo topic in psychology, almost everywhere.

The scenario at IIUM was different in terms of what was taught because the institution was the hub of the Islamization of knowledge, a movement started by Al-Faruqi in the United States and Syed Naqib Al-Attas in Malaysia. I was among people who tried to recast knowledge from the Tauhidic paradigm. Two books that greatly influenced me were *Crisis in the Muslim Mind* by Abdulhameed Abu Sulaiman, IIUM Rector, and *A Young Muslim's Guide to the Modern World* by Sayyed Hussain Nasr. My perspective on psychology changed, and from the very first year I was there, I started writing on psychology from Islamic perspectives (e.g., Haque, 1996, 1998). I also remained involved at IIUM in organizing national and international conferences on topics related to IP.

Incidentally, there was some interest shown by a group of Muslim psychology students from the University of Western Sydney (UWS), Australia, to learn about IP. The head of psychology program at UWS (now WSU) invited Malik Badri and me on a five-day visit to Sydney to talk about IP. Badri had worked in my department (I was department chair then) but assigned to ISTAC as a research professor. Badri and I again went to Sudan the following year for another IP conference.

My interest in IP continued to grow and, as department chair, I had to ensure that Islamic perspectives were incorporated into all psychology courses. This was a University requirement. I developed and taught an IP course to master's students between 2002 and 2004, which resulted in a paper on the contributions of early Muslim scholars to psychology (Haque, 2004). However, in 2004, I moved to the UAE, but working in a Gulf country was a different story. All my colleagues were Arabs, but unfamiliar with IP. It reminded me of what Badri had once said that Muslim psychologists are often more ardent supporters of secular psychology than Westerners, and if IP was to take root and become a formal discipline, it would most likely be spearheaded by Western psychologists who revert to Islam. Hooman Keshavarzi and I came in contact soon after he established the Khalil Center in 2010 and we published two papers on theoretical and practical approaches in therapy from Islamic perspectives (Haque & Keshavarzi, 2014; Keshavarzi & Haque, 2013).

Abdallah Rothman contacted me when I lived in the UAE, and he wanted to study IP at my university. Since we did not have any IP courses, he went for his doctorate to the UK. This is when I first met Abdallah and saw a great deal of enthusiasm in him for IP. I thanked Allah for bringing in younger people who could help to advance the field. After a few years, Badri moved to Istanbul Zaim University in Turkey and established the International Association of Islamic Psychology (IAIP), with Abdallah as its CEO. The scenario at IIUM had changed because the zeal for nationalization had taken over, and many international scholars had left for other countries.

### ABDALLAH'S STORY

My own journey into IP started well before I embraced Islam. While I would not come to identify as a Muslim, nor recognize my calling as "Islamic Psychology" until I was 29 years old, it was in my early teens that my journey along this path began. I was born into a family who were not religious, but were oriented in the helping professions, and particularly in psychology. My grandfather, Leonard Schneider, was a pioneer in the development of humanistic psychology, studying directly under Abraham Maslow, and later working as a close colleague with Fritz Perls. This humanistic approach, which makes room for the soul and insight from the world's wisdom traditions, therefore influenced my understanding of psychology from the beginning of my career. I recognized my calling in psychology only just before my grandfather passed away. In one of the last conversations I had with him, he told me he wished he had paid more attention to religion, as he came to recognize later in life that it had a lot to offer in our understanding of psychology. After he passed away in 1998, I spent time following his footsteps, at places like Esalen Institute and Tassajara in California, where he used to teach. I then began a more serious exploration of religion, based on his final words to me. I very much saw myself as following in the footsteps of my grandfather and continuing his legacy.

To me, psychology was never about the study of behavior or the brain, nor was it limited to cognitive dimensions of the human experience. My orientation to the field was very much rooted in the assumption that it was the study (ology) of the soul (psyche). Thus, I was naturally drawn to an interest in religion and spirituality, since these domains seemed to be more familiar with the realm of the soul, and had more to offer in this sense than did the mainstream field of psychology as was taught in most academic institutions. In fact, I attempted to study psychology as an undergraduate at the University of California Santa Cruz (1994), but could not bring myself to complete the major, after taking the only class that interested me, Psychology and Religion, and realizing that the remaining classes were concerned with a materialist view of the human being and, for some reason, seemed more focused on rats than humans.

My interest in psychology (the study of the soul) was then directed more towards an exploration of the world's religions and spiritual traditions. Parallel with my undergraduate studies, I took on my own dedicated self-study which involved reading any book I could lay my hands on that concerned the soul and spirituality, and traveling around the world. I studied Hinduism, yoga and pranayama breathing practices with a guru from India, lived with a Rastafarian elder in the hills of Jamaica, studied the Torah and tended sheep with a shepherd in the Holy Land, learned meditation from a Buddhist monk in the jungles of Thailand, and other traditions in my various adventures in spiritual exploration. I eventually returned to the academic study of psychology because I was still convinced of the usefulness of the field as an avenue for applying the study of the soul to helping people through their struggles in life. For this reason, rather than apply to a PhD program in psychology, all of which seemed to take a materialist view of the human being, I undertook a master's in psychology with a focus on mental health counseling, at Antioch University.

With my continual exploration of religion and spirituality, it was around the completion of my master's, in 2005, when I discovered Islam. I had been looking specifically into spiritual frameworks for healing and personal growth and was introduced to the practices of spiritual healing within the Islamic tradition. It was through this door, of a framework for the development of the soul, that I was introduced to Islam and how I came to eventually embrace it as my own spiritual path and religion. I studied Islam with a few shayukh in the US and then went to Sudan where I met a Sudanese shaykh who taught me about the inner depths of the deen and how the tradition of *ilm an nafs* is integral to the study of Islam. I was learning to integrate these concepts and practices within my clinical work at the very start of my career as a professional counselor. The shaykh I was studying with paired me up with one of his top students, who had been doing the work of integrating these concepts into clinical practice for many years, and wanted me to be mentored by him. It turned out that this person with whom the shaykh paired me was Dr. Malik Badri. At that point I had never heard of the term IP, nor had I heard of Malik Badri. I spent a week with Dr. Badri, attending conferences with him, listening to him speak, and traveling with him to his birthplace, Rufaa, an island on the Nile River. Little did I know that I had been blessed with the opportunity to be mentored by the father of IP.

Over the course of the following 15 years, I developed as a counseling psychologist in the US, traveling every year to Sudan to continue my study of Islam and learning to integrate IP into my clinical practice. I learned from the shaykh in Sudan how to access the heart, and the intricacies of *tazkiyat an nafs* (purification of the self), while learning from Dr. Badri how these traditional concepts and practices can be integrated into therapeutic approaches in counseling. I developed a relationship with Dr. Badri that began to feel as though he was a stand-in for my grandfather. It was as though he was taking off where my grandfather had left off, in guiding me to the integration of psychology and religion. In addition to this feeling of spiritual family, it turned out that Dr. Badri and I were in-laws twice over, through my wife's family in Sudan. We stayed in close contact over the years, spending time in Sudan together at family weddings and sitting at the feet of the shaykh, speaking over the phone about my clinical practice in the US, and visiting him when he moved to Turkey. I felt fortunate to have his guidance and to be ushered into the field of IP by such a giant of a man, and such a gentle soul.

Throughout our conversations about the development of the field, Dr. Badri and I spoke about the need for formalized training in IP for practitioners, and in 2008 we conceptualized the idea of an association. At that time, we called it the "American Islamic Psychology Association", since Dr. Badri had said it was more likely to be taken seriously and have legitimacy in the field of psychology if it was coming out of the US rather than the Muslim world, and I was living in the US at the time. It remained an idea as I focused on the development of my career and eventually decided to go back to my studies to get a PhD, with the intention of trying to establish more of a theoretical grounding in the development of IP and psychotherapy with the vision of training more practitioners in this field. I had moved to the UAE and was looking for a PhD program there when I discovered that Amber Haque was teaching at the United Arab Emirates University. I approached him to see if I could to a PhD there under him, but it turned out not to be a possibility, so I wound up doing my doctoral studies in the UK and asked Amber to be an external supervisor in partnership with my first supervisor, Adrian Coyle, at Kingston University London. From this point forward there was a great deal of momentum in the global development of the field of IP. Amber and I, along with Hooman Keshavarzi and Fahad Khan went on to write a review article (Haque et al., 2016) on the development of IP research over the previous ten years, and around the same time Dr. Badri and I, along with Professor Rasjid Skinner, went on to establish the IAIP. This feels like the beginning of what has become a rapid surge in the proliferation of IP around the world.

## How This Book Came About

Following the establishment of the IAIP, since 2017, we witnessed a noticeable wave of interest, particularly in the West, with a sudden surge of publications and conferences discussing IP. There was no longer a need to convince Muslims that this was acceptable or necessary, as experienced by Professor Malik in the early part of his career. He had laid the groundwork for this next phase. There appeared to be a collective consciousness of the utility and vastness of the possibility for viewing psychology and psychotherapy through an Islamic lens. This surge brought an entirely new generation and a new group of interested parties, most of whom had never before heard of IP. Within this context we often heard claims that IP was a "new" field, and that it was just now becoming recognized and developed in the West, among first- and second-generation Muslims in the United States, the United Kingdom, and Europe. This phenomenon gave the impetus and need for this book.

As discussed earlier, much of the early work in the development of IP was happening in various countries throughout the Muslim world, where IP conferences were taking place from the late-1990s. At the same time, many less obvious developments were taking place in parallel, either as an organic response to the need for such work or the inspiration that Muslims around the globe found in Dr. Badri's published works. Even in the West, IP work was happening earlier on, but went largely under the radar, without the awareness and attention from the larger Muslim community. Therefore, we wanted to highlight these early developments around the world to draw attention to the fact that IP had been emerging and developing well before this recent surge of popularity in the West. We also believe that we are at a crucial point in the history of the field where it is beginning to formalize as a distinct discipline, with the evolution of textbooks, academic courses, degrees, and organizations. Thus, the need to understand this history will be of the utmost importance and utility for prospective students of IP in the years to come. We understand and hope that this book will soon be out of date as IP continues to evolve. Yet we believe that this will not detract from the significance of the time period captured within the pages of this book, as the accounts from the chapter authors detail the foundational international developments in the emergence of IP as a recognized field.

How we chose the authors to contribute to this volume depended largely on personal contacts and our network of professional colleagues around the world. We sent out a call for Chapters, and authors from almost 20 countries agreed to submit a manuscript. However, some were unable to finalize their chapter due to lack of materials and/or a lack of a clear trajectory of what could actually be considered IP, versus Muslim psychology. The reality of this state of affairs within the global development of the field is such that each country has experienced a very different trajectory. Thus, the chapters in this book will look different from country to country, due to the varying degree to which IP has manifested, either explicitly within an academic or professional discipline, as opposed to that at a more grassroots level, without much literature or overt developments to reference. The criteria that we gave authors was to include only those activities and developments which specifically address an approach to psychology that is grounded in the ontological paradigm of the Islamic tradition, and not the developments of psychology more generally with Muslim populations in their countries. Following the chapter guidelines, each author in this book has shared where IP currently stands in their country today, the challenges faced, and prospects for the future.

## Chapter Descriptions

CHAPTER ONE sketches a brief history of IP as an emerging field in Australia. In 1996, the Federation of Australian Muslim Students and Youth invited Malik Badri to Sydney to discuss Raising Muslim Awareness in the Muslim Youth. The author considers this as the first serious discussion on introducing IP in academic projects and societal bodies. This was followed by the Psychology Department's support at the University of Western Sydney (UWS) for initial talks about IP projects for students of the Muslim faith. In 2002, the Department of Psychology at UWS (now WSU) partnered with the newly established Australian Society for Islamic Psychology (ASIP) and sponsored a conference in which they invited international speakers. The ASIP members initiated and formalized an IP interest group within the Australian Psychological Society (APS) in 2004 and changed the name in 2020 to the Islam and Psychology Group. In 2019, the Islamic Studies Research Academy (ISRA) proposed a new graduate certificate in IP that would benefit health professionals, community workers, chaplains, and others interested in working with Muslim clients. As the approval process from the local authorities can take almost three years, the outcome is still awaited. In 2020, ISRA also signed an MoU with the International Association of Muslim Psychologists (IAMP) to teach an IP course through Charles Strut University, to conduct mental health research from Islamic perspectives, and to organize a biannual conference on IP. More work is needed to introduce IP at the tertiary level.

CHAPTER TWO on Bosnia starts with a brief historical context of Islam and Muslims in that region and notes how communist rule influenced life, including religious and academic liberties. Social scientists' work, including psychology from an Islamic perspective, started merely three decades ago. The authors identify three groups responsible for IP development in the country, that is, Sufis, Muslim intellectuals, and Muslim psychologists/psychiatrists. Theologians' role is highlighted in different institutions in Bosnia that deal with topics of human nature, humans as the spiritual and psychological being, and incorporating such beliefs in all aspects of life. As far as Muslim psychologists are concerned, they do not use the term IP, but many are engaged in the Islamization of knowledge movement. These scholars helped translate some notable books on IP, while the psychiatrists published studies integrating spirituality and mental health. It is interesting to note that locally standardized tests were developed quickly, and some foreign tests have been translated. The authors lament about factors hampering IP development in Bosnia, including the need to connect local scholars and psychologists interested in IP, to promote IP in theological and academic circles, to network local psychologists with the international IP community, and to secure financial support.

CHAPTER THREE discusses how psychology in Egypt was influenced markedly by Western theories and developed significantly over the last century. IP has a relatively recent history here. The author classifies IP efforts at both organizational and individual levels. At the organizational level, conferences, periodicals, and associations started in the 1970s. A few important conferences include the Islamization of Knowledge conference organized by the IIIT in 1989, where a set of recommendations highlighted the need for IP as a discipline, and another conference on an Islamic orientation of the sciences in general, at Al Azhar in 1992. Many books were published, and websites were developed offering educational content to the public. The influence of IOK and IIIT is acknowledged, especially for their published work on psychological sciences in the Islamic heritage supervised by eleven Egyptian scholars, who surveyed, summarized, and annotated 400 treatises written by more than 100 Muslim scholars. However, IP has not found its way into mainstream university education. Various scholars offered ontological discourses; some also offered Sufi perspectives in understanding human nature. Usman Nagati (1914–2000) is seen as the forefather of IP with overarching intellectual contributions over the decades. The chapter highlights Nagati's contributions, depicting his views on key psychological principles derived from the Quran and Sunnah and his seven-step strategic plan for establishing IP as an independent discipline.

CHAPTER FOUR mentions that the foundations of IP in India were laid by the revered Islamic scholar Maulana Ashraf Ali Thanvi (1863–1943), who wrote more than 800 manuscripts related to his descriptions of the Qalb, Nafs, and Aql derived from the Quran and Sunnah. In addition to theorizing about the nature of the self, Thanvi taught his disciples ways to cleanse the nafs for spiritual enhancement. The chapter outlines Thanvi's therapeutic methods and objectives that are followed by many in the subcontinent. The author lists IP-relevant books published, and international conference(s) organized by the Institute of Objective Studies based in New Delhi and the Center for Study and Research based in Hyderabad. Notably, a large part of India's IP work is done at the Aligarh Muslim University (AMU) and headed by the author, whose works focus mainly on spirituality in mental health. Several empirical works are underway at AMU's psychophysiology lab. The author lists locally standardized psychological scales on taqwa, prayers, religious coping, Islamic personality, fitrah, spiritual practices, and so on. The University Grants Commission approved the course on Islamic Perspectives of Psychology in 2016. The author notes that to take IP seriously, the students should be introduced to the understanding of humans from Quranic perspectives and link it with contemporary issues of the modern world. He is optimistic that IP will expand its study, methods, and applications in the coming years.

CHAPTER FIVE on Indonesia starts with the history of psychology in the country and IP development from 1970 onwards. While a book on psychology and religion was written by Zakiya Darajat in 1970 and used in the universities, the book *The Dilemma of Muslim Psychologists* by Badri (1979) had a significant influence on students at Gadja Madah University, since they were already active in IP. In 1991, they started the Indonesian Muslim Psychology Students Organization and the *IP Journal* in 1992. The national symposiums were organized in the 1990s, followed by the establishment of foundations to promote IP in the country. The authors name a few books published in the 1970s and many published starting from the 1990s. The Indonesian Islamic Psychology Association (API) was formed in 2002, leading to the formal recognition of IP in most universities. IP study programs started in 2005, and by 2019, 20 universities had an IP curriculum. These programs led to research-based initiatives and focused on Islamic-based CBT. The authors recommend that IP's objectives be to focus on improving the development of mental health systems, family strengthening, IP in education and organizations, and crisis and disaster management.

CHAPTER SIX on Iran covers five major areas, including the fundamentals of the science of IP, the history of IP in Iran, an introduction to academics' and researchers' works in Iran, discussions on limitations, and the future of IP in Iran. The process of Islamization has both proponents and opponents with differing views on what constitutes IP. There is much discussion on the role of Qalb and Aql and the purpose of life, as explained by Iranian thinkers. The authors classify IP works in 20thcentury Iran in four stages: preparation, refinement, establishment, and comparison, resulting in the establishment of the IP Association in 2004 and introduction of courses in 2010. The authors agree that IP has faced the challenges of course titles, sources, methods, and professors, and to counter these challenges, the IPA organizes quarterly training courses. The chapter covers scientific associations, service centers, and IP professionals' networks in the country. While there are the challenges of methodology, secular psychology, and a gap between theory and practice in IP, there is also a severe communication gap with other Islamic countries to develop IP. Despite these challenges, the authors feel there are positive prospects for IP in Iran with the design of recent methodology models and methods of psychological understanding of religious texts.

CHAPTER SEVEN on KSA reviews what is termed the Islamic rooting movement in Saudi Arabia and points out that at least five different terminologies are simultaneously used to work on the same goal: (a) IP defined differently by three groups; (b) Islamization of knowledge including psychology proposed by Ismail Raji Al Faruqi and the efforts of this movement organized by the International Institute of Islamic Thought around the world; (c) Islamic guidance for psychology, a term used for academic courses in Saudi universities and the five principles on which it is based; (d) Islamic interpretation of behavior, also a term used in some universities for the courses they offer; and e) Islamic rooting of psychology used at Imam Muhammad bin Saud University. The author highlights that Islamic rooting does not contradict any scientific methodology or progress if these approaches do not contradict Islamic principles. The chapter lists the Islamic rooting of the primary goals for the disciplines of social sciences and elaborates on the various psychology department courses. The author concludes that Muslim psychologists must refer to Islamic sources in understanding human behavior, primarily the Quran and Sunnah, scientific wealth available in Muslim heritage books, and those of non-Muslims by reading the commentaries and criticisms on both. Although IP work started in the 1970s, the author laments that it did not take off with seriousness and hopes that sincere effort will promote IP in Saudi Arabia.

CHAPTER EIGHT on Malaysia divides the growth of IP into three eras, starting in the 1950s. The first book on IP was published in 1956, followed by other books in the following years until the 1980s. While the first era was more individual based, the second witnessed the establishment of IP programs in the institutions. The third era was when IIUM-trained students returned from their training abroad. The author mentions all prominent Malaysian and international scholars' names who contributed to IP development over the years. He opines that the topical-based books published from IIUM and UKM could pave the way for more student-friendly texts where Islamic perspectives can be embedded in every subtopic and sub-disciplines of psychology. The author recommends a crash course on how to teach IP, the translation of IP books from various languages into English, the development of theories and interventions addressing local Muslim cultures, and psychological tests that consider spiritual aspects. The author points out that IP in Malaysia has expanded to the non-academic sector and in the community.

CHAPTER NINE on Nigeria illustrates one thousand years of Islamic history in the African region that has shaped the culture and which has been further reinforced by the reformist movements' intellectual progress. The influence of local luminaries has resulted in hundreds of books and treatises and thousands of seminaries producing many high-caliber scholars. The Makkah World Conference on Education reinforced all this in 1977,as did the acceptance speech by the late Wazir Junaid of Sokoto at Ahmadu Bello University, who emphasized that while knowledge is universal, there is always a socio-cultural stamp on it that determines its worldview. Al-Faruqi's IOK movement and Badri's book *The Dilemma of Muslim Psychologists* only reinforced what was already in the making for social sciences. These writings inspired faculty members, mainly at Bayero University, in the Department of Education, who published books and articles on IP and taught courses at the university. The two main challenges for IP are a lack of confidence among psychology faculty researching Islamic perspectives because it is considered an area of Islamic scholars and there is also a lack of reference and teaching materials. However, the author believes that there is an increased awareness and interest of IP in the Nigerian faculty. The emergence of a new generation of intellectuals learned in the Quran and Hadith and integration of knowledge suggests a brighter future for IP in Nigeria.

CHAPTER TEN on Pakistan describes the transformative journey of a course on Muslim psychology to a comprehensive IP syllabus. While the authors point out some influential theologians and Sufis' names in the subcontinent, they focus on what has been done since Pakistan's independence. Muhammad Ajmal established psychology as an independent department in 1962 and viewed the discipline as interlinked with spirituality. His paper on the Introduction to Muslim Traditions in Psychotherapy was an impetus for developing the first Muslim psychology course in 1978. Ajmal's student, Syed Azhar Ali Rizvi, introduced this course at Government College Lahore. Rizvi also established the Society for Advancement of Muslim Psychology, which has been active since 1978. These initiatives led to research output in psychology and religion over the years and the formation of the Muslim psychology course at Peshawar University. In 2006, the Higher Education Commission (HCE) approved the Muslim psychology course, and it is now taught at the International Islamic University Islamabad (IIUI) as a core subject for PhD students. While the authors commend individual efforts over the years, they lament the lack of consensus on IP definition. They suggest that psychologists should work collaboratively with Islamic theologians to define and refine religious terminologies. The authors also outline IP at Riphah Institute of Clinical and Professional Psychology, Lahore, and the Center for Islamic Psychology, Islamabad.

CHAPTER ELEVEN on Somalia, introduces the Somali people, indicating that they carry their traditions on understanding human nature and mental health even internationally. The chapter is based on the authors' experiences working in the mental health field, claiming no previous written material on IP in Somalia. The authors indicate that there are professionals related to IP who have been working for the last three decades in academia and practice. It is essential to know that Somali society is traditional, and most people seek Islamic-based services. Although it is unclear what credentials the authors attributed to IP psychologists, they indicate six IP psychologists' practices in the wider Somali peninsula. However, there is no record of publications, conferences, associations, or think tanks in the Horn of Africa. The authors note how Somali Muslims have blended their tribal culture with Islamic interpretation, and that the people's first person of recourse for psychological disorders is usually an

Islamic sheik or clergy. Quran reading sessions have become a form of group therapy and offered by clergy not trained in psychology or counseling services. The authors underscore the value of IP in many areas and expect collaboration and training from IAIP and the creation of a Somali Islamic Psychology Association that will develop an IP code of practice in the country.

CHAPTER TWELVE on South Africa asserts that mainstream psychology has not met the needs of various groups of peoples from different religious, racial, and ethnic backgrounds, including Muslims. To fill this void, Muslim professionals and academics initiated the integration of Islamic traditions into the practice of psychology, but the term IP only became popular in the 2010s. After a brief history of the apartheid regime and how it affected different Muslim sects, the authors highlight the increased utilization of Islamic interpretations and integration of religion in Muslims' everyday lives. Realizing the injunctions from the Quran that believers are helpers of one another, various Muslim volunteer organizations have evolved over the years. Addressing the contributions in academia, the authors name essential organizations that have for many years contributed indirectly to IP by integrating religion in their counseling and mental health practices. The most exciting development was the establishment of the Islamic Careline, which was started in 1992 by three Muslim women and expanded to other parts of the country, assisting Muslim women in their communities. The establishment of the Ibn Sina Institute of Tibb offering diploma programs, undergraduate degrees, and Unani-Tibb medication are discussed. The work of some NGOs offering various services to the Muslim community are highlighted. The authors discuss their Islamic-oriented private practice and believe there is a desperate need for IP practitioners and training programs in the country.

CHAPTER THIRTEEN sketches the development of IP in Sudan with Malik Badri's return from his studies in the UK and some Arab Universities back to his home country of Sudan. Badri taught an Islam and Psychology course in the fourth year of college when students reviewed all previous psychology courses from an Islamic perspective. Although unfamiliar with the concept of IP at the time, the students liked this approach, and it opened the treasures of knowledge inherent in Islamic heritage. In 1979, Badri published his seminal book, The Dilemma of Muslim Psychologists, when he taught at the University of Khartoum and then continued to write other popular books on IP that left an indelible impact on the development of IP. Besides the important contributions of some other prominent scholars in Sudan, the chapter highlights IP syllabus contents, thesis and research samples, psychological measurements, and conferences. It also discusses the conceptual issues followed by the prospects of IP in the country.

CHAPTER FOURTEEN on Turkey points out that IP dates to the Ottoman State's last century (1865–1923). The interest in IP had subsided after Turkey became a republic, but from the early 2000s, there is renewed interest among mental health professionals and theologians. There is particular interest in the perspectives of Sufi traditions in Islam. The chapter outlines the contributions of prominent scholars to IP, some of whom are psychiatrists. Those from outside the clinical field also endeavor to form the theoretical background of IP and strengthen the university academic programs. Some associations like the Transpersonal Psychology Association, the Psychology in Islamic Thought Platform, Ibn Haldun University-Department of Psychology, and the Khalil Center in Turkey are currently active in promoting IP. Besides the regular symposiums and conferences, the radio and TV programs on Sufism and human psychology, books have also increased in recent years.

CHAPTER FIFTEEN on the UK takes us into the IP journey starting in the 1970s with clinicians' efforts. The mental health clinicians had begun to recognize that mainstream theories were inadequate for explaining clients' struggles, especially those of Muslims. The author narrates his shahada story from 1977 and the influence of notable Islamic scholars who described the meanings of key IP concepts that helped make sense of personal and clinical experiences, and which led to the understanding of the self and case formulation's conceptual framework. The author mentions how Malik Badri's book, *The Dilemma of Muslim Psychologists*, and Halim Salim Khan's book on *Islamic Medicine* influenced the author. The author developed and discussed his model of the self which helps diagnose the clients from an Islamic perspective. He narrates his experiences with many clinicians and organizations in addressing Muslims' mental health needs and sketches the individual contributions of different NGOs. In 2008, some psychologists met to design a short syllabus on IP that resulted in a five-day international course. He points out that the Cambridge Muslim College has been instrumental in developing IP in the UK.

CHAPTER SIXTEEN on the US points out that while it is impossible to pinpoint precisely when IP arrived in the US, some contexts led to its emergence. Based on the author's previously published writings and her discussions with known IP figures, she outlines the story of IP development in the US and the scenario of psychology in the 1960s and 1970s, when people had started to "look East" for spirituality. While Islam has existed in the US for centuries, it became more vital in the 20th century. At the academic level, the Islamization of knowledge movement facilitated the emergence of IP in the US. In 1998, the *American Journal of Islamic Social Sciences* published a special edition on IP perspectives.

The chapter highlights the development of Muslim mental health, resulting in the growth of important centers which provide services to clients, conduct research, and provide student training. The IAIP, established in the State of Washington in 2017, offers certification courses and conferences outside the US, and has certified individual practitioners, academic institutions, and clinics in IP. IP's growth is also seen by psychologists presenting IP-related papers in APA Annual Conventions. The chapter outlines the challenges and opportunities for IP and is optimistic that it seems to be linked to divine destiny, since the discipline is continuously unfolding.

CHAPTER SEVENTEEN on Western Continental Europe sketches IP's growth from the mid-2000s, especially in Germany. The authors contend that there has been more interest in Muslim mental health than IP theory development and point out that, in the German context, a top-down Islamically Integrated Psychotherapy (IIP) approach is more feasible than a bottom-up approach, which is to construct a separate school of psychology based on Islamic perspectives. They emphasize that spiritual and religious treatment methods can be employed in a scientifically validated manner. The scenario of spirituality and religion in Europe has changed over the years, and it is now more acceptable for Muslim clients in the German healthcare system. The chapter outlines the historical precursors of IP, starting in 1868 with a manuscript entitled *Psychology of the Arabs* followed by similar works by German authors in 1912, 1967, and 1971. The major works on IP is then categorized into two phases. In the 1990s, works were published on the psychological thoughts of early Muslim scholars who highlighted the value of Islamic perspectives in treating Muslim patients. From 2000 onwards, the works focused on investigating religious and spiritual resources in therapy and a growing interest among non-Muslims. A new generation of Muslim psychologists in Europe has started to critically reflect upon the European IP literature, networking, and organizing IP conferences to exchange ideas.

## Key Takeaways and the Future of IP around the Globe

Our hope in putting together this book is that what was once a scattered and disconnected series of developments in silos around the world can now begin to become an interconnected global network of IP professionals and students. Whereas in the past people spread across various countries were left mostly on their own to attempt haphazardly or to independently construct theories and devise therapeutic approaches based on Islamic conceptions, we now have the opportunity to build on one another's contributions and to collaborate in order to advance the field of IP. As people become more aware of what has been going on in this regard in the 17 countries represented in this book, much of which will be the first time many have heard of such developments, this can illuminate a path forward. Instead of continuing to operate in localized enclaves, we can strengthen our collective resources, knowledge, and experience to grow as an international community.

It becomes clear after reading the accounts of the authors in this book that there exists a consensus on the need for IP, and that there is glaring gap in our communities where there is a lack of awareness and understanding in this body of knowledge and practice. We are one *ummah* (Muslim community) and what affects our brothers and sisters around the world also affects us and should be just as much our concern as it is theirs. Just as the original community of believers around the Prophet (peace be upon him) at the advent of Islam, the global Muslim community is made up of people from all cultures, ethnicities, and walks of life. Each of those cultures and geographic experiences has a unique perspective and a special take on how to live life in the way of Islam, and therefore have the potential to offer a unique contribution. We are like the pieces of a puzzle that we must link together to recognize our potential and to see the full picture. We must embrace this diversity, recognize our interconnectedness, and maximize the vast resources we have as a global Muslim community.

From this point forward, we hope that the field of IP develops in a more organized, inclusive, and confident way. We see this happening through international partnerships, joint research projects across countries, student exchange programs, international conferences, and established standards for the professional practice of IP that maintains integrity to both the Islamic tradition and the helping professions. The IAIP aims to be a catalyst and a facilitator for that work to flourish, and for more existing and prospective IP scholars and practitioners around the world to connect and build networks of support and collaboration. This volume is intended as a step in that direction. We thank the chapter authors for their valuable contributions and hope that this book will become an impetus for collaboration, future research, and further development of the field of IP around the globe.

## REFERENCES

Badri, M. (1979). *The dilemma of Muslim psychologists*. MWH London.

Haque, A., Khan, F., Keshavarzi, H., & Rothman, A. E. (2016). Integrating Islamic traditions in modern psychology: Research trends in last ten years. *Journal of Muslim Mental Health, 10*(1), 75–100. http://quod.lib.umich.edu/j/jmmh/10381607.0010.1

Haque, A. &Keshavarzi, H. (2014). Integrating traditional healing methods in therapy: Enhancing cultural competence in working with Muslims in the West. *International Journal of Culture and Mental Health,*7(3), 297–314.

Haque, A. (2004). Psychology from an Islamic perspective: Contributions of early Muslim scholars to psychology and the challenges to contemporary Muslim psychologists. *Journal of Religion and Health,*43(4), 367–387.

Haque, A. (1998). Psychology and religion: Their relationship and integration from Islamic perspective. *The American Journal of Islamic Social Sciences, 15,* 97–116.

Haque, A. (1996). Cognitive restructuring of Muslim psychologists toward developing a firm faith: A prerequisite of Islamization of psychology. *Islamic Thought and Scientific Creativity,* 7, 102–108.

Kaplick, P. M., & Skinner, R. (2017). The evolving *Islam and Psychology* Movement. *European Psychologist,* 22(4), 198-204.

Keshavarzi, H., Khan, F., Ali, B., &Awaad, R. (Eds.) (2020). *Applying Islamic principles to clinical mental health care: Introducing traditional Islamically integrated psychotherapy.* Routledge.

Keshavarzi, H.,& Khan, F. (2018). Outlining a case illustration of traditional Islamically integrated psychotherapy. In C. York Al-Karam (Ed.), *Islamically integrated psychotherapy: Uniting faith and professional practice.* Templeton Press.

Keshavarzi, H.& Haque, A. (2013). Outlining a psychotherapy model for enhancing Muslim mental health within an Islamic context. *International Journal for Psychology of Religion,* 23, 230–249.

Misra, G.,&Paranjpe, A.C. (2012). *Psychology in modern India, encyclopedia of the history of psychological theories.* Springer. https://doi.org/10.1007/978-1-4419-0463-8_422

Rothman, A. (2021). *Developing a model of Islamic psychology and psychotherapy: Islamic theology and contemporary understandings of psychology.* Routledge.

Rothman, A., & Coyle, A. (2020). Conceptualizing an Islamic psychotherapy: A grounded theory study. *Spirituality in Clinical Practice,* 7(3), 197–213. http://doi.org/10.1037/scp0000219

Rothman, A.,& Coyle, A. (2018). Toward a framework for Islamic psychology and psychotherapy: An Islamic model of the soul. *Journal of Religion and Health,* 57(50), 1731–1744.

Sinha, D. (1965). Integration of modern psychology with Indian thought. *Journal of Humanistic Psychology,* 5(1), 6–17.

Taylor, E. I. (1988). Contemporary interest in classical eastern psychology. In A. C. Paranjpe, D. Y. F. Ho, & R. W. Rieber (Eds.), Asian contributions to psychology (pp.79–122). Praeger

CHAPTER ONE

# Islamic Psychology in Australia: An Emerging Field

HANAN DOVER

ISLAMIC PSYCHOLOGY (IP), starting in the early 2000s, was introduced in Australia as an interest area for psychologists of Muslim faith. There have been community-based professional associations, societies, interest groups, and conferences that have introduced and advanced the knowledge and practice of the integration of Islam in the discipline of psychology. IP integrated in clinical practice is a salient feature of psychologists of Muslim faith, which is why conferences and seminars in this area have been successful. Predominantly in Australia, psychologists have been demonstrating the effects of integrating religious and spiritual perspectives into their therapeutic approaches, interventions, and clinical practices. Recent attempts have been made to formally introduce a graduate certificate in IP in Australia.

## Introduction of Islamic Psychology to Australia

In 1996, Malik Badri was invited to Australia as an international keynote speaker at the conference held by the Federation of Australian Muslim Student and Youth. The theme of the conference was "Raising Muslim Youth in the West." This was the first time an international speaker was invited into Australia who was a psychologist. This was also the first time an academic discussion on Islamic psychology (IP) was introduced in Australia. Badri's presentation was instrumental in developing initiatives, projects, and societal bodies of IP in Australia.

In 2001, discussions with Emeritus Professor Jim McKnight, Head of the School of Psychology at Western Sydney University (WSU; formerly the University of Western Sydney), supported initial discussions on IP projects with a small group of psychologists and postgraduate psychology students of Muslim faith. At the time, WSU was at the forefront of the research and interface of the psychology of religion. The idea was to formalize the aim of IP in alignment with the growing Muslim population in Western Sydney. At the time, the School of Psychology also had a postgraduate subject, "Psychology of Religion," and the school was engaging in research across specific, local topics related to religion and psychology. In 2002–2003, the School of Psychology sponsored and partnered with the newly formed Australian Society of Islamic Psychology(ASIP), founded in 2002 using its discretionary funding:

> *The Australian Society of Islamic Psychology is an organization comprised mainly of Australian psychologists with an interest in Islamic Psychology. Our mission is to contribute to the raising of standards of psychological care and treatment utilizing Islamic approaches. We aim to facilitate research on best practice models of culturally sensitive psychological service provision and to disseminate the findings of such research to psychologists and other health professionals in the form of conferences, seminars, lectures, workshops and literature.*[1]

ASIP was the first formal IP association outside of Muslim-majority nations. It was formed with enthusiasm because it followed scientific methods of the discipline of psychology. Itwas also unique in the understanding of Islamic beliefs and practices as foundational to understanding human nature from a psychological perspective. Holding community events, seminars, and conferences run by ASIP in the early 2000s resulted in the awareness of the integration of Islam within the discipline of psychology and popularized its pursuit as a career among Muslims attempting to enroll in psychological studies at a university. In the early 2000s, there were a few Muslim graduates of psychology at universities. Today, this number has increased to more than 60 registered psychologists.

## International Islamic Psychology Conferences at UWS

The Inaugural International Islamic Psychology Conference 2002 was held from September 30 to October 4th at the University of Western Sydney. It was organized by the ASIP and supported by the University of Western Sydney's School of Psychology.

Theme of conference: *Islamic Perspective of Psychology.*

| TOPIC | PRESENTER |
|---|---|
| Opening Address | Jim McKnight, Head of School of Psychology, University of Western Sydney |
| Interface of Psychology and Religion: Trends and Developments | Amber Haque, Head of Psychology Department, International Islamic University Malaysia |
| Islamization of Psychology: It's Why, It's Who, It's How, and It's Who. | Malik Badri,<br><br>International Institute of Islamic Thought and Civilization, Malaysia |
| Contributions of Early Muslim Scholars to Psychology and the Role of Present-Day Muslim Psychologists | Amber Haque |
| Are the Contributions of Early Muslim Scholars Relevant to Modern Muslim Psychotherapists? | Malik Badri |
| Developing Morally and Psychologically Sound Muslim Youth | Malik Badri |
| Attitudes of High School Students and teachers Towards Muslims and Islam in a South Eastern Australian Community. | Amber Haque |
| Proposed Syllabus for Islamic Psychology | Amber Haque |

Professor Malik Badri also presented at local masjid a series of presentations on IP, *Developing morally and psychologically sound Muslim youth.*2

International Islamic Psychology Conference 2003 was also sponsored by WSU's School of Psychology. It was held on October 1 and 2, 2004, at WSU.

| TOPIC | PRESENTER |
|---|---|
| Islamic Perspectives of Psychology | Mohsen Labhan |
| Halway Houses of Renegotiation: Islamic rites and passages among the Oromo refugees in Melbourne | Greg Gow, Centre for Cultural Research, UWS |
| A case study: Living with Post-traumatic Stress Disorder | Suzanne Tzannes– Psychologist |
| Immigration Detention Stress Syndrome (IDSS) amongst Long-Term Asylum Seekers in Australia | Aamer Sultan |

| | |
|---|---|
| The Effect of 11th of September 2001 on Traumatized Refugee Clients from the Middle East: Retraumatization of a vulnerable group of clients | Nooria Mehraby, Senior Mental Health Clinician, STARTTS |
| Disruption of Sense of Coherence during the Uncertain waiting time for asylum in Sweden – Trauma before arrival, post-migration stress and mental health consequences | Solvig Ekblad & Shervin Shahnavaz – Psychologist (Sweden), Head of Immigration, Environment and Health |
| Panel Discussion | Ethics in the 21st Century |

On October 3, 2003, Psychologist Dr. Mohammad Sadiq (Canada) presented a post-conference workshop called "Counseling Muslim Clients: Obstacles and Solutions." It highlighted obstacles and challenges experienced by Muslim counselors and psychologists counseling Muslim clients within an IP framework in Western nations. The AISP's two international conferences included presentations on topics grounded in the theology of IP, for example, the development of IP and IP in the literature. The first conference produced a handbook of paper presentations from the presenters.

## Psychology from an Islamic Perspective Interest Group (PPIG)

After the ASIP's two international conferences, its members attempted to formalize an IP interest group within the Australian Psychological Society (APS). Achieving this objective required that a minimum of 20 signatures of support be collected from full members of the APS by May 2004. This goal was achieved. The interest group was initially called the Islamic Psychology Interest Group. Two years later, the name was changed to the Psychology from an Islamic Perspective Interest Group (PPIG).

Psychology from an Islamic perspective has nine aims for Psychology from an Islamic Perspective Interest Group3:

1. Provide a network for psychologists interested in IP.
2. Provide a forum for discussion regarding the definition and nature of IP.
3. Liaise and maintain alliances with other Muslim professional and community groups.
4. Promote and support theory and research relevant to understanding Muslim community groups in the context of their social systems and settings.
5. Promote and support theory and research toward the development of culturally sensitive psychometric tests and best practice interventions for the Muslim community.

6. Promote the use of psychometrics and interventions relevant to the Muslim culture by providing educational and training programs.
7. Provide relevant consultations on the Muslim culture to the APS and other bodies on topics related to IP.
8. Promote the field of psychology to members of the Muslim community.
9. Promote the knowledge of IP from its historical origins to the present.

In the last PPIG Annual General Meeting, in November 2020, an objective was changing the interest group's name to "Islam and Psychology." This name was decided to be the most appropriate for the group because it was similar to those of other religion and spirituality psychology interest groups (e.g., Christianity and Psychology, Buddhism and Psychology) and would thus help in achieving the goals of IP inside and outside the Islamic world.

Since PPIG's inception, they have held seminars and professional development workshops on the integration of IP in clinical practice and its effects on psychological disorders.

## Advancements in Muslim Mental Health and the Intersection of IP

Academic research at WSU began attempting to fill a gap in the literature: there were few religiously appropriate measures for Muslims in the psychological research of Muslims. The importance of understanding the psychology of Muslims and their lifestyles from an Islamic psychological perspective started within the school. In 2007, research was published that measured Muslim religious reflection; this research applied concepts from the Quran to design and structure the unique measure (Dover et al., 2007). Subsequently, academics at WSU identified the absence of a religiously sensitive measure of attachment to God among Muslims. Thus they developed the Muslim Spiritual Attachment Scale (M-SAS), and it was used in an Australian study of the psychological health of Muslims (Bonab et al., 2013).

Mission of Hope (MoH) was formally founded in 2003 by Muslims studying psychology and other health professionals. Their aim was to fill the gaps within the Muslim communities where mental health problems were concerned. MoH is a not-for-profit, charitable organization that runs mental health projects for Muslim communities. MoH currently runs a culturally responsive drug and alcohol counseling service and a telephone crisis line. MoH also organizes annual Muslim mental health conferences. In 2020, their conference was held on December 4 and 5, and the first day was devoted to the topic of IP. The aim of that day was to share knowledge on IP, namely, theology and applied and clinical practice.

The conference presentations were as follows:

| TOPIC | PRESENTERS |
|---|---|
| Tazkia Therapy: Theoretical Foundation and Simple Cases | Bagus Riyono (Indonesia)<br>President, International Association of Muslim Psychologists (IAMP) |
| What exactly is Islamic Psychology, and does it apply to us today?" | Rania Awaad – Psychiatrist (US)<br>Director, Stanford Muslim Mental Health Lab, Clinical Director, Khalil Center (US) |
| Theoretical developments in Western psychology, current state of mental health, and the need for Islamic psychology | Fahad Khan – Clinical Psychologist (US)<br>Concordia University Chicago and College of DuPage Deputy and Clinical Director, Khalil Center (US) |
| The Importance of Integrating Islamic Principles of Human Nature When Working Clinically with Muslims | Hanan Dover, Clinical and Forensic Psychologist,<br>Vice President, International Association of Muslim Psychologists (IAMP) |

## Development of Training in IP

In 2019, ISRA in Australia submitted a proposal for a new graduate certificate called the "Graduate Certificate in Islamic Psychology."

The course's aim is to provide students with introductory broad-based knowledge and critical skills in the study of IP. The students will study subjects that will provide a good understanding of the teachings of human psychology within the framework of the Islamic perspectives of human nature, their psyche, and their bio-psycho-social realities in comparison to Western psychology. IP incorporates and builds on recognized classical Muslim scholars (e.g., al-Ghazali, al-Balkhi, al-Harith Al-Muhasibi) and integrates their contributions with modern psychological sciences and practical applications. The course prepares students for further academic study on the clinical applications of Islamic psychotherapy and counseling. This course would benefit individuals interested in Islam and its adherents, which would benefit health professionals, community workers, chaplains, teachers, or individuals or institutes managing Muslims regularly. The duration for course approval is approximately three years; thus, this course has not yet been approved.

In 2020, ISRA signed a Memorandum of Understanding with the International Association of Muslim Psychologists. This agreement covers three areas:

1. Design and delivery of the Graduate Certificate in IP course through Charles Sturt University.
2. Conducting research on mental health and well-being from an Islamic perspective and in relation to Muslims.
3. Organizing a biannual conference on IP.

Inshallah this collaboration contributes to IP disciplines.

Unlike the Muslim-majority nations or Western institutions that have established learning centers for IP, Australian Muslims' centers remain in their initial stages but are determined to increase awareness and knowledge in the area.

The hope is that institutions that have Islamic sciences and Islamic studies departments in Australian universities explore and adapt seminars and conferences that present the fundamental aspects of psychological and emotional problems in Australian society.

Australian Muslims are 2.6% of Australia's population, constituting 604,200 adherents of Islam. This number is 15% higher than the number of Muslims five years prior. Despite Muslims being a minority community in Australia, the movement toward the appreciation of IP has been concentrated in the Greater Sydney area, where 42% of the Muslims in Australia reside. IP was unknown before Professor Malik Badri's conference presentations in the later 1990s in Australia.It was quickly adopted by very few Muslim psychologists at the time and is enthusiastically adopted by psychologists of the mid-2000s. The addition of the growing number of private Islamic schools and community-based religious lectures and seminars has made it easier for Muslim psychologists to access religiously sound knowledge related to human nature and Islam to be able to integrate Islamic knowledge into their clinical practices and service delivery of IP. This addition also resulted in the increasing number of Muslim psychologists working in private practice. In these practices, Muslim clients seek psychologists who can identify with their faith and provide them therapeutic strategies in line with their religious worldviews and spiritualities.

## Conclusion

The development of IP in Australia by psychologists of Muslim faith began instrumentally with the support from Western Sydney University and was furthered by the formation of IP-related societies and interest groups conveying and participating in disseminating knowledge on IP to mental health professionals and raising awareness of their applications in clinical practice. Muslims in Australia are a young population, and psychologists led the pioneering of IP by popularizing it among their clinical peers of Muslim faith and mental health professionals. More work needs to be done to introduce IP subjects and courses at the tertiary level because this paradigm is crucial in furthering psychology from the perspective of its Islamic contributions and future contemporary applications.

## References

Bonab, B. H, Miner, M., & Proctor, M. (2013). Attachment to god in Islamic spirituality. Journal of Muslim Mental Health, 7(2).https://doi.org/10.3998/jmmh.10381607.0007.205

Dover, H., Miner, M. H., & Dowson, M. (2007). The nature and structure of Muslim religious reflection. Journal of Muslim Mental Health. http://www.informaworld.com/smpp/content~content=a783323514~db=all~jumptype=rss

---

1 See https://www.asip.org.au (discontinued website)

2 See http://web.archive.org/web/20060823014005/http://www.famsy.com/salam/Psychol1002.htm

3 See https://groups.psychology.org.au/ipig/

4 See https://missionofhope.org.au/australian-muslim-mental-health-conference-2020/

5 See https://web.archive.org/web/20170710020910/http://abs.gov.au/ausstats/abs@.nsf/Lookup/by%20Subject/2071.0~2016~Main%20Features~Religion%20Data%20Summary~25

CHAPTER TWO

# Islamic Psychology from a Bosnian Perspective: Experience and Contributions of Muslim Psychologists and Thinkers

AID SMAJIĆ
SELVIRA DRAGANOVIĆ

AS INDIGENOUS PEOPLE in southeast Europe, Muslims for centuries have been inhabiting lands of what is today Bosnia and Herzegovina. Their encounter with Western, non-Muslim worldviews and understandings of humankind accordingly has been long lasting and an intensive experience. In a similar fashion, local thinkers and psychologists identifying with Islam as a worldview inevitably were predestined to make attempts at reconciling Islamic religious anthropology with the modern scientific understanding of human psyche and behavior. For much of the 20th century, however, their homeland was an integral part of the antireligious communist political order of socialist Yugoslavia. Therefore, contributions of Bosnian Muslim thinkers, scholars, and psychologists in this regard, later to be named *Islamization* or integration of Islam and psychology, up to the disintegration of Socialist Yugoslavia in the early 1990s have been negligible. Similarly, more active and engaging attempts to (re)consider theories and practice of so-called Western psychology from an Islamic perspective, as a part of ongoing discourse of integration of knowledge and social sciences in the Muslim mainland, belong to the last three decades. Furthermore, it has been an uncoordinated endeavor undertaken usually by religious scholars, individuals, and non-governmental organizations (NGOs) close to Muslim religious circles and institutions in Bosnia. Most notably these activities include (a) explicating basic premises of the general discourse on the integration of Western knowledge to the local academic community; (b) translating texts of their main proponents in main Muslim lands into Bosnian language; (c) promoting Islamic understanding of humanity, anthropology, and various psychological concepts; (d) calling for recognition of the role of religion and religiosity/spirituality in human life, mental health, behavior, development, and education; (e) engaging in empirical research on the mentioned themes as well as investigating the contributions of Muslim classical thinkers to psychotherapy; and (f) making attempts to integrate religiosity and religious motivation in the practice of upbringing, education, and psychotherapy.

## Introduction

Bosnia and Herzegovina (hereafter Bosnia) is a relatively small country located in southeast Europe and, for many, a place where "the East meets the West" in various ways. Given early conversion of its inhabitants to Islam in the 15th century, Muslims for centuries have been inhabiting this part of the European continent and identifying with Islam as a religion and worldview. As a result, their Islamic identity largely determined their historical experience of the other, including the latter's cultural, scientific, and ideological achievements, making this tiny country a sort of battlefield for confronting armies as well as a meeting point of different cultures, worldviews, and ideas about nature, society, and humanity throughout a considerable part of its (pre)modern history.

In a symbolic manner the above remark proved to be true also at the end of the 19th century. In 1878, representatives of the great powers in Europe at that time convened a meeting in Berlin resulting in the historical treaty with annexation of Bosnia, previously a province in the Muslim Ottoman Empire, to the Christian Austro-Hungarian Empire, as one of the treaty's major conclusions. Only one year later, Wilhelm Wundt, known as the father of experimental psychology, established the first laboratory for psychological research in the German city of Leipzig. According to historical accounts, Bosnian Muslims fiercely reacted to the first event that resulted in annexation, laying down numerous lives to defend the land and its autonomy. Conversely, what was the reaction of Bosnian Muslims, their scholars, and intellectuals in decades and the century to come to the *cultural invasion* of the West? More precisely, how did they react regarding the second event mentioned above marking the *official establishment* of a new psychology and approach in understanding of humankind, personality, behavior, and destiny in this world and, (in)directly, in the Hereafter? In terms of a prompt and systematic answer, could it be possibly compared with the reaction of the Catholic Church, its clergy, and intellectuals or even European Protestants (Smajić, 2017a)? Was there already a clearly conceived notion of so-called Islamic Psychology (IP) present and used by local Muslim scholars and intellectuals, or were the latter satisfied with Islamic indigenous terminology of *Sufism*? Given their status as a minority in majority Christian lands, to what extent could Bosnian Muslim scholars have and had benefited from the overall reaction of the Muslim world to cultural and scientific achievements of the West in systematically conceiving Islamically oriented psychology? What have been their contributions in this regard so far, and what factors should be referred to account for such situations and prospects of IP in Bosnia?

Providing a fair answer to these questions requires two important considerations. First, we need to consider the broader context in terms of the overall status and position of Islam, Islamic institutions, and Muslims in Bosnia within existing sociopolitical and legal order in a particular time of history, including the former's connections with mainland Muslim countries and their Islamic educational institutions. Second, given that so far Muslim scholars have not agreed on definitions of IP (Al-Karam, 2018), Islamization of psychology and IP here should be understood in their broad and fluid sense. Therefore, here we do not intend to reduce the former to efforts of adapting modern psychology to Islam, as suggested by definitions of Islamization by some Muslim authors (Othman &Raba, 1996). In the context of this chapter, by Islamization of psychology we mean various endeavors taken by local Muslim religious scholars, intellectuals, and social scientists aiming to promote an Islamic understanding of human nature, personality, and behavior. Only this broad approach, bearing in mind specific historical circumstances of Islam and Muslim presence in Bosnian lands, would allow us to provide reasonable amounts of meaningful material regarding the above topic.

Having this in mind, this chapter has two primary aims. First, it seeks to briefly delineate a history of Islam and Muslims in Bosnia. Second, it attempts to present contributions and achievements of local Muslim scholars and intellectuals in promoting an Islamic understanding of humanity, human psychology, and behavior over the years up to today.

## Brief History of Islam and Muslims in Bosnian Land

It is generally accepted that Muslims have inhabited Bosnia since the 15th century after local people converted to the religion of Islam brought to this region by the Ottomans. Being a part of the Ottoman Empire for more than four centuries, Bosnia became a place where Islam, Islamic culture, and Islamic learning were flourishing as manifested in numerous mosques and religious sites, and Islamic historical monuments and educational centers known worldwide. Ghazi

Husraw-bay Madrasa, founded in 1537 in the capital city of Sarajevo, for example, had a ranking almost equal to that of *Sahn-i Saman,* the highest and most prestigious schools of higher learning in the Ottoman Empire in which rational and traditional sciences were taught (Nakičević, 1983). In a similar manner, it is both interesting and telling that Muhammad 'Abduh (d. 1905), famous Muslim reformer from Egypt, referred to the Shari'a School for Muslim Judges in Sarajevo, established in 1887, as an exemplary of successfully reformed and modern educational institution of Islamic higher learning at that time (Karčić, 2004). Accordingly, it is not surprising that Muslim religious scholars from Bosnia also served as *Shaykh al-Islam,* the highest position of religious authority in the Ottoman State (Popara, 2006). Eventually, *Sufism,* understood as Islamic mysticism aiming at intensification of faith and psycho-spiritual purification of an individual by some and as an authentic Islamic Psychology itself by some others (Shafi'i, 1985), with its proponents and orders, was present in the country since the first days of Islam in the Balkan Peninsula (Beglerović, 2015).

The aforementioned altogether shows that by the third quarter of the 19th century, Bosnian Muslims, ethnic Bosniaks, seemingly had enough religious, intellectual, and institutional resources to produce scholarship capable of articulating Islamic understanding of the world and humanity as well as an authentic Islamic response to ongoing cultural and scientific developments in the Christian West, including the establishment of a *new* psychology. The sociocultural developments in the country in the last quarter of the 19th century onwards, however, significantly delayed, undermined, and shaped their *Islamic* response in (this) regard in the post-Ottoman history of Bosnia, which is marked by four distinctive periods: Hapsburg monarchy (1887–1918), Monarchic Yugoslavia (1918–1941), Socialist Yugoslavia (1945–1992), and the independent state of Bosnia and Herzegovina (1992–present).

Most notably, beginnings of modern psychology, symbolized by the establishment of the first psychological laboratory in Leipzig in 1879, coincided with the Berlin Treaty in 1878. According to the Agreement, this former Ottoman province was annexed to the Catholic Hapsburg monarchy, whereby local Muslims overnight were turned into a minority in the country ruled by their former enemy and conqueror from the Christian West. Consequently, many of them, including their religious and intellectual elite, decided to migrate to the Muslim lands of the Ottoman Empire, thus initiating an emigration process that lasted until the 1960s, significantly weakening the Muslim academic community in the country and creating the biggest diaspora of ethnic Bosniaks until today. Those who stayed in their homes, on the other side, largely took an antagonistic and defensive attitude toward cultural and scientific achievements of the West, paying no special attention to a new and, for them, still largely unknown science of psychology. Instead, they were preoccupied with seemingly more important and existential concerns brought about by living in a non-Muslim environment as to how to preserve the tenets of Islamic religious identity, their religious rights, as well as the autonomy of newly established and reformed Islamic institutions, infrastructure, and endowments (*waqf*). Eventually, for various reasons, connections with educational institutions in the Muslim world were reduced and seriously limited (Karčić, 2004).

Similar challenges continued to burden Bosnian Muslims, their scholars, and religious and cultural institutions in the days to come under the rule of Monarchic Yugoslavia (1918–1941). The end of World War II and establishment of Socialist Yugoslavia (1945–1992) by communists, with Bosnia and Herzegovina being one of its six republics, for the greatest part of this period only worsened an already dire situation in terms of the status of Islamic institutions as well as religious literacy and awareness of Bosnian Muslims as a necessary precondition for a new and appropriate articulation of IP. With the exception of Ghazi Husraw-bay Madrasa in Sarajevo, all other Islamic schools and institutions of higher learning soon were closed by the new regime, confining basic religious education of Muslims to weekend classes in mosques, while Sufi orders were prohibited and religious literature significantly limited. In accordance with the communist ideology and understanding of secularism, religion furthermore was proclaimed to be a strictly private matter and even a sign of backwardness with no relevance for politics, society, culture, and science. Eventually, exchange of visits and ideas between Muslim religious scholars and students in Bosnia and major Muslim countries were scrutinized and controlled by the regime authorities. The status of religious freedom in Bosnia and other Yugoslav republics, however, considerably improved in the 1970s, which in years to come would create more, albeit still largely limited, space for (re)establishing institutions of Islamic learning, (re) opening of Sufi orders, and improving connections with the Islamic scholarship in the Muslim world. That the doors of the religious freedom for Muslims and other religious traditions in the country would widely open soon was heralded by the first multiparty and democratic elections in Bosnia in 1990 and definitely confirmed by privileged legal and societal position of religion in post aggression (1992–1995) Bosnian state, legislature, society, and culture (Smajić, 2010; Smajić, 2017b). Interestingly, only one year before, in 1989, the Department of Psychology at the Faculty of Philosophy in Sarajevo was established as an independent academic and administrative unit after 30 years of existing as part of the Department of Pedagogy and Psychology at the same Faculty. Given global and local developments in the world of politics and psychological science, it was a ripe time in Bosnia for a fresh (re)consideration of modern psychology from an Islamic perspective in a proper sense.

## "Who," "What," and "How" of Islamic Psychology in Bosnia and Herzegovina

Bearing in mind the above outlined short introduction to Bosnia, here we will portray individuals and institutions that affirmed Islamic worldview, ethics, and psychology accordingly either as part of a defense against new culture, science, and psychology in the West, or a more proactive attitude of integrating modern psychology in Islamic teaching and thus creating a body of knowledge that could be termed *Islamic psychology* in its broad sense. Hence, we will begin with the *who, what,* and *how* of Islamic Psychology in Bosnia.

In a broad sense, these bearers of IP in Bosnia could be categorized into three categories: (1) Bosnian Sufis, their followers and activists; (2) Muslim intellectuals, theologians, and religious scholars, the latest usually being attached to Islamic religious educational institutions; and (3) Muslim psychologists, psychiatrists, and psychotherapists.

## Bosnian *Sufis*

Sufi orders generally for centuries focused their efforts on personal, social, and intellectual pathways with the purpose of purifying the human heart as an ultimate locus of human psyche in Islamic orthodox understanding of humanity, personality, and behavior. Bosnian Sufis accordingly nourished and transmitted knowledge about Islam and their understanding of humankind and human nature and development from the moment of conception to the death and afterlife. Sufi orders in Bosnia alongside with individuals gathering around them and their followers contributed with their views on humanity, human nature, and the human spiritual dimension. Some of their work focuses on history of Sufism in Bosnia, barely providing the number of Sufi orders, their length of existence in this part of the world, and their contribution to various fields (Beglerović, 2015) without considering Western psychology. Some others also try to incorporate Islam and psychology coining the term "Sufi psychology" (Kukavica, 2016), while some attempt to compare and critically analyze missing points in Western psychology, adding Islamic contributions to it (Hasanović, 2017), discussing personality development in *Tasawuf,* indicating the path to a mature personality through seven phases of *nafs* (Gaši&Pajević, 2002), and investigated and discussed the impact of prayer on shaping some mature personality structure and personality structure of those who pray and do not pray (Pajević & Sinanović, 2002). Significant contribution to promoting an Islamic notion of human psychology has also been made by Bosnian Muslim thinkers, theologians, and Islamic scholars. We discuss them in more detail below.

## Bosnian Muslim Thinkers/Intellectuals, Theologians, and Islamic Scholars

Bosnian Muslim thinkers and intellectuals should also be acknowledged for their contributions and discussion on humanity, human nature, body and soul, spirituality, and spiritual dimension and needs of humankind discussed in light of the Qur'an and Sunnah. Alija Izetbegović, for example, has been known and recognized in the Muslim world not only as a politician and the first president of the independent state of Bosnia and Herzegovina but also as a profound thinker who wisely contemplates the ongoing state and fate of Muslim Umma. In his famous book *Islam between the East and the West,* he also discusses Islamic understanding of man where he, for instance, asserts that "Islam means a call for developing a man as a carrier of a harmony between body and soul and a society whose institutions help maintaining and not violating it" (Izetbegović, 1990: 26). Contrary to the ingrained Western understanding, in his work, Izetbegović discussed a different understanding of anthropology and the structure of man emphasizing the need for freedom. In that sense, Izetbegović criticized materialism, which supports totalitarian regimes in which people lose dignity and freedom, and remarkably points that freedom cannot be attained without ideas of God and monotheism. Criticizing conditions in both Eastern (only religion matters, no place for materialism) and Western (science and materialism matter only) societies, Izetbegović (1990) points to the need for balance in both orientations. By that he strongly reaffirmed a balanced approach in understanding both world and humanity, which is an important tenet in every attempt of exposing an Islamic notion of human psychology.

Furthermore, in Bosnia we can identify various religious scholars mostly attached to Islamic religious educational institutions (i.e., Faculty of Islamic Studies in the capital of Sarajevo, Islamic Pedagogical Faculties in Zenica and Bihać, and Islamic High Schools or *Madrasas*) who can be described as Muslim thinkers, theologians, or Islamic scholars. In their work they often deal with topics of human nature and spiritual, physical, moral, and psychological being, encompassing human belief, needs, and incorporating all human dimensions in this life and Hereafter, contrary to Western teachings. These issues are usually discussed regarding the themes pertaining the moral crises of a modern man (Spahić, 2002) or a man as a synonym for a very complex and crown-shaped personality in God's hands (Hafizović, 2002), or the impact of the mosque on human psyche (Terzić, 2002), or understanding the phenomena of a stable personality within the context of Islamic notion of freedom and universal order (Karić, 2002). In opposition to the new Western culture, science, and psychology, these scholars explicitly or implicitly try to (re)affirm Islamic worldview and understanding of man and human nature.

Their approach to the matter, however, usually lacks deep understanding of contemporary psychology, thus creating an impression that the topic of Islamic psychology belongs to theology rather than an interdisciplinary field of science trying to critically tackle Western understanding of man and human psychology. The traces of similar impression often can be found in public and popular Muslim literature as well. Using this approach, Muslim theologians, for example, tend to refer to and quote Qur'anic *ayats* and Prophetic *ahadith,* thus exposing an Islamic notion of man and his nature, while simultaneously discussing contemporary psychological concepts albeit in a way lacking an analytical and investigative rigor. In a similar manner and for similar reasons, they also interchangeably use psychological and theological terminology to prove that discussed psychological terms can be found in the text of the Qur'an or Sunnah. Thus, they not only miss offering clear IP counterparts but also neglect tending to matter of the psyche in a scientific manner.

## Bosnian Muslim Psychologists, Psychotherapists, and Psychiatrists

The term IP as an interdisciplinary scientific field trying to critically tackle Western understanding and the science of human psychology and behavior from an Islamic perspective is still not commonly used in Bosnia. As far as Bosnia is concerned, this understanding of IP has its origin in works on a broader topic of Islamization of knowledge. Accordingly, it is correct to claim that IP, in its narrow meaning, has a recent origin going back, most probably, to the return of Bosnian graduates in the late 1990s from universities in main Muslim lands where the notion of Islamization has been already promoted and firmly established. It is beyond doubt that the International Islamic University of Malaysia (IIUM) deserves to be mentioned as one of educational institutions where the first Bosnian students had an opportunity to learn about Islamization of knowledge and Islamic psychology to later on introduce the very same concepts in their homeland.

The Islamization project caught the attention of a broader Muslim intellectual community, while it was Muslim psychologists in the country who showed the greatest interest in the idea of Islamic psychology. Both groups, however, have promoted these ideas through translation of relevant original works into Bosnian language, publications promoting the idea of Islamization of knowledge as well as works, and thesis and research studies exposing psychological ideas of early Muslim scholars and the role of religiosity in mental health and behavior. Here we would like to mention some of these contributions.

In addition to the translated work of Al-Attas on *Islam and Secularism*, further elaboration of the term Islamization of knowledge, its origin, and its current condition has been also presented in numerous publications (Smajić, 2012) that tried to present it as a never-ending intellectual task. In some other research studies (Smajić & Đapo, 2019) the role of religiosity in predicting value orientation of Muslim youth has been investigated, while others talked about the encounter of religion and modern psychology (Smajić, 2017a) or researched psychological dimensions of religion and religious motivation (Jusić, 2006). As far as a master thesis is concerned, several of them should be mentioned here, including *Personality Concept in the Work of Abu Hamid al-Gazali* (Memić, 2020), *Psychological Wellbeing and Marital Satisfaction among Bosnian Sufi Women* (Kilic, 2017), and *Behavioral Therapy in the Works of Selected Early Muslim Scholars* (Smajić, 2003).

In addition to these, there are also significant and important pieces of research studies and publications mostly done by the team of enthusiastic psychiatrists from the town of Tuzla. Their contribution to Islamic psychology is reflected in research and publications investigating concepts of spirituality (Hasanović *et al*, 2011), religious moral beliefs, religious cognitive behavioral patterns and their impact on mental health, psychological wellbeing, and mental illness (Hasanović & Pajević, 2010; Hasanović & Pajević 2013, Hasanović & Pajević 2015). In their research, for instance, they point to the professional necessity to address the spiritual needs of Muslim clients, including the need to explain life and death and their meaning as well as the role of individual or group Islamic prayer (*salah*) in individual or group PTSD treatment processes (Pajević, Sinanović, & Hasanović, 2017). Hasanović and colleagues (2015), furthermore, tested moral religious beliefs in relationship with trauma, depression, and anxiety among Bosnian war veterans and adolescents and found that religious moral beliefs are inversely related and tend to be protective factors in mental health (Pajević, Hasanović, & Delić, 2007) and spiritual and Islamic perspective of PTSD healing (Hasanović, Pajević, & Sinanović, 2017). Hasanović and Pajevićalso investigated the role of religious cognitive–behavioral patterns in appearance and reduction of psychopathology. In conclusion they state that religious cognitive patterns help neutralize psychopathology efficiency and health by providing the true perception of reality, fostering socialization, providing greater resistance to frustration, overcoming conflict, providing greater content and aspiration toward higher goals, rational arrangement, and psychical energy use (Pajević, Sinanović, & Hasanović, 2005).

It is noteworthy that this group largely refers to Sufi psychological tradition in discussing contemporary psychology and similarities between the two. Their area of interest, nevertheless, is mainly limited to the role of religion and spirituality in the context of mental health. In a way, this could be seen as an attempt to find touching points between Islam and contemporary psychiatry and psychology without, however, discussing the differences.

## Tests, Scales, Questionnaires, Books

As we mentioned earlier, considerable efforts of local Muslim psychologists have been devoted to developing new psychometric instruments of Islamic religiosity and spirituality as well as exposing psychological dimensions of Islamic religion and worldview. The latter task has been done either in the form of original works or translation of earlier ones written in foreign languages.

In that sense, Isić (Isić, Pehlić, & Neimarlija, 2014), for example, developed a Muslim religiosity psychometric instrument that contains five religiosity scales, three pertaining to internal (Islamic belief, performing prayer, religious experience) and two to external aspects of religiosity (cognitive belief level and behaviors toward the others in accordance with Islamic postulates). Pajević similarly (Pajević & Sinanović, 2002) created a Spirituality profile scale, *salah* questionnaire, and practicing religion questionnaire.

Some Muslim psychologists in Bosnia wrote about psychological dimensions of Islam and its rituals and sources and should probably be included under a broad umbrella of IP. Noteworthy by their content and writing style, these publications mostly have been meant for the broader public and not psychology experts. Their titles are usually catchy, bearing Islamic reference, while their content rarely offers profound scientific elaborations. The following are books that could be included in this type of publication: *Psychology of Islam* (Selimović, 1995), *Psychology of Prayer* (Selimović, 2002), *Qur'anic Treatment of Stress* (Tule, 2011), *Socio-psychological Dimensions of Qur'an* (Tule, 2010), and *Architecture of a Soul* (Tule, 2018).

In terms of translation, the following works should be mentioned here: Malik Badri's *Contemplation: An Islamic Psycho Spiritual Study*, Najjati' s book *Qur'an wa Ilm ul nefsi* (Qur'an and Psychology), and Husein's book *Uslubul Qur'an ives Sunneti fi Tenmijeti Shahsijjeti*, or Shafi''s book *Freedom from the Self* and Wilcox's book *Sufism and Psychology*, Ubeydi's Qur'an, *Nervous System and Psychology*, Badri's article "Counseling and Psychotherapy from an Islamic Perspective: Are Counseling and Psychotherapy One or Two Different Areas?,"Nasr's *The Encounter of Man and Nature, The Spiritual Crisis of the Modern Man,* Nasr's *The Heart of Islam: Enduring Values for Humanity,* Abu Sulaiman's *Ar-Ru'yah al-kawniyya al-ḥaḍariyyaalqur'aniyya,* Al-Gazzali's *Muslim Character,* Yasin's *Nature of Man in Islam,* and classic works of Abu Hamid Gazali's and Ibn Qayyim al-Jawzijja. The translations are usually done by local experts coming from different disciplines, including psychology, psychiatry, and theology. On the other side, the translated works usually refer to master and pioneer pieces, which have been recognized in the Muslim world for their excellence and contribution in exposing Islamic perspective regarding given topics. It is probably important to note that the mentioned contributors to IP in Bosnia rarely have interdisciplinary educational backgrounds. Except for one person, all others have earned their formal education in one area of science, usually psychology or psychiatry, to combine their scientific interests with their zeal for religiosity, spirituality, or Sufism.

Thus far, we have discussed individuals who in various ways contributed to broad areas of IP in Bosnia. In terms of institutions, we ought to probably mention (1) Sufi orders in Bosnia, (2) Islamic educational institutions, and (3) the most relevant NGOs. Hence, below we discuss contributions of each.

Bosnia is a country rich with Sufi tradition present in this land since the Ottomans. For centuries, Sufis of different orders such as Mevlevis, Naqshbandies, Kadiries, as the most common in Bosnia, contributed to Islamic sciences, teaching, and Muslim education by spiritualizing everyday Islam. Since the entire Sufi tradition and teaching revolves around the experience of divine love and wisdom, their activities have intended to help in purification of the inner heart in man and strengthening his spirituality. In accordance with Sufi tradition in Bosnia, Sufi rituals and group *dhikr* have been held either on specific days during a week, annually, or on special occasions related to important dates in the Islamic calendar. *Dhikr* is usually practiced under supervision of a Sufi master whose responsibility is to help his disciples to reach a state of human completeness of *al-insan al-kamil*, thus attaining personal and inner freedom and improving their level of spirituality. Contrary to philosophy and practice of Western psychology, and in accordance with the Islamic notion of human wellbeing, the final aim is to attain intellectual, emotional, and spiritual completeness.

Islamic educational institutions in Bosnia (i.e., Faculty of Islamic Studies in the capital of Sarajevo, Islamic Pedagogical Faculty in Zenica, and Islamic Pedagogical Faculty in Bihać) should also be recognized for their contribution to the IP. As expected, their curricula and educational activities at these institutions of higher learning mainly focus on basic Islamic courses. However, their undergraduate, postgraduate, and PhD programs often teach courses that tackle topics and concepts related to the broader area of IP. In that sense, undergraduate theology programs usually offer courses on Introduction to Sufism and Theological Epistemology, which discuss concepts pertaining to Sufi anthropology and epistemology as well as ontological and psychological dimensions of cognitions. Religious pedagogy programs, on the other side, usually offer courses like Qur'anic Concept of Education, Introduction to the Study of Religion, Sunnah Concept of Education, Theological Anthropology, Psychology of Religion, Religious Education, and Occult Culture. A Concept of Qur'anic Education course deals with man and philosophy of his education in the light of Qur'an, viewing God to be a primary educator, as well as with concepts of moral, freedom, and law according to Qur'an. Religiosity, new age, and crisis of religious education are discussed within Introduction to the Study of Religion, while the role of Islamic rituals and the Prophet's educational methods are discussed within a Sunnah Concept of Education course. Topics of the nature of man's soul and its categorizations as well concepts of love and man's sexual identity are discussed within the course of Theological Anthropology. Seemingly the most relevant IP concepts are discussed within the course of Psychology of Religion, which deals with constructs of religiosity and spirituality, religion, emotion, meaning, mental health, and coping at the time of existential anxiety. Crisis of religious and cultural identity and the concept of occult and contemporary problems are covered within Religious Education and Occult Culture. Also, a number of other syllabi partially cover topics that could be included in the area of IP. Islamic Philosophy, for instance, discusses Farabi's contribution to achieving happiness and Ibn Sina's contribution to understanding being, while Theological Epistemology covers psychological dimension of cognition, relationship between theology and other sciences knowledge, and social reality and knowledge as a power and the highest educational value. Similarly, Hadith Texts deals with issues pertaining to spiritual, intellectual, and moral education, while Traditional Educational Themes covers topics such as honesty, repentance, conscience, modesty, perseverance, kindness toward parents, evil, and sources of moral and ethics (please check, Faculty of Islamic studies, www.fin.unsa.ba). In conclusion, to the best of our knowledge, a course of Islamic Psychology has not been offered yet in Islamic educational institutions in Bosnia. Significant portion of topics and concepts relevant for the field, however, can be identified as a part of syllabi for other regular courses at these faculties. Likewise, it should be noted that Bosnia is a secular country in which other local faculties strictly abide to a secular worldview where religion and science should be clearly separated from each other.

Finally, among relevant NGOs we probably ought to mention Center for Advanced Studies(*Centar za naprednestudije*, www.cns.ba), the Bosnian branch of International Institute of Islamic Thought (IIIT). In line with the general philosophy and policy of IIIT, for the last 15 years the Center perhaps has been the most active NGO in promoting the idea of Islamization of knowledge and psychology by the means of selectively providing the most recent publication on the topics and its translation into local language.

## Conclusion

As far as IP in Bosnia is concerned, local achievements in this regard should be understood in its rather broad and fluid sense as various endeavors aiming to promote an Islamic understanding of human nature, psychology, and behavior. Contrary to its reduction only to efforts of adapting modern psychology to Islam, this approach has enabled us to identify a reasonable amount of meaningful material that could be included under the umbrella of IP. Most notably, the identified achievements include a robust presence of *Sufism*, *Sufi* orders, and terminology in Bosnian society and Islamic educational institutions as well as, relative to the size of Muslim population in the country, a significant number of Muslim theologians, intellectuals, psychiatrists, psychologists, educational institutions, and NGOs that have been active in elaborating and promoting an Islamic concept of man, mental health, and contributions of early Muslim scholars in this area. Furthermore, contrary to the potential expectations of some, the term *Islamic Psychology* has not been used by them, unlike that of *Sufi* psychology, which for those who employed it obviously was equal to IP. Similarly, Islamization of knowledge as an initiative, and to some extent Islamization of psychology, has been popularized in Bosnian society and the academic community to a limited extent and usually by those identifying with Islamic religious circles and educational settings. Eventually, adapting theory and practice of modern psychology to Islamic worldview in Bosnia so far has usually been a matter of popular literature, individual practice, and translating relevant foreign works undertaken by enthusiastic Muslim theologians, mental workers, and university professors rather than a planned group project and matter of systematic theoretical elaborations.

Causes of the current situation in the IP field in Bosnia, in our opinion, should be attributed to cumulative effect of various factors, including (1) a relative global novelty of the Islamization project; (2) due to unfavorable historical circumstances, preoccupation of the responsible Islamic institutions with more urgent issues at the time and their disconnection from advanced scholarship in some major Muslim lands; (3) intensive and more than one century-long secularization of knowledge and social sciences; (4) relatively recent and delayed educational institutionalization of psychological science in Bosnia, which wrongly sometimes has been identified with antireligious views of Freud and pseudoscience by local Muslim scholars; and (5) lack of support and funding for a purposeful long-term project that would gather prospective Muslim theoreticians and practitioners in the field of IP. In a similar manner, it is our firm belief that the prospects of IP in Bosnian land are promptly and systematically addressing the very same issues. Accordingly, recommended steps in this regard should possibly concern (1) gathering Bosnian scholars and psychologists interested in the idea of IP; (2) organizing efforts in further elaborating and promoting the idea of integration of knowledge and IP in theological and academic circles in the country;(3) establishing stronger connections with Muslim psychologists, relevant educational settings, and associations in major Muslim lands and the West for the purpose of networking, exchange of ideas and literature, as well as purposeful additional education and training in the area of IP; and (4) securing organizational and financial support for the above activities.

## References

Al-Karam, C. Y. (2018). Islamic psychology: Towards a 21st century definition and conceptual framework. *Journal of Islamic Ethics, 2,* 97-109.

Badri, M. (2001). The Islamization of Psychology: Its Why, Its What, Its How and Its Who. Paperdelivered at *National Conference of Psychology,* IIUM, July 14-19.

Beglerović, S. (2015). TassavufiTarikat u BosniiHercegovini (Tasavuf and Tariqat in Bosnia and Herzegovina). Časopis *za filozofijuireligiju Logos, 2,* 29-45.

Centar za naprednestudije (Center for Advanced studies). Retrieved from www.cns.ba

Gaši, A., &Pajević, I. (2002). Faze razvojaličnosti u Tesavvufu (Phases of personality development in Tasawwuf), pp. 221-237. In Sinananović, O., Hafizović, R., &Pajević, I. (Eds). *Duhovnostimentalnozdravlje (Spirituality and Mental Health).* Svjetlost, Sarajevo. Fakultetislamskihnauka (Faculty of Islamic Studies in Sarajevo). http://fin.unsa.ba

Hafizović, R. (2002). Čovjek kao sveto podzemlje duha Božijeg i Njegov mikrokozmički hram (Man as a holly underground of God's spirit and His microcosmic temple), pp. 201-219. In Sinananović, O., Hafizović, R., &Pajević, I. (Eds). *Duhovnostimentalnozdravlje (Spirituality and Mental Health).* Svjetlost, Sarajevo.

Hasanović, M. (2017). Tesavvuf– srceislama je nepravaziđenametodaodgojakojavoid integracijiličnosti (Tasawwuf – the heart of Islam is unsurpassed nurturing method which leads to personality integration). *Kelamu'l Šifa' – Historijskonaslijeđe, tesavvufikultura"Eseji o tesvvufu",* 1438; 45-47, XIII:32-39.

Hasanović, M., Hodić, A., Hodić, S., &Pajević, I. (2015). The association of the religious moral beliefs, anxiety, depressiveness, aggressiveness, family relations and addictive behaviors of the school adolescents in the postwar Bosnia-Herzegovina. *European Psychiatry, 30 (S1),* 1-1.

Hasanović, M., &Pajević, I. (2010). Religious moral beliefs as mental health protective factor of war veterans suffering from PTSD, depressiveness, anxiety, tobacco and alcohol abuse in comorbidity. *PsychiatriaDanubina, 22 (2),* 203-210.

Hasanović, M., &Pajević, I. (2013). Religious moral beliefs inversely related to trauma experiences severity and depression severity among war veterans in Bosnia and Herzegovina. *Journal of Religion and Health, 52 (3),* 730-739.

Hasanović, M., & Pajević, I. (2015). Religious moral beliefs inversely related to trauma experiences severity and presented posttraumatic stress disorder among Bosnia and Herzegovina war veterans. *Journal of Religion and Health, 54 (4),* 1403-1415.

Hasanović, M., Pajević, I., &Sinanović, O. (2017). Spiritual and religious Islamic perspectives of healing of posttraumatic stress disorder. *Insights on the Depression and Anxiety,* Heightened Science Publications (1), pp. 23-29.

Hasanović, M., Sinanović, O., Pajević, I., &Agius, M. (2011). The spiritual approach to group psychotherapy treatment of psychotraumatizedpersons in post-war Bosnia and Herzegovina. *Religions, 2 (3),* 330-344.

Isić, A., Pehlić, I., &Neimarlija, M. (2014). Konstukcijaimetrijskekarakteristikeupitnika religioznosti (Creation and psychometric characteristics of religiosity questionnaire), ZbornikradovaIslamskogpedagoškogfakulteta u Zenici, Islamic Pedagogical Faculty in Zenica (*Proceedings*), pp. 17-39.

Izetbegović, A. (1990). Islam izmeđuIstokaiZapada (Islam between the East and the West. Self-publication, Sarajevo.

Jusić, M. (2006). Psihološkadimenzijareligijeireligioznemotivacije. *Novi Muallim, (25),* 60-65.

Karčić, F. (2004). *Bošnjaciiizazovimodernosti: kasniosmanlijskiihabsburški period (The Bosniaks and the Challenges of Modernity: Late Ottoman and Habsburg Times*). El-Kalem, Sarajevo.

Karić, A. (2002). Razumijevanjefenomenapsihičkistabilneličnosti u kontekstuislamskog poimanjaslobodeiuniverzalnogreda (Understanding phenomenon of psychologically stable personality within the context of Islamic understanding of freedom and universal order), pp. 245-249. In Sinananović, O., Hafizović, R., &Pajević, I. (Eds). *DuhovnostiMentalnozdravlje (Spirituality and Mental Health*). Svjetlost, Sarajevo.

Kilic, Z. (2017). Psychological wellbeing and marital satisfaction among Bosnian Sufi women. Unpublished master thesis. International University of Sarajevo, Bosnia and Herzegovina.

Kukavica, E. U. (2016). Promišljanje o duhovnosti u sadašnjemvremenu (Reflecting on spirituality in contemporary time). Živabaština, *Vol 2, 5,* 113-133.

Memić, A. (2020). Pojamličnosti u djelimaEbu Hamida Gazalija (The concept of personality in the works of Abu Hamid Al-Gazali). Unpublished Master thesis. Faculty of Islamic Studies, Sarajevo.

Nakičević, O. (1983). Mjesto Gazi Husrev-begove medrese u sistemuOsmansko-Turskogškolstva i system školstva u OsmanskojTurskoj (Ghazi Husraw-bay Madrasa in the Ottoman-Turkish School System and School System in Ottoman Turkey). *Anali Gazi Husrev-begovebiblioteke,* 6:9-10, 241-262.

Othman, A.H., & Raba, A.M. (1996). Toward Islamization of guidance and counseling. Paper delivered during *National Seminar on Islamization of Psychology*, IIUM (November 30–December 1, 1996), pp. 106-148.

Pajević, I., Hasanović, M., &Delić, A. (2007). The influence of religious moral beliefs on adolescents' mental stability. *PsychiatriaDanubina, 19(3)*, 173-183.

Pajević, I., &Sinanović, O. (2002). Utjecajnamazanaoblikovanjenekihkaraktersitikacrtazrele ličnosti (Impact of prayer on shaping some mature personality characteristics), pp. 237-245. In Sinananović, O., Hafizović, R., &Pajević, I. (Eds). *DuhovnostiMentalnozdravlje (Spirituality and Mental Health)*. Svjetlost, Sarajevo.

Pajević, I., Sinanović, O., & Hasanović, M. (2005). Religiosity and mental health. *Psychiatria Danubina, 17(1-2)*, 84-9.

Pajević, I., Sinanović, O., & Hasanović, M. (2017). Association of Islamic prayer with psychological stability in Bosnian war veterans. *Journal of Religion and-Health, 56(6)*, 2317-2329.

Popara, H. (2006). Bošnjacisuimalidvašejhu-l-islama (Bosniaks had two shaykh-al-islam).

*Preporod*,Retrieved19 November 2020 from https://www.islamskazajednica.ba/index.php?option=com_content&view=article&id=1619%3Abosnjaci-su-imali-dva-sejhu-l-islama&catid=195%3Apromicljanja&Itemid=76

Selimović, E. (1995). *Psihologijaislama. (Psychology of Islam)*. TimaşYayinlari.

Selimović, E. (2002). *Psihologijanamaza. (Psychology of Prayer)*. Self-publication.

Shafi'i, M. (1985). *Freedom from the Self: Sufism, Meditation and Psychotherapy.* Human Sciences Press, New York.

Smajić, A. (2003). Behavioral therapy in the works of selected early Muslim scholars. Unpublished Master thesis. International Islamic University of Malaysia, Kuala Lumpur.

Smajić, A. (2010). Bosnia and Herzegovina: Country report. In Nielsen, J. S., Akgonul, S., Alibašić, A., Marechal, B.,& Moe, C. (Eds). *Yearbook of Muslims in Europe*. Vol. 2, Brill, Leiden, pp. 89-105.

Smajić, A. (2012). Projekatislamizacijeznanja: Osnovneideje, razvojitrenutnostanje(Islamization project: Basic ideas, development and current condition). *Zbornikradova* (Collection of Papers), Faculty of Islamic Studies, No. 16, pp. 252-266.

Smajić, A. (2017a). Religija u susretu s modernompsihologijom: iskustvoKatoličkecrke (Religion in the encounter with modern psychology: The experience of Catholic Church). *Context, 4 (1)*, 7-26.

Smajić, A. (2017b). Islamic leadership in Bosnia and Herzegovina. In Racius, E.,&Zhelyazkova, A. (Eds). *Islamic Leadership in the European Lands of the Former Ottoman and Russian Empires*. Brill, Leiden, pp. 68-88.

Smajić, A.,&Đapo, J. (2019). Religioznostkaoprediktorvrijednosnihorijentacijamladih (Religiosity as a predictor of value orientation of youth). *Zbornikradova-*

*KongresapsihologaBiH* (*Collection of papers from Congress of BiH Psychologists*), pp. 155-177.

Spahić, H. (2002). Islamskiodgojimoralnakrizasavremenogčovjeka (Islamic education andmoral crisis of a contemporary man), pp. 227-237. In Sinananović, O., Hafizović, R., &Pajević, I. (Eds). *Duhovnostimentalnozdravlje* (*Spirituality and Mental Health*). Svjetlost,Sarajevo.

Terzić, I. (2002). Džamijainjenutjecajnapsihuljudi (Mosque and its impact on human psyche), pp. 57-67. In Sinananović, O., Hafizović, R., &Pajević, I. (Eds). *DuhovnostiMentalnozdravlje* (*Spirituality and Mental Health*). Svjetlost, Sarajevo.

Tule, A. (2018). *Arhitekturaduše.*Self-publication. Sarajevo.

Tule, E. (2010). *Socio psihološkedimenzijeKur'ana*. Emanet d.o.o., Zenica.

Tule, E. (2011). *Kur'anskitretmanstresa*. Amos Graf, Sarajevo.

CHAPTER THREE

# The Journey of Islamic Psychology in Egypt: The Case of Muhammad 'Uthman Nagati (1914–2000)

KHALID ELZAMZAMY
ROAA MOUSTAFA AHMED
WALID HASSAN
MOHAMED EL MAHDI

ALTHOUGH PSYCHOLOGY IN Egypt has been dominated by Western-centric theories, methodologies, and approaches, many Egyptian organizations and scholars played a key role in developing and shaping the field known today as Islamic Psychology (IP). This chapter will shed light on the organizational and individual contributions to the emerging field of IP. The chapter will also offer an in-depth examination of the intellectual contributions of Muhammad 'Uthman Nagati (1914–2000), one of the forefathers of IP in Egypt and the Muslim world.

## Introduction

Psychology has been progressively becoming a well-established discipline in Egypt since the educational reform of the 1950s. Scholars who completed their graduate education in European and American universities were influential in the development of the field in Egypt and the region at large. Although psychology in Egypt has been dominated by Western-centric theories, methodologies, and approaches, many Egyptian organizations as well as individual scholars played a key role in developing and shaping the field known today as Islamic

Psychology (IP). This chapter starts with a brief history of the development of psychology in Egypt. The chapter will then explore organizational contributions to IP such as conferences, journals, and professional associations as well as various factors influencing those contributions. Individual scholarly efforts in various domains of IP will be presented followed by an in-depth examination of the contributions of Muhammad 'Uthman Nagati (1914–2000). Nagati's contributions are the focus of the latter part of the chapter due to the encompassing nature of his works and his entire IP endeavor, which serves as a role model for emerging IP scholars and efforts.

## History of Psychology in Egypt

German psychologist Hermann Ebbinghaus (d. 1909) said that psychology has a long past but a short history. This statement precisely describes the development of psychology in Egypt. Descriptions and classifications of human behavior, personality, mental states, and mental disorders can be found sculptured on ancient Egyptian temples. The ancient Egyptians believed that the human soul was made up of many parts, with the "ka" (or vital essence) being the most important. The "ka" was thought to determine individual human traits such as character, nature, or temperaments (Mohamed, 2012). Additionally, Egyptians were interested in psychological experiments. An Egyptian king is believed to have conducted behavioral experiments during the seventh century BC to study the influence of environment on language development (Hunt, 1993, p.1).

In modern Egypt, since the early twentieth century and the establishment of Cairo University, psychology has been markedly influenced by Western psychological schools. This was partly due to the influence of returning Egyptian scholars who had been sent to complete their graduate education in European and North American universities. Decades later, two other prominent universities were established: Ain Shams University and Alexandria University. Currently, psychology departments are housed within the Faculty of Arts across all Egyptian universities. European and American textbooks, in their original or translated forms, as well as Arabic sources deriving directly from them, are the cornerstones of psychology didactics in Egyptian universities. Prominent authors whose works have been utilized include Anne Anastasi, Hans Jurgen Eysenck, Sigmund Freud, Joy Paul Guilford, Ernest Hilgard and Arab scholars such as Yousef Murad, Abdel-Moneim Elmiligui, Louis Kamil Meleika, Muhammad 'Uthman Nagati, and others (Ibrahim, 2014; Mohamed, 2012).

Many developments in the field of psychology in Egypt ensued. The Egyptian Association of Psychological Studies was the first professional body to be established. Other organizations have followed, such as the Egyptian Psychoanalytical Society, Egyptian Society of Clinical Psychology, Egyptian Global Association for Psychological Consultation and Services, and Egyptian Psychological Union. The Egyptian National Translation Center, established by the Egyptian Ministry of Culture, assigned Professor Abdel-Sattar Ibrahim to chair two working groups of experienced professors to translate two major American Psychological Association (APA) and Oxford University Press publications: *The APA Dictionary of Psychology* (Vanden Bos, 2007) and *The Oxford Handbook of the History of Psychology: Global Perspectives* (Baker, 2012; Ibrahim, 2014). The former was published in 2015, while the latter is yet to be published.

## Islamic Psychology in Egypt: Organizational Efforts

Mainstream Western-centric psychology dominates the scene in Egyptian universities. Islamic orientations to psychology do not seem to be popular or prominent, even at Islamically oriented institutes such as Al-Azhar University. There are multiple factors that might contribute to this lack of organizational support for IP. Egypt has experienced increasing political tensions from the 1960s onwards, the majority of which have revolved around Islam's involvement in public life. Governments have played a role in marginalizing, alienating, and ostracizing some religious authorities, figures, and organizations under the cover of countering terrorism and extremism while bringing forth and supporting others (Alzubairi, 2019; Barraclough, 1998; Campagna, 1996; Farah, 2013). The social and psychological ramifications of these ongoing conflicts have conceivably created a degree of sensitivity towards addressing religion in public and academic spaces and, more importantly, in psychological and psychotherapeutic discourses. In such an atmosphere, it takes courage for individuals to bring up religion in academic spaces. That being said, Egyptian society is frequently described as being "religious by nature," and religion shapes the day-to-day activities of millions of Egyptians (Abou-Youssef et al., 2015; Klevesath, 2014).

Despite this sociopolitical atmosphere, the field of psychology in Egypt witnessed the emergence of a few organized efforts advocating for an Islamic orientation for psychology. These organized efforts took the form of conferences, magazines, and periodicals and establishing professional associations.

One of the earliest organized efforts with an overreaching impact was the establishment of *Jam'iyyat Al-Muslim Al-Muaser* (The Modern Muslim Foundation). The foundation was an educational and research platform founded by Dr. Gamal 'Atiyya in 1974. Through its magazine *Majallat Al-Muslim Al-Muaser (Journal of the Modern Muslim)*, which carried the same name, and many other publications, the foundation focused on dealing with contemporary life issues in view of Islamic teachings. Over the years, the foundation facilitated discussions on the Islamic roots of sciences, including psychology. The magazine was still actively publishing in 2021:https://almuslimalmuaser.org.

Another organized initiative geared toward a clinical application of IP was the World Islamic Association for Mental Health (WIAMH), founded in 1983 by Gamal AbouElazayem, Mohammed Rashid Chaudhry, Osama El-Rady, Omar Shaheen, Arshad Hussain, and Farouk Sendiony. The association's main objective was to promote Islamically adapted models of care to Muslims via conducting culturally appropriate research. The central notion of the WIAMH was that modern psychiatry had to be adapted to the needs of Muslim cultures in all aspects, including diagnosis, treatment, and the establishment of psychiatric facilities. Since its foundation, the WIAMH has conducted numerous national and international conferences around the world, including Cairo, Egypt, in 1987 and 1994. It also pioneered global work in trauma psychology for Muslims. However, the focus of the association's work was more to advance the field commonly referred to as Muslim mental health (MMH) rather than purely IP. *Al-Nafs Al-Motmaena*(*The Peaceful Soul*) was a bimonthly magazine published by WIAMH that promoted topics related to its mission(for more information, see http://arabpsynet.com/Associations/WIAMH.ass.htmand https://www.elazayem.com/wiamh).

In the 1980s and 1990s, a few important conferences and seminars took place in Egypt. Some of these conferences concerned the Islamic orientation of sciences in general, such as the one organized by Al-Azhar University in 1992. Other conferences were geared predominantly towards IP, such as the 1989 conference organized by the International Institute of Islamic Thought (IIIT) in collaboration with local Islamic societies. Thirty-four research papers were presented, and the seminar concluded with a set of recommendations highlighting the need for the emerging IP field to develop accurate terminology as well as proper curricula (Al-'Isa, 2015).

In support of the above efforts, various publishers showed an interest in the field of IP and published many of the books that will be mentioned in the following sections. These publishers included Dar Al-Shurouq, Nahdet Misr Publishing Group, General Egyptian Book Organization, Dar Al Salam, and Iqraa Establishment.

In addition to printed publications, a few websites supervised by prominent psychiatrists have been offering educational content to the public, and a significant proportion pertains to mental well-being. These websites include www.maganin.com, which is supervised by Dr. Wael Abu Hindi, and www.elazayem.com, supervised by Dr. Mahmoud Gamal Abou Elazayem.

Finally, the status of IP curricula in Egyptian universities bears mentioning. The general observation is that IP has not found its way into mainstream Egyptian university education. Most curricula and syllabi revolve around Western-centric disciplines, themes, and methodologies. One might think the situation would be different at Al-Azhar University; however, anecdotal reports from students at Al-Azhar highlight this trend. Although the undergraduate psychology syllabus at Al-Azhar University (which was reviewed by one of the authors, "KE") does mention Islamic values as being central to its mission and learning objectives, this does not seem to reflect teaching psychology from within an Islamic paradigm. Rather, there are courses on *fiqh*, ethics, Quran, and Hadith that are taught from a religious perspective but not a perspective that explores their interaction with psychology.

## Islamic Psychology in Egypt: Individual Efforts

The IP scene in Egypt is believed to have been spearheaded by the written initiatives of a few scholars in the 1950s and 1960s. One of the forefathers of IP in Egypt with overreaching intellectual efforts was Muhammad 'Uthman Nagati (1914–2000), whom we discuss at length below. Another prominent early figure was Qutb (1919–2014), who taught at Umm Al Qura University and whose writings influenced the founders of modern IP, such as Malik Badri. The contributions of Egyptian scholars to IP can be classified into various themes and approaches.

Many earlier works attempted to offer an Islamic ontological discourse on human nature and faculties. These included Muhammad Qutb's (1952, 2005) work. The former book may be considered one of the earliest Islamic criticisms of modern psychological theories, including Freud's theories and behaviorism. Qutb advocated for an Islamic grounding of all social and psychological sciences away from the Eurocentric views that emerged in what can be described as an anti-religious environment. Along the same lines of building an Islamic understanding of human nature from the ground up, a series of books were written by Sayyid Abdulhamid Morsi and more recently by Sa'd Riyad (Morsi, 1983, 1985, 1989, 1992, 1994; Riyad, 2004a, 2004b, 2008). Elmahdi (2002a) attempted to portray an Islamic view on various components of a human being, namely *fitrah* (natural disposition), psyche, mind, heart, and soul. He also offered an Islamic perspective on various psychological disciplines such as perceptions, thoughts, motivation, and emotions.

Sufi scholarly perspectives on the nature of humans and the treatment of various psycho-spiritual ailments were expounded by 'Amir Al-Najjar and Hasan Al-Sharqawi. Al-Najjar is a scholar of Islamic philosophy known for his passion to revive the Islamic intellectual heritage. In his treatise titled *Al-Tasawwuf al-Nafsi (Psychological Sufism)*, Al-Najjar (2002) presented the views of three Sufi scholars who lived in the third century: Al-Muhasibi, Al-Hakim Al-Tirmidhi, and Al-Tusturi. Al-Sharqawi's (1976) *Nahw 'Ilm Nafs Islami (Towards an Islam-*

*ic Psychology*)addressed ontological and foundational concepts and explored various psycho-spiritual illnesses as well as psycho-spiritual healing strategies. He launched a staunch attack on certain modern psychological theories such as Freud's. Al-Sharqawi proposes that the Sufi discourse is in the best position to produce an Islamic vision for psychology and psychological well-being.

Other scholarly works attempted to provide the emerging field of IP with a working operational framework that includes definitions and foundational principles. Ibrahim Ragab was a central Egyptian figure in the Islamization movement of social sciences. Although Ragab's major contributions were not purely on IP, his works provided central concepts relevant to the Islamization of psychology (Ragab, 1992, 1996). Nagati (2001b) and Omar (1983) wrote *An Introduction to Islamic Psychology* and *Characteristics of Islamic Psychology*, respectively. Another attempt, *Towards an Operational Constitution for Muslim Psychologists*, was undertaken by Mahmoud (1990), former Head of the Psychology Department at Cairo University. Mahmoud shed light on the importance of Muslims paying attention to the field of psychology and making use of the rational, empirical, and objective findings in the Western field while retaining and emphasizing an Islamic identity. He encouraged Muslim psychologists to turn to the Quran, the Sunnah, and the rich Islamic traditions to extract Islamically grounded and informed psychological approaches. On a practical note, Mahmoud proposed 33 examples of research domains to be undertaken by Muslim researchers. Abu Hatab (1992), from Ain Shams University, wrote *Towards an Islamic Paradigm for Psychology*. In this paper, Abu Hatab critically surveyed the existing works by Muslim psychologists on IP. He explored their major critiques of Western psychology as well as the major reactions and positions held by them. He also identified the following six main directions in the emerging IP field:

- Psychology of religion
- Arabic Islamic Psychology
- Quranic Psychology
- Sufi Psychology
- Shi'i Psychology
- Psychological studies in the Islamic intellectual tradition

As a natural inclination for any emerging Islamic discourse, some Egyptian scholars turned to the Quran, the Sunnah, and the rich intellectual Muslim tradition to extract guidance and wisdom. Although all IP books and publications drew from the Quran, the Sunnah, and Islamic tradition in one way or another, what is meant here are direct attempts to explore Islamic scriptures and intellectual tradition for psychological themes and topics. Many of the books written in this genre were given titles that reflected psychology in the Quran, psychology in the Sunnah, and psychology in the Islamic intellectual tradition. Nagati (2001a, 2005) and Riyad (2004a, 2004b) each published books titled *Psychology in the Quran* and *Psychology in the Sunnah*. Al-Sharqawi (1989), in his *Foundational Psychological Concepts in the Quran and The Question of Terminology*, focused on Quranic psychological terminology to advocate the use of Islamically informed psychological language in Muslim research. The rich Islamic intellectual heritage was the subject of extensive investigation and exploration by Nagati (1993) and Rabi' (2004). The abovementioned *Al-Tasawwuf al-Nafsi*by Al-Najjar (2002) may also be considered one of these attempts, exploring in particular the Sufi tradition for psychological wisdom. Finally, a massive collective undertaking was launched by IIIT to explore, survey, summarize, and present more than 400 classical treatises written by more than 100 Muslim scholars spanning the first *hijri* century to the fourteenth *hijri* century. It was published in four volumes titled *'Ilm al-Nafs fi al-Turath al-Islami* (*Psychological Sciences in the Islamic Heritage*). This project was a collaborative effort supervised by Egyptian scholars Muhammad 'Uthman Nagati, Abd Al-Halim Mahmoud, Tarif Shawqi Faraj, and Abdel-Moneim Shehata Mahmoud. All contributors to this project (more than 20 professors) were professors of psychology from Egyptian Universities (Abd Al-Hamid et al., 2008; Majariyya et al., 2011).

Another angle that received attention in Egypt was the clinical applications of IP in the domains of health and well-being. The relationship between Islamic religiosity, psychology, psychiatry, and mental well-being was the focus of many works written by Gamal Madi Abu-l-'Azayem, a renowned Egyptian psychiatrist who held many leadership positions in Egyptian and international psychiatric organizations; Mohamed El Mahdi, former Chair of the Psychiatry Department at Al-Azhar University; and Mohamed Omar Salem, who was originally from Alexandria and held teaching positions at the University of London and the UAE University and is currently practicing in Qatar (Elmahdi, 2002b; Salem & Foskett, 2009). A few other books drew on themes of psychological well-being from the Quran and the Islamic teachings (Abu-l-'Azayem, 1994; Morsi, 1994). Elmahdi (1990) and Abu Hindi (2002) tackled psychopathology and psychotherapy through an Islamic psychological lens. They addressed topics such as the history of psychiatry in the Muslim world, common myth surrounding mental illness in Muslim societies, foundations of Islamic psychotherapies, and the role of spiritual phenomena and spiritual interventions in Muslim mental health. Other scholars also proposed Islamically informed models of assessment and treatment in clinical settings. Mohammad Sharif Salem and Wael Abu Hindi dedicated special monographs to the topic of OCD and its assessment and treatment, both of which were best-sellers and widely recognized (Abu

Hindi, 2003; Salem, 2008). Mohamed Omar Salem proposed an Islamic theory for the mind as well as models of Islamically integrated therapy (Salem, 2003, 2007, 2009, 2010; Salem & Hamdan, 2010). Another area that Salem pioneered was the study of sleep and dreams from an Islamic perspective. He conducted empirical studies and offered theoretical frameworks, all of which were featured at international conferences and in encyclopedias on the study of dreams (Elzamzamy& Salem, 2020; Salem & Yousef, 2010; Salem et al., 2009, 2013).

The following section will focus on the contributions of an Egyptian scholar who contributed profusely to IP, Muhammad 'Uthman Nagati.

## Muhammad 'Uthman Nagati (or Mohamed Osman Nagaty, 1914–2000)

As early as 1948, the term *'ilm al-nafs al-Islami*(IP) appeared in the writings of Professor Muhammad 'Uthman Nagati, who some consider to be the first to coin the term (Nagati, 2001b). The way Nagati defined the term in his earlier writings, however, did not reflect the sophistication and maturity used in his later IP works. In his earlier works, he used the term IP to denote the contributions of classical Muslim scholars to the understanding of the human psyche (Nagati, 1980). As the field of IP became mature to some extent, Nagati offered more detailed and nuanced conceptual definitions of IP.

Nagati was not an ordinary psychologist who simply developed an interest in the Islamic perspective on human beings. Rather, he established himself as one of the most influential Arab psychologists of his time. After completing his PhD at Yale University, Nagati was instrumental in developing the field of psychology in the Arab region. In fact, he established the first psychology department and program in the Gulf region at Kuwait University (Ibrahim, 2012). His mainstream psychological contributions ranged from supervising countless graduate dissertations; writing authoritative texts on various disciplines of psychology in the Arabic language; translating key English psychological texts, especially texts written by Freud; and translating psychometric tests into Arabic (Al-Shinnawi, 1996, p. 249; Freud, 1982a, 1982b, 2006, 2018; Nagati, 1960a, 1960b; Zahran, 2005, p.225). In recognition of his contributions to the field of psychology, Nagati was awarded the *Mustafa Ziwer Award in Psychological Sciences* in 1993. The award, offered annually by the *Center for Psychological and Psychosomatic Studies* in Lebanon, is named after another Egyptian giant in the field of psychology, Professor Mustafa Ziwer (Markaz Al-Dirasat Al-Nafsiyya, n.d.).

Nagati's IP contributions were no less significant than his contributions to mainstream psychology in the Arab region. In addition to supervising the massive collaborative encyclopedic IP three-volume publication by IIIT titled *'Ilm al-Nafs fi al-Turath al-Islami* (*Psychological Sciences in the Islamic Heritage*),which provided annotations for hundreds of classical Islamic psychological texts, Nagati himself surveyed, summarized, and analyzed the efforts of numerous classical Muslim scholars in his study *Al-Dirasat al-Nafsaniyya 'ind al-'Ulama' al-Muslimin* (*Psychological Studies of Muslim Scholars*) (Nagati, 1993). Nagati's IP efforts included works that drew directly from Islamic roots and scriptures (Quran and Sunnah) as well as from the Islamic intellectual heritage. He also attempted to offer the newly born field of IP a sense of direction and framework by offering his insights in *Madkhalila 'Ilm al-Nafs al-Islami* (*An Introduction to Islamic Psychology*) (Nagati, 2001b). He brought his passion about IP to the classroom by establishing an independent course on IP, which was taught in the undergraduate psychology program at Kuwait University (Ibrahim, 2012). He also taught a graduate course on IP at the Imam Muhammad Ibn Saud Islamic University in Riyadh during the years 1985–1987 (Nagati, 2001b, p.29).

The originality, brilliance, and impact of Nagati's ideas were widely recognized. Many editions have been printed of all his IP books, which speaks to their positive reception in the field and among the public. His work on Ibn Sina's theory on human perception was forwarded and praised by Shaykh Mustafa Abd al-Raziq (1885–1947), the former Grand Shaykh of al-Azhar and former Egyptian Minister of Awqaf. Some sources claim that Nagati was honored with the notable King Faisal Prize as well as the Award of the Islamic Conference in Kuwait (Abdulaziz Saud Al-Babtain Cultural Foundation, n.d.), but this information could not be verified.

Another unique aspect of Nagati's brilliance is his poetry, which he infuses with psychological vibes. His name is featured in the *Al-Babtain Directory*, a contemporary index of Arab Poets from the nineteenth and twentieth centuries. Nagati's eloquent poetry is laden with emotions, psychological expressions, and descriptions of nature. His family possesses a handwritten collection of his poetry (Abdulaziz Saud Al-Babtain Cultural Foundation, n.d.).

Nagati was born in Khartoum, Sudan, in 1914, and lived in Sudan, Egypt, the United States, Kuwait, and Saudi Arabia. He completed his undergraduate and graduate studies at Cairo University (formerly known as King Fuad I University), where he later served as a professor and in other academic leadership positions (Abdulaziz Saud Al-Babtain Cultural Foundation, n.d.; Prothro &Melikian, 1955). He completed his postgraduate studies at Yale University, as mentioned earlier. Alongside his academic studies, Nagati was a close student of Shaykh Mustafa Abd al-Raziq, the former Grand Shaykh of al-Azhar. Shaykh Mustafa was an enthusiast of Islamic philosophy, which immensely impacted Nagati's career and writings. Perhaps his choice of writing on Ibn Sina's works very early in his career reflected the influence of Shaykh Abd al-Raziq.

The following section delves into Nagati's three main areas of contribution to IP: (1) his vision and proposed plan for the emerging field of IP, (2) his exploration of the Islamic scriptures in search of psychological truths, and (3) his historical journey as he attempted to unveil the contributions of classical Muslim scholars to the understanding of human beings.

### NAGATI'S VISION FOR THE IP FIELD

One of the last books to be published by Nagati summarized his vision for the emerging field of IP. The book was published in 2001, a year after his death, and titled *Madkhalila 'Ilm al-Nafs al-Islami* (*An Introduction to Islamic Psychology*). Nagati wrote this book to offer some foundational principles on which the field of IP can be built. The book may be considered a capstone project for his IP journey, which followed his extensive exploration of the psychological themes in the Quran, the Sunnah, and the Islamic scholarly tradition. One of the strengths of the book is its thorough historical tracing of the IP movement, its terminology, and its major contributors (Nagati, 2001b).

The first task Nagati attempted to accomplish in this book was to clarify the terminological and conceptual foundations of IP. He highlighted how, considering the emerging nature of the field, there has not been a consensus among scholars on a title or a term for the IP field. From among all the terms used to denote the IP movement—such as Islamization, Islamic orientation, Islamic foundations, and Islamic perspectives—Nagati favored the term *'Ilm al-Nafs al-Islami* (IP). He traced the historical usages and meanings of the various terms used by contemporary scholars and responded to critics. The definition he proposed for IP was "Psychology that is based on the Islamic conception of the human being, the Islamic principles, and the truths of the Islamic *shari'a*." (Nagati, 2001b, p.16).

The epistemological and ontological aspects of modern psychology were appraised by Nagati. He presented an overview of the Islamic epistemological foundations of sciences (sources of knowledge in Islam). Nagati proposed that IP should adopt a moderate position regarding Western psychology in terms of acceptance vs. rejection. He favored a position that does not reject modern psychology and its findings in their totality. In fact, he did not believe that Islam contradicts the objective, evidence-based research findings in psychology. He sided with Malik Badri in his conclusion that the major objections towards modern psychology lie within the baseless theories proposed by some of its founders rather than the objective findings. Nagati applauded the contributions of modern psychology in applied fields like educational psychology, organizational psychology, military psychology, and cognitive psychology. His central critiques of modern psychology revolved around the materialistic and reductionist view of human beings found in the behaviorist and Freudian schools of thought. Nagati drew attention to the revisionist approaches and new theories emerging within the field of modern psychology that indicate its evolving and changeable nature. This very nature opens the door for indigenous psychological approaches to arise. Nagati established five central notions pertaining to the Islamic epistemology of science and ontology of human nature. These five notions are presuppositions for the emerging IP and include the following:

- Belief in Allah, the angels, the revealed texts, the messengers, and the Day of Judgment.
- Unity of the truth, which refers to the fact that rational truths do not contradict revealed truths.
- Human beings are created by God and are made up of a body and a soul.
- Human beings by disposition are inclined towards goodness.
- Human beings have a free choice and a free will.
- The Quran and Sunnah are sources for ultimate knowledge about humans.

Prior to presenting his proposed plan for the foundation of an IP discipline, Nagati brought light to the situation of the field of psychology in universities throughout the Muslim world. He criticized the reliance on social sciences produced in the West, which reflected the values and culture of those societies and not necessarily of the universal human experience. He highlighted some of the historical, political, and social root causes for this phenomenon in Muslim universities, a major one being the split of the educational trajectory into a religious track and a secular track. This split leads to two types of scholarship produced in isolation of each other. Nagati expressed his hope that Muslim universities and scholars will take the lead in establishing the field of IP through serious academic efforts in research and teaching as well as through collaborations with experts in Islamic studies.

Nagati proposed a strategic plan for the foundation of IP that consisted of seven vital steps, shown in Table 1. These steps are to be undertaken collaboratively by the IP scholarly community.

**Table 1. Seven-step strategic plan proposed by Nagati for the establishment of IP**

| | | |
|---|---|---|
| 1 | Mastery of modern psychology | Subject matter expertise in all aspects of the field is critical including knowledge of its history, methodology, theories, findings, and problems, in addition to subject matter expertise in the subfields of psychology. |
| 2 | Mastery of the Islamic tradition | Knowledge of the Islamic principles and foundations is necessary to enable IP scholars to formulate sound psychological theories and foundations. This can be substituted by collaborating with scholars of Islamic studies. |
| 3 | Knowledge of the Muslim intellectual psychological heritage | A key point to investigate is how Muslim scholars reconciliated between ancient and Greek philosophies and the Islamic tradition. |
| 4 | Critique of modern psychology | Once the above the three steps are accomplished, Muslim scholars will be able to use a filter-approach to examine modern psychology and to adopt only with is aligned with the Islamic tradition and to scrutinize what is not. |
| 5 | Conducting Islamically oriented theoretical and empirical research studies | This is a proactive step which attempts to produce knowledge from within an Islamic frame of reference. This step requires collaboration between Muslim universities and attempts to find solutions to problems facing humanity. The main domain of study proposed here are: 1. Theoretical and 2. Empirical. The theoretical domain includes writings on the Islamic perspective on psychological concepts as well as writings surveying the psychological views of classical Muslim scholars. |
| 6 | Organizing academic conferences and seminars | This requires collaborative efforts between scholars and universities. It also requires a collaboration between Muslim psychologists and scholars of Islamic studies. |
| 7 | Rewriting psychology within an Islamic framework | This step is the culmination of all the above steps which allow the rewriting of a psychological discipline from an Islamic perspective. |

## PSYCHOLOGICAL TRUTHS IN THE QURAN AND THE SUNNAH

Nagati published the first editions of his renowned works, *The Quran and Psychology* and *The Prophetic Hadith and Psychology*, in 1982 and 1989, respectively. To our knowledge, both works are the most extensive in the genre that explore the psychological discourse in the Islamic scriptures. Each of these works exceeded 300 pages and included a wide range of themes and subthemes. Nagati portrayed how a full image of the human being can be painted based on the Quran and Hadith traditions. He described human nature, its various states and traits, its drives and emotions, its ailments and deviations, and its means to attaining well-being. Throughout his discourse, Nagati displayed the core distinction between modern psychology and a psychology that is based on the Islamic tradition. This core distinction lies in the reductionism of modern psychology to human nature and what is objective and measurable. On the other hand, the Islamic scriptures look at the human being more holistically. This can be seen throughout the chapters of both books (Nagati, 2001a, 2005).

Table 2 highlights the key psychological principles and remarks attained through Nagati's exploration of the Quran and the Sunnah in the abovementioned books.

**Table 2. Key psychological principles and remarks in the Quran and the Sunnah as portrayed by Nagati**

| | MAIN THEMES | KEY POINTS |
|---|---|---|
| 1 | Drives and Motives | • The role of drives and motives in driving human behaviors has been recognized in the scriptures including physiological, psychological, and spiritual drives.<br>• Physiological drives serve an existential purpose while spiritual drives seek to attain a connection with the Divine.<br>• These drives are partly dispositional and partly acquired and they influence behaviors consciously and unconsciously.<br>• Scriptures aim to regulate and strike a balance between these drives to attain happiness in this world and the hereafter for individuals and societies.<br>• Unrestrained drives can lead to destruction, deviation, and pathology.<br>• Regulating sexual drives is an important theme in the scriptures.<br>• Emotions play a significant role in regulating or unleashing human drives. |

| | | |
|---|---|---|
| 2 | Emotions | • Various emotional states have been described such as love, fear, happiness, hatred, jealousy, envy, sadness, guilt, and bashfulness (*ḥaya'*).<br>• Emotional regulation and balance is a praiseworthy state while uncontrolled emotional states can lead to negative outcomes.<br>• Scriptures recommended approaches for regulating emotions and offered comprehensive measures for treating unhealthy emotional reactions.<br>• Emotions are associated with physical manifestations. |
| 3 | Sensory perception | • Sensations are faculties created by God to serve an essential purpose in human existence.<br>• External and internal factors may alter or hinder sensory perceptions. Internal factors include emotional states as well as drives, motives, and values.<br>• Scriptures referred to extra-sensory perception as well as illusions. |
| 4 | Cognition | • Cognitive abilities are what distinguishes humans from other creatures.<br>• Scriptures endorsed and encouraged thinking, reflection, observation, creativity, and searching for answers.<br>• Practical steps for problem-solving are exemplified in the scriptures, particularly in the stories of the Prophets.<br>• Scriptures referred to thinking errors which may lead to rigidity and faulty conclusions. |
| 5 | Learning | • Humans are created with a natural disposition and potential to learn and acquire knowledge and skills.<br>• Two sources of knowledge are acknowledged, namely human and Divine, both of which complement each other.<br>• The virtues of knowledge and seeking knowledge are unsurpassed.<br>• Learning languages is of utmost significance.<br>• Some learning principles and methods were laid in the scriptures such as modelling, experimenting, trial and error, repetition, active participation, rewarding, questioning, and reasoning.<br>• Motivation is a key driving force for learning and scriptures show various ways of igniting the learner's motivation.<br>• Scriptures emphasized the role of attention in learning.<br>• Gradual teaching which is spaced over time is an endorsed approach for teaching. |

| | | |
|---|---|---|
| 6 | Divinely inspired knowledge (*al-'ilm al-ladunni*) | • Abilities of the human brain are limited and hence humans need Divine guidance in the form of revelation, prophethood, and dreams.<br>• Modern psychology ignores Divine revelation and inspiration as epistemological sources of knowledge. The term 'inspiration' in modern psychology exclusively refers to the realm of creativity.<br>• Biological and psychological determinants of human behaviors are not independent of Divine destiny and omnipotence. |
| 7 | Development | • The miraculous stages of embryonic development are mentioned in the scriptures which call upon pondering on the creation and the beginnings of human beings.<br>• Many references are found in the scriptures to early childhood development and its interactions with the environment.<br>• Prerequisites of healthy development across various stages are dispersed within the verses and *ahadith*. |
| 8 | Memory | • Scriptures, particularly the Quran, refer to various kinds of forgetfulness and heedlessness. However, being a religious text, most of these references pertain to spiritual heedlessness rather than biological or organic types of memory impairment.<br>• Some remedies for heedlessness were offered in the Quran.<br>• Repetition and remembrance are recognized as aids to memory development. |
| 9 | The nervous system | • Scriptures referred to the decline in cognitive abilities associated with senility.<br>• Scriptures associated certain functions with the brain and associated accountability with activities executed by the brain. |

| | | |
|---|---|---|
| 10 | Personality | • All modern attempts to provide a comprehensive theory of human personality have failed and have ignored the spiritual aspect of existence.<br>• Scriptures are rich with texts describing key aspects of the human personality including various healthy and maladaptive states and traits as well as ways to develop and modify traits.<br>• Individual differences are acknowledged in the scriptures.<br>• Role of biological (genetic) and environmental factors in the development of personality is acknowledged in the scriptures.<br>• Scriptures offered various typologies and classifications of personalities.<br>• Healthy and maladaptive traits, states, and coping mechanisms are described. |
| 11 | Psychological well-being | • Religion and spirituality play a significant role in mental health and are considered indicators of mental well-being.<br>• Striking a balance between the needs of the body and the needs of the soul is key to mental health which was exemplified in the life of the Prophet (peace and blessings of God be upon him).<br>• The Islamic spiritual approach to achieving well-being has three pillars: belief in Allah and worshipping Him alone; God-consciousness (taqwa); Acts of worship.<br>• The Prophet instilled in his follower's positive psychological states such as an internal sense of safety, self-confidence, sense of responsibility, independence and autonomy, contentment with God's destiny, patience, productivity, and efficiency.<br>• A positive mental state will reflect on one's relationship with God, with themselves, with their society, and with the universe at large. |
| 12 | Psychological treatment | • The Islamic scriptures had a transformational impact on the characters of early believers.<br>• Religion and spirituality are central in any effort aiming at psychological wellbeing, including prevention or treatment efforts.<br>• Religious communities can be a source of strength and resilience.<br>• Scriptures aim at changing people's beliefs, ideas, behaviors, and perspectives into positive ones which is the same aim of psychotherapy.<br>• Scriptures are rich with behavioral modification strategies.<br>• Physical and mental health are interrelated. |

## NAGATI'S JOURNEY INTO THE ISLAMIC PSYCHOLOGICAL HERITAGE

Nagati firmly believed that a critical step in building IP as a discipline lies in the exploration of the Islamic intellectual heritage. This exploration serves multiple functions. First, it allows IP scholars to utilize and draw upon contributions that spanned the course of 15 centuries. Second, it bridges a historical gap frequently found in the writings of modern psychology historians who tend to bypass the Islamic civilization. Third, it builds upon psychological knowledge that was produced by Muslim scholars in Muslim communities. Fourth, it exemplifies approaches exerted by Muslim scholar to reconcile Islamically driven knowledge and knowledge acquired from other cultures and traditions. Fifth, it allows for the development of a holistic understanding of human beings. Finally, it complements the psychological truths derived from the Quran and the Sunnah.

Nagati launched his own journey as well as supervised a major effort directed by the IIIT. His journey started in the early 1940s when he published the first edition of *Al-Idrak al-Hissi 'Ind Ibn Sina* (*Sensory Perception in Ibn Sina's Works*). In this book, Nagati conducted an extensive historical study of one psychological theory, sensory perception, in the works of one scholar, Ibn Sina. However, the findings of the study were well-situated in the historical context and were analyzed in relation to Greek literature, which predated Ibn Sina's work, as well as Islamic literature, which surrounded the time of Ibn Sina. Nagati correlated his findings with modern psychology as well. Nagati's personal interest in the psychological legacy of Muslim scholars culminated in the publication of a 300-page monograph titled *Al-Dirasat al-Nafsaniyya 'ind al-'Ulama' al-Muslimin* (*Psychological Studies of Muslim Scholars*) (Nagati, 1993). This monograph originally started as lectures Nagati taught to undergraduate students at the Imam Muhammad Ibn Saud Islamic University in Riyadh during the years 1984–1987. The monograph dedicated sections to explore the psychological themes found in the writings of the following fourteen scholars:

- Al-Kindi (801–866 CE)
- Abu Bakr Al-Razi (864–925 CE)
- Al-Farabi (872–950 CE)
- Miskawayh (unknown to 1030 CE)
- Ikhwan Al-Safa (10th Century CE)
- Ibn Sina (Avicenna) (980–1037 CE)
- Ibn Hazm (994–1064 CE)
- Al-Ghazali (1058–1111 CE)
- Ibn Bajah (1082–1138 CE)
- Ibn Tufail (unknown to 1185 CE)
- Ibn Rushd (1126–1198 CE)

- Fakhr Al-Din Al-Razi (1150–1210 CE)
- Ibn Taymiyya (1263–1328 CE)
- Ibn Al-Qayyim Al-Jawziyya (1292–1350 CE)

The themes explored included theory of knowledge, ontology of the *nafs*, mental faculties, human states and traits, sleep and dreams, emotions and emotional regulation, happiness, behaviors and behavior modification, treating psychological ailments, and parenting and childhood development. Nagati made it clear that he focused on the psychological rather philosophical themes proposed by these scholars. He drew comparisons and associations between some of the ideas of the scholars and modern theories and applications.

In addition to this monograph, Nagati was selected by the IIIT, alongside the Egyptian scholar Abd Al-Halim Mahmoud Al-Sayyid (1936–2010), to supervise a massive project that surveyed, summarized, and annotated more than 300 treatises written by more than 100 Muslim scholars. This effort was published in 2008 in three volumes spanning 1,500 pages titled *'Ilm al-Nafs fi al-Turath al-Islami* (*Psychological Sciences in the Islamic Heritage*). The three volumes were organized chronologically starting with Ibn Sirin (d. 729 CE) and ending with Abu Al-'Ula Afifi (d. 1966 CE). Eleven professors of psychology from various Egyptian universities annotated the treatises. The aim of the project was to act as a guide for researchers in the field of IP. The project had intended to include published and unpublished classical treatises; however, due to lack of resources, it ended up including only published treatises (and not all of them). The IIIT initially printed 100 copies and distributed them to scholars and experts in the field, hoping to collect their feedback and appraisal of the methodology and content of the encyclopedia. However, they were disappointed by the fact that, over the course of six years, only two responses were received (Abd Al-Hamid et al., 2008). A fourth volume was later published in 2011 in the same series by a larger group of Egyptian professors supervised by Abd Al-Halim Mahmoud, Tarif Shawqi Faraj, and Abdel-Moneim Shehata Mahmoud (Majariyya et al., 2011).

## Discussion

It is evident from IP's journey in Egypt that an enthusiasm about this emerging field existed at one time, especially among individual scholars. However, individual efforts seem to have declined in the past two decades, especially since 2010. As evident from the information presented earlier, the degree of organizational support for IP in Egypt has been limited to a small number of entities. Apart from some IP conferences held in the 1980s and 90s, there did not appear to be a continued effort to host further conferences or seminars in Egypt. Organizations such as the World Islamic Association for Mental Health (WIAMH) exist in theory; however, active efforts to propagate their mission and develop new knowledge and future IP scientists is in question. The last activity on their website dates many years back. Universities across Egypt do not seem to be formally offering IP courses or integrating IP into mainstream courses. Perhaps this lack of organizational support, in addition to other sociopolitical factors, might have led to the declining productivity.

Moreover, apart from the IIIT collaborative project on the Islamic psychological heritage, the individual scholarly efforts seem to be disjointed and largely lacking engagement with each other. Some of these efforts were originally papers presented at IP conferences held in Cairo in the 1980s and 90s. There were many attempts then by Egyptian scholars to propose a framework for the field of IP, including the one undertaken by Nagati. Other attempts are still being offered to date on the global scene of IP (Al-Karam, 2018, 2020; Jakhdal, 2018). The impact of the earlier frameworks offered by Egyptian scholars needs to be investigated.

The works of Egyptian scholars, in general, might be invisible to the international IP community due to language barriers. Given that many IP efforts are taking place today in non-Arabic speaking scholarly communities, there is a need to translate and present the works of Egyptian scholars to the international community. Some of the books and efforts published by Egyptian scholars have the potential to move the field forward if considered and if disseminated properly. Doing so saves new scholars the need to reinvent the wheel.

Al-Azhar University is in a unique position to advance the field of IP. Students at Al-Azhar University are dually trained. They complete their professional degrees while advancing their knowledge of Islamic studies, which equips them with the necessary tools to accomplish important tasks for the IP discipline.

Muhammad 'Uthman Nagati can be safely considered one of the most prolific and influential contributors to IP in the last century. He not only proposed a comprehensive, seven-step vision and strategy for the foundation of IP, but he individually and collaboratively undertook many projects that served to accomplish this vision and strategy in his lifetime. He mastered modern psychology and obtained his PhD from Yale University, and he mastered the Islamic tradition to a certain extent as evident from his writings. He extensively explored the Muslim intellectual tradition and criticized certain aspects of modern psychology in almost all his writings. He actively participated in and organized academic conferences and seminars and taught undergraduate and graduate psychology courses from within the IP vision that he pioneered. Indeed, Nagati's contributions surpass those accomplished by entire communities of IP scholars.

## Conclusion

The authors attempted to present a glimpse of the overall scene of IP in Egypt, and it is possible that the chapter did not capture every single IP activity in Egypt. One of the limitations of this chapter is its reliance largely on accessible printed material, anecdotal and personal reports, and information available on the internet. As the adage in the medical field goes, "'If it [something you did with the patient] is not written down [in the patient's file], then it didn't happen!" Chronological and physical distance between the authors and some of the abovementioned scholars, organizations, and events might have limited the information available. Although there is a massive religious publication industry in Egypt with a plethora of works on themes of spiritual development and self-purification, which may be indirectly considered IP literature, this chapter focused on works published within the framework of psychology and IP. The authors hope that the information presented above inspires aspiring scholars and organizations to continue carrying on the legacy of Nagati and other scholars, despite the sociopolitical challenges.

## References

Abd Al-Hamid, I. S., Muhammad, T. S., Abu Sari', U. S., Khalifa, A. M. Abd Al-Mun'im, A. M., Mahmoud, A. S., Yusuf, J. S., Shalabi, M. A., Ridwan, S. G., Al-Sabwa, M. N., Abd Allah, M. S., Al-Sayyid, A. M., &Nagati, M. U. (2008). *'Ilm al-nafs fi al-turath al-Islami* (Psychological sciences in the Islamic heritage) (Vols. 1–3). Dar Al Salam & International Institute of Islamic Thought.

Abdulaziz Saud Al-Babtain Cultural Foundation. (n.d.). *Muhammad 'Uthman Nagati.*Almoajam. https://www.almoajam.org/lists/inner/6647

Abou-Youssef, M. M. H., Kortam, W., Abou-Aish, E., & El-Bassiouny, N. (2015). Effects of religiosity on consumer attitudes toward Islamic banking in Egypt. *International Journal of Bank Marketing, 33*(6), 786–807.

Abu Hatab, F. (1992). NahwwijhaIslamiyya l-'ilm al-nafs (Towards an Islamic Paradigm for Psychology). *AlMuslimAlMuasir, 62,* 135–184.

Abu Hindi, W. (2002). *NahwtibbnafsiIslami* (Towards an Islamic psychiatry). NahdetMisr Publishing Group.

Abu Hindi, W. (2003). *Al-waswas al-qahri min manzur Arabi Islami*(OCD from an Arabic Islamic perspective). Alam Al-Maarifa - Kuwait.

Abu-l-'Azayem, G. M. (1994). *Al-Quran wa al-sihha al-nafsiyya* (Quran and mental health). Dar Al-Hilal.

Al-'Isa, I. (2015). Waqi' buhuth al-ta'silwa al-tawjih al-Islami li-l-'ulum al-tarbawiyya fi jami'at al-mamlaka al-'Arabiyya al-Su'udiyya (The current state of research on the Islamic orientation of educational sciences in the Saudi universities). *Journal of Educational Sciences, 7*, 15–74.

Al-Karam, C. Y. (2018). Islamic psychology: Towards a 21st-century definition and conceptual framework. *Journal of Islamic Ethics, 2*(1–2), 97–109.

Al-Karam, C. Y. (2020). Islamic psychology: Expanding beyond the clinic. *Journal of Islamic Faith and Practice, 3*(1), 111–120.

Al-Najjar, A. (2002). *Al-Tasawwuf al-Nafsi*(Psychological Sufism). General Egyptian Book Organization.

Al-Sharqawi, H. (1976). *Nahw 'IlmNafsIslami*(Towards an Islamic Psychology). General Egyptian Book Organization.

Al-Sharqawi, H. (1989). Al-Mafahim al-nafsiyya al-asasiyya fi-l-Quran al-Karim wakhuturat al-istilah (Foundational Psychological Concepts in the Quran and The Question of Terminology [pp. 53–64]). *Research Papers Presented at the Seminar on Islamic Psychology—International Institute of Islamic Thought.*

Al-Shinnawi, M. M. (1996). *Al-'Amaliyya al-irshadiyya* (The process of counseling). Dar Ghareeb.

Alzubairi, F. (2019). *Colonialism, neo-colonialism, and anti-terrorism law in the Arab world.* Cambridge University Press.

Baker, D. B. (Ed.). (2012). *The Oxford handbook of the history of psychology: Global perspectives.* Oxford University Press.

Barraclough, S. (1998). Al-Azhar: Between the government and the Islamists. *The Middle East Journal, 52*, 236–249.

Campagna, J. (1996). From accommodation to confrontation: The Muslim Brotherhood in the Mubarak years. *Journal of International Affairs, 50*, 278–304.

Elmahdi, M. (1990). *Al-'ilaj al-nafsi fi daw' al-Islam* (Psychotherapy in light of Islam). Dar Elwafaa.

Elmahdi, M. (2002a). *Mustawayat al-nafs* (Dimensions of the psyche). Dar El-Bitash.

Elmahdi, M. (2002b). *Saykulujiyyat al-din wa al-tadayyun*(Psychology of religion and religiosity). Dar El-Bitash.

Elzamzamy, K., Salem, M. O. (2020). Dreams and their role in Islamically integrated mental health practice. In Keshavarzi. H., Khan, F., Awaad, R., Ali, B. (Eds.), *Applying Islamic principles to clinical mental health care: Introducing traditional Islamically integrated psychotherapy*(pp. 141-167). Routledge.

Farah, N. R. (2013). *Religious strife in Egypt (RLE Egypt): Crisis and ideological conflict in the seventies.* Routledge.

Freud, S. (1982a). *The ego and the id* (M. Nagati, Trans.). Dar Al-Shurouq (Original work published in 1923).

Freud, S. (1982b). *Inhibitions, symptoms and anxiety* (M. Nagati, Trans.). Dar Al-Shurouq (Original work published in 1926).

Freud, S. (2006). *Three essays on the theory of sexuality* (M. Nagati, Trans.). Dar Al-Shurouq (Original work published in 1905).

Freud, S. (2018). *The essentials of psychoanalysis* (M. Nagati, Trans.). Dar Al-Shurouq (Original work published in 1986).

Hunt, M. (1993). *The story of psychology* (1st ed). Anchor Books.

Ibrahim, A. (2012). Saudi Arabia. In Baker, D. B. (Ed.), *The Oxford handbook of the history of psychology: Global perspectives*(pp. 442-461). Oxford University Press.

Ibrahim, A. (2014). Psychology and psychologists in Egypt: Emphasis on cultural psychology research and its growth. *International Psychology Bulletin, 18*(4), 54–59.

Jakhdal, S. A. (2018). Islamic psychology: The question of adaptation, not indigenization. *JiL Journal of Human and Social Sciences, 39*, 95–114.

Klevesath, L. (2014). Religious freedom in current political Islam: The writings of Rachid al-Ghannouchi and Abu al-'Ala Madi. In *Demokratie und Islam* (pp. 45–64). Springer VS.

Mahmoud, A. (1990). Nahwdustur 'amal li-'ulama' al-nafs al-muslimin (Towards an Operational Constitution for Muslim Psychologists). *Rabitat Al-Tarbiya Al-Haditha, 23*, 144–117.

Majariyya, A., Shalabi, A., Al-Shinnawi, U., Ziyada, K., Morsi, S., Anwar, A., Abd Al-Ghaffar, G., Abu Al-Makarim, F., Idris, M., Abd Al-Wahhab, N., Abd Al-Tawwab, N., Hanafi, H., Husain, N. A., Al-Sayyid, A. M., Farag, T. S., & Mahmoud, A. S. (2011). *'Ilm al-nafs fi al-turath al-Islami* (Psychological sciences in the Islamic heritage) (Vol. 4).Dar Al Salam/International Institute of Islamic Thought.

Markaz Al-Dirasat Al-Nafsiyya (Center for Psychological Studies). (n.d.). *Mustafa Ziwer Award in psychological sciences.* Filnafs. http://www.filnafs.com/fil11.html

Mohamed, W. (2012, March).*Psychology in Egypt: Challenges and hopes*. American Psychological Association. https://www.apa.org/international/pi/2012/03/egypt

Morsi, S. (1983). Al-*Nafs Al-Mutma'inna*(The peaceful soul). Maktabat Wahba.

Morsi, S. (1985). *Al-Shakhsiyya al-sawiyya* (The upright personality). Maktabat Wahba.

Morsi, S. (1989). *Al-fardwa-l-mujtma' fi-l-Islam* (The Individual and the society in Islam). Maktabat Wahba.

Morsi, S. (1992). *Wanafswa ma sawwaha* (By the human and its creation). Maktabat Wahba.

Morsi, S. (1994). *Al-imanwa al-sihha al-nafsiyya* (Faith and mental health). Maktabat Wahba.

Nagati, M. (1960a). *'Ilm al-nafs al-sina'i* (Industrial psychology). Maktabat Al-Nahda Al-Masriyya.

Nagati, M. (1960b). *'Ilm al-nafs al-harbi*(Military psychology). Dar Al-Nahda Al-Arabiyya.

Nagati, M. (1980). *Al-Idrak al-Hissi 'Ind Ibn Sina* (Sensory Perception in Ibn Sina's Works). Dar Al-Shurouq.

Nagati, M. (1993). *Al-Dirasat al-nafsaniyya 'ind al-'ulama' al-Muslimin*(Psychological Studies of Muslim Scholars). Dar Al-Shurouq.

Nagati, M. (2001a). *Al-Quran wa 'ilm al-nafs* (The Quran and psychology). Dar Al-Shurouq.

Nagati, M. (2001b). *Madkhalila 'ilm al-Nafs al-Islami* (An Introduction to Islamic Psychology). Dar Al-Shurouq.

Nagati, M. (2005). *Al-hadith al-nabawiwa 'ilm al-nafs*(The Prophetic Hadith and Psychology). Dar Al-Shurouq.

Omar, M. M. (1983). *Malamih 'ilm al-nafs al-Islami* (Characteristics of Islamic psychology). Dar Al-Nahda Al-Arabiah.

Prothro, E. T., &Melikian, L. H. (1955). Psychology in the Arab Near East. *Psychological Bulletin,* 52(4), 303.

Qutb, M. (1952). *Al-Insanbayn al-maddiyyawa-l-Islam* (The human being between the material world and islam). Dar Al-Shurouq.

Qutb, M. (2005). *Dirasat fi al-nafs al-insaniyya*(Studies on the human psyche). Dar Al-Shurouq.

Rabi', M. S. (2004). *Al-Turath al-nafsi 'ind 'ulama' al-muslimin* (Psychological legacy of Muslim scholars). Dar Ghareeb.

Ragab, I. (1992). *Madakhil al-ta'sil al-Islami li-l-'ulum al-ijtma'iyya* (Principles of the Islamic rooting of social sciences). *AlMuslimAlMuasir, 63,* 43–79.

Ragab, I. (1996). *Al-ta'asil al-Islami l-il-'ulum al-'ijtima'iyya* (Islamic paradigms for social sciences). Dar Alam al-Kutub Publisher.

Riyad, S. (2004a). *'Ilm al-nafs fi al-Quran al-Karim* (Psychology in the Holy Quran). Iqraa Establishment For Publishing & Distribution.

Riyad, S. (2004b). *'Ilm al-nafs fi al-hadith al-sharif* (Psychology in the Hadith tradition). Iqraa Establishment for Publishing & Distribution.

Riyad, S. (2008). Mawsu'at*'ilm al-nafswa-l-'ilaj al-nafsi min manzurIslami* (Encyclopedia of psychology and psychotherapy from an Islamic perspective). Dar Ibn Al-Jawzi.

Salem, M. O. (2003). *The spiritual support group at Medway Maritime Hospital experience* (Annual Meeting). Royal College of Psychiatrists.

Salem, M. O. (2007). *The heart, mind and spirit.* WPA Section on Religion, Spirituality and Psychiatry. http://www.religionandpsychiatry.com/Publications/Heart__Mind_and_Spirit__Mohamed_Salem.pdf/

Salem, M. S. (2008). *Al-waswas al-qahri: dalil 'amali li-l-marid wa al-usrawa al-asdiqa'* (OCD: A practical manual for patients and their families and friends). Dar Al-Aqeeda.

Salem, M. O. (2009, January 13–15). An Islamic theory for the mind (p. 83). *The 5th SELF International Biennial Conference, Book of Abstracts,* Al Ain, UAE,.

Salem, M. O. (2010). Integrating spiritual techniques into psychotherapy—Islamic model (p. 129). *Proceedings of the 1st International Conference of Saudi Psychiatric Association*, Al Khobar, Saudi Arabia.

Salem, M. O., & Foskett, J. (2009). Religion and Religious Experiences. In Cook, C. C., Powell, A., & Sims, A. (Eds.), *Spirituality and Psychiatry*(pp. 233-253). Royal College of Psychiatrists Publications.

Salem, M. O., & Hamdan, A. L. (2010). Spiritual and religious interventions in psychiatry and psychotherapy (p. 56). *Proceedings of the 1st International Conference on Psychological Sciences & Applications*, Al Ain, UAE.

Salem, O. M., & Yousef, S. (2010). Effects of watching films on dreams of the UAE university students. *International Journal of Dream Research, 3*(1), S9.

Salem, M. O., El Banna, A., Younis, A., Saleh, B., & Yousif, M. S. (2009, December 13–14). Effect of dreams on psychiatric patients in a UAE Study (p. 143). *Proceedings of the First Annual SEHA Research Conference*, Al Ain, UAE.

Salem, M. O., DeCicco, T. L., Ragab, M. A., Yousif, S., Murkar, A., & Vaswani, M. (2013). Spiritual and religious imagery in dreams: A cross-cultural analysis. *International Journal of Dream Research, 6*(2), 24–27.

VandenBos, G. R. (2007). *APA dictionary of psychology*. American Psychological Association.

Zahran, H. A. (2005). *Al-Tawjihwa al-irshad al-nafsi* (Psychological counseling and guidance). Dar Alam al-Kutub Publisher.

CHAPTER FOUR

# Islamic Perspective of Psychology in India

AKBAR HUSAIN

AN INDIAN MUSLIM scholar, Maulana Ashraf 'Ali Thanvi, deliberated on the nuances of personality development, causes and classification of diseases, and treatment or therapies. He laid the foundation for IP in India and inspired budding researchers to explore this arena of psychology further. Later institutes, such as the Institute of Objective Studies, New Delhi, and the Centre for Study and Research, Hyderabad, were established to foster research and development in the field of IP Psychology in India. Several contemporary Indian scholars from the Department of Psychology have delved into this arena in order to elucidate the possibilities for this field in terms of the Qur'an as the foundation of knowledge. The present chapter attempts to shed light on the extant research, review articles, books, chapters in edited books and articles published in the proceedings of seminars and journals.

## Brief Profile of Maulana Ashraf 'Ali Thanvi

In reflecting on the history of IP, a religious scholar, Ashraf 'Ali Thanvi, was responsible for our understanding of personality theory, psychopathology, and psychotherapy. In India, he has been a source of inspiration to the Islamic perspective in psychology and attempts have been made to explore the roots of IP through his contribution. He was born on 5th *RabiusThani* 1280 A.H. (19th September 1863 A.D.) at Thanaa Bhawan in the province of Uttar Pradesh, India. Referred to by many Muslims as *Hakim al-Ummat* (spiritual physician of the Muslim *Ummat*) and *Mujaddid al-Ummat* (Reformer of the Nation), Thanvi's a towering figure of Islamic revival and re-awakening in the 20th century. Maulvi Mirza Muhammad Beg Malik was the first man to give him the title of *Hakim al-Ummat*. Later, it was adopted by all. Maulana Ashraf 'Ali Thanvi became the most eminent religious personality of his time, a prolific author and the greatest Sufi of modern India.

## Contributions of Thanvi to the field of Psychopathology and Psychotherapy

For Thanvi, the observation of piety (*taqwa*), remembrance of Allah (*dikr*) and meditation (*muraqabah*), will bear fruits in this world but, if God so wills it, can open the doors for mystic illumination, both cosmic (*Kashaf-e Kauni*) and divine (*Kashaf-e Ilahi*), over the aspirants' hearts. Thanvi's writings fit well into the tenets of Islam as seen in his popular texts *Bahishti Zewar*(*Heavenly Ornaments*, n.d,) and *Tarbiyyat-ul-Shalik*(n.d.).

## Bahishti Zewar: (Heavenly Ornaments)

Thanvi wrote many books in simple language for women and children. The most illustrious is *Bahishti Zewar*, which is a summary of the *Qur'an* and *Hadith* teachings. This text and reference book on Islam and Islamic law is based on the *Hanafi School* of Islamic jurisprudence andis considered the most widely read book among Muslims of India after the *Qur'an* in Urdu, Gujarati, Bengali, Hindi and English. It addresses the rules of daily life for a Muslim family and is considered a must for new converts. The book is translated in multiple Indian and European languages. *Bahishti Zewar* is the only book which fully covers the entire *Shari'ah* and essentials of Islam in all its five branches, that is, (i) Beliefs (*'Aqa'id*), (ii) Worship and Prayers (*'Ibadah*), (iii) Transactions and Business (*Mu'amlat*), (iv) Way of Life and Habits (*Mu'ashirah*) and Manners and Morals (*Tasawwuf*, *Akhlaq* and *Tariqah* according to*Shariah* and *Sunnah*).

### THANVI'S CONTRIBUTIONS CAN BE IDENTIFIED BY THE THREE AREAS IN THE FIELD OF ISLAMIC PSYCHOLOGY:

(1) *Personality Theory:* According to Thanvi, a child is born with innocent nature. He learns good and bad things from his environment. Three types of "Nafs" are developed in his personality: (i) *Nafs Ammara* (turning to evil), (ii) *Nafs Lavvama* (reproaching after sin) and (iii) *Nafs Mutmainna* (following divines).

(2) *Causes and Classification of Mental Diseases:* Thanvi explains the causes of mental diseases as follows:

Causes: When a human being becomes detached from religion and goes away from God it makes him worthless. This also removes distinction between good and bad; greed and material gain become the all-important goal of one's life in the world. This worldly gain and greed expose one to mental diseases.

According to Thanvi, there are two forces within a human being: constructive force and destructive force. He lays great emphasis on the training of a child in order to strike a balance between the two forces. In the early days, parents, especially the mother, play a greater role while bringing up the child along the right lines. Incorrect training spoils him, making him prone to mental diseases.

Kinds of Mental Diseases: Thanvi divided the mental diseases into two categories: organic and functional disturbances. The organic diseases may be cured by medicines, but the functional or psychological diseases are to be cured by individual and group therapies. In the individual therapy, the disturbed individual is made to understand his own self-knowledge as the right path. He cured thousands of persons suffering from organic and functional disturbances through his therapeutic approaches.

*(3) Methods of Psychological Treatment:* The methods of treatment can be divided into three types: (i) Cure by reading books, (ii) cure by company and (iii) cure by communication. It includes both individual and group therapy. Those who approached Thanvi for treatment were told that it was necessary for the client (Salik) to have reverence for his therapist, be able to understand his therapeutic method clearly and always be prepared to follow his instruction. His therapy was a directive one. He used to explain to his clients the nature of his therapeutic technique and what a client can expect from the therapist. He named his therapy "Sulook" (treatment) and explains it briefly that:

1. It may not necessarily work out in miracles. Miracles and *Kashf* are not essential.
2. It is not responsible for helping one in gaining salvation on doomsday. There is no guarantee of forgiveness on the Day of Judgment.
3. It does not provide for wish-fulfilment by magic or incantation. There is no promise of material benefits, amulets, ritual, etc. for success in litigation or better material prospects in life.
4. It is not a cure for the disorder by exorcising or making prophecies. Sickness cannot be warded off by occult rituals.
5. It does not ensure that the follower will be automatically reformed by the attention of the mentor or that he will not even think of evil and be always busy in prayers. Therapist attention itself will not automatically cure the patient.

6. It stresses that no accomplishment is achieved without determination. No action is possible without will power.
7. It does not set any time limit for such intrinsic states to develop where one would become ecstatic with pleasure during one's prayers.

Inner experiences are not guaranteed. Here the client is told explicitly that the cure of disorders is not guaranteed through exorcism but will depend on the patient's own cooperation and determination. Thus, Thanvi's emphasis is on the will of the patient to cure the disease, which cannot be alleviated by any ritual. It is the job of the therapist to guide, to give advice, and during the therapeutic session to make his ideas more explicit by reflecting upon them. Here the individual's mental capacity is kept in mind. Both the individual and the group therapeutic methods are directly used. A child is born with many instincts – constructive and destructive, good and evil. At birth, these forces are integrated; the child has no particular bent of mind. Environment directs these forces towards one thing or the other, but there are always individual differences. Therefore, we need social circumstances and stimulant situations of different types and intensity to direct them. Due to this, Thanvi lays great stress on childhood training. He says that an individual's personality reflects his character and reminds us of the necessity of education. In childhood training, first, the child comforts his mother. The mother's character has a great influence on the child's personality. After some speculation on the causes of mental disorders, he came to the conclusion that most of the disorders originate in childhood, and as, during childhood, the child is mostly concerned with his mother, he wrote *Bahishti Zewar* for the training of mothers, which is a thorough and comprehensive guidebook.

Thanvi often used to say that a Muslim has to concern himself mostly with the Islamic divine laws (Shariah), religious rights ordained by Prophet Muhammad (Sunnah) and religious devotion (Tareeqat), which, in short, can be described as, "rights," "limits," and "preservation of limits." Rights are ordained by "Divine Laws", "limits" by the practice of the Holy Prophet (SAW), and "preservation of limits" by devotion to God. The only source for Muslims to attain the sanction and approval of God is doing justice according to these three sources. A traveller needs three things for his travel: A destination or goal, the "pathway" that leads him to the goal and "foresight", that is, vision that enables him to see the pathway clearly. Divine laws are composed of these three elements: they are eyes, the pathway, and the goal which is blessed by them.

The "treatment" method is concerned with two major aspects of a disorder that are so frequent that hardly any client has escaped them. Even the scholars suffer from them. One of these is the desire to master involuntary behaviors, for example, fervour and ecstasy, devotion and eradication of fear and temptation, absorption, and physical exercise, etc. The other is to master voluntary behavior, such as love for physical life, love for wealth, lust for dominance of physical passion and worldly fear or grief.

When a client asked for the cure to a disorder, Thanvi first inquired whether it was voluntary or involuntary. He said the problem of differentiating between voluntary and involuntary behavior is half the treatment. In fact, all the extrinsic and intrinsic behavior concerned with commands and prohibitions is voluntary and everyone is responsible for it. However, all the impressions and reactions to these behaviors (they may be threats, superstitions, constipation, or they may be cause of delight) are involuntary, and we are not responsible for them. They are neither accountable nor can they be called into question. He always laid more emphasis on distinguishing between voluntary and involuntary behavior, intellectual and natural phenomena, behaviors and their circumstances, actions and their reactions, and desired and undesired objectives. When a person adopts irrational behavior as rational, or rational as irrational, and works for their attainment, all his hard work goes in vain. These fruitless attempts give rise to the feelings of failure and depression that burden the mind, and if this load is kept for long, the individual becomes more prone to mental disorder.

Thanvi wrote that some people try to master involuntary behavior and feel dejected by their failure, and some people try to exempt the involuntary behavior. Failure will increase the anxiety and depression and the individual might face some problems:

1. Continued depression will make him ill, and he may lose his advantageous and commanding position in the family.
2. An excess of depression and grief results in moral deterioration and other people suffer from it.
3. Intense grief and anxiety will not allow a man to do full justice to his family and fellowmen, and he may become sinful.
4. He might become so anxious that, being utterly disappointed, he might commit suicide.
5. Sometimes, overpowered by depression, he shuns good deeds and obedience to God, regarding it as useless.
6. He may become disappointed by his leader, as he himself is not able to attain the goal.
7. Sometimes he is angry with God and feels that, although he has worked hard, he has not been rewarded.

In fact, an uncontrolled behavior cannot be exempted. To create fear is voluntary and can be avoided but fear itself is involuntary and one should not worry about it. Man is responsible for his rational behavior, because it is voluntary, but not for natural behavior, because it is involuntary. We should worry about behavior and not the circumstances. In the same way, actions can be controlled, but reactions cannot be controlled.

In *Tarbiyyat-ul-Salik*, many case histories are recorded. People describe their problems and complexes in writing and the psychotherapist gives them their solutions. He advises some people to read books. It is not a face-to-face communication. The client has reverence for his therapist. Both are firm believers of one God and the Holy Prophet. Therefore, the client takes the writings of his mentor as an actual dialogue with him. The patient asks the question; the therapist answers it in writing. The written pieces of advice from the mentor are a substitute for the mentor himself and the client sees the answer to his problems in the writings. He can identify his irrational behavior and find a way of relief – and he is cured.

## Therapeutic Methods

Thanvi emphasised the importance of the client's own will and effort in the cure of disease or illness. The counsellor (pir) only assists the client to understand causes of the disease and overcome adverse factors while organising his own self. The patient should have full faith and confidence in the counsellor and do as advised. The counsellor believes that some individuals need direct guidance and counselling. After reading the contents of a patient's letter, he raises some questions to satisfy and prepare his client for treatment.

### CURE BY COMPANY

For complex problems and psychological disorders, Thanvi invited the client to come to "Khanqah-e-Imdadia". He wrote to one client: "In the present condition, it will be more prudent of you to come here at least for a month, because some matters need your physical presence." Khanqah-e-Imdadia operated with a strict discipline. He had made a timetable for the facility of others as well as for his own comfort.

From morning till noon, such activities were prescribed that needed solitude. There is a discomfort and difficulty in meeting any one at that time, except those who have come for the first time and want to shake hands only, or those who want to take leave and say goodbye, or those who are in some urgent need that cannot be delayed. After performing my noon prayers, when I come to the gathering till evening prayer, everyone can come, sit and discuss his problems.

If someone wants a private session, he will put a note in the box in the portico. He gets the answer usually after sunset.

He had also prepared a questionnaire for the clients in which they were asked to state their names, residence, province or country of origin, duration of stay, their occupation, source of income, inherited land, and practical qualifications, in Urdu, Arabic and English. Further, it required information on the real aim of the visit: whether it was a courtesy call or it had some specific purpose. It also enquired whether the interview was sought in writing or orally (face-to-face dialogue) and whether it was sought in public or in private audience.

In Khanqah-e-Imdadia, Thanvi himself led the prayers five times a day. At noon he used to deliver a lecture and explain solutions to different problems and conflicts. Clients were divided into groups and each group had a leader. The members of the group listened carefully to their leader, held meetings with him and, thus, shared each other's sorrows. Then they would go into quiet meditation. In whatever miserable or depressed mind the client may be, Hazrat Sahib always inspired him to be courageous and hopeful of recovery and cure. By different methods he suggests to the client that man possesses absolute adaptability and so he should use this faculty for his improvement. Unless he does so, the improvement cannot be achieved. The "Sheikh" will only show him the way, but that does not mean he will drag him on the way. Although the Sheikh's prayers and his bounty have influence, they are limited to a certain degree. The teacher can provide a suitable atmosphere, or he can try to guide him to learn it with affection, but even in that case the child will have to learn it by himself. Therefore, the Sheikh's bounty is helpful, but not sufficient.

For healthy behaviour you need courage, and courage is useless without sincerity. It is said that courage and sincerity are the essence of all mysticism, because if one does not have courage, he will not take risk, and without sincerity all actions will be imperfect. In order to develop sincerity, courage is needed, and courage means summoning up all the faculties. It can be achieved in different ways. The way must be chosen as proposed by the Sheikh.

Thanvi adopted different methods for psychotherapy. For some days, the client would attend the meetings after the evening prayer. He would give sermon on some topic. "Sermon" is the counselling device for intrinsic improvement. People have different motives for listening to a sermon. Some listen only as a duty; some listen for beneficence and some intend to avoid sins by attending it. But the people often do not understand the main purpose of a sermon. Its real aim should be spiritual cure, that is, to look seriously into one's disorders and try to find solutions and cure. Intention is a must. God says, we have revealed the Holy Qur'an, so the people should consider and act upon it.

We are made in a manner that means we do not plan for everything. We do not even think and never repeat whatever we listen, although in some diseases the medicine is taken repeatedly. Only if you listen to a part of a sermon and remember it, and repeat it in your mind, and then try to act according to it, you will be cured by listening to only a few sermons. There are five degrees of meditation:

1. "Yajs", when some thought comes in the Qalb, but it does not move the ego.
2. "Khatir", if it starts coming again and again in the ego, but one could not decide about it.
3. "Hadith-e-Nafs", when ego plans to act or not to act in equal degrees, but one does not take preferences over the other. These are three degrees that are penalised if to no avail and are not rewarded if they are good. Only acts are penalised or rewarded.
4. "Hum", when ego plans to do or not do, preferring one over the other, but the preference is not rigid and is only accidental as superstition is. It is rewarded or penalised.
5. "Azm", when the plan to do becomes so strong that it cannot be avoided. It is also rewarded or penalised.

The first three stages of "temptation", that is, "Yajs", "Khatir", and "Hadith-e-Nafs", are not accountable. There is a *Hadith* which says that: "Loneliness is better than bad company and good company is better than loneliness." All those who went to *Khanqah* with pure and pious intentions, easily mixed with each other. They ate together and they lived together. They were a community which performed its daily chores. They listened to the sermons and, if needed, talked to the Sheikh individually and adopted the way proposed by him, which could be in the form of physical exercise or something else. After staying for some days at the centre of guidance, if the client felt his disorders were showing no signs of cure, he could go to some other place. But he was also told that, if the first advice shows no improvement, do not think it is useless. It is also beneficial because it created the capacity to benefit. The second advice will reinforce it, and the third may even achieve it. The benefit is acquired collectively and gradually. He told the clients that there were two types of disturbance: those which block your way and those which are self-created. Try to differentiate between them. If the temptations and superstitions enter the mind, do not block their way. This blockage will depress you and will cause mental disorder.

Thanvi did not follow a fixed procedure. Broadly speaking, his methods are classified into two categories.

1. Face-to-face contact
2. Provision of reading material and *Salik* contact

Thanvi said, "Man has the power to apprehend the physical as well as spiritual world." The first condition for the treatment put forward by Thanvi is that there must be psychological contact between the therapist and the client. Here, in many cases, contact between two persons is maintained through exchange of letters. The client (Salik) must feel some degree of dissonance between his feelings and actions. The therapist should be sensitively aware of the client's experiences.

Thanvi used direct counselling methods, too. His procedure required the *Salik* to write a letter to him describing his problem. After reading the contents of the letter, he asked some questions. Then, after satisfying himself that the client was really facing some difficulties, and that the client had faith in his capacity to care, he asked him to come to the "Khanqah" and stay there with other people.

Every morning, a session, lasting one or two hours, was held in a group. The individual was supposed to live and work with others while staying at *Khanqah*. If Thanvi found that the *Salik* was not making satisfactory progress, he paid individual attention to him. But the *Salik* was at liberty to terminate the session if he was not satisfied with the therapist. During his stay at the *Khanqah*, the *Salik* had to perform some tasks. Thanvi assured that one must diminish worry and that action and behaviour be continued even if this did not result in total consonance. He believed that good intentions brought rewards.

### CURE BY READING BOOKS (READING THERAPY)

The reading therapy of Thanvi is based on the principle that the patient, instead of face-to-face encounters, should read the relevant material suggested by the therapist to gain insight into his problem. Of course, the first condition is that he must have faith in God.

Thanvi always laid great emphasis on a client's writings about the actual state of his disorder, to know whether the disorder was present, and if it was, of what nature. If he felt the need, he would ask for some more information. When the presence of a disorder was proved, and he thought that it was not of a serious nature, he would recommend "Cure by Books" and suggest different books for him to read and try to act upon the advice given in them. God will bless him.

In reading therapy, the technique that he follows is like the existential therapy. The technique is based on the philosophy of life; the individual is treated as whole. Abnormality is due to deviation from Reality – God. In most cases, ignorance is the cause of deviation. Knowledge is the remedy of ignorance. Knowledge without action is useless. Knowledge is provided by books and Thanvi's lecture, as the client indulges in active practices while living in the *Khanqah*. In reading therapy, sentences are provided to the patient to identify with, and gain insight. Emphasis is on the will to act; merely reading will not solve the problem. For voluntary actions, the patient's determination is necessary. Through will and practice the patient can also control involuntary action.

In reading therapy, emphasis is placed upon action, choice and hope with the realistic and clear understanding of one's situation, goals and possibilities. The most important feature of Thanvi's therapeutic technique is that he never encourages the *Salik* to describe the past experiences and repent them. He said that, by enquiring about the past experiences to find the causes of maladjustment, we reinforce the behavior in the individual. But as maladjustment is due to experience, said Thanvi, one must ask forgiveness from God.

Reading therapy is meant for those who can read and write. It is simple, easier, takes less time. It tends to rely on belief and uses encouragement and reassurances. The technique is simple, but requires much more work from the psychotherapist. It requires full confidence in the therapist, as well as complete faith in God. Thanvi cured many patients by using this technique. It is basically a religious therapy, and research is needed to ascertain what influence is due to the client's own personality, and to what extent the technique helped. Reading therapy requires written reports by the client about his problems and experiences.

### CURE BY COMMUNICATION

In this therapeutic method, Thanvi invited patients to his "Khanqah Imdadia" where he used to sermonise on certain topics which the patients had to listen to intently and act upon as advised. He considered sermon as the best spiritual group therapy. The patients were asked to utter repeatedly what they heard. Remaining near to the therapist was important for effective treatment. This method of treatment applies to those who fully believe in religion. Faith relates to purity of thought, uprightness of character and nearness to Allah.

There are many instances where Thanvi experienced the client's feeling indirectly and pointed out the solution to his problem. Communication was a must; he laid great emphasis on it and did not confine himself to face-to-face situations but used correspondence for the guidance of the *Salik*. He believed that some individuals needed direct guidance.

## Institute of Objective Studies' Contribution to the Development of Islamic Psychology

The Institute of Objective Studies (IOS) was established in 1986, in New Delhi, India, and encourages individuals and institutions in writing and editing books, as well as organising national and international conferences and seminars.

BOOKS PUBLISHED BY IOS IN THE FIELD OF ISLAMIC PSYCHOLOGY ARE:

*Qur'anic Concepts of Human Psyche* –by Zafar Afaq Ansari, 1992, published by International Institute of Islamic Thought.

*Psychology and Society in Islamic Perspective* (M.G. Husain, 1996)

*An Introduction to Islamic Psychology* (A.A. Vahab, 1996)

*The Theories of Hi-Photicity and Psychophotics* (Science) (A.A. Vahab, 2007)

*Psyche in Islam* (General editor Shamim Ahmad Ansari, 2018)

An international conference was jointly organized by IOS and Aligarh Muslim University, Aligarh, on the theme *Concept of Psyche in Islam* (2009)

In September 2020, a one-week online orientation programme on Islamic Counselling and Psychotherapy was organised by the Institute of Objective Studies, New Delhi. Research scholars, students and counsellors participated in this programme. Resource persons delivered lectures on Islamic Counselling, Basic Counselling Skills, Quranic Therapy, Assessment of Clients, and Islamic Counselling Interventions.

It may be worth noting that in terms of professional development of the field, the Centre for Study and Research, Hyderabad, which was founded in 2012, also organised national and international conferences on Islamic Perspective in Psychology. The centre also organises several workshops and brainstorming sessions, in which the resource persons deliberate on defining Islamic Psychology and hold discussions on the number of themes related to the field of Islamic Psychology.

## Contribution of the Department of Psychology, Aligarh Muslim University, Aligarh, (India)

### PUBLICATIONS AND PRESENTATIONS BY PROFESSOR AKBAR HUSAIN

Professor Akbar Husain promoted research and practice in the areas of psychological testing and Islamic counselling. The spurt in the growth of Islamic Psychology is also evident by his publications. He wrote three books: *Islamic Psychology: Emergence of a New Field* (2006), *Applied Islamic Psychology – A Fresh Interpretation* (2018a), and *Quranic Guidance, Therapy, and Islamic Counselling Interventions* (in press), and edited a volume on *Contemporary Trends in Islamic Psychology* (2017a). Besides these, Husain, Nazam, and Khatoon (2019) published a *Manual on Islamic Counselling*, and Husain, Khan, Kirmani, and Khatoon (2021) wrote a book entitled, *Psychological Perspectives in Islam and Sufism*.

Professor Husain has published theoretical and empirical papers in refereed national and international journals, as well as proceedings of national seminars, chapters in edited books and standardised psychological tests in collaboration with the faculty members of the department. The department organised the International Conference on Islamic Psychology: Theory, Research and Application, (10–12 November 2018). Thirty-four international participants from six countries, namely, Australia, Bangladesh, Indonesia, Malaysia, Russia, and Sudan attended this conference. One Orientation Programme on Islamic Counselling was organised by the Malapppuram Centre of Aligarh Muslim University, in collaboration with UGC Human Resource Development Centre, in January 2018.

### HUSAIN'S PUBLICATIONS COVER TOPICS SUCH AS:

1. Alleviating mental health problems through Islamic practices, counselling and cultivation of values (Khatoon & Husain, 2019)
2. Scriptures and prayer: paths towards developing inner strength (Singh & Husain, 2019); Islamic spirituality in practice (Husain, 2016a)
3. Spiritual practices as paths to attain spiritual peace (Husain, 2014)
4. Prevention of environmental pollution through Islamic lifestyles (Husain, 2011)
5. Prophetic ways for coping with behavioural disorders (Husain, 2010)
6. What is good for parents for the development of moral behaviour of children? The spiritual virtues! (Husain, 2008)
7. Islamic approaches for the psychological help of AIDS patients (Kirmani & Husain, 2002).

Empirical papers focussed on the following themes: The relationship between Islamic personality and spiritual practices among Muslim students (Gull & Husain, 2018); Spiritual beliefs among Muslim male and female religious devotees (Singh & Husain, 2015).

### CHAPTERS IN EDITED BOOKS COVERED THE FOLLOWING TOPICS:

1. Contributions of Arab Muslim scholars to psychology (Husain &Kirmani, 2017)
2. Muslim chaplaincy and healing of trauma(Husain, 2017b)
3. Prayer and recitation of the Holy Qur'an: Evidence-based Islamic Practices (Husain & Jahan, 2017)
4. Preservation of health: Al-Tibb and the Quranic perspective (Husain, 2016b)
5. Identifying positive behaviour among Tasbih meditators (Husain,

Masood, Parveen, Ikram, Rahman, & Ahmed, 2014)
6. Muslim attitudes toward near-death experiences, death, and the afterlife (Husain, Khan, Krippner, Fracasso, & Friedman, 2013)
7. Islamic lifestyles: the right path for the maintenance of health (Husain, 2005).

PSYCHOLOGICAL TESTS STANDARDISED:

The following tests, which were standardised, fall in the field of Testing-Islamic Psychology. These tests are based on Muslim samples.

1. Nazam, F., Husain, A., & Gull, M. (2020, in press). Standardization of Taqwa (Piety) Scale. Islamic Quarterly, London: Islamic Cultural Centre.
2. Husain, A., Khan, S. M., & Khan, A. (2019). Manual Prayer Scale. New Delhi: Prasad Psycho Corporation.
3. Gull, M., & Husain, A. (2019). Religious Coping Scale. New Delhi: Psychomatrix, 2019.
4. Gull, M., & Husain, A. (2019). Mental Health Scale. New Delhi: Prasad Psycho Corporation.
5. Husain, A., Singh, R., & Khan, S. M. (2016). Spiritual Practices Scale (Muslims). New Delhi: Prasad Psycho Corporation.
6. Husain, A., Singh, R., & Zehra, S. (2015). Spiritual Belief Scale. New Delhi: Prasad Psycho Corporation.

An important development was the establishment of the Psychophysiology Laboratory in the Department of Psychology under the UGC-SAP DRS-1 Programme, Aligarh Muslim University, Aligarh. Islamic Psychology is evident in the empirical studies. The beginning of scientific Islamic Psychology can be traced from 2018 onwards. A number of scientific experiments were conducted by Dr. S.M. Khan and his colleagues, and research scholars started pioneering empirical work in the field of Cognitive Islamic Psychology. As an individual, Khan exemplified the impact of the recitation of verses of the Quran through neuro-biofeedback records, made cautious inferences and relied more on data for alleviating the behavioural problem (e.g., depression). His name is recognised due to three major experiments (in press):

Electroencephalographic measurement was used to determine the hemispheric difference in cognitive tasks performed by participants. The result showed a significant difference among four treatment conditions, inferring that there is a significant difference in left and right hemispheric activities associated with analytical and creative tasks (Khan, Mir, Husain, & Hasan, in press).

Khan, Mir, Husain and Hasan (2020a) designed an experiment to measure sustained attention through frontal EEG. Beta brainwaves dominated in the experimental conditions, indicating the waking state of consciousness when attention is directed towards the cognitive task. The observation was that a decrease in the beta band activity in the task-related brain regions precedes the declined behavioural performance.

Khan, Mir, Husain and Hasan (2020b)reported the results of Quranic listening to brainwaves. Brain signals of Islamic faith in male participants were recorded when eyes were open and closed. The findings indicate that listening to *Surah Al-Rahman* with meaning increases the relative delta and alpha power in the majority region of the brain, compared to the listening of the same verses without meaning. The study concludes that relaxation is achievable by increasing the alpha and theta brainwaves through the Holy Quranic verses – *Surah Al-Rahman.*

## Ongoing research:

Standardization of Fitrah Scale (Husain, Nazam, & Gull)
Standardization of Islamophobia Scale (Khan, Husain, & Rahman)
Idyllic Personality Inventory (Husain, Rehman, & Rahman)

## Author's personal communication to Professor Azizuddin Khan, Indian Institute of Technology, Bombay, July 2020

Professor Khan reported that: "I have been working in Islamic Psychology for the last seven years. My initial reaction towards developing a new discipline within psychology was quite sceptical. However, my interest started to develop as I started comparing western and oriental psychological perspectives. It became amply clear that there is a need to rethink and develop alternative perspectives in Islamic Psychology. The last several centuries have witnessed that nothing much has been done in Islamic Science in general, and Islamic Psychology in particular. However, there has been a renewed interest in Islamic Psychology since the 1970s, around one century after the establishment of the first psychology laboratory in Leipzig in 1879. However, the root of modern Islamic Psychology goes back to the medieval era, in the writing of Ibn Sina, Al-Hathyam, Al-Ghazali, etc.

In India, studies in Islamic Psychology picked up after Prof. Akbar Husain took an interest in the field. Prof. Husain was instrumental in influencing me to start working in the area of Islamic Psychology. Recently, we completed several projects. In 2017 and 2018, we organised an international conference at Delhi and Aligarh Muslim University (AMU), Aligarh. I also contributed to the construction of Prayer Scale. Prayer is the religious practice of improving one's well-being, having a connection with God, and having a definite purpose, to improve health and serenity, and the maintenance of discipline and material benefits. The scale consists of dimensions: Well-being, Health and Security, Maintenance of Discipline, Connection with God, and Material Benefits. We are also in the process of developing a comprehensive tool to measure Islamophobia."

## Future Agenda

*Islamic Psychology Curriculum*: When one organises the content of Islamic Psychology around different historical schools of thought, one needs to consider medieval philosophers', theologians' and scientists' ideas as being only of historical or cultural significance. The result will be that to study they will realise their contribution to the field of Islamic Psychology and will attempt to integrate them in the understanding of the behaviour of Muslims.

In view of the need for the introduction of various fields of psychology as a specialisation at postgraduate level, *Islamic Perspective on Psychology* is also introduced as a field of specialisation in the University Grants Commission, New Delhi Curriculum 2016. The curriculum committee approved the syllabi for the following courses at M.A. level, year 2.

Paper I – Islamic Psychology
Paper II – Psychology and Sufism
Paper III – Human Nature and Personality – Islamic Perspectives
Paper IV – Islamic Practices, Counselling and Psychotherapeutic Interventions
Semester III/IV: Practicum

If we want students and researchers to take Islamic Psychology seriously as a subject of study and research, it is better to start from the understanding and interpretation of the Qur'an, linked to the contemporary issues that are relevant to the contemporary world, but for which modern science has not given due importance. While introducing a Prophetic model of practical know-how related to these issues, one can then focus on their common ground, his intellect as well as his lifestyle, and their effectiveness for spiritual development. Apparent contradictions and differences between the Prophetic doctrine and the Muslim scholars can be introduced in the context of the conditions under which they can be applied. A typical example might be the Quranic theory of personality and Iqbal's theory of personality; both offer practical tools for the assessment of personality. Husain's (2018b) Islamic personality perspective is needed for the understanding of human nature, especially through the personality traits.

To enhance the integration of the study materials based on the Qur'an and Muslim scholarly writings, the following should be included:

- Students can be taught from the beginning that the Qur'an and *Hadiths* are the most valuable resource.
- It also helps to ask students to work on an individually chosen "*project*":
- The project can be any construct or process related to Islamic Psychology that deals with developmental objectives being the most useful.
- The relevant theory should be studied in-depth.
- The effect of various Islamic practices should be observed carefully in one's own daily life.
- The project should include not only generic theory but also a detailed study of how things worked out in their own life, quoting prophetic traditions, where appropriate, and selected verses from the Qur'an.

### RESEARCH

Islamic Psychology in India is a less travelled road in academia. It is an emerging academic discipline of research. Cognitive psychology and psychological testing constituted the major thrust areas of research in India.

Modern psychology has failed to address key questions of human values and human behaviour, especially in the era of machine learning and artificial intelligence. It is high time Islamic Psychology was established as an alternative model for understanding human behaviour. The future of Islamic Psychology should incorporate both qualitative as well as quantitative analyses of human behaviour. We may build on modern Islamic Psychology based on the knowledge and research done by medieval physicians, such as Abu Zaid Al-Balkhi, al-Zahrawi, Ibn Sina, Al Razi, etc. Future IP should integrate with new developments in other fields of psychology, such as Cognitive Psychology, Positive Psychology, Health Psychology, Personality and Social Psychology, Psychological Testing, and Spiritual Psychology. Therefore, we need to focus on not only using the perspective of the natural sciences, but also developing of new methodology to study complexities of human behaviour. Understanding and studying the concepts related to 'NAFSIAT', namely, *nafs, 'aql, fitrah,* spirit, *ilm, al-qalb* and *taqwa*(Husain, 2018a),can also be the subject matter of Islamic Psychology in the future.

## Conclusion

We anticipate in the next few years that IP will extend the prospects in terms of its nature of study, methods, and its applications in various fields of Applied

Psychology. The Qur'an, Ahadith and principles of Islam are the resources through which we can develop a new branch of Psychology, that is, Applied Islamic Psychology. This will have an important impact on the life of *Ummah*. In terms of the benefits from Quranic therapy and Sunnah, mental health professionals will help prevent many diseases, such as grief, sorrow, anxiety, stress, depression, and worry. Negative behaviours weaken the soul and sicken the body and mind. One should work to heal oneself, otherwise the problem will grow, the treatment will be more difficult, and there will be no cure. In recent years, we have been integrating prayer, meditation, or contemplation, and reading scriptures (Qur'an) into treatments. Positive health leads to the health of the body, mind, and heart. The result of foresight is health and happiness. Islamic/ Spiritual values guide *Ummah*, which is good. Imam Ali said: "Good behaviour is honourable in the sight of God, not pretty speech." Muslims are strong morally, religiously, intellectually, and spiritually. Islamic values such as truthfulness, piety, benevolence, wisdom, peace, and righteousness are the means and elements in the destiny of humanity.

Muslim psychologists should persist on opening the door of IP; they will eventually enter through it in their future endeavours. There is a need to persevere when attending to psychosocial and spiritual problems, regardless of how difficult they are. Muslim psychologists should devote themselves to understanding the behaviour of Muslims. This can be a useful framework to guide their behaviour. It is certainly the duty of Muslim Psychologists to become serious and involve themselves in a mystical spirit for the continuous progress of the field of Islamic Psychology and humanity.

## References

Gull, M., & Husain, A. (2018). Relationship between Islamic personality and spiritual practices among Muslim students. *Asian Journal of Multidimensional Research (AJMR), 7*(6), 251-260.

Husain, A. (2005). Islamic lifestyles: The right path for the maintenance of health. In R. Singh, A. Yadava, & N. R. Sharma (Eds.), *Health psychology* (pp. 329-340). New Delhi: Global Vision Publishing House. ISBN: 81-8220-109-08.

Husain, A. (2006). *Islamic psychology: Emergence of a new field.* New Delhi: Global Vision Publishing House.

Husain, A. (2008). What is good for parents for the development of moral behavior of children? The spiritual virtues! *The Preston Journal of Social Sciences, 1*(1), 1-10.

Husain, A. (2010). Prophetic ways for coping with behavioural disorders. *Indian Journal of Positive Psychology, 1*(1-2), 27-29.

Husain, A. (2011). Prevention of environmental pollution through Islamic Lifestyles. *Proceedings of UGC National Seminar on Psychosocial Antecedents and Moderators of Environment.* Department of Psychology, Banwari Lal Jindal Suiwala PG College, Tosham (Bhiwani), Haryana, pp. 73-77.

Husain, A. (2014). Spiritual practices as paths to attain spiritual peace. In M. M. S. Nadwi Azhari (Ed.),*National Seminar on Peaceful Co-existence in multi-cultural societies – The Quranic Perspective* (pp. 169-176). New Delhi: Excel India Publishers.

Husain, A. (2016a). Islamic spirituality in practice. In N. A. Ab. Majeed (Ed.), *Proceedings of the Two-day International Conference on Social and Spiritual Teachings of the Quran in Contemporary Perspective* (pp. 222-230). New Delhi: Excel India Publishers.

Husain, A. (2016b). Preservation of health: Al-Tibb and the Quranic perspective. In S. Aleem &N. Iqbal (Eds.), *Positive vistas on health and well-being* (pp. 1-9). New Delhi: Excel India Publishers. ISBN: 978-93-85777-34-9.

Husain, A. (Ed.). (2017a). *Contemporary trends in Islamic psychology*. Hyderabad: Centre for Study and Research.

Husain, A. (2017b). Muslim chaplaincy and healing of trauma. In A. Husain (Ed.), *Contemporary trends in Islamic psychology* (pp. 26-36). Hyderabad: Centre for Study and Research.

Husain, A. (2018a). *Applied Islamic psychology: A fresh interpretation.* New Delhi: Global Vision Publishing House.

Husain, A. (2018b). *Manual Islamic counselling.* New Delhi: Global Vision Publishing House.

Husain, A., & Jahan, F. (2017). Prayer and recitation of the Holy Qur'an: Evidence based Islamic practices. In A. Husain (Ed.), *Contemporary trends in Islamic psychology* (pp. 135-156). Hyderabad: Centre for Study and Research.

Husain, A., Khan, A., Kirmani, M. N., & Khatoon, Z. (2021). *Psychological perspectives in Islam and Sufism.* New Delhi: Global Vision Publishing House. (In Press)

Husain, A., Khan, S., Krippner, S., Fracasso, C., & Friedman, H. (2013). Muslim attitudes, toward near-death experiences, death, and the afterlife. In J. H. Ellens (Ed.), *Volume Three – End time and after life in Islamic, Buddhist, and indigenous cultures* (pp. 41-52). Santa Barbara, CA: Praeger.

Husain, A., & Kirmani, M. N. (2017). Contributions of Arab Muslim scholars to psychology. In A. Husain (Ed.) *Contemporary trends in Islamic psychology* (pp. 13-25). Hyderabad: Centre for Study and Research.

Husain, A., Masood, A., Parveen, S., Ikram, S., Rahman, S., & Ahmed, W. A. (2014). Identifying positive behaviour among Tasbih meditators. In S. Saini (Ed.), *Positive psychology in the light of Indian traditions* (pp. 656-672). Haryana: Indian Association of Health, Research and Welfare.

Khan, S. M., Mir, S., Husain, A., & Hasan, A. (in press). Hemispheric differentiation in an independent analytical and creative task: An ERP study. *Cognition,*

*Brain, Behavior. An Interdisciplinary Journal.*

Khan, S. M., Mir, S., Husain, A., & Hasan, A. (2020a). An evaluation of sustained attention with frontal EEG. *Advances in Human Biology, 11,* 56-62.

Khan, S. M., Mir, S., Husain, A., & Hasan, A. (2020b). Neurotheology brain waves and state of mind: Auditory verses of Surah Al-Rahman are associated with peacefulness and relaxation. *Quranica Journal* (Submitted).

Khatoon, Z. & Husain, A. (2019). Alleviating mental health problems through Islamic practices, counselling, and cultivation of values. *IAHRW International Journal of Social Sciences Review,* 7(5-11), 1403-1405. ISSN-2347-3797.

Kirmani, M. N. & Husain, A. (2002). Islamic approaches for the psychological help of AIDS patients. *PRASAR: Contemporary Journal of Population and Adult Education, 1,* 89-93.

Singh, R. & Husain, A. (2015). Spiritual beliefs among Muslim male and female religious devotees. *International Journal of Recent Trends in English Language Teaching (ELT), Education, Psychology and Allied Research,* 2(6), 173-183.

Singh, R., & Husain, A. (2019). Reading scriptures and prayer: Paths towards developing inner strength. *IAHRW International Journal of Social Sciences Review,* 7(2), 292-299.

Thanvi, A. A.(n.d.). *Bahishti Zewar.* New Delhi: Adam Publisher.

Thanvi, A. A. (n.d.). *Tarbiyyat-ul-Salik*3 Volumes in 2 Books DarulIsha'at, Reality of Tasawwuf, Morals, Zikr.

CHAPTER FIVE

# Islamic Psychology in Indonesia: History and Research Priority

DIANA SETIYAWATI
BAGUS RIYONO

INDONESIA HAS THE largest Muslim population in the world. Thus, a reasonable expectation for Indonesia is to become a center of Islamic psychology (IP) development. The Islamization of psychology in Indonesia began more than 30 years ago and has yielded many publications, twenty IP study programs with thousands of students enrolled, multiple conferences, many organizations, theory development, and various clinical practices. The movement's progress is observable. IP is evolving from student movement to more structural and institutional movement. This chapter analyzes the achievements to date. Interviews with the pioneers and systematic literature review of Indonesian IP publications have been conducted and are the basis of the analysis.

## Introduction

The first group of Indonesian psychologists returned to Indonesia from their studies in the Netherlands and Germany in 1953. This event marks the start of psychology in Indonesia. The first Faculty of Psychology was established in 1960 at Universitas Indonesia (Dirgagunarsa, 1975). In 1961, the University of Padjajaran Bandung established the second Faculty of Psychology. In 1965, from a discussion that began in 1958, the third Faculty of Psychology was established at Universitas Gadjah Mada (Fakultas Psikologi UGM, 2015). Today, the number of Faculty of Psychology in Indonesia is more than 300 (including study programs).

Psychology became well known in Indonesia. The practice was based on the perspectives of the established science of psychology practiced worldwide, especially in the West, because Indonesian scholars had studied the subject at universities in the West. The nation with the largest Muslim population is Indonesia, and the spiritual nature of its society is evident. With its history of colonialization, Indonesians' opportunity to learn about Islam might have been limited. Islam is transferred mostly through cultural and family inheritance. The establishment of many Islamic universities and other education levels in Indonesia is increasing. Media broadcasts with Islamic content and prayer meetings are common and wearing a hijab for women is becoming more common and fashionable, demonstrating that Muslim society became more knowledgeable of Islamic values and Islam's essence as a way of life, especially in the 1980s and 1990s. Therefore, a version of psychology that fit more with Islamic values than the established science of psychology was necessary (Sudrajat & Setiono, 1996). For this reason, Islamic psychology (IP) was developed in Indonesia. Notably, in 1970, Zakiyah Darajat started the Islamization of psychology Indonesia.

The IP movement is growing along with the increasing number of Faculty of Psychology in Indonesia. The timeline of the IP movement is presented in Figure 1.

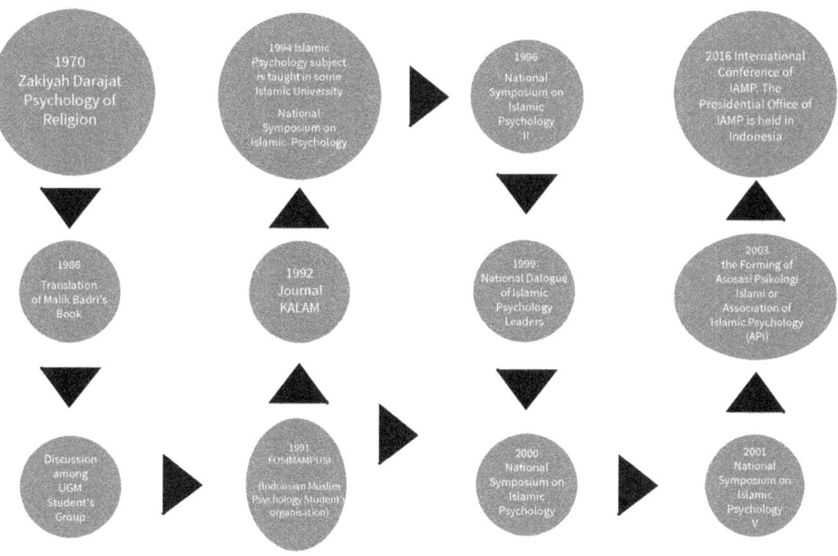

## Zakiyah Darajat Era

One of the pioneers of IP in Indonesia is Zakiyah Daradjat, who began to voice her opinions on IP in 1967 when she was appointed to teach Psychology of Religion at University of Indonesia (UIN) Syarif Hidayatullah Jakarta. In 1970, Zakiyah Daradjat wrote a book entitled "The Psychology of Religion" (*Ilmu Jiwa Agama*). In this book, she defined the psychology of religion as how religious beliefs influence psychological conditions. She also proposed the research area and methods that can be developed on this topic and discussed the history of Western psychology from Edwin D. Starbuck to Sigmund Freud (Daradjat, 1970).

She then discussed religion and its relationship with mental illness and mental health. There are various verses in Al Quran on various psychological states of a human being. Next, she discussed verses on mental health and mental illness. She posited that Islamic teaching contains the science of psychology. Many verses are on the psychological condition of the believers and non-believers. These psychological states are represented in their prayers, attitudes, behaviors, and states of mental health. Based on her clinical practice, she posited that psychotherapy without acknowledging patients' religious beliefs would be a slow process and trigger other illness types. Later, she highlighted that the core of the psychology of religion is understanding the development of religious beliefs in each human developmental stage. In her book, she then focused on the young generation and how this stage is critical. She then proposed how individuals can help youth overcome this age crisis and the importance of women's roles in this stage (Daradjat, 1970). Zakiyah Darajat posited that the vision of Islamic education could be achieved with the application of IP. The students would develop good mental health based on religion, faith, and taqwa. Zakiyah was among the first women and first "santri" (students of Islamic Boarding school/pesantren) who earned her master's degree abroad. She received a Master of Arts in Mental Hygiene in Cairo, Egypt (Nunzairina, 2018).

She wrote many other books, for example, *Peranan Agama dalam Kesehatan Mental* (The role of religion in mental health, 1970), *Pendidikan Agama dalam Pembinaan Mental* (Religion education and mental coaching 1970), and *Membinanilai-nilai moral di Indonesia* (Developing morality in Indonesia).

## Malik Badri's Book, *Fosimamupsi and Kalam*

The second milestone of the IP movement in Indonesia was Malik Badri's book: The Dilemma of Muslim Psychologists (Badri, 1979). In this book, Badri warned Muslim psychologists *not to go inside a lizard's hole.* He reminded readers that the science of psychology is based on established philosophies and backgrounds that omit spirituality and focus only on logical thinking. He discussed the limitations of each psychological paradigm. In summary, he reminded Muslim students of psychology to apply critical thinking in studying psychology. Zainab Luxfiaty translated this book in 1986 into the Indonesian language (Badri, 1979/1986). She graduated from an undergraduate program in the Department of Psychology at Universitas Indonesia, which she enrolled in 1978 or 1979. According to her brother, Luxfiaty wanted to study Islam and psychology. This enthusiasm resulted in her connecting with Malik Badri, who confirmed that she discussed this topic with him in Malaysia. This relationship inspired Zainab to translate his book.

Since then, this book has become famous among Muslim students of the Faculty of Psychology, especially those at Universitas Gadjah Mada. As one of the oldest Faculty of Psychology in Indonesia, this school has an active Muslim student organization. Fuad Nashori Suroso was among the students who led the development of discussions among Gadjah Mada and outside of and across Java island. This active movement triggered the establishment of the Indonesian Muslim Psychology Students Organizations on Islamic Psychology (FOSIMAMUPSI) in 1991. The discussions among students at Universitas Gadjah Mada also produced the first journal on IP, named KALAM, in 1992. This journal connected students and lecturers interested in IP.

FOSIMAMUPSI, the Indonesian Muslim Psychology Students Organization for IP, has also been active in creating a national symposium. The symposium was held in many areas and students gathered at various universities, especially on Java island. Later, some of the activists of this students' movement became lecturers and brought IP into their institutions with new power and positions.

In 1996, Yayasan Insan Kamil (Insan Kamis Foundation) was established by Fuad Nashori, Bagus Riyono, Emy Zulaifah, Subandi, Sumaryono, Ratna Syifaa, Sentot Haryanto, Darwin Ahmad, and Afifah Inayati, to facilitate discussions and development of IP. One of the articles yielded from this discussion is "The principles of Islamic Psychology," by Riyono (1998).

## IP Books and National Conferences

Books on IP were published, as was those on the history of the IP movement. Fuad Nashori published his first book on IP in 1994 with a well-known professor in psychology in Indonesia, Prof. Djamaludin Ancok (Ancok & Suroso, 1994). This book was launched at the 1994 National Symposium of IP in Universitas Muhammadiyah Solo. In this book, they classified Islamic Psychology into two main approaches: the first is filtered modern psychology according to Islamic perspectives, and the second approach is use Al Qur'an and Hadist to develop the concept of man and psychology in general (Ancok & Suroso, 1994).

Since 1994, starting with the National Symposium in Solo, more lecturers in the IP movement, not only students, became active. Some Islamic universities started to offer IP courses at their universities. Islamic National University Jakarta, Muhammadiyah University of Surakarta, and Islamic University of Indonesia are among the pioneers who offered this subject. Universitas Diponegoro is the only state university that has an IP as a subject. At some other state universities, lecturers were still debating the necessity of this course. Therefore, one of the resolutions among IP activists was to make it simultaneously more exclusive and more acceptable among wider audiences (Bastaman, 2005).

In 1995, Hanna Jumhana Bastaman published the book *Integrasi Psikologidengan Islam*/Integration of Psychology and Islam (Bastaman, 1995). He defined IP as psychology based on Islamic teaching. The subject matter discussed in IP is behavior patterns, the interaction between humans and their surroundings, and the spiritual aspect of life. Its objective is to discuss human mental health and quality of religious life. However, Bastaman stated that parts of Western psychology should be applied to IP and that IP should critically review this established science and make it more complete and perfect and provide a new framework. Thus, Bastaman was proposing that a new analysis of psychology that applied Islamic perspectives was necessary to evaluate the Western concepts.

Since 1994, regular national meetings or symposiums have been regularly held by universities in Indonesia, mainly on Java island with national participants (Bastaman, 2005). The National Symposium on Islamic Psychology II was held at Universitas Padjajaran Bandung in 1996 and discussed IP research methods. The next symposium was in 1999 at Universitas Darul Ulum Jombang. Since this national symposium, the discussions have been less on the definition of IP and how to develop IP and more on applying IP in multiple settings and IP's roles in various aspects of life. Thus, the 1999 symposium was on the application of IP. The 2000 Symposium at Universitas Indonesia was on the role of IP in Building a Personality of the Future. The 2001 National Symposium in Bandung discussed optimizing IP's role in improving the quality of the self, the family, and Indonesian society. These topics demonstrated that IP activists intended to contribute to the nation, solving society's problems, and creating better conditions.

## The Establishment of the Indonesian Islamic Psychology Association (API)

The national meeting in 2002 was a historical moment. It marked the establishment of the Islamic Psychology Association (Asosiasi Psikologi Islam/API). This organization later became a formal association under the Indonesian Psychology Association (Himpunan Psikologi Indonesia/HIMPSI). It is a formal acknowledgment of IP in Indonesia as a branch of science and professional practice. With the establishment of the API, the IP movement in each university will become more recognizable. The lecturers involved in this organization and movement were recognized as being part of a professional organization.

Later, more activists wrote more books. Although IP in Indonesia was influenced by the Islamization of Knowledge (Riyono, 1998), according to Abdul Mujib, one of the pioneers at UIN Jakarta (Jakarta Islamic National University), there were two streams of Islamization and books. One stream was from psychologists, and the other stream was from activists with Islamic studies backgrounds, such as Ahmad Mubarok and Abdul Mujib. Mubarok was the first Professor in IP in Indonesia. The examples of books that come from Islamic studies streams were *Fitrah dan Kepribadian Islam: Sebuah Pendekatan Psikologis*/Fitrah and Islamic Personality: A Psychological Perspective (Mujib, 1999), *Jiwa dalam Al-Quran*/A Soul in Al-Quran (Mubarok, 2000), *Psikologi Qurani* (Quranic Psychology) (Mubarok, 2001), *Fitrah dan Kepribadian Islam: Sebuah Pendekatan Psikologis*/Fitrah and Islamic Personality: A Psychological Perspective (Mujib, 1999), and *Nuansa-nuansa Psikologi Islam*/Nuances of Islamic Psychology (Mujib & Mudzakir, 2001). The examples of books that come from psychologists were *Membangun Paradigma Psikologi Islami*/Building Islamic Psychology Paradigm (Nashori, 1994), *Agenda PsikologiIslami: Seri Psikologi-Islami*/Islamic Psychology Agenda: A series of Islamic Psychology (Nashori, 2002a), *MimpiNubuwat: Seri PsikologiIslami*/Prophetic Dream: An Islamic Psychology Series (Nashori, 2002b), and *Potensi-potensi Manusia*/Human Potentials (Nashori, 2003). The list of IP books is presented in Table 1. The list of journals is presented in Table 2.

**Table 1: List of Books 1994–2020**

| TITLE | WRITER | YEAR |
|---|---|---|
| Islamic Psychology: A Solution to psychological problems | Djamaludin Ancok & Fuad Nashori Suroso | 1994 |
| Building Islamic Psychology Paradigm | Fuad Nashori (Editor) | 1994 |
| Integrating Psychology and Islam: Toward Islamic Psychology | H. D. Bastaman | 1995 |
| Islamic Psychology: An Agenda toward action | H. Fuad Nashori | 1997 |
| Fitrah and Islamic Personality: A Psychological Perspective | Abdul Mujib, Darul Falah | 1999 |
| A Soul in Al-Quran | Achmad Mubarok | 1999 |
| Islamic Psychological Method | Rendra Krestyawan (Editor) | 2000 |
| Quranic Psychology | Achmad Mubarok | 2001 |
| Nuances of Islamic Psychology | Abdul Mujib dan Jusuf Mudzakir | 2001 |
| Prophetic Dream: An Islamic Psychology Series | H. Fuad Nashori | 2002 |
| Islamic Psychology Agenda: A series of Islamic Psychology | H. Fuad Nashori | 2002 |
| Developing Creativity in Islamic Psychology Perspective | H. Fuad Nashori | 2002 |
| Love Stories: A Series in Islamic Psychology | Abdul Mujib, Sri Gunting | 2002 |
| What is the Meaning of Your Tears?: A Series in Islamic Psychology | Abdul Mujib, Sri Gunting | 2002 |
| Human Potentials | Fuad Nashori | 2002 |
| A Paradigm of Islamic Psychology | Baharuddin | 2002 |
| Motivation and Personality: Islamic Perspective on Dynamic of the Soul and Human Behavior | Bagus Riyono | 2020 |
| *Islamic Psychology: Concept and Application* | Jalaluddin | 2020 |

**Table 2: List of Journals.**

| TITLE | WRITER | DATE |
|---|---|---|
| An Islamic Psychological Thought Journal | Mahasiswa Yogyakarta | 1992 |
| Islamic Psychology Journal | API HIMPSI | - |
| Islamic Psychology Journal: A Qalb | UIN Imam Bonjol Padang | - |
| Journal of Islamic Psychology and Culture | UIN Sunan Gunung Djati | - |
| Psikoislamika: Journal of Psychology and Islamic Psychology | UIN Maulana Malik Ibrahim Malang | - |
| Psikologika: Journal of Thought and Research in Psychology | Universitas Islam Indonesia (UII) | - |
| An Nafs: Journal of Faculty of Psychology | Universitas Islam Riau | - |
| International Journal of Islamic Psychology | International Association of Islamic Psychologists (IAMP) | - |
| Journal of Islamic Psychology | UIN Raden Fatah Palembang | - |
| Happiness: Journal of Psychology and Islamic Science | IAIN Kediri | - |
| Journal of Studia Insania | UIN Antasari Banjarmasin | - |
| (*Nathiqiyyah:* Journal of Islamic Psychology) | Sekolah Tinggi Agama Islam (STAI) Diniyah Pekanbaru | - |

In addition to these two streams, some books written by psychiatrist Dadang Hawari influenced IP's development. Those books are *Al Quran: Ilmukedokteranjiwa dan Kesehatan jiwa/* Al Quran: Science of psychiatry and mental health (Hawari & Sonhadji, 1995), *Gerakan nasional anti "Mo-Limo" (madat, minum, main, maling, dan madon)/*National movement anti Napza , zina and robbery (Hawari, 2000),and Konsep agama (Islam) menanggulangi HIV/AIDS/*Islamic concept in fighting HIV/AIDS* (Hawari, 2002b).Dadang Hawari also wrote the book *Dimensireligidalampraktekpsikiatri dan psikologi/*Religious dimension of psychiatry and psychology professional practice (Hawari, 2002a). In this book, he stated that psychiatry and mental health are the only subjects with a close relationship with religion among the medical literature. Religion, psychiatry, mental health, and psychology meet at some points in the meaning of health and well-being. He said that the World Health Organization's definition of health is comprehensive and includes the biopsychosociospiritual.

API held more national conferences regularly with more support from universities. However, until approximately 2005, according to Bastaman (2005), research was not well developed. The discussions were mostly on paradigms and the gaps in the research; thus, improving the research was necessary.

IP study programs have been well accepted and developed in some national Islamic universities and institutes or Muhammadiyah universities. The first program was established at Universitas Islam Negeri Imam Bonjol Padang in 2005, and the second program, at Universitas Muhammadiyah Yogyakarta in 2006. In 2019, twenty universities had IP study programs. The list of those universities is presented in Table 3.

The curriculum of the IP study programs was a combination of the established science of psychology taught worldwide and the IP perspectives. Badri's book "The Dilemma of Muslim Psychologists" (Badri, 1979/1986) had influenced this curriculum. According to Sudrajat and Setiono (1996), the structure IP curriculum attempted to follow the national standard of competence that Department of Higher Education had stipulated.

There were four main parts:

1. General psychology and other related courses. It comprised psychology's general concepts, its positions, and its differences from other sciences. It included other related courses such as psychology, sociology, anthropology, philosophy, and statistics.
2. Islamic-oriented general psychology and other related courses. It comprises the determinant of human behavior based on Islamic teachings, such as Islamic teachings on rearing children and adolescents, the benefit of Islamic Tarbiah, and the benefits of prayer and zikr in psychological well-being.
3. Subdivision of psychology. It covered basic psychology, applied psychology, and psychological techniques such as psychotherapy.
4. Islamic-oriented of Subdivision of Psychology. It supplemented the basic, applied psychology and psychological techniques with Islamic perspectives.

**Table 3: List of universities with an Islamic psychology program**

| INSTITUTION | AREA | ESTABLISHMENT |
|---|---|---|
| Universitas Islam Negeri Imam Bonjol Padang | West Sumatra | 2005 |
| Universitas Muhammadiyah Yogyakarta | Yogyakarta | 2006 |
| IAIN Kediri | East Java | 2007 |
| STAIN Kediri | East Java | 2007 |
| IAIN/Universitas Islam Negeri Antasari Banjarmasin | South Kalimantan | 2008 |
| Institut Agama Islam Tribakti Kediri | East Java | 2012 |
| Universitas Islam Negeri Raden Fatah Palembang | South Sumatra | 2012 |
| IAIN Batusangkar | West Sumatra | 2016 |
| Universitas Islam Negeri Raden Intan Lampung | Lampung | 2016 |
| IAIN Manado | North Sulawesi | 2017 |
| IAIN Pontianak | West Kalimantan | 2017 |
| IAIN Salatiga | Central Java | 2017 |
| IAIN Surakarta | Central Java | 2017 |
| IAIN Tulungagung | East Java | 2017 |
| Universitas Muhammadiyah Riau | Riau | 2017 |
| IAIN Jember | East Java | 2017 |
| STAI Diniyah Pekanbaru | Riau | 2017 |
| IAIN Syaikh Abdurrahman Siddik Bangka Belitung | Bangka Belitung | 2019 |
| Institut Agama Islam Sumbar | West Sumatra | 2019 |
| Universitas Muhammadiyah Ponorogo | East Java | 2019 |

## Research-Based IP

As the number of IP study programs increases, the number of academic forums and the amount of research from activists at universities will increase. The research-based theory has started being developed. One of the doctoral research programs at Universitas Gadjah Mada was on theory building regarding motivation by Bagus Riyono. The result was about anchor-based motivation. How a God anchor would be the everlasting motivation source (Riyono, 2012). Other publications related to this anchor motivations theory are the journal articles

"Motivation according to Islamic Psychology Perspectives" (Riyono, 2012), "In Search for Anchors; The Fundamental Motivational Force in Compensating for Human Vulnerability" (Riyono & Himam, 2012), and "Internal Structure Review of Anchor Personality Inventory" (Riyono, 2020). They mark the effort of producing a research-based paradigm.

Research to understand Muslim values' uniqueness in mental health and illness and help-seeking behavior in the mental health system has also been conducted. Additionally, research to understand how to incorporate Muslim values into the most evidence-based therapies worldwide and in cognitive behavioral therapy in Indonesia is also being investigated, especially in the last four years (Bouman et al., 2020). This also marks another approach to IP.

## Islamic Psychology in Indonesia and International Movement

The formalities of API and the support from universities make it possible for Indonesian IP activists to connect with international audiences. Funding for conferences and workshops to invite international IP scholars is available from universities. Many lecturers also receive funding to participate in international conferences abroad. The International Institute of Islamic Thought (IIIT) has strengthened these connections. Badri visited Indonesia to attend many conferences, making the IP movement in Indonesia more connected to the international movement. The Indonesian audiences learned from and clarified concepts with Badri directly. The list of conferences is presented in Table 4.

**Table 4: List of Conferences**

| EVENT | ABOUT | ORGANIZER | DATE |
|---|---|---|---|
| National Symposium on Islamic Psychology I | (Theme: The Concept of Islamic-Minded Psychology as an Alternative Approach to Modern Psychology) | Universitas Muhammadiyah Surakarta | 1994 |
| National Symposium on Islamic Psychology II | (Theme: Building Methodology of Islamic Psychology as a Strategic Step in Building Islamic Psychology) | Universitas Padjadjaran Bandung | 1996 |
| National Dialogue of Islamic Psychology Figures | (Theme: Application of Islamic Psychology) | Universitas Darul Ulum, Jombang | 1999 |

| | | | |
|---|---|---|---|
| National Symposium on Islamic Psychology IV | (Theme: Building a Personality of the Future) | Universitas Indonesia | 2000 |
| National Symposium on Islamic Psychology V | (Theme: Optimizing the Role of Islamic Psychology in Improving the Quality of Self, Family, and Indonesian Society). | Universitas Islam Bandung | 2001 |
| Workshop on Islamic Psychology | (A moment that gave birth to a professional association "Association of Islamic Psychology" [API]) | UIN Jakarta | 2002 |
| Congress I Association of Islamic Psychology | - | Universitas Muhammadiyah Surakarta | 2003 |
| Human Development Program according to Islam and Psychological Perspective | (Training to develop the potential and competition of human resources that are necessary to increase the endurance of people in living the XXI century that is full of challenges as well as opportunities) | IMAMUPSI Fakultas Psikologi UI | 2003 |
| National Seminar on Islamic Psychology | (Theme: Understanding the Diversity of Indonesian Society) | Universitas Gadjah Mada | 2004 |
| National Seminar on Islamic Psychology | (Theme: Islamic Psychology as the Antithesis of Ego Psychologists) | Universitas Gadjah Mada | 2004 |
| 1st National Conference on Islamic Psychology (NCIP) and The 1st Inter-Islamic National University Conference on Psychology (IIUCP) | - | Universitas Islam Indonesia | 2015 |
| International Association of Muslim Psychology (IAMP) Conferences | Child Psychology: Islamic Perspectives | Universitas Gadjah Mada | 2016 |

| | | | |
|---|---|---|---|
| National Symposium on Islamic Epistemology in Modern Scientific Theories | - | Universitas Al Azhar Indonesia | 2017 |
| International Conference on Islamic Psychology | Theme: Reviving the Roots and Responding to Today's Challenges | Universitas Islam Indonesia | 2018 |
| 1st Annual Conference of Applied Islamic Psychology and 5th Inter-Islamic University Conference on Psychology (IIUCP) | Theme: Application of Psychology and Islamic Perspective to Respond Challenges in Modern Civilization | Universitas Muhammadyah Malang | 2018 |
| International Conference on Religion and Mental Health (ICRMH) | Theme: Embracing Life Through Religion and Mental Health Awareness | UIN Syarif Hidayatullah | 2019 |
| 1st International Intensive Course on Islamic Psychology | - | Universitas Islam Indonesia in collaboration with IIIT-Indonesia and IAMP | 2019 |
| 2nd International Intensive Course on Islamic Psychology | - | Universitas Islam Indonesia in collaboration with IIIT-Indonesia and IAMP | 2020 |
| 7th Inter-Islamic University Conference on Psychology and The 3rd National Conference on Islamic Psychology | (Theme: Islamic Psychology: Mental Health Solution to Undergo New Normal Adaptation) | Universitas Muhammmadyah Sidoarjo | 2020 |
| Virtual International Conference on Islamic Studies Today | Theme: Empirical Discourses on Islam, Muslim, and Psychology | UIN Walisongo | 2020 |
| Islamic Psychology Convention | Theme: Education in the Digital Era from Islamic Psychology Perspective: Challenge and Solution | Universitas Gadjah Mada | 2020 |
| Virtual International Student Conference on Islamic & Positive Psychology | Theme: Islamic and Positive Psychology | UIN Ar-Raniry | 2021 |

Observing the enthusiasm of Indonesian universities and students, in 2016, Badri held the International Association of Muslim Psychology (IAMP) in Yogyakarta, Indonesia. The conference entitled "Child psychology: Islamic perspective" attracted a broad audience from within Indonesia and abroad. At this conference, the board of IAMP moved the IAMP presidency and secretariat to Indonesia. Since then, Bagus Riyono has run this organization from Indonesia with the support of Indonesian scholars. Hanan Dover, an Australian psychologist, who involved in IAMP since its establishment, was appointed to be the vice president of IAMP.

## Future Direction and Research Priorities

After thirty years of development, the objective of IP should be increasing human mental health by understanding its existence and the concept of living directed by Quranic teaching. As progress is made toward achieving this objective, society's quality of life will increase, and the contributions to the literature and humanity will flourish. To achieve this goal, IP can be advanced in two directions:

1. Developing the original concept from the Quran with psychology as the subject matter.
2. Studying psychology by applying an Islamic worldview on the evidence-based modern psychology.

Further research directions of IP in Indonesia should also focus on responding to the problems of Indonesians.

1. Mental Health System Development
2. Research has demonstrated that the beliefs and values of societies influence their help-seeking behavior. The mental health professional's ability to incorporate patients' values and beliefs is expected to increase the efficacy of the psychotherapy. Therefore, IP should play important roles in strengthening the Indonesian mental health system.
3. Family Strengthening
4. The health of families is essential to the well-being of both current and future generations. Islamic teaching contains a comprehensive concept of family. Researchers of IP could produce more research in this field to help the government strengthen families.
5. IP in the Education System
6. School is a major part of building the character and well-being of the children. Thus, IP should develop, research, and propose a concept of education.
7. IP in Organization system/Workplace well-being

8. The balance of family life, individual life, and work performance is essential to productivity and well-being. IP also should develop research in this area.
9. IP in Crisis and Disaster
10. Disaster is always an opportunity for humanity to discuss mental health and well-being. Indonesia, is a disaster-prone country that should develop strong disaster management. IP can discuss the Islamic concept of managing calamity and its application in disaster management.

## Conclusion

IP in Indonesia has evolved from an informal movement by students to formal institutions by professional associations. It has also evolved from a local movement to becoming a significant part of IP's international movement. At first, informal discussions were triggered by the influential book "The Dilemma of Muslim Psychologists," and today, many books, journals, and research-based publications have been published. For thirty years, this movement has involved psychologists, psychiatrists, and scholars from an Islamic studies background. IP in Indonesia is now expected to have additional roles in responding to the nation's problems in many sectors.

## References

Ancok, D., & Suroso, F. N. (1994). *Psikologi Islam [Islamic psychology]*. Pustaka Pelajar.

Badri, M. (1979). *The dilemma of Muslim psychologists.* MWH London.

Badri, M. B. (1979/1986). *Dilema Psikolog Muslim [The Dilemma of Muslim Psychologists]* (p. 74) (Siti Zainab, Trans.). Pustaka Firdaus.

Bastaman, H. D. (1995). *Integrasi Psikologi dengan Islam [The Integration of Psychology and Islam]*. Pustaka Pelajar.

Bastaman, H. D. (2005). DARI KALAM SAMPAI KE API: Psikologi Islami Kemarin, Kini, Esok [From KALAM to API: Islamic Psychology, Yesterday, Today and Tomorrow]. *Jurnal Psikologi Islam, 1*(1), 5–16.

Bouman, T., Setiyawati, D., &Lomen, M. (2020). *The acceptability of cognitive behaviour therapy in Indonesian community health care* (submitted for publication).

Daradjat, Z. (1970). *Ilmujiwa agama [The Psychology of Religion]*. Bulan Bintang.

Dirgagunarsa, S. (1975). Clinical child psychology in Indonesia. *Journal of Clinical Child Psychology, 4*(2), 33–35. https://doi.org/10.1080/15374417509532641

Fakultas Psikologi UGM. (2015). *Setengah Abad Sepenuh Hati [A Half Century Full of Dedication]*. Fakultas Psikologi, UGM.

Hawari, D. (2000). *Gerakan nasional anti "Mo-Limo" (madat, minum, main, maling, dan madon) [National Movement on No Drug Abuse, No Alcohol and, No Gambling, No Stealing and No Adultery]*. Dana Bhakti Prima Yasa.

Hawari, D. (2002a). *Dimensi religi dalam praktek psikiatri dan psikologi [Religious Dimension on Psychiatry and Psychology Practice]*. Fakultas Kedokteran, Universitas Indonesia.

Hawari, D. (2002b). *Konsep Agama (Islam) Menanggulangi HIV/AIDS [Islamic Concept on Anticipating HIV/AIDS]*. Dana Bhakti Prima Yasa.

Hawari, D., & Sonhadji, H. M. (1995). *Al Qur'an: ilmu kedokteran jiwa dan kesehatan jiwa [Al Qur'an: Knowledge on Psychiatry and Mental Health]*. Dana Bhakti Prima Yasa.

Mubarok, A. D. (2000). *Jiwa dalam Al-Quran [Soul in Al-Quran]*. PT. Paramadina.

Mubarok, A. (2001). *Psikologi Qur'ani [Qur'anic Psychology]*. Pustaka Firdaus.

Mujib, A. (1999). *Fitrah dan kepribadian Islam: sebuah pendekatan psikologis [Fitrah and Islamic Personality: A Psychological Approach]*. Darul Falah.

Mujib, A., & Mudzakir, J. (2001). *Nuasa-nuansa psikologi Islam [Nuances of Islamic Psychology]*. Raja Grafindo Persada.

Nashori, F. (1994). *Membangun Paradigma Psikologi Islami [Building an Islamic Psychology Paradigm]*. Sipress.

Nashori, F. (2002a). *Agenda psikologi Islam [Islamic Psychology Agenda]*. Pustaka Pelajar.

Nashori, F. (2002b). *Mimpi Nubuwat [Prophetic Dream]*. Pustaka Pelajar.

Nashori, F. N. (2003). *Potensi-potensi manusia [Human Potentials]*. Pustaka Pelajar.

Nunzairina, N. (2018). Sejarah Pemikiran Psikologi Islam Zakiah Daradjat [History of Zakiyah Darajat's opinion on Islamic Psychology]. *JUSPI (Jurnal Sejarah Peradaban Islam), 2*(1), 99–112.

Riyono, B. (1998). Prinsip-Prinsip Psikologi Islam [The Principles of Islamic Psychology]. *Psikologika: Jurnal Pemikiran Dan Penelitian Psikologi, 3*(6). https://journal.uii.ac.id/Psikologika/article/view/8467

Riyono, B. (2012). *Motivasi dengan perspektif psikologi islam [Motivation based on Islamic Perspective]*. Quality Publishing.

Riyono, B. (2020). Internal Structure Review of "Anchor Personality Inventory" [Kajian Struktur Internal "Anchor Personality Inventory"]. *ANIMA Indonesian Psychological Journal, 35*(2). https://doi.org/10.24123/aipj.v35i2.2907

Riyono, B., & Himam, F. (2012). In search for anchors the fundamental motivational force in compensating for human vulnerability. *Gadjah Mada International Journal of Business, 14*(3), 229–252.

Sudrajat, W., & Setiono, K. (1996). The basic for an Islamic oriented tertiary education curriculum in psychology. *Psikologika: Jurnal Pemikiran Dan Penelitian Psikologi, 1*(1), 14–2.

CHAPTER SIX

# Islamic Psychology in Iran: Past, Present, & Future

HAMID RAFIEI-HONAR
MASOOD AZARBAYEJANI

AS ONE OF The Abrahamic religions, Islam pays special attention to the human psyche. Islamic Psychology (IP) is the science of studying the "*Nafs*" (Psyche) and its functions and norms to discover or produce the rules that govern it, to provide mental health, and to create a good life in line with the transcendent goal that God has set for humans. Although this science is not recognized in the scientific community, in Islamic countries, for example, Iran, it has been studied for more than three decades. This chapter reviews the following: 1. Fundamentals of the science of IP; 2. the history of IP in Iran; 3. works of IP in the form of books, quarterlies, and conferences, and disciplines as educational programs; 4. introduction to the scientific institutions working on IP, including educational research centers, scientific associations, and psychological service centers; and 5. limitations and future prospects of IP in Iran.

## Introduction

Psychology is the study of phenomena that provide the psychological norms and means for ensuring the mental health and well-being of individuals, families, and communities. The divine religions are aware of this basic human need, and Islam, with more than 1.5 billion followers, pays special attention to the human psyche. "Islamic Psychology (IP)" is the science of studying the "*Nafs*" (Psyche) and its functions and norms to discover or produce the rules that govern it, aiming to provide mental health and create a good life in line with the transcendent goal that God has set for man. We begin this chapter with the theoretical foundations of IP, divided into two sections: "Fundamentals of Science" and "Fundamentals of Anthropology."

## Fundamentals of Science of IP

The fundamentals of the science of IP refer to the study of the subject, purpose, and methods of IP (Rashaad, 2011). IP in Iran, and its general flow in the world, has always faced scientific challenges. Regarding the Islamization of knowledge, there are both proponents (e.g., Gharavi & Azarbayejani, 2012; Khodayarifar, 2019; Khosravi & Bagheri, 2006) and opponents (e.g., Paya, 2007; Soroush, 2011).

### THE SUBJECT OF IP

Regarding the Islamization of psychology, Iranian thinkers have various views. The most important ideas in this field are "*Fitrah*" (Ahmadi, 1983; Ale Ishaaq (1990), the immaterial factor of life; the "*Ruh*" (Soul; Hosseini, 1985), the "*Nafs*" and its functions (Azarbayejani, 2019; Gharavi, 1995; Hosseini, 1994; Haqqani, 1999; Khodayarifar, 2019), "*A'mal*" or deed (Bagheri et al., 1995), behavior and mental processes (Kavyani Arani, 1998a, 2018; Shojaei, 2015), and "*Qalb*" (Bagheri, 2018). The difference between "A'mal" (the deed) and behavior is that the *A'mal* is based on principles such as cognition, desire, and will, but behavior can occur without these cases (Bagheri et al., 1995). However, the subject matter of "*Nafs*" has received more attention among researchers. Notably, the "*Soul*" cannot be well known in this world; and "*Fitrah*" because of its limitation and inactivity in many situations cannot be the subject of IP. Conversely, the *Nafs* is so general that it covers other concepts, including *A'mal*, behavior, and mental processes, and can be a more appropriate subject for IP (Khodayarifar et al., 2021). Although the *Nafs* refers to the aspect of human identification, the "*Qalb*" refers to the area of change of the *Nafs* in emotional, cognitive, and motivational dimensions (Rafiei-Honar et al., 2020).

### THE PURPOSE OF IP

The purpose of IP among Muslim psychologists has expanded from the usual behavioral approach goals in mainstream psychology (describing, explaining, predicting, and controlling) to human happiness and nearness to God. This issue is partly influenced by the choice of the subject of this science. For the individuals who consider the *Nafs* to be the subject of IP, they consider knowing the Nafs, its functions, strengths, and laws to be the prelude to knowing God. Moreover, according to Misbah (2009), a contemporary Iranian Islamic thinker, knowing God will provide the ground for reaching nearness and divine perfection, the true happiness of human beings. Therefore, the goals that can be imagined for IP are set in line with that great goal, including achieving mental health, a good individual life, and cohesion in a collective life to achieve divine perfection (Rafiei-Honar, 2019a).

### THE METHOD OF IP

One of the most challenging debates in the field of religious science in general and in IP in particular is the methodology of this science. IP must prove both its scientific and Islamic nature. Therefore, a strategy of Islamic psychologists has been to emphasize multimethod studies over single-method studies (Abu Torabi & Misbah, 2019). The most recent review studies in Iran (Fadakar et al., 2020) have also revealed that most researchers agree that in the production and development of IP, all methods can be used, including those that are rational, experimental, narrative (based on revelation), and intuitive. However, the emphasis on experimental methods has always been an approach to proving the scientific nature of IP.

Religious researchers (Gharavi & Azarbayejani, 2012; Khosravi & Bagheri, 2006; Shojaei, 2015) with different but consistent readings have emphasized that after determining the hypotheses and presuppositions of a research problem based on Islamic sources and principles, it must be tested, and this scientific process must continue until the result is obtained (confirming or rejecting the hypothesis). These researchers argue that if religious hypotheses are rejected or refuted in the process, the correctness of religion will not be harmed, because an assumption is that the hypotheses arose from a researcher's perception of religious sources, and these are the researcher's perceptions that must be corrected. Of course, there may also be errors in the use of experimental methods. However, the following remains unclear: which of the aforementioned methods (rational, empirical, narrative, and intuitive) follow which methodological paradigm, and which methods are the best for data collection and analysis. These ambiguities are discussed in "Limitations and Prospects," at the end of this chapter.

## Fundamentals of Anthropology of IP

According to some Iranian researchers (Azarbayejani, 2012a), mainstream psychology has limitations, for example, a purely materialistic view of humans, determinism, no focus on human free will, human–animal homogenization, and Darwinian evolution. Therefore, the principles of anthropology in Islamic thought should be considered.

## ISLAM'S DUAL VIEW OF HUMANS

According to Iranian Islamic thinkers (e.g., Motahhari, 2010), Islam has a dual view of humans as comprising nature (body) and the supernatural (soul). The Holy Quran's description of the human and his characteristics are both praiseworthy and reproachful. These descriptions indicate that humans have strengths and weaknesses simultaneously, different needs, and various desires and aspirations, which they choose voluntarily and that determine the course of their lives. By explaining these principles, it is possible to present a correct view of human in the Islamic tradition.

In the Holy Quran, the term *Nafs* and its derivatives have been used more than 290 times. According to the Iranian Exegetes (*Mufassir*) of the Holy Qur'an (Tabatabai, 1995, vol. 14), *Nafs* in the Qur'an is generally used in one main meaning and two common meanings. Regarding the one main meaning, a) *Nafs* basically means what is added to it, and thus "*Nafs al-Insaan*" means man himself, and "*Nafs al-Shei*" means the thing itself. The two common meanings are as follows: b) the human being who is a BEING composed of soul and body (e.g., Al-Ma'idah: 32), and c) the human soul (e.g., Al-An'am: 93). According to this thinker, what makes a person a human is awareness, life, and power. These three are dependent on the human soul; thus, the identification of human with the human soul has been made. It is called the *Nafs* as long as it is with the body. This is the same truth that each of us speaks with the phrase "I." Of course, the *Nafs* is united with the body and governs the body through consciousness, will, and other perceptual attributes (Tabatabai, 1995). According to various verses of the Holy Qur'an (e.g., Az-Zumar: 2; Al-Baqarah: 154), the *Nafs* has characteristics other than the characteristics of the body. Among other things, the talent of perfection and deficiency is hidden in him, and the factors of achieving each of them have been identified to and understood by the Creator of the *Nafs* (verses 7 to 10 of Surah Shams; Tabatabai, 1995, vol. 20).

In the Holy Qur'an, at least 12 abilities (positive attributes, e.g., guidance, faith, certainty, patience, insight), and 15 negative attributes (e.g., misguidance, arrogance, stinginess, stupidity, rebellion) are ascribed to the *Nafs*, which is also attributed to another concept called "*Qalb*" (Rafiei-Honar et al., 2020). Islamic scholars (Azarbayejani & Shojaei, 2014; Azarbayejani et al., 2020) from another perspective have divided the Qur'anic functions of the *Nafs*, including positive–negative functions (Al-Muzzammil: 20 and An-Nisa: 128), worldly–hereafter (At-Tahreem: 6 and Az-Zukhruf: 71), physical–spiritual (Al-Baqarah: 54 and Az-Zumar, 42), moral–spiritual (Faatir: 18 and Al-A'raf: 205), developmental (Ash-Shams: 7 and 8, Yusuf 53, Al-Qiyamah: 2 and Al-Fajr: 27–30), and cognitive–emotional–behavioral (As-Sajda: 17, Faatir: 8 and Luqmaan: 34).

## THE PLACE OF QALB AND AQL IN IRANIAN ISLAMIC THOUGHT

In the Holy Qur'an, the word *Qalb* has been used 132 times, in which at least 25 states or traits of health such as guidance, faith, and confidence and approximately 30 diseases or traits such as cruelty, hypocrisy, and arrogance have been attributed to it. Some states such as "*Hidayah*" (guidance) and "*Tafaqqoh*" (deep thinking) have been attributed to both the *Nafs* (As-Sajda: 13) and the *Qalb* (At-Taghabun: 11; Al-A'raf: 179). Thus, there is a relationship between the *Qalb* and the *Nafs*.

Iranian Islamic thinkers (Motahhari, 2011; Tabatabai, 1995, vol. 9) posit the *Qalb* and the *Nafs* have one meaning. According to *Allamah* Tabatabai (1995, vol. 9), the *Qalb* is a phenomenon that has the power of perception and cognition, different emotions have emerged from it, and it is the source of different emotions; additionally, from the perspective of other Islamic scholars (Majlesi, 1982, vol. 1), because the states and characteristics of a human's *Nafs* can change and transform, it is called the *Qalb* (the Qalb in Arabic means change and transformation). However, Islamic researchers (Rafiei-Honar et al., 2020), through analyzing Islamic texts, have shown that the ability of the *Nafs* to change itself is a main psychological action of humans. The human's *Nafs* can make changes in a positive direction *al-Saadah* (spiritual and eternal happiness) and negative direction *al-Shaqaavah* (eternal misery); and these changes occur not all at once but hierarchically.

The study of Islamic sources shows that humans' *Nafs* causes changes in itself through forces and mechanisms, the most important of which is the capacity of "*Aql*." However, the meaning of the *Aql* in Islamic sources has been much debated among Islamic scholars. Rafiei-Honar et al. (2014) conducted content analysis and examined the opinions of the commentators of the Holy Quran (Tabarsi, 1992; Tabatabai, 1995), Islamic *Muhaddith*s (narrators, e.g., Majlesi, 1982), researchers of Islamic humanities (e.g., Mirdrikvandi, 2010; Shojaei, 2009) and the verses and first-hand Islamic hadiths and found at least two common elements in the nature of the *Aql*: "Cognition" and "Control." Accordingly, the *Aql*is a cognitive-controlling capacity that equips the individual with factual cognitions; it prevents him from deviating from the standards in accordance with healthy and sublime goals.

## HUMAN WILL

In Islamic philosophy, humans have Will (*Iraadah*), and this claim is supported by various verses of the Holy Qur'an, for example, in one's free will in accepting the guidance of the prophets (Al-Insaan: 3; Al-Isra: 15), the necessity of examining human (Al-Insaan: 2), being responsible for a human's deeds (Al-Muddaththir: 38), encouraging or condemning a human for his deeds (Al-Baqarah:

155), the afterlife of having human deeds (At-Tawbah: 72), sending Bibles and Prophets to guide human beings and inviting them to education (An-Nahl: 36; Ibrahim:1), and training and cultivation (Al-Jumu'ah: 2). From the collection of these verses, we conclude that human beings are free and independent beings and can voluntarily step on the path of healthy and transcendent goals (*Saadah*) or pathological and inhuman goals (*Shaqaavah*).

### THE PURPOSE OF LIFE

What emerges from Islamic sources is that any change that serves to lead a person to lofty goals is desirable for Islam and that any change in the opposite direction of the well-being of individuals will not be desirable for the religion of Islam. From the perspective of Iranian Islamic thinkers (Javadi, 2004), the ultimate, transcendent goal of humans is the "*Falaah*," which means rising from evil, achieving good, and staying in it, and the human's *Falaah* in achieving absolute perfection is "*Leqa Allah*" (Meeting God).

The important point is that the place of purposeful movement and change toward the transcendent goal is the human's *Nafs*. According to Tabatabai (1995, vol. 6), the path of humans to God is the *Nafs* of man because there is nothing other than the man himself that is the way of man. It is he who has different evolutions and different degrees and stages. Therefore, considering the ultimate goal determines the current type of life of a human has and the direction of his changes in the world. Attention to the final destination will significantly affect the type of human behavior in life such that it compels one to change the existing conditions and perform righteous deeds, and these righteous deeds become a source for human perfection and happiness. Therefore, with the determination of human purpose, the type of interaction of the individual with himself and others is also determined.

## History of IP in Iran

Although the term "Religious Psychology" was first used in its current conception in the 20th century (MacDonald, 1909), and the idea of "Islamic Psychology" was first observed in the 1940s (Nejati, 2001), the origins of the intellectual roots and discussions of the branches of this science are in the *Hadith* works of Islamic scholars and the scientific works of Islamic thinkers.

### IRANIAN PIONEERS OF IP

Well-known Islamic scholars, especially from the 8th century AD (3rd century AH), have placed the *Hadiths* of the Prophet of Islam and the Twelve Shiite Imams on the basis of methodical understanding and intellectual processing (*religious Ijtihad*) in the form of *Fiqh*: Islamic jurisprudence and theological and moral books. Much of the content of these ethical books relates to psychology. Some of the ethical importance of these works (quoted by Tabatabai, 2011) from the 8th to 13th century AD are as follows: the book *al-Aqlva al-Jahl* (Wisdom and Ignorance), *al-Iman va al-Kufr* (Faith and Disbelief), *al-Ishra* (Companionship, Social Ethics), *al-Ma'isha* (of living), and *al-ziva l-Tajammul* (Garment and Beautification and Etiquette). Following the influential book *Al-Kafi* (the Sufficient; Sheikh al-Kulayni, 836–907 AD), *Musadaqat al-Ikhwan* (Friendship of religious brothers), *al-Mawa'iz* (Sermons), *Al-Khisal* (The Traits; Sheikh al-Saduq, 883–959 AD), *Nahj al-Balagha* (The way of Eloquence; al-Sharif al-Radi, 937–984), *Misbah al-Mutahajjid va silah al-Muta'abbid* (Sheikh al-Tusi, 963–1038 AD), *Kashf al-Mahajjah l-Samaratel Muhajah* (ethic and encompasses for children), and *Muhasibah al-Nafs* (spiritual self-monitoring; Sayyed ibn Tawus, 1167–1242 AD) were the books that ensued. These books examine the semantics of the *Nafs* and *Aql*, human psychospiritual strengths and weaknesses, lifestyle principles, religious education of children, principles of interpersonal and social relations, connection with God, spiritual self-supervision, and psychology of spirituality.

The Islamic world is also proud of Islamic scholars who have developed ideas and theories in various branches of psychology. Some of these Iranian ideas (Zakaria Qazvini, 1176–1260) have been introduced by European Islamic studies scholars (Taeschner, 1912), while others (Farabi and Ibn Sina) have been considered by early psychological historians (Brett, 1921). Additionally, Haque (2004) discusses the participation of early Muslim scholars, including Iranian scientists, in the formation of psychology in a detailed article that includes the theories of At-Tabari (838–870), Al-Balkhi (849–934), Al-Razi (864–932), Al-Farabi (872–950), Ali Ibn Abbas Al-Majusi (995), Ibn Miskawayh (941–1030), Ibn Sina (980–1037), Al-Ghazali (1058–1111), and Fakhr Al-Razi (1149–1209). However, the role of Islamic scholars from the 12th to the 19th century has received less attention, including Sheikh Ishraq, Nasir al-Din Tusi, Mulla Sadra, Fayz al-Kaashani, and Mullah Ahmad Al-Naraqi. To complete the history of IP, introducing the psychological ideas of some of these scientists is necessary.

### *Shahab ad-Din" Yahya Suhrawardi (Sheikh Ishraq)*

Sheikh Ishraq (1154–1191) is an Iranian Muslim philosopher. In the Islamic period, there were two major schools of thought in Iran: the *Peripatetic* (the Greek heritage Islamized under the leadership of Ibn Sina) and the *Ishraq* (the Islamized Iranian heritage led by Sheikh Ishraq). *Ishraqian* philosophers, unlike peripatetic philosophers, discover the truths of the universe by combining the spiritual dimension of man and mystical intuition with reason and argument (Maleki, 2017).

Self-knowledge is a prominent issue of the Ishraqian system of wisdom, and its goal is to recognize the position of the "self" in the system of existence and to find its ultimate happiness. Sheikh Ishraq, unlike the peripatetic scholars, has brought *Ilm al-Nafs* (philosophical psychology) closer to theology, and its topics are mostly used to provide a means to save man from the darkness of the material world (Azhir & Elyasi, 2019). In the book *Hayaakil al-Noor* (The Temple of Light), the Sheikh considers the human soul as a heavenly truth imprisoned by the earthly body and returns to its original truth after acquiring virtues and perfections (Sharifi & Fanaei Eshkevari, 2018).

Sheikh Ishraq has described human personality in the form of a "cognitive-emotional-spiritual" model. In the book *Fi Haqiqat al-'Ishq* (On the Reality of Love; Suhrawardi, 1993), in the form of a mysterious story, he describes the human *Nafs* (soul), its various dimensions, forces, and mechanisms. In this model, the existential core of the human *Nafs* is the *Aql* (intellect), which has dimensions of cognition and emotion, which include God knowing (with goodness affect), self-knowledge (with love affect), and awareness of poverty (with sadness affect). He considers these three to be hierarchical. Goodness (*al-Hosn*) is at the highest level, and the happiness and perfection of every human are in achieving it. Love (*al-'Ishq*) is equipped with forces that both help and prevent the achievement of the ultimate goal. Love is very interested in goodness, and with the help of sadness (*al-Hozn*), seeks to achieve it. He introduces goodness with the metaphor of *Joseph,* love in the form of *Zuleikha,* and sorrow in the form of *Jacob*. He considers the human *Nafs* (soul) akin to a sad lover who has left his homeland, and in the form of a risky journey, and passing through different stages; it seeks to achieve well. In explaining this model, the Sheikh has provided evidence from the verses of the Holy Quran and some Hadiths.

*Muhammad ibn al-Hasan al-Tusi (Khajeh Nasir al-Din)*

Khajeh Nasir al-Din (1201–1274) is one of the greatest and most influential Iranian scientists and philosophers of the Islamic era in the 12th and 13th centuries. He was a leader in jurisprudential, philosophical, theological, moral, mystical, astronomical, and mathematical sciences and wrote several works in the mentioned fields (Masoumi Hamedani, 2012).

Among his psychological works is the book Nasirean Ethics (*Akhlaq-I Nasiri (2008)*). According to this book, he believes in the "longitudinal pyramid of perfection" (Abolhasani Niaraki, 2013) and considers the health of the *Nafs* (*Tazkiyah* and *Tahliah*: cultivation and refine) as the first level of human perfection (a necessary and not sufficient condition). Part of the book is entitled *Moaalija amraaz al-Nafs* (Treatment of Mental Illness). For example, he explains depressive disorder (Poor Hossein, 1996), and by accepting *al-Kindi*'s

(866–801) definition of depression, he defines it as psychological suffering, which is rooted in the two factors of losing a beloved subject and not achieving the desired goal. According to Khajeh Nasir al-Din, all mental states require a type of psychological projection in or out, and they can be divided into two categories, internalized and externalized, of which depression is part of the first category (Hosseini Alawi, 2002). He proposed the idea of *Ilaaj al-Hozn* (treatment of depression) to offer some cognitive solutions (including correcting the belief in the stability of the world and the possibility of achieving all the desires in it and managing dependencies in the field of economic possibilities and physical lusts) and exploit some positive capabilities (e.g., gratitude). It has been used to treat depression (Nasir al-Din Tusi, 2008).

*Sadr al-Din Muhammad Shirazi (Mulla Sadra)*

Mulla Sadra (1571–1640) is the originator of the famous theory of substantial motion (*al-harakat al-jawhariyyah*), substantial change, and transformation of everything in the order of nature, as a result of the self-flow (*al-fayd*) and penetration of being (*sarayan al-wujud*). He has been the most influential Iranian thinker from the 17th to the 20th century (Zekavati Qaragozloo, 1999). Mulla Sadra has provided more than 50 scientific works to the intellectual and narrative sciences, the most famous of which is The Transcendent Philosophy of the Four Journeys of the Intellect (*al-Hikmat al-muta'aliya fi-l-asfar al-'aqliyya al-arba'a*). More than 3,000 articles specifically on Mulla Sadra' s philosophical, mystical, psychological, and educational ideas have been registered in the *database of Noor specialized journals* (noormags.ir, 2020), and this shows the importance of this thinker's point of view among Iranian scholars. In the field of psychology, first, his special explanation of the *Nafs*, its types, how it appears and occurs, its intensification-complementary movement, and the type of its relation to the body must be considered. Thus, the ideas on the psychological strengths and dimensions of man, the meaning and purpose of life, human perfection, and the relationship between cognition and emotions must be analyzed, which does not fit into a brief discussion in this article due to space constraints.

According to Mulla Sadra, a human's *Nafs*, because it is the Nafs, occurs with the creation of the body, but because their spiritual truth existed in divine knowledge, it should be considered eternal (*qadím*). Therefore, the *Nafs* is bodily in its origination in time (*jismaniyyat al-huduth*), and when it has been transformed from potentiality (*quwwa*) to actuality (*fi'l*) and reached perfection, it will be spiritual in its timeless existence (*ruhaniyyat al-baqa*) (Mulla Sadra, 1981a, vol. 8; quoted by Rafiei-Honar, 2018). The human soul (*nafs*) has different degrees and levels from the beginning of its formation until it reaches its end: at the beginning of its formation is the physical essence, then it gradually grows intensively and has degrees to the extent that he becomes upright and moves from this world to the Hereafter and returns to his Lord. Thus, it is a physical occurrence and a spiritual survival (Mulla Sadra, 1982).

The *Sadrian* perspective (quoted by Rafiei-Honar, 2018) on personality, pathology, and health is a developmental view. According to Mulla Sadra, the human soul (*Nafs*) has four levels: vegetative, animal, human, and immaterial (holy), which is expanded in a continuous continuum from this world to the Hereafter (Mulla Sadra, 1984). The child is in the womb and possesses only the vegetative soul *(nafs al-nabaati)*—that which is nourished, and which grows—and all other levels of the soul are only possessed in potentiality. When the embryo develops into an infant and is born, the animal soul *(nafs al-haywaani)*—that which senses and imagines—is actualized; then, in a gradual process, his faculty of thought and understanding grows. When the child reaches the age of reason, the rational soul (*nafs al-Insaani*) is actualized. Once the human soul has reached this level, it possesses "practical" intellect, the faculty through which it may realize its intellectual perfection (at approximately 40 years old). Finally, after this stage, there is a talent for promotion to a higher level called the Holy Soul (nafs al-qodsi) (Mulla Sadra, 1981a, vol. 8; quoted by Rafiei-Honar, 2018). Perhaps one in thousands of individuals will attain the status of the Holy Spirit (*ruh al-qodos*; Mulla Sadra, 1981b). Of course, it is an inference from Mulla Sadra's words that each level of the soul (*nafs*) has the characteristics of the previous level plus more things. Therefore, a human can be healthy (obedient and calm) or sick (rebellious and restless) at any stage of the soul (especially animal and human souls) and achieve happiness or misery. Notably, the human soul (*nafs*) is changeable, and the sick animal soul, even in the Hereafter, after enduring punishment, can be criticized and move toward health (see Mulla Sadra, 1981b). Sadra's thought seems to be a solid, suitable basis for IP.

*Mulla Muhsin al-Fayz al-Kaashani (Fayz Kaashani)*

Fayz Kaashani (1585–1669) is an Iranian Twelver Shi'a Muslim, mystic, philosopher, and Muhaddith. He is also a student and a son-in-law of Mulla Sadra. One hundred and sixteen titles of books and treatises have been registered for Fayz. One of his famous moral books is *Al-Mahajjatal-bayda'fitahdhib al-ihya' (1995)*. He compiled this book to correct, refine, and explain al-Ghazali's book; *Ihya' 'Ulum al-Din* (The Revival of the Religious Knowledge). Influenced by Mulla Sadra and Ghazali, Fayz presented a cognitive–motivational theory to explain behavior and personality development. According to him, the human soul (*nafs*) is governed by five internal and external cognitive–motivational sources—intellect and temperament (internal sources), sharia and custom (external sources), and habit (internalized external source)—for performing its behaviors. However, intellect and sharia are more in harmony with each other, and nature (temperament) and habit are more in harmony with each other, and a custom is a law set by the common people among themselves because it changes with time, place, and ethnicities, sometimes with the first group and sometimes with the second group.

According to Fayzal-Kaashani (2001), there is always the possibility of a conflict between the mentioned forces or the disruption of the individual's cognitions in recognizing the appropriate option and, as a result, loss in the path of ultimate health and happiness. Resolving or not resolving these conflicts will place the human soul (*nafs*) in one of the levels of The Inspired Nafs (*nafs al-mulhamah*), the nafs at peace (*nafs al-mutma'innah*), the self-accusing /blaming nafs (*nafs al-lawwamah*), and the inciting nafs (*nafs al-'ammarah*). Fayz provided strategies for conflict resolution. In addition to the theory of Fayz that explains personality, he draws attention to the cognitive–spiritual development of individuals in five stages: sensory, imaginary, intellectual, abstract, and sacred (Qolizadeh, 2010). The sensory stage is the reception of information through the five senses. The imaginary stage (after the infant period) is related to the recording and maintenance of information obtained from the previous stage. Fayz, at this stage, implicitly refers to the two phenomena of "*Constance*" and "*Conservation*,". These two phenomena have been used in the works of some cognitive psychologists (such as *Jean Piaget*) in the 19th century. After childhood, and in the intellectual stage, the human realizes the general and necessary meanings beyond the imagination, and in the abstract stage processes pure intellectual knowledge and combines them to create more abstract conclusions. The higher order of abstraction is called the "Holy Spirit," which not all individuals have attained and is specific to the prophets and some divine saints. At this stage, one gains an understanding of the findings of the unseen world, some of the teachings of the kingdom of heaven and earth, and the teachings of the Lord—a subject that cannot be understood in the intellectual and abstract stages.

### *Ahmad Ibn Muhammad Mahdi al-Naraqi (Mulla Ahmad Naraqi)*

Mulla Ahmad Naraqi (1771–1829) is an Iranian scholar and Shiite *Mujtahid* and the author of 35 works in the field of jurisprudence, principles, Hadith, and ethics. One of his famous books is *Mi'raj al-sa'ada* (Ladder of happiness), based on Aristotelian virtuous ethics and its elaboration with Islamic texts to explain the psychological characteristics of human, pathology, and providing its treatment. This book is an interpretation of the book *Jami' al-sa'adat* by Mullah Mahdi Naraqi, the father of Mullah Ahmad, a famous Shiite scholar. Notably, most of Mullah Ahmad's writings are commentaries on his father's works.

Naraqi, one of the pioneers of Islamic positive psychology, likens the human psyche to a mountain (or cone) whose only peak is good, difficult to climb, and easy to descend from, and individuals who ascend (Health–happiness) or descend (disease-cruelty) use the main psychic forces, namely, lust (*al-Shahvah*), anger (*al-ghazab*), and intellect (*al-Aql*). The goal of each force is to bring the person pleasure or to repel suffering. The mental health of a person is in maintaining the moderation of the three forces, and his illness is in extremism or wastage of it or corrupting that force .Naraqi offers the "choice–monitoring" model for health–happiness (the aspect of climbing the mountain) and explains the stages of "self-cultivation" (*Tazkiyah al-nafs*), and for the disease–misery (the aspect of descending from the mountain), by using the method of "Counter in a contrasting way," the ways introduce the person to returning to the balance line. In the choice-monitoring model, the person with the aim of maintaining and promoting a Kholq (operationalized strength that arises from the three virtues of chastity, courage, and wisdom) chooses it. Next are the two strategies of environmental care and action monitoring. In monitoring actions, a person is always careful that anger, lust, and intellect do not go beyond moderation. However, in a contrasting manner, the type of disorder and its cause must first be identified.

In the Naraqi theoretical system, mental disorders are divided into seven general categories (rational, lustful, angry, rational–lustful, rational–angry, lustful–angry, and rational–angry–lustful), and each category is divided into three types (disruption as extremism, disruption as wastage, disruption as a corruption of force; Naraqi, 1372/1993). After diagnosis, a person in a continuous treatment process must first perform some countering behavior, and then perform cognitive-behavioral activities, imagining the harms of the disease, and then correct himself with guided self-talk. Next, he engages in contradictory behaviors by drowning and forcing himself to do them (e.g., staying in the dark for someone with a phobia), and finally, if the prior steps were ineffective, he performs difficult acts (*al-Riaazah*) (e.g., depriving oneself of light; Naraqi, 1372/1993). Of course, Naraqi (1372/1993) emphasizes treatment under the supervision of a specialist.

## IP IN THE 20TH CENTURY IN IRAN

Although the beginning of modern psychology in Iran dates back to the 1930s (Siasi, 1938), studying the historical trend of IP is difficult for at least two reasons. The first reason is the lack of formulation in terms of the subject matter, methods, purpose, theories, and the specific structure of this science. The second reason is the dispersion of works and research throughout the 20th century. Recently, based on the idea of some Muslim psychologists (Kaplick & Skinner, 2017), Rafiei-Honar (2021), in a meta-synthesis study among psychological works, examined "*Islamic psychological Currentology in the present age*" and classified the historical process of this science into four phases: the *Preparation* period, the *Refining* period and the first wave of *Establishment*, the *Comparison* period, and the second wave of the establishment. However, as we demonstrate in this paper, these phases do not have a precise cut point, and in some sections, they overlap. During the period of Preparation, approximately from 1910 to 1950, only the ideas of Muslim thinkers in the field of Islam and psychology were introduced. In the second phase, which spread from approximately 1950 to 1990, there are two simultaneous approaches of Refining mainstream psychology and the first wave in the establishment of IP.

In this period, some thinkers have criticized the principles or theories of contemporary psychology, and others have attempted to establish psychology based on Islam. The article "*Human personality in terms of modern psychology and religion*" (Saeedi, 1950) is one of the first works written by Iranian thinkers with a critical view; it criticized psychological theories from the perspective of the Holy Qur'an. The article "*Again God or Man*" (Sahib al-Zamani, 1975) and the book "*Schools of Psychology and its Critiques*" (Gharavi, 1990) are also among the Iranian critical works in the mentioned period. By contrast, a series of articles entitled "*Islamic Psychology*" written by Hawzah (seminary) thinkers (Yazdi, 1966) in this period indicates the adoption of a founding approach. Additionally, the books "*Education Based on Islamic Psychology*" (Riaazi, 1981), "*Fitrah: The Foundation of Islamic Psychology*" (Ahmadi, 1983), "*Preliminary Study of the Principles of Islamic Psychology*" (Hosseini, 1985), and "*Islam and Psychology*" (Ale Ishaaq, 1990) are among the works of psychologists of this period. However, some authors in the period had neither an academic psychological education nor comprehensive knowledge of the science of psychology, and others did not properly consider the requirements for establishing a science. This subject aroused the criticism of experts and caused the establishment of IP to be delayed for approximately two decades.

Thus, the third phase, from approximately 1980 to 2010, attempts to compare psychological perspectives, models, and concepts with Islamic perspectives. The comparative approach provides a dialogue between the parties more than any other approach does. A large part of the research conducted in Iran, especially among psychologists in the *Hawzah of Qom*, has followed the comparative approach. The two scientific centers of *Research Institute of Hawzah and University (RIHU)* and *Imam Khomeini Education and Research Institute (IKERI)*, in *Qom*, have published approximately 90 volumes of books in the field of psychology, and the main approach of most of these books in the mentioned period has been the comparison.

Finally, with the provision of necessary arrangements and the formal gathering of some Muslim psychologists with common goals and policies, the establishment of scientific associations such as the *Islamic Psychology Association* (*IPA*, 2004) and formal academic disciplines (e.g., *Positive-oriented Islamic Psychology*, 2010; Table 4) was started as the second wave of the establishment of IP. During this period, measurement tools and defensible models are being designed, and specialized descriptive and experimental books and articles are being compiled; we discuss the latter in this paper (Rafiei-Honar, 2020a).

WORKS OF IP

The works of IP are introduced in four formats: books, journals and quarterlies, scientific conferences, and educational programs. The introduction of all works requires a detailed review, and here, the most important ones will suffice.

## Books

As aforementioned, most of the works of IP have been published by Hawzah centers and theological psychologists in Qom. However, other Muslim psychologists have entered this field in recent years. Table 1 summarizes the most important books in various branches of psychology that have been published or reprinted in the last two decades. All these publications have been published in Farsi.

**Table 1. The most important books of IP in Iran from 2000 to 2020**

| BRANCH | TITLE-AUTHOR |
|---|---|
| Basic topics of Islamic psychology | A Look at Islamic Psychology (Gharavi & Azarbayejani, 2012)<br>Psychological Perspectives of Ayatollah Misbah Yazdi (Shojaei, 2013)<br>Psychology in Nahj al-Balagha (Azarbayejani & Shojaei, 2014)<br>Psychology from the perspective of Islamic scholars: Islamic psychology (Kajbaaf, 2016)<br>Psychology from the perspective of Muslim thinkers (Narooei, 2017a)<br>Generalities and Concepts in Islamic Psychology (Kalaantari, 2018)<br>Psychology from the perspective of Islamic scientists (Ejeii, 2019)<br>Psychology in the Quran (Kavyani Arani, 2019)<br>Psychology in Quran and Hadith (Shojaei, 2019) |

| | |
|---|---|
| Personality | The model of a perfect human being with a psychological approach (Bashiri, 2010)<br><br>Healthy human theories in the Light of Islamic Sources (Shojaei & Heidari, 2010)<br><br>The Unconscious Mind in the Qur'an (Araafi, 2014)<br><br>Psychology of Self-control with an Islamic attitude (Rafiei-Honar, 2016)<br><br>Personality theories with a view to religious sources (Bashiri & Heidari, 2017)<br><br>Self-Awareness with an integrated monotheistic approach (Sharifinia, 2017)<br><br>Personality Psychology from an Islamic Perspective (Ahmadi, 2018)<br><br>Personality from the perspective of traits: Psychological and Islamic theories (Shojaei, 2018a)<br><br>Consciousness and Unconsciousness: A Comparison of Psychoanalysts' Perspectives and Allamah Tabatabai's Thoughts (Abdoli, 2019) |
| Psychometrics | Religiosity Scale Based on Islam (Azarbayejani, 2003)<br><br>Religious Aql and construction of its scale (Mirdrikvandi, 2010)<br><br>Theoretical foundations and methodology of religiosity scales (Khodayarifar et al., 2012)<br><br>Islamic lifestyle and its measurement tools (Kavyani Arani, 2013)<br><br>Criteria for choosing a spouse from the perspective of Islam and construction of its scale (Hosseinkhani, 2018)<br><br>Marital satisfaction from the perspective of Islam and construction of its scale (Jodeiri, 2018) |

| | |
|---|---|
| Psychopathology and Psychotherapy | Psychology of Sexual Behavior (Kajbaaf, 2006)<br><br>Critique of normative criteria in psychology in the Light of Islamic Sources (Abu Torabi, 2007)<br><br>Introduction to the Psychology of Behavior Regulation in The Light of Islamic Resources (Shojaei, 2009)<br><br>Psychotherapy Integration Models with Focused on Monotheistic integrated therapy (Sharifinia, 2012)<br><br>Principles and techniques of Psychotherapy and counseling: an Islamic approach (Janbozorgi, 2016)<br><br>Semantics of Depression from the Perspective of the Quran (Bahrami Ehsan et al., 2016)<br><br>The Theory Islamic Self-Discovery for treatment of Obsessive-Compulsive Disorder (Narooei, 2017b)<br><br>Methods of Behavior Change in Religious and Psychological Teachings (Sedaaqat, 2017)<br><br>Treatment of depression from the perspective of the Quran (Bahrami Ehsan et al., 2017)<br><br>Spiritually Multidimensional psychotherapy: a God-oriented Approach (Janbozorgi, 2019)<br><br>Couples therapy with Islamic approach (Salarifar, 2019)<br><br>Esteem-based psychotherapy (Pourebrahim & Rasouli, 2019)<br><br>Qur'anic Attitude to Psychotherapy, Behavior Therapy and Personality Therapy (Mortazavi, 2020)<br><br>Counseling and treatment of mourning with an Islamic attitude (Nematipour, 2020) |

| | |
|---|---|
| Mental Health | Mental health and the Role of religion (Marashi, 2008)<br>Mental health with an attitude towards Religious Teachings (Qasemi, 2009)<br>Mental health In the Light of Islamic Resources (Salarifar et al., 2011)<br>Anger Control from the Perspective of Islam (Kiomarthi, 2012)<br>Introduction to Addiction Prevention with an Islamic Approach (Pasandideh & Kiomarthi, 2014)<br>Mental health model based on Iranian Islamic model (Ghobari Bonab & Nosrati, 2016)<br>Life skills based on Islamic teachings (Khatib, 2017)<br>Pattern of regulation of sexual behavior with Islamic approach (Abbaasi, 2017)<br>Sexual health of spouses: Islamic and Psychological Approach (Nooralizadeh Mianaji, 2018)<br>Introduction to the Psychology of Aspirations with an Islamic Approach (Rafiei-Honar, 2019b)<br>Critique of Mental Health, Based on the Teaching of the Quran (Azizi Abarghuei & Nodehi, 2020) |
| Family | Marriage from the perspective of religion with a psychological approach (Panaahi, 2015)<br>Family in the attitude of Islam and psychology (Salarifar, 2018)<br>The role of men and women in the family with an Islamic approach (Panaahi, 2019)<br>Family in Islam and Psychology (Safouraii Parizi, 2019) |

| | |
|---|---|
| Psychology of Religion | Hajj in the Mirror of Psychology (Ahmadi, 2011a)<br><br>God-seeking and its role in the attitude towards death (Olianasab, 2012)<br><br>Introduction to the Psychology of Religion (Azarbayejani & Mousavi Asl, 2014)<br><br>From God-awareness to self-awareness and its psychological effects (Nooralizadeh Mianaji, 2015)<br><br>Religious experience in Islamic culture (Azarbayejani et al., 2016)<br><br>The Role of Affection in Faith (Haqqani, 2017)<br><br>Psychology of the Development of religiosity (Nozari, 2018) |
| Positive Psychology | The Islamic Model of Happiness (Pasandideh, 2013)<br>Positive traits: A study and analysis of the narrations of "Makarem al-Akhlaq" (Abdi & Pasandideh, 2018)<br>The role of positivist Islamic psychology in purposefulness in life (Zaakeri, 2019)<br>Positive Thinking in Psychology and Islam (Yousefi Najafabadi, 2020)<br>Theoretical foundations of Islamic Positive Psychology (Rafiei-Honar, 2021) |
| Social Psychology | Social Psychology in the Light of Islamic Sources (Salarifar et al., 2019) |
| Motivation and Emotion | Motivation and Emotion: Psychological and Religious Theories (Shojaei, 2018b)<br><br>Quran and human Emotions (Afifi, 2019) |
| Developmental Psychology | Developmental Psychology with a View to Islamic Sources (Saqaaye Biria et al., 2004) |
| Methodology in Psychology | The Method of psychological Understanding of Religious Texts (Pasandideh, 2019)<br><br>Islamic Humanities Model: Theoretical Framework and Operational Model (Taqavi, 2020) |

Table 1 presents some of the hundreds of works available, and most are scientific dissertations and research articles. For example, extensive activities have been conducted in the field of religious psychometrics in Iran. According to Rafiei-Honar's (2020b) review, among the scales designed in Iran from 1970 to 2019, approximately 70 scales have been identified based on Islamic sources in the fields of positive virtues (e.g., trust in God, hope, humility, contentment, gratitude, patience, forgiveness, courage, optimism, and dignity), moral vices (e.g., arrogance, greed, jealousy, self-deception, neglect, worldliness, and bigotry), and psychological constructs (e.g., desire regulation, moral intelligence, willpower, self-control, diligence, and self-esteem). Additionally, according to Khodayarifar et al. (2012), from 1973 to 2003, 19 scales of religiosity based on Islam were designed in Iran. Azarbayejani (2012b) also introduced five scales that measure moral concepts in the Light of Islamic Sources.

Thus far, conceptual models and educational–psychological protocols have been designed in the form of master's and doctoral dissertations, and their feasibility and initial efficacy have been tested. Some examples of these are *al-Zohd* (regulation of worldly desires) to control anxiety (Abdi et al., 2015), Islamic hope therapy to increase the psychological well-being of patients with MS (Salehi et al., 2016), the conceptual model of identity from an Islamic perspective (Nouri et al., 2016), Islamic Couples Therapy (Jodeiri et al., 2017), the Religious Self-Regulation Protocol to Reduce Marital Conflict (Jahangirzadeh, 2017), the Intervention Package of Nearness to God to Control Anxiety (Aynehchi, 2018), the Islamic Self-Regulation Protocol for Depression Treatment (Rafiei-Honar, 2018), the conceptual model of "Fear of God" based on Islamic Thoughts (Khalilian et al., 2018), Treatment of OCD based on the Islamic cognitive-behavioral approach (Ansari et al., 2019), and the Islamic Eudaimonic Pleasure Protocol for the Treatment of Depression (Abbaasi, 2019).

### QUARTERLY

According to the statistics in the reputable scientific databases of Iran (Noormags, 2020), 1,919 professional journals in the humanities and Islamic sciences have been identified and published in Iran. Approximately 96 of these journals are related to the field of psychology and health, of which 14 journals are mostly related to the field of Islam and psychology. These journals have been launched since 2007 and published more than 1,600 scientific articles. The information on these journals is presented in Table 2.

**Table 2. The most important professional journals of Islam and psychology in Iran**

| TITLE | TYPE<br>YEAR OF ESTABLISHMENT<br>NUMBERS | AFFILIATION |
|---|---|---|
| Studies in Islam and Psychology | Semi-annual Journal<br>2007<br>25 Numbers | Research Institute of Hawzah and University (RIHU) |
| Ravanshenasi va Din<br><br>(Psychology and Religion) | Quarterly Journal<br>2008<br>50 Numbers | Imam Khomeini Education and Research Institute (IKERI) |
| The Islamic Journal of Women and the Family | Quarterly Journal<br>2008<br>34 Numbers | Al-Mustafa International University (AMIU) |
| Sadra Islamic Humanities | Quarterly Journal<br>2011<br>33 Numbers | Sadra Research Center of Islamic Humanities (SRCIH) |
| Religion and Health | Semi-annual Journal<br>2012<br>14 Numbers | Mazandaran University of Medical Sciences (MUMS) |
| Islam and Health | Semi-annual Journal<br>2014<br>12 Numbers | Babol University of Medical Sciences (BUMS) |
| Pizhuhish dar din va salamat<br>(Research on Religion & Health) | Quarterly Journal<br>2014<br>24 Numbers | Shahid Beheshti University of Medical Sciences (SBUMS) |
| Islamic Studies of Women and the Family | Semi-annual Journal<br>2014<br>11 Numbers | Jameah Al-Zahra<br>(Al-Zahra University) |
| Islam and Psychological Research | Semi-annual Journal<br>2015<br>8 Numbers | the Academic Institute for Ethics and Education (AIEE) |
| Journal of Islamic Psychology | Semi-annual Journal<br>2015<br>8 Numbers | Research Institute of Quran and Hadith (RIQH) |
| Research Bulletin for Lifestyle | Semi-annual<br>2015<br>10 Numbers | Research Institute of Islamic Lifestyle (RIIL) |

| Fundamental Research Humanities | Quarterly Journal<br>2015<br>17 Numbers | Sadra Research Center of Islamic Humanities (SRIH) |
|---|---|---|
| Islamic Life Journal | Quarterly Journal<br>2016<br>15 Numbers | Cultural and Student Deputy of the Ministry of Health, and Medical Education (MHME) |
| Islamic Psychology Research | Semi-annual Journal<br>2018<br>2 Numbers | AMIU |

### SCIENTIFIC CONFERENCES

The authors of this chapter have identified at least 13 national and international conferences on Islam and psychology held in Iran from 2000 to 2020. The most important permanent conference is related to the *International Congress of Islamic Humanities,* held every two years under the auspices of the *Supreme Assembly of Islamic Humanities (SAIH).* The policy-making council of this conference comprises 17 real and legal members from 16 scientific centers of Iran. The Secretariat of the Congress has organized 5 international congresses since 2011. The IP Commission has thus far received 252 scientific articles, 72 of which have been accepted, presented, and published. Additionally, in the past few years, the SAIH has held annual meetings of professors active in various fields of Islamic humanities. A one-day meeting of professors of IP was held in December 2018 in Mashhad, and the experts presented their latest findings in the field of IP (www.icih.ir). See Table 3 for information on the conferences.

**Table 3: Scientific Conferences on Islam and Psychology in Iran: 2000–2020**

| TITLE | GOALS/AXES | ORGANIZER INSTITUTION DATE OF HOLDING | DESCRIPTION |
|---|---|---|---|
| International Congress on the Role of Religious Knowledge in the Humanities & Social Sciences: From Dialogue to the Establishment of Religious Science | Identifying the dimensions and characteristics of religious science and methodology in religious knowledge | RIHU<br>October 2020 | 29 speakers (9 non-Iranian speakers) attended; 30 scientific articles presented<br><br>One of the panels was dedicated to psychology<br><br>http://rihu.ac.ir |

| | | | |
|---|---|---|---|
| International Congress of Islamic Humanities | Creating change in humanities, producing thought and theory and establishing new scientific foundations based on religious principles and foundations using the capacities of the Islamic world | SAIH<br>From 2011, Every two years; Continued<br>Sixth Congress: 2021 | The IP Commission is one of the 18 specialized commissions of this congress<br>http://icih.ir |
| The first National Conference on the Qur'an and Psychology | Coordination and alignment of different currents of Islamic psychology in the country and reviewing and evaluating the latest research in the field of Quran and psychology | Faculty of Psychology and Educational Sciences (FPES),<br>University of Tehran<br>June 2019 | https://qpsy.ir |
| Annual Conference on Spiritual Health | The Axes: Islam and the basic theory in spiritual health<br>Religious forms and methods of promoting spiritual health<br>Spiritual care<br>Spiritual health and psychological well-being | Department of Spiritual Health,<br>Academy of Medical Sciences (AMS)<br>From 2011 to present; The seventh edition was held in 2019. | http://www.ams.ac.ir/ |

| | | | |
|---|---|---|---|
| The first festival of top dissertations in the field of psychology with the religious approach | Promoting research and ideation and designing interventions in the field of counseling with a religious approach and expanding the field of psychological knowledge and counseling based on religious teachings | Comprehensive Center for Counseling, Growth and Empowerment (CCGE)<br>in<br>Astaan Quds Razavi<br><br>June 2019 | 14 dissertations selected from 126 works sent to the Secretariat<br><br>https://www.razavi.ir/ |
| The first international conference on religion, spirituality and quality of life | The Axes: the relationship between religion and spirituality, psychology of religion, spirituality in Islam and other religions, the effect of spirituality on individual and social health, and the relationship between order and security in an Islamic lifestyle | AMIU<br>June 2019<br><br>The second conference will be held in January 2020. | Selected 55 articles from 300 articles.<br>http://icrsl.ir |
| First International Congress of Quran and Humanities | The Axes: Qur'anic scientific authority in the field of humanities, Quran and basics of humanities, Quran and humanities goals, role of Quran in orienting to humanities methods, and methodology of interdisciplinary studies of Quran and sciences | Higher School of Quran and Hadith<br>of<br>AMIU<br><br>April 2017 | Publication of a collection of articles in the book *Quran and Psychology* (Rezaei Isfahani et al., 2017) |

| | | | |
|---|---|---|---|
| National Conference on the Islamic-Iranian Model of Counseling | Objectives:<br><br>Utilizing the capacity of religious resources in the fields of psychology and counseling, extracting the concepts of counseling from the Qur'an and hadiths, and increasing the knowledge of reference groups in this field | Institute of Counseling, Youth and Social Research Services<br><br>in<br><br>Astaan Quds Razavi<br><br>November 2013 | https://www.razavi.ir |
| National Conference on Islamic Lifestyle | Objective: Pathology of the current lifestyle and an explanation of a monotheistic and Islamic lifestyle | Department of Psychology of<br><br>IKERI<br><br>January 2013 | Select 18 articles from 332 submitted.<br><br>Articles. http://qabas.iki.ac.ir |
| National Conference on Gender from the Perspective of Religion and Psychology | Axes: Sexual identity and its development from the perspective of religion and psychology, the role and function of gender differences in the family, the impact of secular perspectives on male and female psychology, male–female communication pattern. | Department of Psychology of<br><br>IKERI<br><br>October 2011 | Publication of a collection of articles in the book *Gender from the Perspective of Religion and Psychology* (Ahmadi, 2011b) |

| | | | |
|---|---|---|---|
| Second National Conference on the Role of Religion in Mental Health | Axes: Religious Role, Religious and Islamic Attitudes and Beliefs in Primary Prevention and Promotion of Mental Health, Position of Islamic Psychology and Community Psychology and National Religious Behavior in Health | Iran University of Medical Sciences (IUMS) & Tehran Psychiatric Institute (TPI) 2008 | Accepted 32 articles. Publication of a collection of articles in the book *The Role of Religion in Mental Health* (Khamsehai & Tavabaki 2012) |
| The First Conference on Theoretical Foundations and Psychometrics of Religious Scales | Axis: Theological foundations of religious scales, methodological and psychological foundations, and limitations and barriers to measuring religiosity | Department of Psychology of RIHU February 2004 | Publication of articles in the book *Theoretical Foundations and Psychometrics of Religious Scales* (Salarifar et al., 2011) |
| First International Conference on the Role of Religion in Mental Health | Axes: Religious Role, Religious and Islamic Attitudes and Beliefs in Primary Prevention and Promotion of Mental Health, Position of Islamic Psychology and Community Psychology and National Religious Behavior in Health | (IUMS) & (TPI) 2001 | 130 articles presented in Persian and English. (Secretariat Of Religion Researchers, 2001) |

Additionally, from 2000 to 2020, scientific chairs and meetings in the field of IP have been held by various scientific centers, some of which are mentioned while introducing the aforementioned centers.

### EDUCATION PROGRAMS

IP education programs can be introduced in the framework of formal academic programs and seasonal courses. According to the Higher Education Planning

Office (HEPO) of The Ministry of Science, Research and Technology (MSRT) of the Islamic Republic of Iran (https://prog.msrt.ir), there are 37 fields of study in psychology and 11 fields in counseling at different levels of study in the country's universities and scientific centers. Of these, 8 disciplines (2 bachelor's degrees, 5 master's degrees, and 1 doctoral degree) are related to the field of Islam and psychology (Table 4). Additionally, with the approval of the *Supreme Council of Hawzah,* the field of "Islamic counseling" as one of the professional fields of seminaries has operated since 2013. Table 4 presents information on academic disciplines.

**Table 4: Information on academic disciplines of Islam and Psychology in Iran**

| DISCIPLINE TITLE | COURSE SPECIFICATIONS | TARGETS | YEAR OF APPROVAL |
|---|---|---|---|
| Islamic Sciences and General Psychology | Undergraduate<br>Combining Hawzah University courses in the field of Islam and psychology<br>190units<br>10semesters | Contributing to the effectiveness of Islamic concepts and updating them in the field of psychology | 2003 |
| Islamic Knowledge, and Psychology | Undergraduate<br>Combining Hawzah University courses in the field of Islam and psychology<br>183units<br>10semesters | A simultaneous acquaintance of learners with the basic ideas of Islam and professional topics of psychology<br>Training a psychologist based on the teachings of Islam | 2004 |
| Quran and Science with Psychology oriented | PHD<br>Combining seminary–university courses in the field of Qur'anic sciences and psychology<br>68units (50 educational and 18 for dissertation)<br>10semesters | Training of researchers and experts in the field of Quran and sciences (psychology), expanding the boundaries of knowledge and theorizing in the field of Quran and psychology | 2007 |

| | | | |
|---|---|---|---|
| Positive-oriented Islamic Psychology | M.Sc.<br>The interdisciplinary approach and combining the two perspectives of positive psychology and Islamic teaching<br>32 units (28 educational and 4 for dissertation)<br>4 semesters | Familiarity with the existing views of positive psychology, understanding the views of Islam in positive psychology and using the views of religion in research, educational, and executive activities | 2010 |
| Islam and Social Psychology | M.Sc.<br>The interdisciplinary approach and combining the two perspectives of social psychology and Islamic teaching<br>32 units (28 educational and 4 for dissertation)<br>4semesters | Familiarity with existing views of social psychology, understanding the views of Islam in social psychology, and using the views of religion in research, educational, and executive activities | 2011 |
| Personality Psychology | M.Sc.<br>Combining Hawzah University courses in the field of Islam and personality psychology<br>84units<br>6 semesters | Training a researcher in the field of personality psychology for Islamic missionaries | 2011 |
| Development and Promotion of Religious Culture, by Counseling | M.Sc.<br>Multidisciplinary approach and integration of communication, religious *Tabligh* (*al-Dawah*) and counseling psychology<br>32 units (28 educational and 4 for dissertation)<br>5 semesters | Training capable people to propagate religion and advise and guide students in religious-cultural affairs | 2012 |

| | | | |
|---|---|---|---|
| Islamic counseling | Level 3 seminary (equivalent to master's degree)<br>For students of Hawzah (*Tollab' e Ulom' e Dini*)<br>Combining seminary–university courses in the field of counseling psychology and Islam<br>123units<br>8semesters | Understanding the basics and issues of Islamic counseling based on the teachings of the Qur'an and hadiths.<br>Creating and improving the necessary skills to provide counseling and psychotherapy services to students of religious sciences | 2013 |
| Psychology, with Psychology of Religion-oriented | M.Sc.<br>Interdisciplinary approach: the study of religion from psychology and Islam perspectives<br>32units (28 educational and 4 for dissertation)<br>4 semesters | Recognize and critique the views of psychologists on religious beliefs and behaviors, formulate Islamic views on the explanation of religious beliefs and behaviors, and lay the groundwork for the development of religious psychology based on Islamic teachings | 2016 |
| Islamic Psychology | M.Sc.<br>32units (28 educational and 4 for dissertation)<br>4 semesters<br>* Introducing a Syllabus on Future Prospects | Understanding the Islamic perspective in the field of human psychological issues and topics and developing psychological knowledge with an Islamic orientation | 2020 |

Despite the official courses mentioned by some universities and scientific centers of Iran, the realization of IP has experienced the challenge of title, source, method, and professor. Recently, efforts have been made to design new disciplines, including the field of "Islamic Psychology" at the graduate level, which is further discussed in Future Prospects. However, to cover some of the limitations, some scientific-noncommercial institutions have held quarterly courses in IP, the most important of which are introduced. The *Level 1 IP* training course was held in 2019–2018 by the *IPA*. During this course, 20 postgraduate and doctoral graduates in psychology were trained in one semester. The 7 topics presented were the philosophy of psychology, general topics of IP, the history of indigenous IP, the methodology of IP, developmental psychology from the perspective of Islam, the psychology of personality from the perspective of Islam, and motivation and emotion with an Islamic approach (http://islamicpa.com).

Three courses of the *Seasonal School of IP* were held by the *CCGE* of *Astaan Quds Razavi* in February 2018, and in September and February 2019 with the participation of 60 graduates and doctoral students. The topics presented in these courses were the philosophy of IP, challenges and opportunities of IP, method of psychological understanding of religious texts, evolution of IP in Iran and the world, and treatment protocols and psychological interventions with an Islamic approach.

*Quran and Psychology Workshops* was the title of a two-day course held in July 2019 by *the Quran and Psychology Research Core (QPRC)*, affiliated with the *FPES, University of Tehran.* The course was held online on the sidelines of the First National Conference on the Qur'an and Psychology. The topics of these workshops were anthropology from the perspective of the Qur'an, the system of thinking in the Qur'an, the system of growth in the Qur'an, parenting and Qur'anic teachings, the theory of monotheistic personality in the Qur'an, and the position of IP on the role of biological factors in mental disorders.

The *Seasonal School of Positive Psychology and Religion* was organized online by the *Vice-chancellor for Social and Cultural Affairs* of *Kharazmi University* for 60 undergraduate and graduate students in the summer of 2020. In this intensive training course, the following topics were taught: philosophy of psychology, critical study of the history of psychology, method of critique of scientific texts, familiarity with applied fallacies, and critique of schools of psychology (https://sociocul.khu.ac.ir).

## Scientific institutions working in IP

Scientific institutions working in IP have three forms: educational research centers, scientific associations, and psychological service centers. The main educational research centers in the field of Islam and psychology operate in *Qom*. At least 8 educational or research centers are in this field, which we briefly introduce.

The *Department of Psychology* of the Institute of Behavioral Sciences of *RIHU* is one of the 17 departments of this institute, operating since 1982. The objectives of this group are to extract Islamic principles and perspectives in psychology, theorize about the fundamental issues of psychology and interdisciplinary issues between psychology and religion, realize the humanities localization project based on the principles of religion in psychology, and fulfill the research needs of Iran in psychology with a religious approach. The research works of this department include the authorship of 43 books and a scientific research journal (Table 2). The department has 7 faculty members who are graduates of both Islamic sciences and psychology. To conduct research in the field of psychology with an Islamic perspective, with the permission of the Ministry of Science, the department has organized two psychology training courses for doctoral students, with 10 graduates (http://rihu.ac.ir).

The *Department of Psychology* of *IKERI* is one of the 17 scientific groups of this institute that started its educational activities in 1991 at three levels: bachelor, master, and doctorate. The main goal of the department is to train experts, researchers, and theorists who, by mastering Islamic principles, can critique and study theories in psychology, explain the Islamic view in this field, and fulfill the social, intellectual, and cultural needs of Islamic society. The department has 10 faculty members who specialize in both Islamic sciences and psychology. The department has thus far had 721 graduates at the three levels, of which 136 were masters and doctorates. The department publishes a scientific research quarterly (Table 2) and has published 20 volumes of research books. (http://iki.ac.ir).

The *Islamic Psychology Department* of the *Institute of Ethics and Psychology* of the *RIQH* is one of 15 departments that has been operating since 2011 with four faculty members. A methodical and scientific explanation of psychological teachings based on the Qur'an and Hadith and theorizing in the field of IP is one of the most important goals of this group. A scientific research journal (Table 2) and 24 books are the works of this scientific group (www.riqh.ac.ir(.

Other educational and research centers include *University of Quran and Hadith* (www.qhu.ac.ir), The *AIEE* (www.ueae.ir), and *Hodaa College* (www.hu.jz.ac.ir) for teaching the fields of *Positive-oriented Islamic Psychology*; *AMIU* (www.miu.ac.ir) for teaching two fields of *personality psychology*, and *Quran and Science with Psychology Orientation*; *Imam Khomeini Professional Center* (*IKPC*; www.mtik.ismc.ir) and *Imam Reza Higher Education Institute* (www.iri.dte.ir) to present the field of *Islamic counseling*; *University of Islamic Studies* (www.maaref.ac.ir) to present the field of *Development and Promotion of Religious Culture, by Counseling* (Table 4); and the *Research Institute of Ethics and Spirituality* affiliated with *the Islamic Sciences and Culture Academy* (www.isca.ac.ir) for interdisciplinary research in Islam, psychology, and ethics.

Scientific associations of psychology are other active institutions of psychology in Iran. At least 14 scientific associations of psychology have been registered in Iran, one of which is the *IPA*, established in 2004. The association comprises psychologists who also have higher education at the seminary and currently has 130 *Associate Members* and 300 *Affiliated Members*. The association is governed by a board of directors whose members are elected every two years by the members of the general assembly (the authors of this chapter have both been president [Azarbayejani] or vice president [Rafiei-Honar] of the association). The association has held training courses (e.g., *Level 1 IP*) and applied workshops (e.g., principles of Islamic counseling, *God-oriented* therapy), extended scientific chairs (approximately 40 seats; e.g., personality formation and treatment of disorders based on *religious self-discovery, self-control* based on Islamic sources and building its scale, components of *Islamic Lifestyle* and its pathology, and IP: Reality or illusion?), and offered book review sessions (e.g., book review of religious *Aql* and psychological intelligence; book review of the Principles and Techniques of Psychotherapy and Counseling: an Islamic approach; www.Islamicpa.com).

*The QPRC* affiliated with the *FPES,* University of Tehran, is another department directing doctoral dissertations in the field of Qur'anic-psychological studies and began its informal activities in 2011. The regular meetings are chaired by several psychologists and Quran scholars who discuss research topics in front of psychology students interested in this field.

*Ishraq Network* is another collection of applications that comprises a collection of psychologists and counselors working in the field of Islam and psychology. This network has recently been formed under the auspices of the *National Family Foundation.* One of the goals of this network is to align the psychological activities of concerned psychologists in the field of IP (https://eshraghy.com).

Finally, psychological service centers are notable. Clinics and centers of psychological services in Iran with the permission of the *Psychology and Counseling Organization* (PCO) *of I. R. Iran* (www.pcoiran.ir) are allowed to operate. At least six official centers have provided psychological services with an Islamic approach by obtaining a license: *Mawaa Counseling Center* (affiliated with IKERI, Qom), *Family Counseling Center* (affiliated with RIHU, Qom), *Comprehensive Center for Counseling, Growth and Empowerment* (affiliated with Astaan Quds Razavi, Mashhad), *Sadra Counseling Center, "Life in the Color of God" Counseling Center* in Qom, and *Sobol al-Salam Counseling Center* in Tehran. Additionally, the *Qom Hawzah Counseling Center* is operating informally under the supervision of the IKPC. However, in 2015, the PCO announced the formation of a "specialized commission for the religious psychology approach," to organize Islamic psychological service centers.

## Limitations and Future Prospects

Despite many advances in the field of IP over the past three decades, the realization of the knowledge of *Islamic Psychology* has experienced various limitations. This section discusses the general limitations and future prospects, including limitations in science methodology, the challenge of secular psychology education, the distance between theory and practice in Islamic findings, the type of interaction between cultural psychology and IP, and the lack of communication with Islamic countries to develop IP.

## LIMITATIONS

The first and one of the most important limitations of IP from 2000 to 2020 has been the methodology of this science. As aforementioned, IP must prove both its scientific and Islamic nature, and in this regard, researchers in IP have emphasized the use of all methods, including rational, experimental, narrative, revelation, and intuitive. However, the generality of this claim has not been able to determine the methodological position in this knowledge. First, which methodological paradigm (positivist, interpretive, critical) have researchers based each of the aforementioned methods on (see Iman, 2012), and does the acceptance of all the aforementioned methods mean the simultaneous acceptance of all the methodological paradigms in IP? Second, there is no distinction between data collection methods and data analysis methods. Third, the place of qualitative methods in IP is not well defined (Azarbayejani, 2012a), and the place of analysis of religious text from non-text is not determined. Fourth, the following remains unclear: where and at what stage of the development of IP can each of the aforementioned methods be used? Of course, in response to some of these questions, Islamic thinkers have recently begun to make efforts, which we discuss next.

The second limitation relates to the challenge of teaching secular psychology and the distance from theory to practice in Islamic findings. The field of modern psychology in Iran has been officially offered and taught in academic centers for approximately 80 years (Rafiei-Honar, 2010), and the first official field related to Islam and psychology was established 17 years ago (Table 4). As aforementioned, 16% of all psychology and counseling majors in Iran (48 majors) are related to Islam and psychology and most are offered at non-profit universities, and the remaining 84% is related to mainstream psychology with secular foundations taught at public universities. Thus, the prevailing theories among professors and students in this field are the United States and European theories. By contrast, the topics of most disciplines in the field of Islam and psychology are a simultaneous but separate education of the courses of the two aforementioned fields, rather than leading to the teaching of theories and models of IP. Notably, religious theories in the field of psychology conducted by Muslim scholars have not found their place in the field of formal education or in practical spaces. According to researchers, in these Islamic fields, there are challenges of titles, textbooks, methods, and professors (Amrayi, 2019), and according to the decision of the *HEPO* of *MSRT*, most of the mentioned fields have been applicable for five years, and after that, they must be reviewed. Of course, the approval of new disciplines may compensate for some of these limitations, which we discuss next.

The third challenge concerns the position of cultural psychology and its relationship with IP. Fifty-six years ago, Nasefat (1343/1964), one of the pioneers of psychology in Iran, for the first time in an article entitled *The Future of Psychology in Iran: Imitation or Research* drew the attention of the scientific community to the important issue that current psychology is not general. That is, its findings cannot be generalized from one country to another without regional research. He warned against the mere adaptation and imitation of theories from Europe and the United States and the lack of attention to the indigenous–cultural characteristics of Iranian society in the study of growth and personality and stressed the importance of cultural psychology.

Additionally, Jean Piaget, a famous psychologist, in 1977, in an introduction to the book *PIAGET's Standpoint: Essential Texts, Developmental Stages,* written by two of his Iranian students, Mahmoud Mansour and the late Parirokh Dadsetan (2000), wrote that despite the stability of the *Sequence,* "The average ages of development may vary according to the subjects' intelligence and their cultural environment." Dadsetan supported this finding in experimental studies of Iranian children (1998; quoted by Dadsetan, 2007). However, the study of cultural psychology in Iran has not become an influential trend; and its position has received little attention; additionally, in line with Kuo-Shu Yang on psychology in China (1997; quoted in Shweder, 2000), Probably, it can be said that psychology in Iran has also become the *Americanized Iranian psychology without the "Iranian" spirit.* The more important issue is the relationship between cultural psychology and IP. If the focus of cultural psychology is to demonstrate the differences and distinctions in the psychological development and personality of individuals in each society, will IP be a universal or regional phenomenon? Does Islam have a universal explanation for the human, or does it have a specific explanation based on the Islamic culture of human? Is IP the psychology of the Muslim culture, or is it applicable to all cultures? These questions require further investigation.

Finally, the important challenge of the lack of communication with Islamic countries for the development of IP should be noted. In 2000, the *Encyclopedia of Psychology* of the *American Psychological Association* acknowledged that "there are unofficial reports of ongoing experimental activities in the Iran that use the Muslim belief to educate individuals and treat a variety of individual and social pathologies, but studies published, they are not available" (Moughrabi, 2000). Unfortunately, this issue is observed in the database of works of IP (*Islam and Psychology Research Group: Islamic Association of Social and Educational Professions* [*Germany*]), published in 2019 under Kaplick's supervision: no Persian language works are in this database (Kaplick, 2019). In addition, in IP conferences in Iran, we have rarely observed presentations of Muslim psychologists from other countries. Among this group, the presentations of Haque (2001) and Koenig (2020) are notable (Table 3). Of course, a limited number of Iranian works in the field of IP (Hosseini, 1985) have been translated into Arabic,

English, or French, and few articles by Iranian psychologists (e.g., Fatemi, 2018; Ghobari Bonab & Koohsar, 2011; Khalili, 2008; Khodayarifar et al., 2016) have been published in Latin books and magazines. Notably, thinkers and academic centers in different countries are only somewhat aware of Persian language works in the field of IP and overcoming this low awareness has become one of the biggest challenges in this area.

## FUTURE PROSPECTS

Because of the aforementioned limitations, upcoming events promise significant changes in the field of IP in Iran. In the field of methodology, Islamic thinkers have recently designed models. For example, Hassani (2018), Khosropanah (2018), Bostan (2019), and Pasandideh (2019) have explained the *Ijtihadi Paradigm* model of practical knowledge, the *Hekmi and Ijtihadi* Model of Islamic Social Sciences, the *Ijtihadi-Experimental Model* of Religious Science, and the method of psychological understanding of religious texts. Khosropanah (2016) fit the method for and the paradigm of religious knowledge, provided a combined version of the two paradigms of positivism and interpretivism called "network realism," and explained the "Ijtihadi method" in religious science based on this paradigm.

Recently, with the efforts of several Islamic psychologists, for example, Azarbayejani, Ahmadi, Gharavi, Salarifar, Narooei, et al. (2020), a course on "Islamic Psychology" has been developed at the master's degree level, approved by the MSRT, and is being implemented. The purpose of this course is to introduce the Islamic perspective in the field of human psychology, to develop psychological knowledge with an Islamic orientation, and to apply the results tailored to the needs of society. This new program comprises 32 units, which include a specialized syllabus (16 units) and an elective syllabus (24 units, of which students choose 16 units for education). Table 5 shows the syllabus.

**Table 5 Titles of the specialized and elective syllabus in *Islamic psychology***

| ROW | SPECIALIZED SYLLABUS | NUMBER OF UNITS |
|---|---|---|
| 1 | Fundamentals of Islamic Psychology 1 (Knowledge of Science) | 2 |
| 2 | Fundamentals of Islamic Psychology 2 (Knowledge of Nafs) | 2 |
| 3 | The methodology of understanding the Qur'an and Hadith | 2 |
| 4 | Psychometrics of religious concepts | 2 |
| 5 | Social psychology with an attitude toward Islamic sources | 2 |
| 6 | Mental health in Islam | 2 |
| 7 | Thesis | 4 |

| | ELECTIVE SYLLABUS | |
|---|---|---|
| 1 | Advanced research method | 2 |
| 2 | Advanced inferential statistics | 2 |
| 3 | Developmental psychology from the perspective of Islam | 2 |
| 4 | Anthropology from the perspective of Islam and psychology | 2 |
| 5 | Motivation and Emotion in the Light of Islamic Sources | 2 |
| 6 | Psychopathology in the Light of Islamic Sources | 2 |
| 7 | Theories of psychotherapy in Islamic sources | 2 |
| 8 | Moral Psychology in the Light of Islamic Sources | 2 |
| 9 | Psychology of religion and its critique | 2 |
| 10 | Positive psychology in the Light of Islamic Sources | 2 |
| 11 | Personality psychology in the Light of Islamic Sources | 2 |
| 12 | Religious science | 2 |

In the field of cultural psychology, in 2017, the launch of the journal *Cultural Psychology* by the Department of Behavioral Sciences of the Institute for Research and Development in the Humanities at the Organization for Researching and Composing university textbooks in the Humanities (SAMT) was an attempt to fill this gap in Iran. Perhaps, because Shweder (2000) distinguished between absolute psychology and cultural psychology, one subject is considered the study of *"mind"* and the other subject is called *"mentalities."* It can be said that IP initially sought to study the Nafs (soul); it will then study the *Nafsaniyah* (The manifestation of the characteristics of the *Nafs* in each person) in different societies, thereby becoming integrated psychology.

Finally, to address the challenge of the lack of communication with Islamic countries, the following proposals are presented:

- Active communication between scientific institutions and prominent personalities by holding national and international joint conferences and meetings on IP.
- Increasing the translation of scientific works of IP of Iran into Arabic, English, and other languages .
- Active communication between Iran and other Islamic countries to share experiences and develop IP through joint conferences, international scientific associations, and joint sites.
- Relations between Iran and Islamic countries with Western psychology centers and holding joint conferences.

- Providing applied disciplines of IP to solve global problems such as peace, family, and cyberspace, with a psychological approach.
- Establishment of community-based IP to pay more attention to social issues from a psychological perspective.

Perhaps the activation of the international section of the SAIH in Iran would facilitate the realization of the aforementioned proposals. God willing.

## References

Abbaasi, M. (2017). Pattern of regulation of sexual behavior with Islamic approach [Persian]. Qom: Dar-al hadith Publications.

Abbaasi, M. (2019). *Development of eudaimonic pleasure conceptual model and treatment protocol based on Islamic sources in depressive syndrome.*(Unpublished PhD thesis [Persian]]). Qom: IKERI.

Abdi, H., Janbozorgi, M. Gharavi, S. M. Pasandideh, A., & Rasoulzadeh Tabatabai, S. K. (2015). Introduction of a pattern for adjusting the interest-based on the Islamic *Zohd* (piety) and making comparisons between the pattern and the cognitive-behavioral therapy in reducing the anxiety., *Studies in Islam and Psychology [Persian], 17*, 57–86.

Abdi, H., & Pasandideh, A. (2018). Positive traits: A study and analysis of the narrations of "Makarem al-Akhlaq" [Persian]. Qom: Dar-al hadith Publications.

Abdoli, H. (2019). Consciousness and Unconsciousness: A Comparison of Psychoanalysts' Perspectives and Allamah Tabatabai's Thoughts [Persian]. Qom: IKERI.

Abu Torabi, A. (2007). Critique of normative criteria in psychology in the Light of Islamic Sources [Persian]. Qom: IKERI.

Abu Torabi, A. & Misbah, A. (2019). The necessity of establishing unitary psychology in the framework of the Islamic approach. *Ravanshenasi va Din [Persian] (Psychology and Religion), 45*, 55–72.

Abolhasani Niaraki, F. (2013). Scientific and ethical perfection from Khajeh Nasir's viewpoint. *Research Quarterly in Islamic Ethics [Persian], 22*, 169–192.

Afifi, H. (2019). Quran and human Emotions [Persian]. Qom: Maaref (Religious teachings) Publishing Office.

Ahmadi, A. (1983). *Fitrah: Islamic psychology foundation [Persian]*. Tehran: Amirkabir Publishing House.

Ahmadi, A. (2018). Personality Psychology from an Islamic Perspective [Persian]. Tehran: Amir Kabir Publications.

Ahmadi, M. (2011a). Hajj in the Mirror of Psychology [Persian]. Qom: IKERI.

Ahmadi, M. (2011b). Gender from the Perspective of Religion and Psychology (Papers Abstract of National Conference on Gender from the Perspective of Religion and Psychology) [Persian]. Qom: IKERI.

Ale Ishaaq, M. (1990). *Islam and psychology [Persian]*. Qom: Ale Ishaaq Publisher.

Amrayi, M. (2019). Islamic psychology has no share in a public university: Lack of expertise or academic credibility? *The educational report [Persian]*. Retrieved: https://snn.ir/fa/news/791266

Ansari, H., Janbozorgi, M. Hosseini, S.S., Gharavi, S. M., & Rasoulzadeh Tabatabai, S. K. (2019). Design an Islamic approach of CBT in the treatment of OCD. *Clinical Psychology Studies, 34*, 167–196.

Araafi, A. (2014). The unconscious mind in the Qur'an [Persian]. Qom: Enlightenment Institute.

Aynehchi, A. (2018). Development of conceptual model and intervention package of nearness to god: Based on Allamah Tabatabai"s thoughts, and its feasibility study in reducing anxiety. (Unpublished PhD thesis [Persian-Unpublished]). Qom: IKERI.

Azarbayejani, M. (2003). Religiosity Scale Based on Islam [Persian]. Qom: RIHU.

Azarbayejani, M. (2012a). Shortcomings of psychology in Iran. *Strategy for Culture, 19*, 7–26. A

Azarbayejani, M. (2012b). Measuring moral concepts. *Revelatory Ethics [Persian], 1*, 7–32. b

Azarbayejani, M., &Shojaei, M. S. (2014). *Psychology in Nahj al-Balagha: Concepts and teachings [Persian]*. Qom: Research Institute of Hawzah and University (RIHU).

Azarbayejani, M. & Mousavi Asl, S. M. (2014). Introduction to the Psychology of Religion[Persian]. Qom: RIHU.

Azarbayejani, M. Shirazi, A., Lavasani, S.M., & Habibi, M. (2016). Religious experience in Islamic culture [Persian]. Qom: RIHU.

Azarbayejani, M. (2019). In the path of the school of Islamic psychology. *Fundamental Research Humanities [Persian], 27 and 28*, 23–35.

Azarbayejani, M. Ahmadi, M., Gharavi, S. M., Salarifar, M., Narooei, R., Mahkam, R., Jahangirzadeh, M. R., Janbozorgi, M., Pasandideh, A., Kavyani Arani, M., Rafiei-Honar, H., & Mosavi, H. (2020). General details of the program and the title of the master's degree courses in Islamic psychology. *Committee on Psychology and Religion in the Special Working Group on Psychology of the Council for the Transformation and Promotion of the Humanities of the MSRT of IRI [Persian—Unpublished]*, Unofficial Publication.

Azhir, A., & Elyasi, A. (2019). Symbolical anthropology in Sheikh al-Ishraq"s mystic narratives. *Religious Thought [Persian], 71*, 1–22.

Azizi Abarghuei, M., & Nodehi, D. (2020). Critique of Mental Health, Based on the Teaching of the Quran [Persian]. Tehran: Golden Thought Publications.

Bagheri, K., Eskandari, H., Khosravi, Z., & Akbari, M. (1995). Assumptions of

Islamic psychology. *Methodology of Social Sciences and Humanities [Persian], 5,* 19–30.

Bagheri, A. (2018). *Psychology of Qalb-based or mind-based? [Persian],* available at http://tasrifeandisheh.ir

Bahrami Ehsan, A., Fayyaz, F., & Okhovvat, M. (2016). Semantics of Depression from the Perspective of the Quran [Persian]. Tehran: Tehran University Publications.

Bahrami Ehsan, A., Fayyaz, F., & Okhovvat, M. (2017). Treatment of depression from the perspective of the Quran [Persian]. Tehran: Quran and Ahlul Bayt of Prophethood Publications.

Bashiri, A. (2010). The model of a perfect human being with a psychological approach [Persian]. Qom: IKERI.

Bashiri, A. & Heidari, M. (2017). Personality theories with a view to religious sources [Persian]. Qom: IKERI.

Brett, G. S. (1921). *A history of psychology* (Vol. 2). G. Allen, Limited.

Bostan, H. (2019). Revising Ijtihadi—Experimental model of religious science. *Methodology of Social Sciences and Humanities [Persian], 49,* 29–98.

Dadsetan, P. (2007). *Eighteen psychological studies [Persian].* Tehran: SAMT.

Ejeii, J. (2019). Psychology from the perspective of Islamic scientists [Persian]. Tehran: Islamic Culture Publishing Office.

Fadakar Davarani, F., Borjali, A., Esmaeily, M., & Bagheri, K. (2020). An investigation and analysis of the essence [Quiddity] of Islamic psychology in the so-called studies of Islamic psychology. *Counseling Culture and Psychotherapy [Persian], 41,* 1–26.

Fatemi, S. M. (2018). Integrating Duaa Arafa and other Shiite teachings into psychotherapy. In Al-Karam, C. Y. (Ed.), (pp. 222-234). Islamically integrated psychotherapy (Vol. 3, pp. 222–234). Templeton Foundation Press.

Fayz al-Kaashani, M. M. (1995). *Al-Mahajjat al-bayda'fitahdhib al-ihya (A clear way in refining the book of Al-Ahya) [Arabic].* Qom: Islamic Publications Office.

Fayz al-Kaashani, M. M. (2001). *Al- Haqaaeq Fi Mahaasen al-Akhlaaq [Arabic]* (The truths in the virtues of ethics). Research by H. M. Aqeel, H. M. Qom: Islamic Publications Office.

Gharavi, S. M. (1995). Methodology and conditions of research in psychology, and gaps in the compilation of Islamic psychology. *Knowledge [Persian], 15,* 84–89.

Gharavi, S. M. (1990). *Schools of Psychology and its Critiques [Persian].* Qom: RIHU.

Gharavi, S. M., & Azarbayejani, M. (2012). *A look at Islamic psychology [Persian].* (M. Forghani, A. Sheikh Shojaei, & N. Nouri, (Eds.). pp. 1-304. Qom: RIHU.

Ghobari Bonab, B., & Koohsar, A. A. H. (2011). Reliance on god as a core construct of Islamic psychology. *Procedia—Social and Behavioral Sciences, 30,* 216–220.

Ghobari Bonab, B., & Nosrati, F. (2016). *Mental health model based on Iranian*

*Islamic model [Persian].* Tehran: Center for the Iranian Islamic Model of Progress.

Hassani, H. R. (2018). *An introduction to the Ijtihadi paradigm of practical knowledge [Persian].* Qom: IKERI.

Haqqani, A. (2017). *The Role of Affection in Faith [Persian].* Qom: IKERI.

Haqqani, Z. H. (1999). The difference between Islamic psychology and modern classical psychology. *The School of Islam [Persian],* 3, 39–45.

Haque, A. (2001). Psychology and religion: Two approaches to mental health (summary). *Religion Researcher Newsletter [Persian],* 2. 76-77.

Haque, A. (2004). Psychology from Islamic perspective: Contributions of early Muslim scholars and challenges to contemporary Muslim psychologists. *Journal of Religion and Health,* 43(4), 357–377.

Hosseini, S. A. (1985). *A preliminary study of the principles of Islamic psychology [Persian].* Mashhad: Astaan Quds Razavi.

Hosseini, A. A. (1994). Introductory discussion on the ""Principles"" of psychological knowledge in Islam. *Psychology and Educational Sciences [Persian],* 53, 137–148.

Hosseini Alawi, M. A. (2002). *Alaqah al-Tajrid [Persian],* (vol. 1). (The Connection of Abstraction. Persian explanation of *Tajrid al-Etqad*'s Khajeh Nasir al-Din al-Tusi). Tehran: Association of Cultural Works and Honors.

Hosseinkhani, H. (2018). *Criteria for choosing a spouse from the perspective of Islam and construction of its scale [Persian].* Qom: IKERI.

Iman, M. T. (2012). *Philosophy of research methods in humanities [Persian].* Qom: RIHU.

Jahangirzadeh, M. R. (2017). Couple therapy program based on self-regulation with Islamic approach. (Unpublished PhD thesis [Persian-Unpublished]). Qom: IKERI.

Janbozorgi, M. (2016). *Principles and techniques of Psychotherapy and counseling: an Islamic approach [Persian].* Qom: RIHU.

Janbozorgi, M. (2019). *Spiritually Multidimensional psychotherapy: a God-oriented Approach [Persian].* Qom: RIHU.

Javadi, A. A. (2004). *Tasnim: Interpretation of the Holy Quran (Vol. 2) [Persian].* (A. Eslami, (Ed.). Qom: Isra Publishing Center.

Jodeiri, J. (2018). *Marital satisfaction from the perspective of Islam and construction of its scale [Persian].* Qom: IKERI.

Jodeiri, J., Fat'hi Aashtiani, A., Motaabi, F., & Hassanabadi, H. (2017). Theoretical foundations of lifestyle from the view of the Holy Quran. *Studies in Islam and Psychology [Persian],* 20, 7–36.

Kajbaaf, M. (2006). Psychology of Sexual Behavior [Persian]. Tehran: Ravn (Psyche)Publications.

Kajbaaf, M. (2016). Psychology from the perspective of Islamic scholars: Islamic psychology [Persian]. Tehran: Ravn (Psyche) Publications.

Kalaantari, M. (2018). Generalities and Concepts in Islamic Psychology [Persian]. Tehran: Asrekankash (The age of research) Publications.

Kaplick, P. M. (2019). *A preliminary compilation of texts in Islamic Psychology*. Project IP Literature Database, Islam and Psychology Research Group: Islamic Association of Social and Educational Professions (Germany). Available in: https://www.researchgate.net.

Kaplick, P. M., & Skinner, R. (2017). The evolving Islam and psychology movement. *European Psychologist, 22*(3), 198.

Kavyani Arani, M. (1998a). Preliminary plan for research in Islamic psychology. *Knowledge [Persian], 27*, 89–96.

Kavyani Arani, M. (1998b). The perspective of Islamic psychology as a school., *Studies in Islam and Psychology [Persian], 23*, 69–100.

Kavyani Arani, M. (2013). Islamic lifestyle and its measurement tools [Persian]. Qom: RIHU.

Kavyani Arani M. (2019). Psychology in the Quran [Persian]. Qom: RIHU.

Khajeh Nasir al-Din al-Tusi, M. (2008). *Akhlaq-iNasiri* (Nasirean Ethics) *[Persian]*. (M. Minavi, & A. Heidari, Ed.). Tehran: Kharazmi.

Khalili, S. (2008). *Psychologie, Psychotherapie und Islam – Erste Entstehungsphasen einer Theorie aus islamischer Psychologie* (Psychology, psychotherapy and Islam - first phases of development of a theory from Islamic psychology view). VDM Verlag.

Khalilian Shalamzari, M., Hassanabadi, H. R., & SaqaayeBiria, M. N. (2018). Psychological reading of ""Fear of God"" based on Allamah Tabatabai's thoughts: Presenting a model of appearance. *Ravanshenasi va Din (Psychology and Religion) [Persian], 43*, 38–23.

Khatib, S. M. (2017). Life skills based on Islamic teachings [Persian]. Qom: Dar-al hadith Publications.

Khamsehai, S., & Tavabaki, F. (2012). *The Role of Religion in Mental Health* (Papers Abstract of Second National Conference on the Role of Religion in Mental Health) [Persian]. Mashhad: Astan Quds Razavi Publications.

Khodayarifar, M. (2019). A paradigmatic confrontation between modern psychology and Islamic psychology, *Sadra Islamic Humanities Quarterly [Persian], 28 and 29*, 107–120.

Khosravi, Z., & Bagheri, K. (2006) Towards Islamic psychology: An introduction to crossing theoretical barriers. *Psychological Studies [Persian], No. 4 and 5*, 161–172.

Khodayarifar, M., Azarbayejani, M., and & Shahabi, R. (2021)., *Introduction to the fundamentals of Islamic psychology [English]*. (Working paper).

Khodayarifar, M., Ghobari-Bonab, B., Akbari-Zardkhaneh, S., & Zandi, S. (2016). Positive psychology from an Islamic perspective. *International Journal of Behavioral Sciences, 10*(1), 77–83.

Khodayarifar, M., Faqihi, A. N., Ghobari Bonab, B., Shokohi-Yekta, M., & Rahimi-Nejad, A.(2012). *Theoretical Foundations and Methodology of Religiosity Scales [Persian]*. Tehran: Avaye Noor.

Khosropanah, A. H. (2016). *Social science methodology [Persian]*. Tehran: Research Institute of Iranian Wisdom and Philosophy.

Khosropanah, A. H. (2018). An introduction to the Hekmi and Ijtihadi model of Islamic social sciences. *Fundamental Research Humanities [Persian], 13*, 7–35.

Kiomarthi, M. (2012). Anger Control from the Perspective of Islam [Persian]. Qom: Dar-al hadith Publications.

Koenig, H. (2020). *Religion, Spirituality, and Health: Clinical Research and Practice*. Taken from http://rhc.rihu.ac.ir/fa/news/37225 MacDonald, D. B. (1909). *The religious attitude and life in Islam*: Being the Haskell lectures on comparative religion delivered before the University of Chicago in 1906. University of Chicago Press.

Majlesi, M. B. (1982). *Behaar Al-Anwaar (Seas of Light) [Arabic]*. Beirut: Al-Wafaa Establishment.

Maleki, M. (2017)., Revelation-—Mystical philosophy and approach of Sheikh Ishraq. *Research Encyclopedia [Persian]*. Available: http://pajoohe.ir

Mansour, M., & Dadsetan, P. (2000). *PIAGET"s standpoint: Essential texts, developmental stages*. Tehran: Beast Publishing.

Marashi, S. A. (2008). *Mental health and the Role of religion [Persian]*. Tehran: Scientific and cultural publishing company.

Masoumi Hamedani, H. (2012). *Master of human: Research in the life and science of Khajeh Nasir al-Din Tusi [Persian]*. Tehran: Written Heritage Research Center.

Mirdrikvandi, R. (2010). *Religious Aql and construction of its scale [Persian]*. Qom: IKERI.

Misbah, Y. M. T. (2009). *Ethics in Quran 1 [Persian]*. In (M. H. Eskandari, (Ed.). pp. ??-??. Qom: IKERI.

Mortazavi, S. J. (2020). *Qur'anic Attitude to Psychotherapy, Behavior Therapy and Personality Therapy [Persian]*. Tehran: Dar Al-Irfan.

Motahhari, M. (2010). *Human in the Quran [Persian]*. Tehran: Sadra.

Motahhari, M. (2011). *The perfect human [Persian]*. Tehran: Sadra.

Moughrabi, F. (2000). Islam and psychology. In A. E. Kazdin (Ed.),. *Encyclopedia of psychology*. (Vol. 4, (pp. 366–368). Washington, DC: American Psychological Association. Wadsworth: Cengage Learning.

Mulla Sadra, M. (1981b). *Al-Shawahid al-Rububiyyah fi al- Manahij al-Solukiah* (Evidence of

lordship in behavioral methods) *[Arabic]*. Mashhad: Public Center for Publishing.

Mulla Sadra, M. (1982). *Arshiyyah* (The Wisdom of the Throne) *[Arabic]*. Tehran: Maola

(Majesty) Publications.

Mulla Sadra, M. (1984). *Mafatih al-Gheib* (The keys of the unseen) *[Arabic]*. Tehran: CulturalResearch Institute.

Naraqi, M. A. (1372/1993). *Mi'raj al-sa'ada (Ladder of happiness) [Persian]*. Qom: Hijrat Publishing House.

Narooei, R. (2017a). *Psychology from the perspective of Muslim thinkers [Persian]*. Qom: RIHU.

Narooei, R. (2017b). *The Theory Islamic Self-Discovery for treatment of Obsessive-Compulsive Disorder [Persian]*. Qom: IKERI.

Nasefat, M. (1343/1964). The future of psychology in Iran: Imitation or research. *Iran Issues [Persian], 22*, 418–424.

Nasir al-Din Tusi, M. (2008). *Akhlaq-i Nasiri (Nasirean Ethics) [Persian]*.Tehran: Kharazmi.

Nejati, M. O. (2001). Introduction to Islamic psychology *[Arabic]*. Cairo: Dar El-Shorouk.

Nematipour, Z. (2020). *Counseling and treatment of mourning with an Islamic attitude [Persian]*. Tehran: Parents and Teachers Association.

Nooralizadeh Mianaji, M. (2015). *From God-awareness to self-awareness and its psychological effects [Persian]*. Qom: IKERI.

Nooralizadeh Mianaji, M. (2018). *Sexual health of spouses: Islamic and Psychological Approach [Persian]*. Qom: IKERI.

Noormags (2020). Taken from https://www.noormags.ir

Nozari, M. (2018). *Psychology of the Development of religiosity [Persian]*. Qom: RIHU.

Nouri, N., Asgari, A., & Narooei, R. (2016). The conceptual structure of identity-based on Islamic sources. *Ravanshenasi va Din (Psychology and Religion) [Persian], 36*, 5–24.

Olianasab, S. H. (2012). God-seeking and its role in the attitude towards death [Persian]. Qom: IKERI.

Panaahi, A. (2015). Marriage from the perspective of religion with a psychological approach

[Persian]. Qom: RIHU.

Panaahi, A. (2019). The role of men and women in the family with an Islamic approach [Persian]. Qom: RIHU.

Pasandideh, A. (2013). The Islamic Model of Happiness [Persian]. Qom: Dar-al hadith

Publications.

Pasandideh, A. (2019). *The method of psychological understanding of religious texts [Persian]*. Mashhad: Astaan Quds Razavi.

Pasandideh, A., Kiomarthi, M. (2014). Introduction to Addiction Prevention with an Islamic Approach [Persian]. Qom: Dar-al hadith Publications.

Paya, A. (2007). Critical considerations about the concept of religious knowledge and indigenous knowledge. *Hekmatva Falsafeh (Wisdom and philosophy) [Persian], 11*, 39–76.

Poor Hossein, R. (1996). Grief and sorrow and its treatment from the perspective of Khajeh Nasir al-Din al-Tusi. *Payvand (Connection) [Persian], 206*, 32–35.

Pourebrahim, T., & Rasouli, R. (2019). *Esteem-based psychotherapy [Persian]*. Tehran:

Publications of the sound of light.

Qasemi, S. (2009). *Mental health with an attitude towards Religious Teachings [Persian]*. Qom: IKERI.

Qolizadeh, A. (2010). Anthropology from the point of view of Fayz al-Kaashani. *Kowsar Maaref (Endless Knowledge) [Persian], 13*, 3–34.

Rafiei-Honar, H. (2010). A look at two different translations in Iran and the Islamization of psychology. *Pouya Farhang (Dynamic Culture) [Persian], 16*, 99–102.

Rafiei-Honar, H. (2016). *Psychology of self-control with an Islamic attitude [Persian]*. Qom: IKERI.

Rafiei-Honar, H. (2018). *Self-regulation therapeutic pattern for depression based on Islamic sources: Conceptual modelling, treatment protocol development, feasibility, and reviewing its preliminary results.* (Unpublished PhD thesis [Persian-Unpublished]). Qom: IKERI.

Rafiei-Honar, H. (2019a). Islamic psychology and scientific movement: Looking at the challenges of psychological knowledge in Iran. *Sadra Islamic Humanities [Persian], 28 & and 29*, 92–77.

Rafiei-Honar, H. (2019b). *Introduction to the Psychology of Aspirations with an Islamic Approach [Persian]*. Qom: Dar-al hadith Publications.

Rafiei-Honar, H. (2020a). Islamic psychological currentology in the present age: Meta-analysis study. *Cultural Psychology [Persian], 7*, 176–205.

Rafiei-Honar, H. (2020b). Review of Iranian scales in the field of moral *psychology*. (Research project of the Research Institute of Ethics and Spirituality [Persian]). Qom: The Islamic Sciences and Culture Academy (ISCA).

Rafiei-Honar, H. (2021). *Theoretical foundations of Islamic positive psychology [Persian]*. Qom:

Research Institute of Quran and Hadith (RIQH). (Working paper).

Rafiei-Honar, H., Janbozorgi, M., Pasandideh, A., & Rasoulzadeh Tabatabai, S. K. (2014). A review of self-control, according to Islamic thought. *Ravanshenasi va Din (Psychology and Religion) [Persian], 27*, 5–26.

Rafiei-Honar, H., Janbozorgi, M., Narooei, R., & Hassanabadi, H. (2020). Analysis of the Concepts of ""Added-Nafs"" in the Islamic narrations, and explanation of the psychological construct of self-regulation based on it. *Ulum-I Hadith (Hadith Sciences) [Persian], 95*, 61–29.

Rashaad, A. (2011). Logic of classification of humanities. *Conference on the Transformation of the Humanities [Persian].*, Tehran: University of Tehran., Available: http://Rashaad.ir/

Rezaei Isfahani, M., Kavyani Arani, M., & Aqajani-Kopaie, M. (2017). *Quran and Psychology (Papers Abstract of First International Congress of Quran and*

*Humanities) [Persian]*. Qom: Al-Mustafa International University (AMIU).
Riaazi, H. (1981). *Education Based on Islamic Psychology [Persian]*. Tehran: Ganjineh (Treasure).
Safouraii Parizi, M. (2019). *Family in Islam and Psychology [Persian]*. Qom: Al-Mustafa International University (AMIU).
Sahib al-Zamani, N. (1975). Again God or Man: An Introduction to the Psychology and Sociology of Ideals [Persian], *Negin* (Jewel), *111*, 35-38.
Salarifar, M. (2018). Family in the attitude of Islam and psychology [Persian]. Qom: RIHU.
Salarifar, M. (2019). Couples therapy with Islamic approach [Persian]. Qom: RIHU.
Salarifar, M., Azarbayejani, M., & Rahimi-Nejad, A. (2011). Theoretical Foundations and Psychometrics of Religious Scales [Persian]. Qom: RIHU.
Salarifar, M., Shojaei, M., Mousavi Asl, S. M., & Dolatkhah, M. (2011). Mental health In the Light of Islamic Resources [Persian]. Qom: RIHU.
Salarifar, M., Azarbayejani, M., Tabik, M., Mousavi Asl, S. M., & Kavyani, Arani, M. (2019).
Social Psychology in the Light of Islamic Sources [Persian]. Qom: RIHU.
Salehi, M., Janbozorgi, M., & Rasoulzadeh Tabatabai, S. K. (2016). The effect of Islamic hope therapy on the subjective well-being of people with multiple sclerosis: And its comparison with hope therapy based on Snyder theory. *Ravanshenasi va Din (Psychology and Religion) [Persian]*, *35*, 29-50.
Saeedi, S. Gh. (1950). Human personality in terms of modern psychology and religion [Persian], *Forough Elam* (The light of science), *7 & 8*, 17-23.
Saqaaye Biria, N., Shameli, A. Zarean, M., Rahnama, S.A., AqaaTehrani, M., & Mesbah, A. (2004). Developmental Psychology with a View to Islamic Sources [Persian]. Qom: RIHU.
Secretariat of Religion Researchers. (2001). The Role of Religion in Mental Health (Abstract of Conference Papers). *Religious Studies Newsletter* [Persian], 2, 76-84.
Sedaaqat, M. (2017). Methods of Behavior Change in Religious and Psychological Teachings [Persian]. Qom: Al-Mustafa International University (AMIU).
Sharifinia, M. (2012). Psychotherapy Integration Models with Focused on Mono-theistic integrated therapy [Persian]. Qom: RIHU.
Sharifinia, M. (2017). Self- Awareness with an integrated monotheistic approach [Persian]. Qom: RIHU.
Sharifi, M. A., & Fanaei Eshkevari, M. (2018). The precedence of the soul (nafs) over the body from the point of view of Ibn Sina, Sheikh Ishraq and Sadr al-Muta'allehin. *Philosophical Knowledge [Persian]*, *59*, 5–24.
Shojaei, M. (2009). Introduction to the Psychology of Behavior Regulation in The Light of Islamic Resources [Persian]. Qom: Dar-al hadith Publications.
Shojaei, M. (2013). Psychological Perspectives of Ayatollah Misbah Yazdi [Per-

sian]. Qom: IKERI.

Shojaei, M. (2015). *Islamic psychology (basics, history and territory) [Persian]*. Qom: AMIU.

Shojaei, M. (2018a). Personality from the perspective of traits: Psychological and Islamic theories [Persian]. Qom: RIHU.

Shojaei, M. (2018b). Motivation and Emotion: Psychological and Religious Theories [Persian]. Qom: RIHU.

Shojaei, M. (2019). Psychology in Quran and Hadith [Persian]. Qom: RIHU.

Shojaei, M. & Heidari, M. (2010). Healthy human theories in the Light of Islamic Sources [Persian]. Qom: IKERI.

Shweder, R. A. (2000). The psychology of practice and the practice of the three psychologies. *Asian Journal of Social Psychology, 3*(3), 207–222.

Siasi, A. A. (1938). *Ilm-al-Nafs or psychology in terms of education [Persian]*. Tehran: University of Tehran.

Sohrawardi, S. (1993). *Fi Haqiqat al-'Ishaaq (On the reality of love) [Persian]*. In H. Corbin, N. Habibi, & H. Nasr, (Eds.), Collection of the works of Sheikh Ishraq, (Vol. 3, pp. 267–293), Tehran: Institute for Humanities and Cultural Studies.

Soroush, A. K. (2011). Islam and social sciences: Critique of the religionization of science. In *The collection of religious science articles, views, and considerations* [Persian, Unpublished].

Tabarsi, F. (1992). *Majma'al-Bayan fi-Tafsir al-Qur'an (*Collection of statements in the interpretation of the Qur'an) *[Arabic]*. Tehran: Nasser Khosrow Publications.

Tabatabai, M. H. (1995). *Al-Mizan Fi Tafsir Al-Quran*, (Vol. 1). (M. B. Mousavi Hamedani, Persian Trans.). Qom: Islamic Publications Office.

Tabatabai, M. K. (2011). *The logic of understanding Hadith [Persian]*. Qom: IKERI.

Taeschner, F. (1912). Die Psychologie Qazwînis (The psychology of Qazwini). (Inaugural – dissertation). KÖNIGL. CHRISTIAN-ALBRECHTS-UNIVERSITÄT ZU KIEL.

Taqavi, M. (2020). Islamic Humanities Model: Theoretical Framework and Operational Model [Persian]. Tehran: Publications of Aaftab Toseeh (Sunshine of Development).

Yousefi Najafabadi, K. (2020). *Positive Thinking in Psychology and Islam [Persian]*. Tehran: Concentration of thought Publications.

Zaakeri, A. (2019). *The role of positivist Islamic psychology in purposefulness in life [Persian]*. Tehran: Successful Iranian Thought Publications.

Zekavati Qaragozloo, A. (1999). A look at the critique of Mulla Sadra''s thoughts in the last four centuries. *Research Mirror [Persian], 57*, 21–14.

CHAPTER SEVEN

# Islamic Rooting of Psychology in the Kingdom of Saudi Arabia

SALEH BIN IBRAHIM AL-SANIE

THE ISLAM AND psychology movement in the Kingdom of Saudi Arabia (KSA), is referenced by several terms used by researchers to address the topic, namely Islamic psychology (IP), Islamization of psychology, Islamic guidance for psychology, and Islamic interpretation of behavior. The author considers the term "Islamic rooting of psychology" more appropriate and deals with the topic in eight axes: (1) psychology departments in universities and rooting courses; (2) conferences, seminars, and the topics of Islamic rooting; (3) scientific theses in the master's and doctoral stages; (4) books published; (5) psychological measures that deal with fundamental topics; (6) applications in psychotherapy; (7) non-academic organizations interested in the Islamic rooting of psychology; and (8) the outlook of the Islamic rooting movement.

## Introduction

The Islamic rooting movement for psychology began with the emergence of psychology departments in Saudi universities in the 1960s. The question that may arise is *why* there was an Islamic rooting movement for psychology, and the answer is that rooting was not needed among the previous Muslim scholars when they were the leaders and pioneers of the world. Their writings had stemmed from the sources of their religion, and they did not need to root what they presented, unlike what is happening today. Muslims are no longer the leaders, so there is a need to take the Muslims back to their Islamic origins of knowledge.

In the field of psychology, some of those interested in the Islamic rooting movement for psychology, including Malik Badri, presented the reasons for rooting in an article titled "Muslim Psychologists in the Lizard Hole" (Badri, 1976). He showed that the contemporary Muslim psychologists are experiencing dependency on Western knowledge, and what the students in Muslim countries receive is almost the same as what is offered to the students in Western societies, without considering the historical, social, ideological, and cultural environments and conditions among the societies. The Western society has assumptions of knowledge that differ from the beliefs of Muslims in many aspects of life. Therefore, the Muslim researchers must have a path commensurate with their knowledge based on the Qur'an and Sunnah in studying everything related to human behavior.

There are five terms frequently used among Muslim researchers on the topic of Islamic rooting of psychology, that is, Islamic psychology (IP), Islamization of psychology, Islamic guidance for psychology, Islamic interpretation of behavior, and Islamic rooting for psychology. Many terms have appeared on the role of Islamic perception in the social sciences in terms of its foundations, general assumptions, and contributions it can make to serve the social science disciplines and save them from their contemporary crisis at the level of the curriculum or in applications. Muslim researchers have differed in choosing the term that expresses this role of studying human behavior from Islamic perspectives. We will deal with each of the five terms separately in the following.

## Islamic psychology

This term emerged in the introduction written by Ahmed Fuad Al-Ahwani in 1962 in the book *Psychological Studies* among Muslim scholars and Al-Ghazali, which is a master's thesis by Professor Abdul Karim Al-Othman and under the supervision of Al-Ahwani. Morsi (1991) believes that this term was used by three groups in different ways:

1. IP refers to Islamic religious psychology as proposed by Al-Ahwani in his introduction to Al-Othman's book:
2. As long as we open the way to psychologically studying religious phenomena, it is not surprising to say that there is Islamic psychology, just as there is Buddhist and Christian psychology, due to the different characteristics of each of these religions. (Al-Othman, 1981)
3. However, this proposal did not find acceptance by Muslim scholars because of their belief that Islam differs from other religions and that

it is a comprehensive, complete religion that includes everything in life and cannot be a part of any other term.

4. IP is an alternative to Western psychology and is based on a study of humans as mentioned in the Qur'an and Sunnah and what the Muslim scholars have presented in their efforts to explain the verses and hadiths and deduce from them. The opinion of this group reflects the works of Muhammad Rashad Khalil, who wrote that psychology is one of the broadest sciences of Islam. It occupies a large area in Qur'an and Sunnah and the jurists took great care of it. He also wrote that the concepts of advocacy, guidance, and behavior should be understood from the Qur'an and Sunnah. The opinion of this group is that it is forbidden to present what is in Western psychology, but that does not prevent Muslims from benefiting from it if it does not oppose the general assumptions of Islamic principles.
5. IP is the science that researches human nature, human purpose, goals, and relations with God, people, and the universe. This also includes the relation with the soul, its essence, conditions, and components, protecting and treating it, and examining the relationship of the soul with the body, the soul itself, the heart, and the integration among them, and human behaviors, motives and goals, values, habits, directions, thoughts, and whispers. This is the pursuit of life, one's belief in God, one's psychological and social compatibility to this world, and one's faith in the hereafter. Fuad Abu Hatab is considered one of the pioneers of this group. He presented his views at the symposium Toward an Islamic Psychology in Cairo in 1989.

## Islamization of psychology (Islamization of knowledge)

Ismail Al-Faruqi first introduced the term in the symposium held by the International Institute of Islamic Thought (IIIT) in Islamabad, Pakistan, in January 1982. Islamization means "reformulating knowledge based on Islam's relationship to it, and Islamization is defined as redefining and coordinating information, rethinking the introductions and results obtained from it, re-establishing the conclusions reached, and re-defining the objectives so that it makes these sciences enrich the Islamic perception and serve the cause of Islam" (Al-Faruqi, 1993). This can be applied to the Islamization of psychology, but one may ask, how is it done? Faruqi answered by saying: "To achieve this goal, the Islamic methodological conceptions—by which I mean the unity of truth, the unity of knowledge, the unity of humanity, the unity of life, the teleological nature of creation, the exploitation of the universe to man, and the slavery of man from it—must replace Western perceptions and that based on which the realization of the truth and its organization are determined—as well, Islamic values are necessary—and I mean by them the effect of knowledge in achieving happiness for a person, opening his faculties and reviewing creatures in such a way that they embody divine laws, build culture and civilization, and establish prominent human features in knowledge, wisdom, heroism, virtue, and piety—and inevitably these values can replace Western values and guide educational activity in all fields" (Al-Faruqi, 1993).

The IIIT adopted this term and endeavored to hold seminars and conferences to Islamize the various branches of knowledge, especially those related to the sciences, humanities, and social studies. The institute presented a plan that includes the priorities of the Ummah's work in implementing an Islamic plan of knowledge so that the Islamization process would go through two primary stages:

1. The first stage includes two steps:

   a. Mastering the modern sciences, which means that Muslim scholars must master the modern sciences and present them in a holistic way as they understand the goals of these sciences, the conditions of their origins, developments, and historical growth, while acknowledging the objective criticisms of these sciences from both Western and Islamic worldviews.
   b. Mastering the heritage by enabling the students to know the basic principles of Islam and the knowledge of Qur'an and Sunnah. The students should evaluate the texts of their own specialization, study Islamic heritage, and extract knowledge in the spirit of Islam and not based on myths, deviations, or sophistries that have afflicted the nation's spirit and thought for ages.

2. The second stage includes two steps:

   a. Identifying the fundamental problems, meaning that a Muslim thinker must define the nature of issues and challenges and aspire to confront them from an Islamic perspective. Muslims need to realize that the issues and problems are only a consequence of the Ummah's latent disease, which is the obscurity of Islamic vision, atrophy of the foundations of Islamic thought, and deterioration of its methodologies.
   b. Engaging in creativity and Islamic initiative by taking steps to bridge the gap that influenced the Islamic civilization. The Muslim

scholar must find alternatives and standards that express Islam in its Sharia, morals, culture, spirit, and purposes, and use these in performing all tasks and practices.

## Islamic guidance for psychology

The term *guidance* is common among those interested in this topic. Indeed, the names of some academic courses in Saudi universities have this terminology or close to it. In Imam Muhammad bin Saud Islamic University, before the implementation of the new plan (2006–07), two courses replaced it with the name of rooting, and at King Saud University (KSA), a course offered is called Islamic Guidance for Psychological Studies. Among the first to introduce this term was Fuad Abu Hatab in the Psychology and Islam Symposium held by the Department of Psychology at the College of Education at KSA in 1978. Islamic guidance for psychology refers to finding a scientific point of view for this science in Islamic countries, directing Muslim psychologists in their view of humans, explaining behavior in developing programs in mental health, protecting people from deviation or treating deviations, choosing research topics, interpreting results, preparing articles and books, and teaching psychology in the universities and institutes.

Islamic guidance for psychology is based on the following principles:

1. A psychologist is responsible before God for calling to God's approach to life, which is Islam, and for helping people adhere to it in word and deed, so that they may be happy in this world and win in the hereafter.

2. The adoption by Muslim psychologists of the Islamic direction of psychology makes their scientific destination Islamic. It makes psychology appropriate for Islamic societies and distinct from psychology in non-Islamic societies.

3. Every Muslim community is responsible before God for educating researchers in psychology on the Islamic direction, encouraging them to belong to it and build their scientific glories on its basis to willingly obey it. They are convinced of its superiority over other approaches.

4. Islamic guidance for psychology is the responsibility of Muslim psychologists who are the vanguard of its sciences, trained in its methods, absorbed its theories, laws, objectives, topics, and

philosophies, as they are the people of expertise and know-how who can develop, refine, and improve it.

5. Evaluating the jurisprudence of psychologists in Islamic guidance is the responsibility of specialists in Sharia sciences. They are the specialists and knowledgeable of what matches Sharia and what does not. It is wrong to place the burden of Islamic guidance for psychology or any science on the shoulders of Sharia scholars because the responsibility must fall on all specialists in these sciences.

## Islamic interpretation of behavior

This term is used for a course in several departments of psychology including KSA. The guide of the Psychology Department, KSA describes the purpose of this course as follows: "To clarify the foundations of human behavior in Islam while explaining the Islamic approach to achieving psychological balance for an individual by identifying the determining factors of Islamic behavior."

## Islamic rooting of psychology

Imam Muhammad bin Saud Islamic University adopted the term *Islamic rooting* for social sciences and hence the establishment of the Deanship of Scientific Research in 1983–84. The Deanship prepared a memo at the beginning of 1985 on a plan for the Islamic rooting of social sciences at the university level. There was an internal symposium in 1986 under the chairmanship of H.E. the President of the University Abdullah Al-Turki, during which 17 papers, a memo, and a working paper were presented in eight sessions followed by a final statement of the symposium, which read, "The Islamic rooting for the social sciences is an invitation—or rather—a return to the early Islamic origins, as it is the main source from which the sciences derive their foundations and starting points, so that through the rooting process, what is attached to those sciences are theoretical flaws, and Western ideas are inconsistent with what Islam came, the method, purpose, and a path."

It is important to note that Islamic rooting does not in any way contradict any scientific progress or methodological development if they do not contradict the Islamic curriculum as Islam calls for knowledge and its promotion. The recommendation at the symposium was to establish a permanent committee for Islamic rooting for the social sciences in the Deanship of Scientific Research to achieve the recommendations of the seminar, formed from that year and that continued to achieve the objectives but stopped to evaluate its work by the university administration in 2000, and it did not resume its activities after that. The reason for this long pause is not known, and perhaps it will return to work to pursue the Islamic rooting movement within governmental and professional institutions related to psychology.

The university has 19 goals for Islamic rooting of social sciences, nine of which are as follows:

1. Explain Islamic law and what is in the Qur'an and hadith regarding the principles of behavior, motivation, nature of innateness, Sunnah of the meeting, rules of urbanization, methods of education, and foundations of social relations that regulate the conditions of people and determine the nature of their societies and gatherings.
2. Revive the heritage of pioneering Muslim social thinkers to demonstrate the extent of their scientific originality in theory and methodology in social sciences so that the rooting can have a clear background and confirm a vision of Islam, which is the religion of science and work, belief, and worship, in consideration and application.
3. Correct the Muslim vision of social reality so that his righteous thoughts lead to the clarity of a guiding Islamic vision rooted in conscience and define his thinking and behavior in relationship with God, people, and society.
4. Benefit within the framework of the Islamic rooting process from the curricula of modern and contemporary thinkers in studying the reality of humankind, provided that the curriculum is not based on an atheistic idea or an insulting theory of human dignity projecting his fate, such as the theory of evolution and the origin of species, and that the study of social systems and systems in Islamic society through Islamic approach.
5. If the Islamic curriculum is the method for studying social systems in the light of a critical vision of what Western thought produces in terms of social theories and generalizations, the goal goes beyond the curriculum.
6. Establish the Islamic School of Social Sciences that bases its objectives, curricula, theoretical, and applied methods on the principles and rulings of Islam.

7. Purify the social sciences from perceptions and trends stemming from pagan, Jewish, or Christian origins or subversive doctrines such as communism, existentialism, and pornography, and this is done through a scientific evaluation based on the correct Islamic perception of those sciences.
8. Present pure Islamic thought in the fields of social sciences to others in a manner that the owners of other social, psychological, and educational doctrines know the positive features and characteristics of the Islamic school stemming from the Islamic religion and its ability to find solutions to the problems facing humanity in every age.
9. Prepare the Muslim teacher, researcher, and thinker by building the personalities and forming their ideas according to the Islamic conception of the universe, humanity, and life, so that their abilities to educate young people are good, and they can direct the society in a sound manner consistent with the principles of Islam, its ideals, and cultural values. (The Islamic Origins of the Social Sciences, BT, pp. 17–23)

## Axis I: Rooting courses in psychology departments

Many psychology departments in Saudi universities are newly established. Therefore, the focus will be on the first three departments established in KSA: College of Education at King Saud University (KSU) (1972), College of Education at Umm Al-Qura University (UQU) (1973), and College of Social Sciences at Imam Muhammad bin Saud Islamic University (1978).

The Department of Psychology at KSU is the first psychology department to be established in a Saudi university, and concerning the rooting decisions, the department's first plan included courses in Islamic guidance for psychology and psychological heritage for Muslim scholars. In postgraduate studies, only one course, Community Culture and Psychological Disorders, was offered in counseling psychology.

The Department of Psychology at the College of Education (UQU) started as a scientific unit for Education and Psychology affiliated with the Dean of the College in 1963–64, then in the following year transferred to the Department of Education and Psychology. In 1974–75, the Department of Psychology was separated as an independent department but does not offer a program at the bachelor's level, except for psychological preparation courses for other majors. However, a course on Humanistic Psychology from an Islamic Perspective at the master's level and Islamic Educational Theory at the Ph.D. level is offered.

The Department of Psychology at the Imam Muhammad bin Saud Islamic University started in 1976–77, when a department was established in the College of Arabic Language and Social Sciences under the name of the Department of Behavioral Sciences, and it included three majors: Sociology, Education, and Psychology. In the same year, the department name was changed to the Department of Sociology and Psychology. The bachelor's plan went through several changes, including the decisions of Islamic rooting for psychology. In the first plan, three courses were offered: psychological heritage of Muslim scholars, personality in the Islamic perspective, and Islamic direction of psychology, and in the next plan, the course names were changed to psychological heritage in Islamic civilization, introduction to the Islamic rooting of psychology, and studies in the Islamic rooting of psychology. These courses continued until the year 2020, and starting from the academic year 2020, the three courses were reduced to one course called Islamic Rooting for the Science of Self. There is a course at the master's level called Islamic Guidance for Psychology. In the Path of Deviation and Crime, there is a course, The Islamic Perspective of Deviation and Crime.

## Axis II: Conferences and seminars in academic institutions

The Psychology Department at KSU (formerly Riyadh University) held a symposium in 1978 entitled Psychology and Islam, in which 23 research papers were presented (see Table 1).

**Table 1: Studies of the Symposium on Islam and Psychology**

| NO. | TITLE | AUTHOR |
|---|---|---|
| 1 | The Quran and Psychology | Jamal Madi Abu Al-Azim |
| 2 | Islam and Diseases of the Age | Osama Muhammad Al-Radi |
| 3 | Psychology: Between Science Methodology and the Position of Islam | Zaki Muhammad Ismail |
| 4 | Islamic Guidance for Psychology | Fuad Abd Al-Latif Abu Hatab |
| 5 | The Concept of Personality in Islam | Rashid Hamid |
| 6 | Towards an Islamic Psychology of Motives | Muhyiddin Abdul Shakour |
| 7 | The Fundamentals of Psychology and Islam from a Letter Presented to the President of the Symposium | Al-Rakhawi |
| 8 | The Faith among Muslims: A Proposal and a Framework for a Global Study | Shihab al-Din |

| | | |
|---|---|---|
| 9 | The Process of Normalization among Thinkers of Islam and Modern Psychology | Adel Ezz El-Din Al-Ashoul |
| 10 | Preferred Arab and Greek Doctors to Psychotherapy | Hakim Saad Abdul Razzaq |
| 11 | The Theory of Conditional Action in Al-Ghazali | Fayez Muhammad Ali Al-Hajj |
| 12 | The Full Dimension of the Human Soul according to Muhammad Iqbal | Abdulaziz Abdel Qader |
| 13 | The Psychological and Spiritual Role of Islam in Helping Muslims Who Are Addicted to Alcohol | Malik Babiker Badri |
| 14 | A Study of the Relationship of Religious Value to the Productive Sufficiency of Industrial Workers in a Muslim Society | Mahmoud Al-Sayed Abu Al-Nil |
| 15 | Religiosity and Psychological Compatibility | Abdul Majeed Sayed Ahmed Mansour |
| 16 | The Importance of Moral Development in Psychological Formation | Abdul Hamid Muhammad Al-Hashemi |
| 17 | Islam and Overcoming Problems for Outpatients | John Sullivan |
| 18 | The Impact of Faith on the Psychological Accordance of the Individual | Muhammad Qutb |
| 19 | An Empirical Study: Religiosity and Psychological Compatibility | Maher Al-Hawary |
| 20 | The Relationship between Religiosity and Neuroticism, and the Extravagance in Self-Confidence, Drive for Achievement, and Flexibility among University Students | Mustafa Ahmed Turki |
| 21 | An Islamic System for Mental Health Services: A Practical Model for Planning and Exploitation | Muhy Al-Din Abdel Shakour, Rashid Hamed and Attia Sweilem |
| 22 | The Role of Psychology in Education on Islamic Foundations | Ahmed Essam Al-Safadi, Taher Muhammad Abdul Razzaq |
| 23 | Distinguishing Characteristics of an Islamic Approach to Psychology | Muhammad Hamid Al-Effendi, Ibrahim Muhammad Al-Shafi'i |

According to the author's knowledge, it was the first scientific symposium that gathered specialists and dealt with issues of rooting, but not many of those studies were presented in great depth. Therefore, the effect was that many did not continue and are considered only as a part of the first symposium. The Imam

Muhammad bin Saud Islamic University, represented by the Deanship of Scientific Research, also held an internal symposium in 1987 titled Islamic Rooting for the Social Sciences in Riyadh, in which seventeen working papers were presented (see Table 2).

**Table 2: Working papers**

| | | |
|---|---|---|
| 1 | The Deep Roots of the Human Sciences, a Systematic Framework for Understanding, Correcting, and Rooting | H.E. Dr. Abdullah Al-Turki |
| 2 | Building the Islamic Theory and Rooting for Sociology | Abdullah bin Hussein Al-Khalifa |
| 3 | The Islamic Asset for Social Sciences | Zaki Muhammad Ismail |
| 4 | Rooting Social Sciences | Abdel Rahman Al-Essawi |
| 5 | Islamic Rooting for Social Service | Muhammad Ibrahim Nabhan |
| 6 | The Islamic Formulation of Social Thought | Muhammad Aref |
| 7 | Islamization of Social Sciences | Muhammad Othman Najati |
| 8 | A Project Proposal to Prepare the Islamic Encyclopaedia of Sociology | Nabil Al-Samalouti |
| 9 | My Views and Suggestions on the Plan for Rooting the Social Sciences | Miqdad Yajan |
| 10 | Working Paper on the Islamic Rooting of the Social Sciences | Muhammad Azmi Saleh |
| 11 | The Islamic Rooting of Psychology, towards an Islamic Theory of Personality | Abd al-Rahim Bakhit Abd al-Rahim |
| 12 | Vision in the Islamic Rooting for Psychological and Educational Sciences | Abd al-Rahim Bakhit Abd al-Rahim |
| 13 | The Characteristics that Must Be Met in the One Who Works in the Islamic Rooting for the Social Sciences | Saleh Al-Luhaidan |
| 14 | Islam and Behavioral Sciences | Abdulaziz bin Muhammad Al-Nughaimshi |
| 15 | A Proposed Plan for the Islamization of Psychology | Malik Babiker Badri |
| 16 | Action Plan in the Field of Islamic Rooting for the Social Sciences | Ibrahim Wajih Mahmoud |
| 17 | How to Implement the Decision of the Academic Council at Imam University to Write the Humanities on an Islamic Basis | Jaafar Sheikh Idris |

The author believes that the working papers lacked in-depth research dealing with issues of rooting, but important ideas and projects were proposed to develop the rooting process, and a permanent committee for Islamic rooting for social sciences was established at the Imam University, whose work continued in several programs for a decade, including meetings between specialists in forensic sciences with their counterparts in social sciences, issuance of rooting guides for the sciences of education, sociology, and psychology, and issuance of books that serve rooting. The committee stopped in 1999 to evaluate its previous work and has not yet resumed, and it is hoped that Imam University officials will reactivate their efforts.

The Saudi Society for Educational and Psychological Sciences devoted its fifth annual meeting in 1993 to Islamic rooting for education and psychology. Due to circumstances that prevented the meeting from taking place, several research papers presented for the discussion were published in the society's journal, "The Message of Education and Psychology."

From the mid-1990s, the efforts of the institutions to hold seminars or conferences on rooting issues, according to this author's knowledge, were not successful for ten years (1996–2006), and we do not know the reason. However, the Psychology Department at Imam Muhammad Ibn Saud Islamic University held three symposiums, in which much research related to rooting was presented.

The First Symposium. Symposium of Psychology Departments in Saudi Higher Education Institutions: Reality and Future Prospects, Imam Muhammad bin Saud Islamic University in Riyadh (2009). Among research topics discussed were ways to embrace university psychology courses by Malik Badri, teaching books of Islamic heritage in psychology departments and its importance in establishing it by Abdullah Al-Tariqi, and employing the Islamic rooting of psychology in teaching psychology courses by Abdullah Al-Subaih.

The Second Symposium. Psychology and Protection of Youth in the Age of Globalization, Imam Muhammad bin Saud Islamic University, Riyadh, 2013. Among the research presented were Protecting Youth from AIDS by Malik Badri and Psychology between Globalization and Islamic Rooting by Saleh Al-Sanie.

The Third Symposium. Identity and Challenges of the Age, Imam Muhammad bin Saud Islamic University, Riyadh, 2016. Among research presented were Islamic identity and dangers of globalization by Ibrahim Al-Sabati; the identity of the ego as a sufficient basis for national beliefs, feelings, and practices by Hussein Abdel-Fattah Al-Ghamdi; and the Internet and the system of Islamic values among young people, a socio-analytical study from the viewpoint of the youth of Constantine, Algeria by Shiheb Adel.

It is hoped that psychology departments in Saudi universities will return to adopting seminars and conferences that present the fundamental aspect in addressing psychological problems in our Arab and Islamic societies.

## Axis: III: Master and doctoral theses

Academic theses in the master's and doctoral levels that deal with topics related to the Islamic rooting of psychology are presented below from the year 2000 onwards and derived primarily from the bibliography of the King Fahad National Library.

| NO. | THESIS TITLE | RESEARCHER | DEGREE | DEPARTMENT | UNIVERSITY | YEAR |
|---|---|---|---|---|---|---|
| 1 | Self-Counseling from an Islamic Perspective in Light of the Changes among Students of the College of Education | Mariam Binti Abdul Latif Al Najim | Ph.D. | Psychology | Faisal University, Al Ahsa | 2000 |
| 2 | The Islamic Rooting of Psychology in Light of the Directions of the Noble Qur'an and the Sunnah of the Prophet | Jamila bint Abdullah Hasan Saqa | Ph.D. | Islamic Education | Umm Al-Qura University | 2001 |
| 3 | Islamic Education for a Saudi Security Man and Its Impact on His Security Performance | Ali bin Hamid Al-Hamid | MA | Social Sciences | College of Graduate Studies, Naif Arab University for Security Sciences | 2001 |
| 4 | Altruism and Its Relationship to Some Personality Variables among University Students in Riyadh | Abdulaziz bin Ali Al-Sweileh | Ph.D. | Psychology and Social Sciences | Imam Muhammad bin Saud Islamic University | 2001 |

| 5 | The Value Commitment of a Sample of Delinquent and Non-delinquent Juveniles in Makkah | Ghalib bin Muhammad Ali Al-Mashikhi | MA | Education Psychology | Umm Al-Qura University | 2001 |
|---|---|---|---|---|---|---|
| 6 | Effectiveness of Self-Concept Adjustment Program on Achievement of Late Students in Riyadh: An Empirical Study | Ibrahim bin Hamad Al-Naqathan | Ph.D. | Psychology and Social Sciences | Imam Muhammad bin Saud Islamic University | 2001 |
| 7 | Adherence to the Islamic Religion and Its Relationship to both Death Anxiety and Depression among the Elderly in the Holy Capital and Jeddah | Khalid bin Shukri bin Omar Nujoom | MA | Education Psychology | Umm Al-Qura University | 2001 |
| 8 | The Concept of Anxiety and Depression from the Two Points of View of Imam Ibn al-Qayyim al-Jawziya and Some Modern Western Psychological Trends | Amal bint Muhammad Ali al-Nimri | MA | Education Psychology | Umm Al-Qura University | 2002 |
| 9 | Effectiveness of an Islamic Psychological Program for the Treatment of Anxiety Cases among Adolescents in Secondary Level in Riyadh | Abdulaziz bin Abdullah Al-Ahmad | MA | Psychology and Social Sciences | Imam Muhammad bin Saud Islamic University | 2002 |

| | | | | | | |
|---|---|---|---|---|---|---|
| 10 | Faith and Its Role in Crime Prevention: An Empirical and Empirical Study | Tariq Bin Sulaiman Al-Bahlal | MA | Criminal Justice Postgraduate Studies | Naif Arab University for Security Sciences | 2005 |
| 11 | The Effect of Prayer Worship on Crime Prevention | Yahya Bin Naseer Al-Sarhani | MA | Criminal Justice Postgraduate Studies | Naif Arab University for Security Sciences | 2005 |
| 12 | Religious Commitment, Social Responsibility, and Some Demographic Variables among a Sample of Umm Al-Qura University Students | Ali bin Muhammad Mubarak Al-Shalawi | MA | Education Psychology | Umm Al-Qura University | 2005 |
| 13 | The Relationship of the Level of Religiosity and Social Support to Setback: A Study on the Dependent Relapsed from the Inpatients of the Al-Amal Complex in Riyadh | Muhammad bin Ibrahim bin Abdullah Al-Salim | MA | Psychology and Social Sciences | Imam Muhammad bin Saud University | 2006 |
| 14 | The Role of the Mosque in the Prevention of Deviation: A Field Study on Imams and Visitors of Mosques in East Riyadh | Mutaib Bin Ali Al-Mashouf | MA | Social Sciences Postgraduate Studies | Naif Arab University for Security Sciences | 2007 |

| | | | | | | |
|---|---|---|---|---|---|---|
| 15 | Social Skills from an Islamic Perspective and Their Relationship to Emotional Intelligence, Academic Achievement, Social Status, and Age: A Study on Female Students in Riyadh | Modhi bint Muhammad Abdulaziz | Ph.D. | Psychology | Imam Muhammad bin Saud University | 2008 |
| 16 | Feeling of Happiness and Its Relationship to Achieving Goals and Religious Behavior among a Sample of Students from King Saud University | Safa Alawi Hashem | MA | Psychology | King Saud University | 2008 |
| 17 | A Proposed Application Model to Meet the Demands of the Child's Social Development in Light of Islamic Education | Khalid bin Ahmed Al-Saadi | Ph.D. | Education and Social Sciences | Imam Muhammad bin Saud University | 2009 |
| 18 | Islamic Education Methods in Directing Behavior and Teachers' Familiarity with and Application | Zu'air bin Fahd Al-Subaie | MA | Social Sciences Graduate Studies | Naif Arab University for Security Sciences | 2010 |
| 19 | The Role of the Holy Quran Preservation Program in Rehabilitation of Inmates in Correctional Institutions | Muhammad bin Badi Al-Harbi | MA | Social Sciences | Naif Arab University for Security Sciences | 2010 |

| | | | | | | |
|---|---|---|---|---|---|---|
| 20 | Sources of Happiness for a Sample of Middle School, High School and University Students in Light of Some Demographic and Social Characteristics | Aisha bint Abbas bin Muhammad Saeed Al Mahrouqi | MA | Education Psychology | Umm Al-Qura University | 2011 |
| 21 | How Religiosity Influences Consumption: The Impact of Consumer Religiosity on Perceptions of Psychological and Social Risk | Thamer Ahmad Baazeem | Ph.D. | Business | King Abdelaziz University | 2015 |
| 22 | Islamic Psychology and Its Role in the Call to God: An Analytical Study | Mona Bint Majdi Muhammad Hariri | MA | Dawah and Islamic Culture the Call and Fundamentals of Religion | Umm Al-Qura University | 2016 |
| 23 | The Islamic Rooting for the Patterns of the Human Personality and Their Educational Applications | Nasreen bint Atiya Ibrahim Al-Zahrani | MA | Islamic Comparative Education | Umm Al-Qura University | 2016 |
| 24 | The Effectiveness of a Religious Counseling Program in Alleviating the Symptoms of Obsessive-Compulsive | Bandar bin Ali Ahmad Al Ghamdi | MA | Education Psychology | University of Baha | 2016 |
| 25 | Religious Instructions and their Relationship to the Level of Moral Provisions | Aasia bint Mari Al-Zahrani | MA | Education Psychology | King Saud University | 2016 |

| | | | | | | |
|---|---|---|---|---|---|---|
| 26 | Religion, Psychological Distress, and Discrimination Among Arab American | Najwa Alharbi | Ph.D. | | Birmingham, Alabama, USA | 2019 |

## Axis IV: Books

The books concerned with issues of Islamic rooting for psychology published 2000 onwards are listed below:

| NO. | AUTHOR | BOOK TITLE | PUBLISHER | YEAR |
|---|---|---|---|---|
| 1 | Al-Amiri, Ahmed Al-Baraa | The Art of Thinking: An Islamic View, 2nd Edition | Riyadh: Al-Obeikan Library | 2006 |
| 2 | Busbet, Bahia Bint Abdul Rahman | Dive into the Depths of the Human Soul | Riyadh: Dar Alam al-Kutub | 2005 |
| 3 | Al-Habib, Tariq bin Ali | Obsessive-Compulsive Disorder: Mental Illness or Satanic Conversations? | Riyadh: Clinics of psychiatry behavioral therapy and stress therapy | 2004 |
| 4 | Al-Habib, Tariq bin Ali | Towards a Reassuring and Confident Soul | Riyadh: Clinics of Psychiatry Behavioral Therapy and Stress Therapy | 2005 |
| 5 | Al-Habib, Tariq bin Ali | Religious Education in Saudi Society: A Psychosocial View | Riyadh: Jeraisy Foundation for Distribution | 2006 |
| 6 | Al-Habib, Tariq bin Ali | Psychotherapy and Qur'an Therapy: A Legal Psychiatric Vision, 9th Edition | Riyadh: Arab Psychiatrists Union | 2009 |
| 7 | Al-Harbi, Musa bin Hussein Ali | Psychotherapy by Supplication | Jeddah: Society House | 2006 |
| 8 | Hammam, Fadia Kamel | Children's Behavioral and Educational Problems and How to Face Them from an Islamic and Educational Perspective | Riyadh: Dar Al-Zahra | 2002 |
| 9 | Al-Dossary, Muhammad bin Fahid | Sport of the Souls: An Industry for the Human Soul | Al-Kharj: Al-Humaidhi Press | 2005 |

| | | | | |
|---|---|---|---|---|
| 10 | Al-Rashoud, Khalid bin Saud bin Abdullah | The Fragrance of Paradise in the Characteristics of a Reassuring Soul | Riyadh: Dar Al-Qasim | 2005 |
| 11 | Al-Ruwaili, Abdullah bin Awwad | Treating Depression from the Book and the Sunnah of Khair al-Ahbab | Riyadh: Al-Rashed Library | 2009 |
| 12 | Al-Zahrani, Musfer bin Saeed bin Muhammad | Psychological Guidance and Counseling from the Holy Quran and the Sunnah of the Prophet: Religious / Ethical / Educational / Educational / Psychological / Therapeutic | Makkah Al-Mukarramah: The Meccan Library | 2001 |
| 13 | Al-Sanie, Saleh bin Ibrahim | Religiosity and Mental Health, 1st Edition | Riyadh: Imam Muhammad bin Saud Islamic University; Deanship of Scientific Research | 2000, 2nd ed. 2005 |
| 14 | Al-Sanie, Saleh Bin Ibrahim | Family Disintegration; Reasons and Suggested Solutions | (joint author) Kitab Al-Ummah No. 83, the twenty-first year, Jumada Al-Awwal | 2001 |
| 15 | Al-Sanie, Saleh Bin Ibrahim | Studies in Psychology from an Islamic Perspective,1st Edition | Riyadh: Alam Al-Kutub House | 2002 |
| 16 | Al-Sanie, Saleh bin Ibrahim | Introduction to the Islamic Foundations of Psychology, 1st Edition | Riyadh: Al-Rashed Library AD | 2007, 2nd ed. 2015, 4th ed. 2020 |
| 17 | Al-Sanie, Saleh bin Ibrahim | Studies in Psychology from an Establishing Perspective, 1st Edition | Riyadh: Dar Alam Al-Kutub | 2011 |
| 18 | Al-Sanie, Saleh bin Ibrahim | The Psychology of Terrorism: An Islamic Perspective, 1st Edition | Riyadh: Al-Rashed Library | 2014 |

| | | | | |
|---|---|---|---|---|
| 19 | Al-Anoud Bint Muhammad | Mental Health and Human Relations: Reflections on the Psychosocial Miracles in the Qur'an and Sunnah | Riyadh: (The Author) | 2008 |
| 20 | Al-Otaibi, Nouf Bint Faris | How to Achieve Happiness and Eliminate Psychological Pressure? | Riyadh: Dar Al-Qasim | 2005 |
| 21 | Al-Attas, Abdullah bin Muhammad | The Concept of Moral Behavior from the Two-Point of View of Imam Abu Hamid Al-Ghazali and Some Modern Western Psychological Trends | Makkah Al-Mukarramah: Scientific Research Institute at Umm Al-Qura University | 2014 |
| 22 | Ali, Muhammad Mahmoud Muhammad | Mental Health in the Light of Islam | Riyadh: Dar Al-Zahraa | 2009 |
| 23 | Al-Amiri, Muhammad bin Abdullah | Islam's Stance on Terrorism | Riyadh: Naif Arab University for Security Sciences, Center for Studies and Research | 2004 |
| 24 | Al-Aidan, Abdullah bin Abdulaziz bin Abdullah | Faith and Mental Health | Riyadh: (Author) | 2004 |
| 25 | Al-Aidan, Abdullah bin Abdulaziz bin Abdullah | Your Way to Mental and Organic Health, 7th Edition | Riyadh: Dar Al-Waraqat Al-Alami for Publication and Distribution | 2005 |
| 26 | Ghanem, Muhammad Hasan; Alaa al-Din al-Saeed al-Najjar | The Islamic Interpretation of Human Behavior | Riyadh: Al-Shaqri Library | 2009 |

| | | | | |
|---|---|---|---|---|
| 27 | Kurdi, Fawzia Bint Abdul Latif | The Metaphysical Influences on the Human Soul between Religion and Philosophy, 2nd Edition | Riyadh: Al-Taseel Center for Studies and Research | 2016 |
| 28 | Al-Malik, Saleh bin Abdullah | The Islamization of Social Sciences | Riyadh | 2009 |
| 29 | Al-Mikhlif, Muhammad Mikhlif bin Saleh | Psychological Warfare in Early Islam | Riyadh: Aalim al-Kutub House | 2006 |
| 30 | Al-Matroudi, Abdul-Rahman bin Suleiman | A Look at the Concept of Terrorism and the Position on It in Islam | Riyadh: King Faisal Center for Research and Islamic Studies | 2004 |
| 31 | Al-Najjar, Fahmy Qutb al-Din | Psychological War: Islamic Lights | Riyadh: Dar al-Fadila | 2005 |
| 32 | Al-Nughaimshi, Abdulaziz bin Muhammad Abdullah | Emotions: Diagnosis and Treatment from an Islamic Perspective | Riyadh: Dar Al-Fadila | 2001 |
| 33 | Abdul Rahman bin Suleiman bin Abdulrahman | Shyness: Its Causes and Treatment, a Practical Program | Riyadh: Dar Al-Fadila | 2005 |
| 34 | Niazi, Abdul Majeed Tash | The Islamic Perception of Treating Crises | Riyadh: Al-Rashed Library | 2007 |
| 35 | Yarkandi, HanimBint Hamed | Mental Health in the Islamic Concept and Psychological Studies | Riyadh: Dar Alam Al-Kutub | 2000 |

| | | | | |
|---|---|---|---|---|
| 36 | Yaljin, Miqdad | The Compass of Personality and Characteristics of Individuals and Peoples and the Styles of Strong, Influential and Attractive Personalities | Riyadh: Dar Alam al-Kutub | 2013 |

## Axis V: Psychological measures

We were able to obtain the following psychological measures developed and discussed within the master's and doctoral theses in Saudi universities:

<table>
<tr><th>SCALE</th><th>AUTHOR</th><th>YEAR</th><th>DESCRIPTION</th><th>NO. OF ITEMS</th></tr>
<tr><td rowspan="2">The Scale of Faith in Fatalism</td><td>Tarifa Al-Shuwayer</td><td>1984</td><td>A measure of belief in judgment and destiny</td><td>22</td></tr>
<tr><td colspan="4">The half-segmentation constancy had a coefficient of 0.90. Validity of the arbitrators and the validity of internal consistency obtained good validity coefficients (Al-Shuwayer, 1987)</td></tr>
<tr><td rowspan="2">The Scale of Religious Orientation</td><td>Abdul Hamid Al-Nassar</td><td>1988</td><td>Consists of 94 paragraphs with five responses each</td><td>emotional aspects (35 items); behavioral responses (34 items); cognitive aspects (25 items)</td></tr>
<tr><td colspan="4">The scale has acceptable validity and constancy.</td></tr>
</table>

| | | | | |
|---|---|---|---|---|
| Religiosity Index | Saleh Al-Sanie | 1989 | This measure of religiosity was prepared as part of a doctoral thesis. It consists of sixty phrases for each statement, three options, and for each option, one, two, or three levels, and arranged so that the levels were ascending for some expressions and descending for others to reduce the value of the random answer factor. | The scale phrases covered the following topics:<br>1. The Pillars of Faith: God, the Angels, the Books, the Apostles, the Last Day, Fate is good and bad (6 paragraphs).<br>2. The Pillars of Islam: Prayer (4 paragraphs), Zakat (two paragraphs), fasting (two paragraphs), Hajj and Umrah (two paragraphs).<br>3. From the People of Faith (Obligations, 22 paragraphs).<br>4. From the People of Faith (endings, 22 paragraphs). |
| | The scale has acceptable validity and reliability coefficients and is used in several master's and doctoral dissertations and research inside and outside the KSA (Al-Sanie, 1993). | | | |
| The Level of Religiosity Scale | Sulaiman Al-Qahtani | 1996 | | Consists of 78 items divided into four elements: religious sentiment, belief, worship, and transactions. |
| | There are good reliability coefficients, content validity, the validity of arbitrators, internal consistency, and correlation coefficients (Al-\ Qahtani, 1996). | | | |

<table>
<tr><td rowspan="2">The Scale of Ethical Behavior</td><td>Suleiman Al-Duwairat</td><td>1996</td><td></td><td>Consists of 120 items distributed on three dimensions: basic virtues, higher virtues, and preservation virtues.</td></tr>
<tr><td colspan="4">It obtained good correlation coefficients for the validity of the arbitrators, validity of internal consistency, and good stability coefficients (Al-Duwairat, 1996).</td></tr>
<tr><td rowspan="2">Mental Health Scale</td><td>Suleiman Al-Duwairat</td><td>1996</td><td></td><td>Consists of 60 items distributed on four dimensions: religious, psychological, social, and physical.</td></tr>
<tr><td colspan="4">It has good correlation coefficients for the validity of the arbitrators, validity of internal consistency, and good stability coefficients (Al-Duwairat, 1996).</td></tr>
<tr><td rowspan="2">The Criminals' Psychological Characteristics Scale</td><td>Abdullah Al-Saadawi</td><td>1996</td><td></td><td>Consists of 112 items distributed into nine sub-dimensions.</td></tr>
<tr><td colspan="4">Has good reliability and honesty coefficients (Al-Saadawi, 1996).</td></tr>
<tr><td rowspan="2">The Terrorist Personality Manifestations Scale</td><td>Saleh Al-Sanie</td><td>2014</td><td>Aims at the predictive aspect when applied to the target samples in the community so that the researcher touches the manifestations of individuals of the sample who have such manifestations higher and are closer to falling into terrorist behavior. They are subjected to programs that address their appearances and save them from falling into the clutches of terrorism.</td><td>Based on three sources: (a) Explaining theories of terrorist behavior, (b) Islamic perspective and interpretation of terrorist behavior, and (c) Standards in the field. There are six dimensions of the scale and each dimension has six paragraphs: Intolerance and hyperbole, Alienation, Weak faith, and knowledge, Following desires and the Satan, Aggression, and the failure of educational institutions.</td></tr>
<tr><td colspan="4">Two types of validity (arbitration, structural) and two types of stability (half segmentation and Cronbach) were extracted, and it came out with good and scientifically acceptable rates (Al-Sanie, 2014).</td></tr>
</table>

## Axis VI: Applications in psychotherapy

The author did not find a book or paper on the history of psychotherapy in Islamic perspectives, so we used two ways in this research: (a) master's and doctoral theses that applied Islamic methods in treating psychological conditions and (b) the application of some treatments from an Islamic perspective in psychiatric clinics.

The master's and doctoral theses that apply Islamic methods in treating psychological conditions are many, but we will endeavor to mention what we were able to find.

- Islamic Psychotherapy Program for Shyness: An Empirical Study, Abdulrahman Al-Namlah, Master Thesis, Department of Psychology, Imam University, 1995.
- Exercising an Islamic Program for Individuals with Psychological Anxiety: An Experimental Study Applied to a Sample of Male Attendants at the Psychological Clinics of King Fahd University Hospital in Al-Khobar Governorate, Moza Al-Kaabi, Master Thesis, Department of Education and Psychology, Princess Noura University, 1996.
- Evaluation of the Effectiveness of a Proposed Counseling Program for Adolescents to Quit Smoking, Ahmad Al-Zahrani, Ph.D. Thesis, Department of Psychology, Imam Muhammad bin Saud Islamic University, 1998.
- The Effectiveness of Self-Concept Adjustment Program on Achievement of Late Students in Riyadh: An Empirical Study, Ibrahim Al-Naqathan, Ph.D., Department of Psychology, Imam Muhammad bin Saud Islamic University, 2001.
- The Effectiveness of an Islamic Psychological Program for Treating Anxiety States in Adolescents at the Secondary Stage in Riyadh, Abdulaziz Al-Ahmad, Ph.D., Department of Psychology, Imam Muhammad bin Saud Islamic University, 2002 AD.
- The Effectiveness of a Religious Counseling Program in Alleviating the Symptoms of the Obsessive-Compulsive Disorder among a Sample of First-Grade Secondary Students in the City of Al-Baha, master's thesis, Department of Education and Psychology, Al-Baha University, 2016.

In the application of Islamic perspectives in psychiatric clinics, we found many examples and discuss only one here in brief by Dr. Osama Al Radi, the first Saudi psychiatrist (returned from Egypt in 1962), and the second director of a mental health hospital established in 1967. In an interview with him in the Saudi newspaper *Al-Jazirah* (2000), he said, "Islamic group psychotherapy is distinguished from other group therapies, such as analytical, behavioral, and others in that it takes into account the horizontal level in addition to direct contact between the slave and his Creator, and that its main focus is on Islamic values and principles alongside adopting modern scientific methods that prove their effectiveness in some aspects, while the other treatments mentioned above take into account only the horizontal level and are limited to the relationship between the individual and society only. This psycho-religious group therapy is carried out in the form of a session that takes place in the mosque for a period ranging from an hour to an hour and a half, in which the session is held according to the number of patients at a rate of one session per day and it is preferable that the number of patients in one session does not exceed ten patients, and the session is managed by a specialist in medicine, psychologist, social worker, and religious instructor, and the session begins at the time of the Maghrib prayer until the evening prayer, where everyone performs ablution and the religious instructor explains the characteristics of ablution and that it is worship and repentance to God and joining the worship of God and that it includes physical and spiritual cleanliness and atonement for sins and also urges them to make sure that water is delivered to every part. An aspect of ablution is massaging, which leads to physical and psychological relaxation. This is the first stage of reverence, and in this case the prayer begins behind the religious preacher who they follow in performing the prayer with reverence, who is directed to the Creator with all his senses and with his body together and begins to recite the Holy Quran in a voice that everyone can hear, as well as takbir, praise and supplication until the end of the prayer, then everyone sits in the remembrance circle."

## PSYCHOLOGICAL MATERIAL IN ANCIENT ISLAMIC WRITINGS

The author investigated ancient Islamic psychological material and found approximately 80 references. The author then collected all Islamic psychological terms and classified them into five main categories: faith, religiosity, and worship/personal qualities/human relations/lifestyle and living/proper handling of crises and distress.

The Islamic psychological perspective is characterized by features that use Eastern, Arab, and Islamic methods to understand and treat illness. It is a reminder based on the ways of sages, not philosophers, and this method is classified as raising self-awareness. The speech is directed to the soul and not to the mind. It uses Islamic concepts, such as the eschatological dimension, wisdom, and patience, and focuses on the meaning of events and the extraction of wisdom. The self's goodness and happiness are in the ability to acquire good habits and eliminate the bad ones. It places great value on endurance, discipline, and patience and results in a religious change. The more we expand the cycle of change, the better the long-term results. These are changes in personal characteristics, in the ability to adapt, in relationships, religion, and life in general. The treatment method consists of the patient to know first where the defect lies by evaluating one's psychological characteristics. Then, to know more about the characteristics to be identified and acquired, and lastly, to begin a graduated systematic and practical program to discard the old psychological characteristics and acquire new and improved psychological characteristics.

## Axis VI: Non-academic organizations

As per the author's knowledge, there is only the Islamic Rooting Committee established by the World Assembly of Muslim Youth (WAMY) in 2002.

This committee is responsible for implementing the policies of WAMY to lead and coordinate the efforts made by university professors, graduate students, and young researchers in various disciplines and reform the process of modern sciences, especially the social and human sciences, to be guided by the Quran and Sunnah in a way that helps in the mission of authentic civilized construction of Ummah while making use of what is in this modern science of goodness.

It includes the following:

1. Inviting those working in modern and social sciences to exchange opinions and advice on the theories and methods of these sciences and suggest ways to develop them in the light of the Islamic conception of deity, existence, humanity, and society.
2. Documenting previous efforts on integration between Sharia and social sciences and assessing the situation regarding the potentials to benefit from them.
3. Crystallizing appropriate methodologies to benefit from the Qur'an and Sunnah to formulate the theoretical frameworks that reflect the Sunnah of God in the horizons and the souls and which can benefit from and contribute to building young researchers throughout the Islamic world.
4. Proposing the necessary research programs to serve the cause and coordinate the efforts of researchers interested in participating in those programs, in providing the necessary material and literary support, and in inviting capable people of the nation to provide appropriate support for these activities.

5. Publishing the findings of the results, first-hand, for the benefit of young learners who can continue work.
6. Preparing a reference library and an information base that serves the achievement of the previous objectives.
7. Providing aid and support to young researchers and graduate students to enable them participate effectively in these blessed efforts.

The policies and efforts of this committee would result in (1) supporting scientific research, dissertations, and university books dealing with Islamic rooting for science and its applications in various disciplines; (2) holding seminars and lectures that contribute to the exchange of scientific experiences between researchers and scientists; (3) holding training courses to prepare researchers who can participate in the rooting efforts by facilitating forensic sciences for specialists in social sciences and facilitating social sciences for specialists in forensic sciences; (4) organizing discussion sessions in which scholars interested in the issue examine what has been reached in the previous stages and build on it as a means to other young researchers; (5) striving for non-disabled members of the nation to support the programs adopted by the committee; (6) printing and publishing university books and other writings that contribute to achieving the committee's goals; (7) preparing a website for the committee; and (8) cooperating and coordinating with bodies of common interest in serving the cause of Islamic rooting for science.

## Axis VIII: Outlook and conclusion

Based on the aforementioned, we can conclude the following:

1. Researchers in the field of human sciences in general, including psychology, must make use of the scientific wealth in heritage books on foundations that include:

   A. The content of heritage given its appropriate status so that it is not superior to its ability to become a revelation not subject to criticism, and does not degrade it, so the researcher offers to include it in his contemporary research.

   B. Access to literature, especially the materials of the scholars of the righteous predecessors and that is in more than one book, and not being satisfied with what contemporaries report about them.

C. Consider the spatial and temporal conditions in which the books were written and know the effects of those circumstances on the reader.

D. Make the most of the methods of the predecessors in employing the texts of revelation and inferring from those texts.

E. Link the topics taught to all students in universities in keeping with the heritage scholars have written on those topics.

2. Personnel working in the fields of counseling and mental health should benefit from Islamic propositions in studying mental problems and illnesses and how to prevent and treat them, and not be limited to the proposals from non-Muslims.

For researchers and practitioners alike, it is essential to refer to the Islamic sources, most important of which are (a) The Holy Qur'an and its reliable interpretations, (b) the authentic Sunnah and its commentaries, (c) Islamic heritage, ancient and contemporary, with criticisms, and (d) heritage of non-Muslims with criticisms.

Overall, we observe a decrease in decisions on Islamic rootedness of psychology at departmental levels and hope that this will be restored. The conferences and seminars also stopped due to the pandemic but should continue remotely via the Internet. We also hope scientific theses will focus on Islamic rooting, which is largely the responsibility of thesis supervisors. The publication of books is generally good compared to other axes discussed above, but the hope also is to increase these types of books, especially for use in the universities. Psychological measures based on an Islamic vision have also decreased, and the researcher aspires to increase the interest of young students and scholars to create new measures and publish their work in scientific journals. The application in treatment is perhaps the weakest in Islamic rooting services, and the researcher hopes that this also will be given proper attention. In the area of non-academic organizations, the researcher hopes to increase the number of agencies interested in establishing self-knowledge in all areas as the new Saudi association system opened wide opportunities of existence of associations in each discipline.

*Editor's Note: The chapter was translated from Arabic into English and edited for length and formatting. The references from the list below were removed if not cited in the text.*

## References

Al-Duwairat, S. A. (1996). *Ethical behavior and its relationship to mental health from an Islamic perspective: A relational study on university students in Riyadh*(Unpublished doctoral thesis).Department of Psychology, College of Social Sciences.

Al-Faruqi, I. R. (1993). *The Islamization of knowledge: General principles and action plan* (Abd al-Warith Saeed, Trans.). International Institute for Islamic Thought, Kuwait. Scientific Research House.

*Al-Jazirah* (2000, January 23). G No. 9978.*Al-Jazirah*. https://www.al-jazirah.com/2000/20000123/tr.htm

Al-Othman, A. K. (1981). *Psychological studies for Muslim scholars, Al-Ghazali in particular* (2nd ed., p. 5). Wahba Library.

Al-Qahtani, S. M. (1996). *The relationship between the level of religiosity, job satisfaction, and productivity at work: A study on SABIC employees* (Unpublished doctoral thesis). Department of Psychology, College of Social Sciences, Imam University.

Al-Saadawi, A. S. (1996). Building a scale for the psychological characteristics of the criminal: A prepared and codified study on the Saudi environment (Unpublished master's thesis). College of Social Sciences, Imam Muhammad bin Saud Islamic University.

Al-Sanie, S. B. I. (1993). *Religiosity, the treatment of crime*. Scientific Council, Imam Muhammad bin Saud Islamic University.

Al-Sanie, S. B. I. (2014). *The psychology of terrorism (an Islamic perspective)*. Al-Rashed Library.

Al-Shuwayer, T. B. S. (1987). *Belief in fate and its impact on psychological anxiety*. Dar Al-Bayan Al-Arabi.

Badri, M. (1976). Muslim Psychologists in the Lizard's Hole. Symposium conducted at Fourth

Annual Convention of the Association of Muslim Social Scientists.

Morsi, K. I. (1991). *Lectures in the introduction to Islamic guidance for psychology* (pictorial and unpublished memo).

CHAPTER EIGHT

# The Establishment and Growth of Islamic Psychology in Malaysia

ALIZI ALIAS

THE ESTABLISHMENT AND growth of Islamic psychology (IP) in Malaysia can be divided into three different eras: (1) Early contributions to IP since the 1950s, (2) the establishment of IP in the 1990s, and (3) the growth of IP in the 2000s. In reference to the first era, there are several publications related to IP as championed by numerous individuals. The second era was more institution-based and was marked by the establishment of the Department of Psychology, at the International Islamic University Malaysia (IIUM), and the introduction of the course titled Psychology of Da'wah at Universiti Kebangsaan Malaysia (UKM). This was when many international psychologists, including the world-renowned Malik Badri, were working at IIUM and contributed to the teaching, curriculum development, and publications. The third era saw a larger development of IP, marked by the return of many IIUM-trained Muslim psychologists from their postgraduate studies back to IIUM, and the introduction of new clusters of IP at UKM leading to active IP publications in both institutions. Each era also influenced the development of psychology curriculum in Malaysia and led to an increased awareness of IP among the Malaysian population, led by several non-governmental organizations.

## Introduction

This chapter aims to outline the establishment and growth of Islamic psychology (IP) in Malaysia from the 1950s until the 2020s. It excludes, however, the discipline of Islamic guidance/counseling, Islamic psychiatry, and Islamic social work in its discussion. Due to a large number of resources, the chapter will also exclude conference papers and theses unless they are published later in the form of books, book chapters, and journal articles.

It is generally thought that the establishment of the Department of Psychology at the International Islamic University Malaysia (IIUM) in 1990 was a starting point for the growth of IP in Malaysia (Haque & Masuan, 2002). However, little is known about an important figure from a traditional state of Kelantan, Yusoff Zaky Yacob, who had written and translated books on IP from the 1950s to the 1970s, and the contributions of Universiti Kebangsaan Malaysia (UKM) in IP and the Psychology of Da'wah. This chapter will chronologically outline the development of IP in Malaysia in three different periods: (1) early contributions to IP since the 1950s, (2) the establishment of IP in the 1990s, and (3) the growth of IP in the 2000s.

## The Underappreciated Early Contribution to IP in Malaysia

It was quite a surprise to find out that the first book on IP in Malaysia (or on psychology, for that matter) was published in Malaysia in 1956 and written by an Islamic scholar named Yusoff Zaky Yacob, entitled *Saikologi Remaja* (*Adolescent Psychology*), using the old Malay spelling system, and republished using the new spelling system in 1977 (Yacob, 1977). His book is based on Arabic references written by Riyad Muhammad Askar, Mustafa Fahmi, and Anis Hashim and on English references written by Hilgar, Bernard, Cole, Hollingsworth, Paulson, Odium, and also based on his lecture notes from his studies at the Faculty of Education, American University of Cairo.

Yusoff Zaky Yacob further published a book entitled *1,001 Masalah Jiwa Manusia* (*1001 Psychological Problems Faced by Humans*) (Yacob, 1986, 1989), which are two compilations of articles published in a magazine called *Majalah Dian dan Diges*, under a column called "Teropong Psikologi" (Psychological Telescope). He had also translated Muhammad Qutb's book *Memahami Jiwa Manusia: Menurut Perspektif Islam* (originally *Dirasat fi al-nafs al-insaniyah* or *Studies in Human Psychology*) (Qutb, 1996), which is considered one of the earliest Islamic critiques of Western psychology in the Arab world. Hassan (2018) further listed other Yusoff Zaky Yacob books related to psychology, such as *Prinsip-prinsip Ilmu Masyarakat* (*Principles of Social Studies*) in 1957, *Rahsia Kebahagiaan* (*Secrets of Happiness*) in 1957, *Manusia Yang Sempurna* (*The Perfect Human Being* or *Insan Kamil*) in 1958, *Air Mata Abdi* (*The Tears of the Servant*) in 1958, *Psikologi Kanak-kanak* (*Child Psychology*) in 1960, *Ilmu Jiwa* (*Psychology*) in 1970, *Mencari Kejernihan Jiwa* (*Searching for Psychological Tranquility*) in 1988 and *Psikologi Takut* (*The Psychology of Fear*) in 1976. However, Yusoff Zaky Yacob's writings in psychology are not particularly well known to Muslim psychologists in Malaysia since they are not published by famous publishers and are overshadowed by his other works in the areas of Islamic studies, notably his most famous work, the translation of the monumental exegesis (tafsir) of the Qur'an, *Fi Zilal al-Qur'an* by Syed Qutb, into the Malay language (Hassan, 2018).

At the same time, a more recent pre-IIUM era saw the publication of a book by a Malaysian educational psychologist entitled *Teori-teori Kesihatan Mental: Perbandingan Psikologi Moden dan Pendekatan Pakar-pakar Pendidikan Islam* (*The Theories of Mental Health: A Comparison Between Modern Psychology and Islamic Educationists' Approach*) (Langgulung, 1983) and a book chapter entitled *Research in Psychology: Toward an Ummatic Paradigm* (Langgulung, 1989), then a lecturer at Universiti Kebangsaan Malaysia (UKM), before moving to IIUM in the 1990s. In the first book, Langgulung wrote about the norms, concepts, and theories of Western mental health before comparing them with Islamic approaches whereas in the second book, he explored the possibility of Islamization of psychology and pedagogy in educational context. This era also saw a few publications by Abdul Majid Mackeen, another Malaysian scholar, then a lecturer at Universiti Malaya (UM), before moving to IIUM in the 1990s.He wrote about "Human Personality" in the *Islamic Herald* magazine (Mackeen, 1977) and later wrote another article entitled "Al-Ghazali on Negative Human Behavior and Health" (Mackeen, 1997). It can be said that the early contributions of these Muslim scholars have paved the way the establishment of IP in Malaysia in the 1990s.

## The Establishment of IP in Malaysia from 1990 to 2000

The Department of Psychology at IIUM played an important role in the rapid growth of IP in Malaysia in the early 1990s, with scholars such as Shamsur R. Khan, Zafar A. Ansari, Malik B. Badri, Abbas H. Ali, and Mumtaz F. Jafari, later followed by Mahfooz A. Ansari, Nizar Alani, Mustapha Achoui, Fatma Z. Sai, Sabina M. Watanabe, Babiker Badri (Malik Badri's nephew), Mohamad Abdur Rashid, Amber Haque, and four Malaysian scholars, Wan Rafaei Abdul Rahman, Noraini M. Noor, Rahmattullah Khan, and Ghulam Irshad Hussain. This marked the first phase of IP in terms of curriculum development, journal publications, and seminars.

In the early 1990s, two courses were included in the psychology curriculum: (1) Islam and Psychology, and (2) Early Muslim Scholars' Contributions to Psychology. The main references included Badri (1979) and Ansari (1992), who were both teaching at IIUM at that time, and Al-Najati (1987, 1989, 1993) whose books are written in Arabic and are only beneficial to psychology lecturers and psychology students who are well-versed in Arabic. It was during this time that Malik B. Badri delivered his well-received speech at IIUM, entitled "Use and Abuse of Human Sciences in Muslim Countries", later published in the journal *Intellectual Discourse* (Badri, 1992) and later re-published in Badri (2017). In this presentation at IIUM's Al-Malik Faisal Hall, to a jam-packed audience, he outlined the characteristics of an effective "Islamizer" and several methodologies of Islamization in social sciences and humanities, with examples from the discipline of psychology. Haque and Masuan (2002) summarized some of the developments of IP (with additional points on Islamic mental health, psychiatry, Islamic thought, Malay psychology, and spiritual healings) and roles played by Malaysian Muslim psychologists in Malaysia during this period.

From the 1990s until 2005, all psychology major students were required to minor in the discipline of Islamic Revealed Knowledge and Heritage, where they studied traditional Islamic subjects, such as the Sciences of the Qur'an, the Sciences of Hadith, Islamic *Aqidah*, Islamic Ethics, Biography of the Prophet, Introduction to *Fiqh*, *Fiqh al-Ibadah*, and Sciences of Islamic Jurisprudence. Several unique courses were also made available as requirements for psychology majors, such as Man in the Qur'an and Sunnah, and Tauhid and the Methodology of Science. One unique elective course is the Foundation of Psychology in the Qur'an and Sunnah - taught by a Malaysian scholar, Abdul Majid Mackeen, who was previously mentioned, and had written several articles related to IP. IIUM students in general, and IIUM psychology students in particular, benefited during this era from a great Malaysian Muslim scholar-philosopher, Syed Naquib al-Attas, the then President-Founder of the International Institute of Islamic Thought and Civilization (ISTAC), and who wrote *The Nature of Man and the Psychology of Human Soul* (Al-Attas, 1990), which summarized the psychological theories and ideas by early Muslim scholars. He also wrote *The Meaning and Experience in Islam*, which summarized the theory of happiness in Islam (Al-Attas, 1993). The former book was made a compulsory set text by Malik B. Badri in the Islam and Psychology course in the 1990s, and later by Alizi Alias in the same course in the 2000s.

Also, during this period, several works were published that contributed to the Islamization of psychology from 1990 to 2000by international psychologists while teaching at the Department of Psychology IIUM, such as Jafari (1992) on counseling psychology in Islam, Ali (1995) on personality psychology in Islam, Badri (1996) on counseling and psychotherapy in Islam, Achoui (1998) on human nature in Islam, and Haque (1996, 1997, 1998a, 1998b, 1999) on psychology and religion.

Two major seminars were conducted by the Department of Psychology: (1) National Seminar on Islamization of Psychology, held on 30th November and

1st December 1996, (2) International Seminar on Counseling and Psychotherapy: An Islamic Perspective, held on 15th-17th August 1997, and which saw the birth of the International Association of Muslim Psychologists (IAMP) with Malik Badri elected as its first president. Other office bearers included Fouad Abu-Hatab, Nizar Al-Ani, Noraini M. Noor, Zafar A. Ansari, Abdul Halim Othman, Muhammad Yusuf, and Fatma Zohra Sai. It was during this seminar that Malik Badri presented his well-received paper entitled "Are contributions of early Muslim scholars relevant to modern psychotherapists?" later published in Badri (2017)in a chapter entitled Emotional Blasting Therapy: A Psychotherapeutic Technique Invented by Early Muslim Physician, in which he highlighted early Muslim scholars' ideas of classical conditioning, systematic desensitization, flooding technique, and what he would call 'emotional-blasting therapy'. A different kind of contribution to IP during this time happened at Universiti Kebangsaan Malaysia (UKM), with the introduction from the early 1990s of the course *Psikologi Dakwah* (*Psychology of Da'wah*) for undergraduate students at the Department of Da'wah and Leadership, Faculty of Islamic Studies. Another university which offers a single course on the Psychology of Da'wah is Universiti Islam Sultan Zainal Abidin (Unis ZA). One major contribution to the Psychology of Da'wah was a book written by Zin (1999) on the *Psychology of Da'wah*.

It can be said then, although IIUM established IP in Malaysia, UKM and other individuals and institutions had also contributed towards it during the 1990s. This led to the exponential growth of IP during the following two decades.

## The Growth of IP in Malaysia from 2000 to 2020

When the first few batches of IIUM psychology students graduated around 1995–1997, and when some of them pursued their postgraduate studies and returned as academic staff at IIUM around 1998–2000, the second phase of IP at IIUM was in order. These were psychology graduates who had a minor in Islamic studies. Some of them even have double degree in psychology and Islamic revealed knowledge and heritage (IRKH) such as Shukran Abdul Rahman, Alizi Alias, Mariam Adawiah Dzulkifli, and Nazariah Sharie Janon. Other young scholars who joined the Department of Psychology were Khairol A. Masuan, Md. Azman Shahadan, Mardiana Mohamad, Hariyati Shahrima Abdul Majid, Zaki Samsudin Shariffah Rahah Sheik Dawood, and Saliza Karia Zakaria. This mixed working environment between home-grown scholars and several international scholars coming to IIUM, such as Djilali Bouhmama, Mokhdad Mohamed, Ashiq A. Shah, M.G. Husain, Feryad Hussain, Shamsul Haque, and Syed Sohail Imam, led to an exciting growth of IP in terms of curriculum, publications, and seminars. More young scholars joined IIUM later, such as Jusmawati Fauzaman, Harris Shah Abdul Hamid, Lihanna Borhan, Aminatu Zahriah Mohd Ngamal, Nor Diana Mohd Mahudin, Mimi Iznita Mohd Iqbal, Ruhaya Hussain, Intan Aidura Alias, Junita Nawawi, Azlin Alwi, Jamilah Hanum Abdul Khaiyom, Nur Haidzat Abdul Wahid, Maisarah Mohd Taiband one international young scholar, Nadjet Acknouche.

It was during this time, particularly in 2005 during a major curriculum review, that Islamic perspectives were not only covered in a separate course but throughout the entire curriculum. By 2005, it was mandatory that every undergraduate and postgraduate psychology course included references, course assignments, and final examination questions on psychology in order to include an Islamic perspective. In addition to a first-year course, Islam and Psychology, a new course was introduced called Undergraduate Seminar on Islamic Perspectives of Psychology, and which focused on issues and debates in Islamization of psychology. Alizi Alias taught this new course from 2005 up until 2018 and students were required to read major books by, for example, Badri (1979, 2000a, 2000b), journal articles related to the Islamization of psychology, especially those published in the book edited by Haque and Mohamed (2009). In 2018, another major curriculum review was conducted and it then became mandatory for every psychology course to include Islamic perspectives in course learning outcomes, and to cover Islamic perspectives in every sub-topic in a sub-discipline. To put it into a developmental perspective, the terms used in the IIUM psychology curriculum started with "psychology from Islamic perspectives" in the 1990s, "psychology from Islamic and scientific perspectives" in the 2000s, to "psychology from Islamic-scientific perspectives" in the 2010s. Outside IIUM, during this era, several diplomas in psychology programs in Malaysia had included Islamic perspectives in their curriculum, such as Kolej Dar al-Hikmah, Kolej Jaipetra (now Kolej Uniti Kota Bharu) with its major-minor and double-diploma program, and Akademi Darul Tauhid which offered a full-fledged Diploma in IP program and which included both traditional Islamic courses and psychology courses from an Islamic perspective.

During this time, several works were also published by IIUM scholars that contributed to the Islamization of psychology from 2000 to 2020, such as on Islamic approach to AIDS crisis by Badri (2000a), on Islamic contemplation by Badri (2000b), on psycho-pedagogical approaches to Islamization of Knowledge by Langgulung (2001), on different approaches to Islamization of Psychology by Mokdad (2006), on therapy from the Qur'an and Hadith by Hussain (2011), on an early Muslim scholar named al-Balkhi's contribution to psychology by Badri (2013), on a compilation of Question-and-Answers about psychology (Badri, 2015), and a collection of unpublished or out-of-print papers on IP (Badri, 2017). Amber Haque, in particular, was prolific during his tenure at IIUM, publishing articles related to psychology and religion (Haque, 2000, 2001a, 2001b, 2001c, 2001d, 2002a, 2002b, 2002c, 2004; Haque & Masuan, 2002) including a few papers pre-2000 as mentioned previously. Abdul Latif Abdul Razak, an IIUM Islamic studies graduate, also an ISTAC graduate, together with two psychologists, Mardiana Mohamad and Alizi Alias, had written on iman-restoration therapy (Razak et al., 2011). Some contributions by IIUM psychology graduates included a book entitled *Major Personalities in the Qur'an* by Raba (2001), that highlights the issues of human nature, prophets' personalities, faith and worship-related personalities, socially and ethically-related personalities, and intellectually, emotionally, physical, and professionally-related personalities as mentioned in the Qur'an, and a book entitled *Legal Capacity (Al-Ahliyyah) Between the Shari'ah and Developmental Psychology* by Amafua (2008), another IIUM psychology double-degree graduate, that compared the field of Islamic jurisprudence and developmental psychology, showing a unique integration between psychology and the traditional Islamic disciplines of *fiqh* (Islamic jurisprudence) when most IP writings had been focusing on another traditional Islamic study of *tasawwuf* (Islamic mysticism and ethics).

However, one major milestone in the development of IP during this era was the publication of a book in 2009 edited by Noraini M. Noor, entitled *Psychology from an Islamic Perspective: A Guide for Teaching and Learning,* which helped lecturers to teach the basic psychology courses at IIUM and elsewhere from the perspective of Islam. The four major chapters that set the foundation of the books are the "Islamization of Psychology" (Badri, 2009), "Indigenization of Psychology" (Samsuddin, 2009b), "Integrated Methodology" (Alias & Noor, 2009), and "Human Nature" (Alias, 2009). Subsequent chapters dealt with specific courses in psychology from an Islamic perspective, such as "Personality Psychology" (Samsuddin, 2009a), "Psychology of Learning" (Dzulkifli & Alias, 2009), "Physiological Psychology" (Majid, 2009), "Motivation and Emotion" (Samsuddin & Alias, 2009), "Cognitive Psychology" (Dzulkifli, 2009), "Developmental Psychology" (Iqbal, 2009b), "Social Psychology" (Mahudin, 2009), and "Abnormal Psychology" (Iqbal, 2009a). This book has made it easy for both lecturers and students to teach and study Islamic perspectives in undergraduate psychology core courses. Malik Badri introduced to IIUM a book by Taha (1995) that outlined the history of IP, which was topical-based, rather than scholar-based, as with the book by Al-Najati (1993). A translation project has been started but never completed. Nevertheless, some points from the book have been incorporated in the teaching of psychology at IIUM by Alizi Alias.

Two major seminars were conducted by the Department of Psychology: First seminar is the National Seminar on Psychology for Well-Being and Self-Actualization, held in 2001. This was when Malik Badri presented his keynote speech, entitled "The Islamization of Psychology: Its 'why,' its 'who', and its 'how'", later published in Noor (2009). Second seminar is the 3rd Conference of the International Association of Muslim Psychologists (IAMP) on Islamization and Indigenization of Psychological Knowledge, held in December 2011. This was when Alizi Alias presented his keynote address entitled "Islamization of Psychology, Relevantization of Islamic Studies, and Integration between the Two." The same speech (a revised version) was presented by Alizi Alias as an invited speaker at a workshop at Jakarta in 2015 organized by Universitas al-Muhammadiah, at a conference in Istanbul in 2018 organized by the International Association of Islamic Psychology (IAIP), at a roundtable discussion in London in February 2019, organized by the International Psychology Professional Association (IPPA), and at a seminar in London in December 2018, organized by the Alif Institute. Some points on Islamization, relevantization, and integration in psychology were later published as a main book chapter related to Islamization, relevantization, and integration of psychological research (Alias, 2020) in Dzulkifli and Mahudin (2020) and in another book chapter related to quantitative and qualitative research methods from an Islamic perspective (Alizi, in press) that is expected to be published in 2021. The book edited by Mariam Adawaiah Dzulkifli and Nor Diana Mohd Mahudin, *Contextualizing Islam in Psychological Research: Theoretical Foundation, Current Initiatives and Way Forward,* is itself the latest unique contribution from the Department of Psychology, IIUM, with chapters reporting empirical research that use Islamization, relevantization, and integration as a guide in formulating research, reviewing research, conducting research, and interpreting research. These three terms, coined by the former rector of IIUM,M. Kamal Hasan, are formalized in a small booklet published by the IIUM Centre for Islamization (CENTRIS), entitled *IIUM Policies and Guidelines in Islamization,* in which he outlined eight policy statements, 18 connotations of Islamization for academic affairs, four connotations of Islamization for non-academic affairs, and three categories of Islamization of human knowledge efforts at IIUM (International Islamic University Malaysia, 2013).

An exciting development outside IIUM during this time was the introduction of a single course on IP at Universiti Teknologi Malaysia (UTM) for undergraduate psychology students (initiated by an educationist Zulifli Khair in 2008, and currently taught by Alizi Alias in 2020 as a part-time lecturer), at Kolej Universiti Islam Selangor (KUIS) for diploma students since 2009, plus at other colleges, such as Kolej Universiti Islam Melaka (KUIM), and Kolej Universiti Islam Pahang Sultan Ahmad Shah (KUIPSAS). Elsewhere, in the Faculty of Islamic Studies, Universiti Kebangsaan Malaysia (UKM), particularly in the Department of Da'wah and Leadership, at a research institute called Institute

Hadhari, and at a general studies center called Pusat Citra Universiti UKM, interest in IP is growing. Among its main proponents are Fariza M. Sham with several publications related to IP, psychology of da'wah and adolescent psychology (Sham, 2010, 2015, 2016; Sham & Nazim, 2015; Sham & Stapa, 2011). UKM has also made a major contribution to IP with the publication of the book entitled *Psikologi Islam: Falsafah, Teori dan Aplikasi* (*Islamic Psychology: Philosophy, Theory and Applications*) edited by Ismail et al. (2016). This book starts with a discussion about epistemology, philosophy, and paradigms, before discussing specific topics such as intelligence, personality, emotion, plus some measurement issues related to integrity, cognition, and concludes with a summary of early Muslim scholars' contributions to psychology. Another book which comes from UKM psychologists is *Islam & Psikologi Dari Perspektif Kemanusiaan* (*Islam and Psychology from the Perspective of Humanity*) edited by Ismail et al. (2019), of which the second and third editors are IIUM psychology graduates. The book starts by discussing Islam and psychology, followed by specific discussions on behaviors, presumption, love, personality, women and family, prosocial behavior, and morality. Universiti Sains Islam Malaysia (USIM) also published a book written by two psychologists, Sipon and Hussin (2010), entitled *Teori Kaunseling dan Psikoterapi*, with two chapters dedicated to the Islamic perspective on psychotherapy, of which the second author is an IIUM psychology graduate. Recently, at the University of Malaya (UM), Zin (2020) edited a book entitled *Psikologi Dalam Dakwah* (*The Psychology in Da'wah*). This book applies the psychological principles of attention, motivation, emotion, reinforcement, personality, and social psychology to the da'wah (Islamic call) including special segments on society, such as children, adolescents, senior citizens, the disabled, and prisoners.

Therefore, it can be said that, although most of the growth of IP in Malaysia has been centered at IIUM, other universities and colleges have also contributed towards its growth during the two decades from 2000 to 2020. By the end this decade, IP psychology was recognized even outside academia. The shocking and massive changes during the Covid-19 pandemic has made the population more interested in what IP has to say about stress, emotional regulation, and mental illness. In the field, several psychospiritual-oriented, non-governmental organizations were set up by psychologists together with other helping professionals (psychiatrists and counsellors), such as *Pertubuhan Terapi Psikospiritual Malaysia* (Malaysian Psychospiritual Therapy Association) led Mohamed Hatta Shaharom, a renowned Malaysian psychiatrist in Malaysia, *Pertubuhan Kesejahteraan Psikospiritual Malaysia*(Malaysian Psychospiritual Wellbeing Association) led by Kamaliah Noordin, an educational psychologist, the Psychospiritual Institute led by Azlina Roszy Mohamad Ghaffar, a clinical psychologist, and *Psikospiritual IKRAM* (P.S.I) led by Alizi Alias, an organizational psychologist.

It should be noted, that although there are several other NGOs that use the term *psikospritual* (psychospiritual) it mainly refers to either *'ilm al-tasawwuf* (Islamic mysticism) or Islamic healings using *ruqyah* (Qur'anic-based chanting) which is not the focus of this chapter.

## The Future of IP in Malaysia beyond 2020

Although it can be said that there are more publications and programs related to Islamic counseling in Malaysia compared to IP, Malaysia has made significant contributions to the establishment and growth of IP in the South-East Asia region. Most of the contributions, however, have focused on the macro aspects of psychology, such as human nature, or the micro aspects of psychology, such as psychotherapy.

The several pre-1990s publications made a small but significant impact on IP in Malaysia. While the contributions made by Abdul M. Mackeen, Hasan Langgulung, and S. M. N. al-Attas, are well known to students, perhaps due to their later employment at IIUM and ISTAC, the contributions of Yusoff Zaky Yacob are not as familiar. Although not concerned with IP, Al-Attas (1978) in his book, *Islam and Secularism*, provided a balanced view for students about the Islamization of psychology together with the ideas of Al-Faruqi (1992) in his later book, *Islamization of Knowledge*. This was further facilitated by the review of different approaches to IP by Mokdad (2006) and different approaches to *Islamization of Knowledge* by M. K. Hasan in International Islamic University Malaysia (2013). The major-minor curriculum in Islamic studies and opportunities to do double-diploma and double degree has also contributed to the growth of IP in Malaysia.

This may provide a harmonious approach to IP that is possibly unique to Malaysia. It may open doors to offer unique courses on the Islamization of Knowledge in general, and IP in particular at postgraduate level at institutions outside IIUM. It may also provide an opportunity to go beyond disagreements about Islamization approaches and focus on providing every possible Islamic perspective in various sub-topics in psychology at micro level, rather than just on macro level issues, such as human nature and grand psychological theories, for example, psychoanalysis, behaviorism, humanistic perspectives, cognitive perspectives, and biological perspectives. The topical-based books from IIUM (Dzulkifli & Mahudin, 2020) and UKM (Ismail et al, 2016) may pave the way to more student-friendly IP textbooks in the future, where Islamic perspectives (including early Muslim contributions to psychology) can be embedded in every sub-topic in various sub-disciplines in psychology, and not be perceived as being purely focused on human nature or Islamic psychotherapy.

Much has been discussed about the concept of the soul in psychology and the importance of biopsychosocial-spiritual approaches as early as Badri's seminal book, *The Dilemma of Muslim Psychologists*, in 1979 and he even illustrates the role of various types of Muslim psychologists in IP. Alias (2020) and Alias (in press) had suggested a general model that considers the concept of the soul in relation to biological, psychological, and social factors and how to go about Islamizing psychology in the most sub-disciplines of psychology. It would be a great contribution if Malaysian Muslim psychologists could focus on describing the potential of 'soul' as the basis for each sub-discipline in psychology, and perhaps to develop testable models, especially for non-clinical psychology, so that students and teachers alike can see the significance of IP in various psychological issues and settings. One of the barriers to the Islamization of psychology, as mentioned by Badri (1992, 2009, 2017), is a lack of confidence. To overcome this barrier, in addition to student-friendly textbooks, a crash course on how to teach IP would be good for boosting confidence in the teaching of IP, considering there are now many colleges and universities outside IIUM that offer courses in IP. Also, the translation of IP books from Arabic, Malaysian, Indonesian, Urdu, and Turkish languages (to name a few) into the English language may also further facilitate the teaching and learning of IP in various colleges and universities. All these may also attract more psychology instructors to become involved in IP teaching and research in Malaysia, and perhaps all over the world.

In terms of research, as early as 1979, Badri in his book, *The Dilemma of Muslim Psychologists*, emphasized the importance of cross-cultural validity in IP and the role of various types of Muslim psychologists as researchers and as applied psychologists. Malaysian Muslim psychologists can play an important role in developing theories and interventions which consider local Muslim cultures (including different Muslim Malay, Muslim Chinese, and Muslim Indian cultures) and also in developing psychological tests and questionnaires that consider spiritual aspects. Books on IP edited by Noor (2009), Ismail et al. (2016, 2019), and Dzulkifli and Mahudin (2020), had all started the ball rolling on this.

The encouraging development of the Psychology of Da'wah may also complement the flourishing of IP. Since da'wah is an applied discipline, it may facilitate the effort of the Islamization of psychology applied in organizational, educational, health, legal, sport, community, and political settings. Most psychology of da'wah courses are offered to non-psychology students. This provides an opportunity to introduce IP to non-psychology students and to the population in a language easily understood by them. The work of many NGOs in their promotion of IP in various talks, forums, and webinars, especially during the Covid-19 pandemic, has provided an exciting potential for IP to be introduced to, and appreciated by, the masses. It can be said that IP in Malaysia has now expanded its influence to non-academic audiences and the community.

## Conclusion

The history of IP in Malaysia started as early as the pre-independence era and without significant impact on the academic world. Until the end of the 1980s, IP was championed by individuals. Starting in the 1990s, IP has become more recognized since the involvement of academic institutions, such as IIUM and UKM, and has seen the involvement of international scholars in Malaysian research and teachings in IP. With the dawn of the new millennium, a new generation of Malaysian psychologists have become actively involved in developing and promoting IP in terms of teaching, curriculum development, publications, and community engagement. It can be said that IP in Malaysia started modestly in the 1950s, established in the 1990s, grew rapidly in the 2000s, and will continue to expand to the masses beyond the 2020s. The future of IP in Malaysia is bright.

## Note:

This writing is submitted to the editor on 8 February 2021, when Prof. Dr. Malik Badri passed away in Malaysia. The author really feels that Muslim psychologists in Malaysia are expected to continue his legacy so that IP will further flourish in Malaysia and the whole world.

## References

Achoui, M. (1998). Human nature from a comparative psychological perspective. *American Journal of Islamic Social Sciences, 15*, 71-95.

Al-Attas, S. M. N. (1978). *Islam and secularism.* Angkatan Belia Islam Malaysia.

Al-Attas, S. M. N. (1990). *The nature of man and the psychology of the human soul.* Institute of Islamic Thought and Civilization.

Al-Attas, S. M. N. (1993). *Islam and Secularism.* Institute of Islamic Thought and Civilization.

Al-Faruqi, I. R. (1992). *Islamization of knowledge: General principles and work plan.* International Institute of Islamic Thought (IIIT).

Alias, A. (2009). Human nature. In N. M. Noor (Ed.), *Psychology from an Islamic perspective: A guide to teaching and learning* (pp. 79–118). IIUM Press.

Alias, A. (2011, December 6–8). *Islamization of psychology, relevantization of Islamic studies and integration between the two: An experience in teaching Islam and psychology course.* Keynote address delivered at the 3rd Conference of the

International Association of Muslim Psychologists on Islamization and Indigenization of Psychological. International Association of Muslim Psychologists (IAOMPSY) and International Islamic University Malaysia (IIUM), International Islamic University Malaysia, Kuala Lumpur, Malaysia.

Alias, A. (2020). Islamisation, releventisation, and integration: Implications for research in psychology. In M. A. Dzulkifli, & N. D. M. Mahudin. (Eds), *Contextualizing Islam in psychological research: Theoretical foundation, current initiatives, and way forward* (pp .6-23). IIUM Press.

Alias, A. (in press). Islamic-scientific social research: Philosophy, methods, issues and a proposed model. In Ariffin, A. (Ed.), *Enriching the Islamic tradition in research inquiry: Some practical guidelines in using qualitative data collection techniques* (pp. 1-16). International Institute of Islamic Thought (IIIT).

Alias, A., & Noor, N. M. (2009). An integrated methodology for the social sciences. In N. M. Noor, (Ed.), *Psychology from an Islamic perspective: A guide to teaching and learning* (pp. 61–78). IIUM Press.

Al-Najati, M. U. (1987). *Al-Qur'an wa `ilm al-nafs*. Dar al-Shuruq.

Al-Najati, M. U. (1989). *Al-Hadith al-nabawiyywa `ilm al-nafs*. Dar al-Shuruq.

Al-Najati, M. U. (1993). *Al-dirasat al-nafsaniyyah `inda `ulama' al*-muslimin. Dar al-Shuruq.

Ali, A. H. (1995). The nature of human disposition: Al-Ghazali's contribution to an Islamic concept of personality, *Intellectual Discourse, 3*, 51-64.

Amafua, M. K. (2008). *Legal capacity (al-ahliyyah) between the shari`ah and developmental psychology.* IIUM Press.

Ansari, Z. A. (Ed). (1992). *Qur'anic Concepts of Human Psyche*. International Institute of Islamic Thought.

Badri, M. (1979). *The dilemma of Muslim psychologists.* MWH London Publishers.

Badri, M. (1992). Use and abuse of social sciences and the humanities in Muslim countries, *Intellectual Discourse, 1*, 1–22.

Badri, M. (1996). Counselling and psychotherapy from an Islamic perspective. *Al-Shajarah: Journal of ISTAC, 1*, 25–28.

Badri, M. (2000a). *Contemplation: An Islamic psychospiritual study*. Medina Books

Badri, M. (2000b). *The AIDS crisis: A natural product of modernity's sexual revolution.* ISTAC.

Badri, M. (2009). The Islamization of psychology: Its "why," its "what," its "how," and its "who". In N. M. Noor, (Ed.), *Psychology from an Islamic perspective: A guide to teaching and learning* (pp. 13–42). IIUM Press.

Badri, M. (2013). *Abu Zayd al-Balkhi's sustenance of the soul: The cognitive behaviour therapy of a ninth century physician.* The International Institute of Islamic Thought (IIIT).

Badri, M. (2015). *Cultural and Islamic adaptation of psychology: A book of collected articles.* Human Behaviour Academy Ltd.

Badri, M. (2017). *Cultural and Islamic adaptation of psychology: A book of collected articles.* Human Behaviour Academy Ltd.

Dzulkifli, M. A. (2009). Cognitive psychology. In N. M. Noor, (Ed.), *Psychology from an Islamic perspective: A guide to teaching and learning* (pp. 171–182). IIUM Press.

Dzulkifli, M. A., & Alias, A. (2009). Psychology of learning. In N. M. Noor, (Ed.), *Psychology from an Islamic perspective: A guide to teaching and learning* (pp. 127–136). IIUM Press.

Dzulkifli, M. A., & Mahudin, N. D. M. (Eds). (2020). *Contextualizing Islam in psychological research: Theoretical foundation, current initiatives, and way forward.* IIUM Press.

Haque, A. (1996). Cognitive restructuring of Muslim psychologists toward developing a firm faith: A prerequisite of Islamization of psychology. *Islamic Thought and Scientific Creativity, 7*, 102–108.

Haque, A. (1997). National seminar on Islamization of psychology: Seminar report. *Intellectual Discourse, 5*, 88–92.

Haque, A. (1998a). Psychology and religion: Their relationship and integration from Islamic perspective. *The American Journal of Islamic Social Sciences, 15*, 97–116.

Haque, A. (1998b). International seminar on counseling and psychotherapy: Conference eport. *American Journal of Islamic Social Sciences, 15*, 153–157.

Haque, A. (1999). Review of human nature in Islam by Yasien Mohamad. *Intellectual Discourse, 7*, 100–103.

Haque, A. (2000). Psychology and religion: Two approaches to mental health. *Intellectual Discourse, 8*, 85–98.

Haque, A. (2001a). Interface of psychology and religion: Trends and developments. *Counseling Psychology Quarterly, 14*, 1–13.

Haque, A. (2001b). Psychology and religion: Indicators of integration, *North American Journal of Psychology, 3*, 61–76.

Haque, A. (2001c). Report on the First International Congress on Religion and Mental Health, Tehran, Iran held from 16 to 19 April 2001. *American Journal of Islamic Social Sciences,18*, 133–136.

Haque, A. (2001d). Review of *The Psychology of Religion: A Short Introduction* by Kate Lowenthal, pp. 182. Oxford: Oneworld Publications. *American Journal of Islamic SocialSciences,18*, 100–102.

Haque, A. (2002a). Psychology of religion: Analyzing religious development, orientation, and negative social behaviors. *Indian Social Science Review, 4*, 25.

Haque, A. (2002b). *Proposed syllabus for Islamic psychology.* https://www.academia.edu/4361984/Proposed_Syllabus_for_Islamic_ Psychology International Islamic University Malaysia. (2013). *IIUM policies and guidelines on Islamisation.* Centre for Islamisation (CENTRIS). https://www.iium.edu.my/centre/centris/iium-policies-and-guidelines-on-islamisation

Haque, A. (2002c). Review on contemplation: A psychospiritual study by Malik B. Badri.
*American Journal of Islamic Social Sciences, 19*, 128–131.

Haque, A. (2004). Psychology from an Islamic perspective: Contributions of early Muslim scholars to psychology and the challenges to contemporary Muslim psychologists. *Journal of Religion and Health,43*, 367–387.

Haque, A., & Masuan, K (2002). Religious psychology in Malaysia. *International Journal for the Psychology of Religion, 12*, 277–289.

Haque, A., & Mohamed, Y. (Eds.) (2009). *Psychology of personality from Islamic perspective.* Cengage Learning Asia.

Hassan, Z. (2018). Kerelevanan karya Yusoff Zaky Yacob dari perspektif Pendidikan psikologi Islam dalam melahirkan mahasiswa pengajian pendidikan Islam (The relevance of Yusoff Zaky Yacob's literature from the perspective of Islamic educational psychology in producing Islamic education graduates). Unpublished doctoral thesis. Universiti Teknologi Malaysia.

Hussain, F. A. (2011). *Therapy from the Qur'an and Ahadith.* Pustaka Darussalam Sdn Bhd.

Iqbal, M. I. M. (2009a). Abnormal psychology. In N. M. Noor (Ed.), *Psychology from*
*an Islamic perspective: A guide to teaching and learning* (pp. 217–236). IIUM Press.

Iqbal, M. I. M. (2009b). Developmental psychology. In N. M. Noor (Ed.), *Psychology from an Islamic perspective: A guide to teaching and learning* (pp. 183–202). IIUM Press.

Ismail, K., Abu Zahrin, S. N., & Alias, J. (Eds.). (2019). *Islam & psikologi dari perspektif kemanusiaan.* Penerbit Universiti Kebangsaan Malaysia.

Ismail, K., Dakir, J., Md Sham, F., & Hamsan, H. H. (Eds). (2016). *Psikologi Islam:* Falsafah, teori dan aplikasi (Islamic psychology: Philosophy, theory and *applications).* Penerbit Universiti Kebangsaan Malaysia. Jafari, M. F. (1992). Counselling values and objectives: A comparison of Western and
Islamic perspectives. *Intellectual Discourse, 1*, 326–339.

Langgulung, H. (1983). *Teori-teori kesihatan mental: Perbandingan psikologi modern dan* pendekatan pakar-pakar pendidikan Islam (Theories in mental health: A comparison *between modern psychology and Islamic educationists' approaches).* Penerbit Pustaka Huda.

Langgulung, H. (1989). Research in psychology: Toward an ummatic paradigm. In
International Institute of Islamic Thought (IIIT) (Ed.), *Toward Islamization of disciplines* (pp. 115–130). IIIT.

Langgulung, H. (2001). *A psycho-pedagogical approach to Islamization of knowledge.* IIUM Research Centre.

Mackeen, A. M. (1977). The human personality. *Islamic Herald, 3*, 38–41.

Mackeen, A. M. (1997). *Studies in behavioral psychology: Imam al-Ghazali on negative human behaviour and health (special issue).* Ceylon Moor Ladies

Union.

Mahudin, N. D. M. (2009). Social psychology. In N. M. Noor (Ed.), *Psychology from an Islamic perspective: A guide to teaching and learning* (pp. 203–216). IIUM Press.

Majid, H. S. A. (2009). Physiological psychology. In N. M. Noor (Ed.), *Psychology from an Islamic perspective: A guide to teaching and learning* (pp. 137–152). IIUM Press.

Mokdad, M. (2006). Approaches to Islamization of knowledge: The case of psychology. In M. Y. Hussain (Ed.), *Islamization of human sciences* (pp. 167–184). IIUM Research Centre.

Noor, N. M. (Ed.). (2009). *Psychology from an Islamic perspective: A guide to teaching and learning*. IIUM Press.

Qutb, M. (1996). *Memahami jiwa manusia menurut perspektif Islam (Understanding Human Psyche according to Islam)*. (Translated by Yusoff Zaky Yacob). Dian Darulnaim Sdn. Bhd.

Raba, A. M. (2001). *Major personalities in the Qur'an*. A.S. Nordeen.

Razak, A. L., Mohamad, M., Alias, A., Adam, K. W., Kasim, N. M., &Mutiu, S. (2011). Iman restoration therapy (IRT): A new counselling approach and its usefulness in developing personal growth of Malay adolescent clients. *Revelation and Science, 1*, 97–107.

Samsuddin, M. Z. (2009a). Personality psychology. In N. M. Noor (Ed.), *Psychology from an Islamic perspective: A guide to teaching and learning* (pp. 119–126). IIUM Press.

Samsuddin, M. Z. (2009b). Psychology, culture and indigenization: An overview from the Islamic perspective. In N. M. Noor (Ed.), *Psychology from an Islamic perspective: A*
*guide to teaching and learning* (pp. 43–58). IIUM Press.

Samsuddin, M. Z., & Alias, A. (2009). Motivation and emotion. In N. M. Noor (Ed.),
*Psychology from an Islamic perspective: A guide to teaching and learning* (pp. 153–170). IIUM Press.

Sham, F. M. (2010). Pendekatan psikologi dakwah dalam menangani masalah tekanan emosi remaja: Fokus kepada memberi perhatian dan kasih saying (A psychology of da'wah approach in dealing with emotional stress among teenagers: Focusing on giving attention and love). *Al-Hikmah, 2*, 107–118.

Sham, F. M. (2015). Kemahiran psikologi dakwah kepada golongan remaja (The psychology da'wah skill when dealing with teenagers). *Al-Hikmah, 7*, 95–103.

Sham, F. M. (2016). Elemen psikologi Islam dalam silibus psikologi moden: Satu alternatif (The elements of Islamic psychology in modern psychology syllabi: An alternative). *Global Journal at-Thaqafah, 6*, 75–86.

Sham, F. M., & Nazim, A. M. (2015). Pendekatan psikologi dakwah dalam menangani

Remaja berisiko: Fokus pendekatan bimbingan jiwa (The psychology of da`wah approach in dealing with teenagers at-risk: Focusing on guiding the soul approach). *Jurnal Hadhari: An International Journal, 7*, 63–73.

Sham, F. M. & Stapa, Z. (2011). Metodologi dakwah kepada remaja: Pendekatan psikologi dakwah (Da`wah methodology for teenagers: A psychology of da`wah approach). *Al-Hikmah, 3*, 145–166.

Sipon, S. & Hussin, R. (2010). *Teori kaunseling dan psikoterapi (Theories of counseling and psychotherapy).* Universiti Sains Islam Malaysia (USIM).

Taha, Z. B. (1995). *`Ilm al-nafs fi al-turath al-`arabiyy al-Islamiyy (Psychology in the Arabic-Islamic heritage).* Matba`ah Jami`ah al-Khartum.

Yacob, Y. Z. (1977). *Saikologi Remaja (Adolescent psychology).* Sharikat Dian Sdn. Bhd.

Yacob, Y. Z. (1986). *1001 Masalah Jiwa Manusia—Jilid 1 (1001 Human psychological problem-Volume 1).* Dian Darulnaim Sdn. Bhd.

Yacob, Y. Z. (1989). *1001 Masalah Jiwa Manusia—Jilid 2 (1001 Human psychological problem-Volume 2).* Dian Darulnaim Sdn. Bhd.

Zin, A. A. M. (1999). *Psikologi dakwah (Psychology of da'wah).* Jabatan Kemajuan Islam Malaysia (JAKIM).

Zin, A. A. M. (Ed.). (2020). *Psikologi dalam dakwah (Psychology in da`wah).* Universiti of Malaya Press.

CHAPTER NINE

# Islamic Psychology in Nigeria: An Overview of Accomplishments, Challenges and Prospects

SALISU SHEHU

THE INSPIRATION TO present knowledge from an Islamic perspective was first observed at the Makkah World Conference on Islamic Education in 1977. The Islamization of the knowledge movement was a direct outcome of the said conference globally. In Nigeria, however, without dismissing the influence of the two important events, the Sokoto revivalist literature of the 19th century played a remarkable role in shaping the consciousness of Muslim intellectuals in this part of the world. These scholars, through their literature, have been sources of great intellectual influence from the 19th century onward. This history explains the quick and easy manner with which the Islamization of knowledge was accepted in Nigeria, first introduced in the early 1980s by Muslim intellectuals. Islamic psychology (IP) is an area that generated interest. As a result, several efforts at propounding Islamic perspectives of psychology have been made. This chapter reviews the institutional, organizational, and individual efforts and accomplishments in developing the discipline. These efforts include seminars, workshops, conferences, symposia, roundtables, and research and publications on IP and related fields. The prospects of the growth of the discipline and the challenges are discussed.

## Introduction and Background

Nigeria presents unique sociopolitical features and paradoxes to the World. Its population is the largest in Africa, with over 200 million people, per projections based on the 2006 general census that reported 160 million. Another paradoxical feature is that Nigeria is perhaps the only country in the world where both Christian and Muslim communities are almost equal in number and live with incessant tensions and conflicts because of perceived intentions of domination by the other. Lebanon is the only country in the world that may have the same sociopolitical configuration, but its geographic and demographic size is unequal to those of Nigeria. The Muslim population in Nigeria is larger than the entire population of Lebanon and that of Egypt, the largest Arab country in the world. The Nigerian Christian population may also be larger than the entire population of the Democratic Republic of the Congo, the largest Christian country in Africa. There is still a sizeable population of followers of traditional African religions in Nigeria. Hence, unsurprisingly, the Nigerian Constitution expediently described the nation as a multireligious State, not a secular country. This background is relevant when this chapter discusses the challenges of Islamic psychology (IP) in Nigeria.

The tradition of Islamic learning in Nigeria is nearly 1,000 years old, since the time that Islam arrived in Bilad al-Sudan, as the entire sub-Saharan Sahelian region used to be called by Muslim Arab historians, scholars, and traders. Present-day Northern Nigeria, where Muslims predominate, is largely composed of the defunct Kanem-Bornu Empire and Hausaland, which occurred hundreds of years before the advent of colonialism. Birnin Ngazargamu in Borno and Kano, Katsina, Zaria, and Yan-Doto in Hausaland were centers of Islamic learning. In the 19th century, much intellectual and scholastic progress was made because of the revivalist/reformist movements by Sheikh Muhammad al-Amin el-Kanemi in Borno and Sheikh Usman Dan Fodiyo. These two historical phenomena promoted learning, namely, the production of hundreds of books and treatises on many aspects of Islamic and natural sciences; the establishment of thousands of Qur'anic schools, *madrassas*, and *Ilimi* schools; and the production of high-caliber scholars.

Based on the aforementioned backdrop of the well-entrenched tradition of learning and scholarship, an assertion is that in Nigeria, the urge, as well as the consciousness to present knowledge in an Islamic perspective, could neither have been first ignited by the famous Makkah World Conference on Islamic Education of 1977 nor first generated by the Islamization of knowledge movement that was a direct outcome of the said conference. Considering the influence and significance of the two important events, the Sokoto revivalist literature of the

19th century must have played a significant role in shaping the consciousness of Muslim intellectuals in this part of the world. Nothing illustrates this phenomenon more than the assertions made by the late Wazir of Sokoto, Wazir Junaid, in his acceptance speech of an honorary doctorate degree in convocation in 1971 in Ahmadu Bello University, Zaria. In the words of Wazir Junaid, knowledge is universal but has a sociocultural stamp, is always committed to a worldview, and cannot be neutral. Unsurprisingly, once the Islamization of knowledge was introduced to Nigeria, it was quickly and easily accepted by some Muslim intellectuals, especially in the universities in Northern Nigeria where Muslims are predominant. IP is one of the areas that generated interest.

## Islam and Psychology: Shaping a Paradigm and Conceptual Framework

Our discourse focuses on IP within a paradigm and a conceptual framework. Thus, this chapter attempts to examine the relationship between Islam as a worldview and psychology as a modern discipline of knowledge. Islam represents the Tauhidi worldview and episteme, and modern psychology represents the Western, secular worldview and episteme. Hence, there are sharp theological and epistemological differences between the two worldviews, which find expression in their conception of knowledge. Despite the differences, there are commonalities. Additionally, against this backdrop, the relation between Islam and psychology is expounded. An assertion is that there is a positive relationship between Islam and psychology because humans are the central figure of interest in both (Shehu, 2001, July). In psychology, even when animal behavior is studied, the aim is to explain human behavior. In Islam, however, humans occupy a more important and central position. The Qur'anic message is primarily directed at individuals and declares that their creation is in the best of forms (95:4), that they have been elevated and honored above all creatures, and that they have been preferred above them (with knowledge) with marked preferment (17:70; 2:29). Another perspective of the positive relationship between Islam and Psychology (Shehu, 2001, July) also explains that the Qur'an in several verses exhorts the study of all aspects of humans (Qur'an 51:20). Last, the positive relationship between Islam and Psychology is demonstrated by various human psychological traits and tendencies described in the Qur'an (20:204-207; 16:14; 14:34; 17:11; 18:54; 70:19-21; 100:6-8; 11:9-11; etc.).

More importantly, however, human development, in all its aspects, has been elaborately discussed in some cases, even with their psychological and social implications, especially during adolescence. The stage-like nature of human development both in its general and specific terms has been alluded to in the

Qur'an. All the information in this paper supports the need for an Islamic perspective of psychology.

## Making Sense of the Concept of IP in the Nigerian Context

The book "Islamic Psychology Around the Globe" is an overview of efforts done in the field in different countries. The book does not provide conceptual and theoretical propositions or postulations that would necessitate a definition of IP. However, because what should be included or excluded in this chapter must be determined, the following definition is proposed: "IP is the attempt to redefine, recast and reorient psychology to make it conform to the Islamic worldview, belief system and values based on theological, epistemological, intellectual, methodological, jurisprudential, spiritual and moral principles derived from the Qur'an and the Sunnah." This definition includes endeavors such as those in general and applied psychology and related fields, for example, guidance and counseling, special education, and tests and measurement. Works in these areas are included in this chapter.

## Indigenous and Foreign Inspirations on IP in Nigeria

As a precursor to the substance of this chapter, searching for sources of inspiration for research on IP in Nigeria is reasonable. Two categories have been identified and are described loosely as indigenous and foreign sources of inspiration. Indigenous in this case means writings (e.g., books, epistles, pamphlets, speeches) by local scholars, even in precolonial times and after colonialism before the advent of the Islamization of knowledge movement that must have, in the view of this writer, influenced or motivated students and scholars to consider the need to study or present psychology and other disciplines of study from a non-Western perspective. *Foreign sources of inspiration* means the writings of Muslim scholars from outside Nigeria that also inspired research on IP.

Earlier in the introduction, we said that some of the writings of the Sokoto Caliphate leaders might be precursors to research in the natural, physical, and social/behavioral sciences. These 19th-century scholars staged intellectual and sociopolitical reform from approximately 1774 to 1804. This reform occurred because these scholars did not limit themselves to writings in strict religious sciences and also wrote on, for example, politics, security, war and diplomacy, and medicine. One area that received substantial attention, especially in the writings of Sheikh Usman Dan Fodiyo, is psychology. Sheikh Dan Fodiyo extensively wrote on *Tasawwuf,* which has substantially influenced psychology. In several books, he referenced *tasawwuf* as *Ilm al-Suluk* (Science of Behavior).

He often focused on purification of the heart *(tazkiya)* and righteous conducts (*husn al-khulq*), for example, humility, humbleness, modesty, compassion, kindness and generosity, truthfulness and trustworthiness, and honesty, which are encouraged in *Tasawwuf*, and condemnable characters or conducts such as arrogance and haughtiness, miserliness, immodesty, and wickedness. In *"Ihya al-Sunnah wa-Ikhmad al-Bid'ah,"* for example, he focused on the reform of *Tasawwuf*, whereby he stated aspects of its practice that conform to the Sunnah of the Prophet (PBUH) and those that deviate from it.

In *"Bayan Wujub al-Hijrahala al-Ibad,"* Sheikh Dan Fodiyo, while providing advice to the prince (Amir or Sultan) on how to manage his subjects based on their individual psychological dispositions, traits, and tendencies, created "political psychology." Sheikh Dan Fodiyo explained that people differ in their psychological dispositions and that leaders should consider that when interacting with or managing them. He explained that among people, their dispositions can be likened to the behavior or character of an animal, for example, a lion, tiger, horse, ox, donkey, dog, fox, goat, sheep, or cat. He described the behavior of each of these animals and advised the leader to be conscious of that when interacting with or managing his subjects. These speculations on humans' individual tendencies, which are within the purview of the psychology of individual differences, can justifiably be suggested to have influenced many Muslim students of psychology to develop an interest in studying the subject from an Islamic perspective.

Regarding the aforementioned point on the impact of the acceptance speech delivered at the 1971 Convocation Ceremony of Ahmadu Bello University, Zaria, by Wazir of Sokoto, Wazir Junaid Ibn Muhammad, the speech had immense influence on Nigerian Muslim intelligentsia. Wazir Junaid said that Nigerian universities in form and substance, in their philosophy and practice and in their letter and spirit, are mere cultural transplants whose roots lie in another civilization. He also said that knowledge pursued within historical, civilizational, and cultural contexts cannot be neutral or value free, because it is based on a certain worldview. In essence, therefore, based on their curricula and overall dispositions, Nigerian universities only promote Western, European Judo-Christian values and culture. Comparing Nigeria's present-day universities to its ancestral African Islamic University of Sankore, he charged the Nigerian Muslim academia with reclaiming them (our universities) by reviewing their philosophies, course content, and academic orientation. Wazir Junaid might have been the first advocate of the paradigm shift and reorientation and transformation of knowledge in the context of an Islamic worldview and value system. The import of this speech was a strong motivator for the Islamization/Integration of Knowledge movement, which came to the fore from the late 1970s to the early 1980s.

These indigenous inspirers created an environment vulnerable to the foreign influences that influenced Muslim faculty members in Nigerian universities. The motivation to advance IP in Nigeria can be explained broadly from two perspectives: general and specific. At the general level, the entire Islamization of knowledge literature has served as a highly impactful inspiration. The proceedings of the Makkah World Conference on Muslim Education of 1977 (published by the King Abdul Aziz University, Jeddah jointly with Hodder and Stoughton) were highly influential. They were the invaluable assets and principal reference materials of many Muslim scholars and researchers. Of all the volumes, the most influential on social and behavioral scientists was that edited by Al-Faruqi and Ashraf (1978) titled, "Social and Natural Sciences: the Islamic Perspectives.". One strong point made by al-Faruqi in his editorial comment on this volume was that in contrast to the natural and physical sciences, in which the researcher studies inanimate objects devoid of emotions and values and is thus more likely to be "objective," "neutral, and "unbiased," it was not possible to attain that in the social and behavioral sciences and humanities where the object of study is a human being who has, for example, attitudes, emotions, and desires. Al-Faruqi therefore strongly advocated for Muslims to propound their paradigm and philosophical frameworks for the study of humans and society.

At the specific level, the chapter on psychology written by al-Hashimi in the volume edited by Al-Faruqi and Ashraf (1978) was both a source of inspiration and a frequent reference of researchers of IP. Of all the materials that influenced, inspired, and motivated research on IP, none was comparable to Badri's "Dilemma of Muslim Psychologists" (1979/2016). This book arrived in Nigeria in the first half of the 1980s. Dozens of undergraduate education and Islamic studies students at Bayero University, Kano acquired it. The limited number of copies brought to Nigeria sold out within a few days. The influence of Badri's book on Muslim psychologists and other behavioral scientists in Nigeria is such that a psychology lecturer or researcher from an Islamic perspective would refer to that book either in their class or writings.

## Pacesetters and Trailblazers of IP in Nigeria

Our review of the development of IP in Nigeria starts among the scholars that pioneered the efforts. Three scholars, who were teachers of the writer of this chapter and graduated from Bayero University, Kano, Nigeria, fit these criteria: Danjuma Abubakar Maiwada, Musa Ahmad (deceased), and Muhammad Kabir Yunus. The first two belong to the Department of Education where this chapter's author also teaches, and the third belonged to the Department of Islamic Studies before he retired. These three scholars contributed to IP, starting in the mid-1980s. Professor Muhammad Kabir Yunus presented a seminar paper, "Al-Ghazaali's Theory about the Human Nature," in 1986 in the Department of Islamic Studies to which he belonged. This paper was probably never published because it was presented over 30 years ago but is the first attempt at presenting psychology from an Islamic perspective in a formal academic setting.

At approximately the same time, Musa Ahmad and Danjuma Maiwada were making their respective individual efforts in the Department of Education at Bayero University, Kano. Notably, in most Nigerian universities, Psychology is offered only in the Department of Education in the form of educational psychology. Few universities run a full-fledged program that results in a B.Sc. Psychology. The late Musa Ahmad infused aspects of IP in his educational psychology lectures at the undergraduate level. One example of such is his presentation on the depictions of *nafs* in the Qur'an in terms of *"nafs al-ammara," "nafs al-lawwamah,"* and *"nafs al-mutma'innah."* Musa Ahmad later wrote and published three books on IP, Health and Healing in the Qur'an, Developmental Psychology: An Islamic Perspective, and Sociology of Islamic Education.

Unlike the late Musa Ahmad, who wrote books IP as mentioned above, Danjuma Abubakar Maiwada wrote and presented several papers at different academic forums. The first paper he presented on IP (Maiwada, 1982) was shared at a departmental seminar of the Department of Education, Bayero University, Kano, Nigeria. The most important point he made in this paper was that the spirit as an integral component of human nature is either not recognized or neglected in modern social sciences. Maiwada (1995) presented a paper at the African Regional Conference on Cross-Cultural Psychology at the Obafemi Awolowo University, Ile-Ife, and it was published in the Proceedings of the Conference. The title of the paper is: "Parameters and Paradigm of Islamic Psychology" Maiwada (1994) published an earlier article on the therapeutic effects of prayer (*salat*) and supplication *(du'a)*. His most recent contribution was titled "Spirituality in man as a natural dispensation: Its consequential and therapeutic effects" (Maiwada, 2017).

## Overview of Efforts and Accomplishments in IP in Nigeria

From the early 1990s to the present, modest accomplishments and progress have been made in IP in Nigeria. An overview of these is presented here in two perspectives, institutional and organizational efforts and individual efforts. In the first perspective, the efforts made by institutions such as universities, colleges, departments, faculties, learned societies, and organizations are presented, and in the second perspective, the research, presentations, and writings and publications by individual scholars and researchers are reviewed.

## Institutional Accomplishments on IP in Nigeria

On the basis of ordinary inquiries made based on personal contacts and relationships with an array of academics in many universities in Nigeria, Bayero University, Kano, through its Department of Education, is ahead of many universities in the promotion and development of IP. Thus far, only in the Department of Education, Bayero University, Kano, are courses on IP taught at both the undergraduate and graduate levels. Since 1997, the Department of Education has introduced an elective course at the 300 Level (third year of undergraduate studies), Introduction to Islamic Psychology. Subsequently, the same department introduced a course at the master's degree level called Advanced Islamic Psychology. In addition to these courses, there were others introduced in the area of guidance and counseling. All of them, however, are at the postgraduate level. The courses Counselling in Islam and Contributions of Muslim Scholars to Guidance and Counselling are offered as elective courses in the Postgraduate Diploma in Guidance and Counselling, and another elective course called Islam, Guidance and Counselling is offered at the master's degree level.

Although the Department of Education, Bayero University, Kano, has established courses on IP and guidance and counseling, few students and staff have endeavored to research these areas, for example, an inconsequential number of students have undertaken degree projects and research on IP at the undergraduate and graduate levels. However, it is instructive that several colleges of education are affiliated with Bayero University, Kano, through the Department of Education, and, as a rule, all the affiliated colleges must adopt the curriculum of the universities with which they are affiliated. Thus, the IP course of the Department of Education is taught in several colleges of education affiliated with Bayero University, Kano.

## Role of the Nigeria Office of the International Institute of Islamic Thought (IIIT) in Promoting IP in Nigeria

The IIIT has been principally and centrally instrumental to most of the institutional efforts and accomplishments made in Nigeria in IP. The IIIT Nigeria Office is in Kano and has supported several academic activities, for example, the conducting of seminars, workshops, and lectures on IP. The IIIT supported this writer in presenting lectures and conducting seminars at various faculties in several universities and in colleges of education across Nigeria, especially in predominantly Muslim regions. The IIIT Nigeria Office has promoted IP in Nigeria through three channels. First, it published several papers and articles on IP in its journal, *Al-Ijtihad*. This writer has had three papers published in three editions of this journal. Second, the IIIT Nigeria Office has conducted monthly seminars for more than two decades. Although the monthly seminars were not specifically instituted for IP, they provided the platform on which several presentations on IP were and are being made. Examples of presentations on IP in these monthly seminars are as follows:

A. Shehu, Salisu (2001) "Introduction to Islamic Perspective of Developmental Psychology", July 2001.

B. Ayagi, Sani M. (2013 Arabic paper), "Ilm al-Nafs min wijhatnazr al-Qur'an al-Kareem", April 2013.

C. Garba, Rabiu I. (2019). "Positive Islamic Psychology: An Emerging Trend for Achieving Fantabulous Happiness", August 2019

D. Auwal, Mustapha (2020). "Islamic Psychology: A Psychotherapy for Enhancing Muslim Mental Health", November 2020.

Another important support offered by the IIIT Nigeria Office to the development of IP is in collaboration with academic or professional organizations and associations to conduct joint academic activities. In February 2020, the IIIT Nigeria Office in Kano collaborated with the Kano State Chapter of the Counselling Association of Nigeria to conduct a joint one-seminar on "Expounding the Islamic Perspectives of Guidance and Counselling." Four papers were presented at the seminar, (i) "Islamic Perspective of Guidance and Counselling: Basic Concepts and Principles;" (ii) "The Contribution of Muslim Scholars to Guidance and Counselling" ([i] and [ii] were presented by the author of this chapter); (iii) "The Imperative of Propounding the Islamic Perspective of Guidance and Counselling," presented by Abdulrashid Garba; and (iv) "Selected Views of Human Nature and their Implications to Counselling: Islamic Perspective," presented by Muhammad ibn Abdullahi. The IIIT Nigeria Office was already working on facilitating the formation of the Association of Islamic Psychologists in Nigeria (AMPIN). As part of the efforts to achieving that objective, a similar joint seminar on IP with the Kano State Chapter of the Nigeria Society of Educational Psychologists is being organized. The seminar organized for April 2020 was canceled because of the COVID-19 pandemic. The plan was to use the seminar to sensitize the participants on the need for the formation of the organization or even to form it at that time.

## Individual Research Efforts on IP in Nigeria

The prior section focused on presenting the institutional efforts supporting and promoting IP. This section reviews the efforts in, for example, research, publications, and lectures. The early efforts of some scholars, since the early 1980s, have been presented and described as setting the pace of research on IP in Nigeria. As an illustration of these individual efforts, a bibliographical list is presented.

*Editor's Note: To avoid redundancy, the following publications were removed from the reference list.*

SALISU SHEHU


Shehu, S (1996). *A study of the Islamic perspective of cognitive development: Implications for Education.* (Unpublished MEd dissertation). Department of Education, Bayero University, Kano.

Shehu, S. (1998). Toward and Islamic perspective of developmental psychology. *The American Journal of Islamic Social Sciences, 15*(4), 41–70.

Shehu, S. (2000). Cognitive psychology in the Muslim world: A study of the postulations of some early Muslim scholars. *Al-Ijtihad: The Journal of Islamization of Knowledge and Contemporary Issues, 1*(1), 44-63.

Shehu, S. (2001). Introduction to Islamic perspective of developmental psychology. A paper presented at a One-Day Seminar at the Federal College of Education, Kano, Kano State, July 15, 2001.

Shehu, S. (2001). The Islamic perspective of adolescent psychology: Propounding an alternative paradigm and approach. Al-*Ijtihad: The Journal of Islamization of Knowledge and Contemporary Issues,* 2(2), 66-90.

Shehu, S. (2003). Stress management and mental health among adolescents: An Islamic perspective. *Al-Ijtihad: Journal of Islamization of Knowledge and Contemporary Issues,* 4(1). 76-105.

Shehu, S. (2009, October 21–22). *Child psychology: Its relevance to building integrity in primary schools.* Paper presented at a Two-Day Train the Trainer Workshop on Building Integrity in Primary Schools, Organized for Primary School Teachers in the FCT, Education Department of the ICPC, ICPC Auditorium, ICPC Headquarters, Abuja.

Shehu, S. (2010). Stress, depression and emotional instability in adolescent development: Empirical and theoretical issues. In B. A. Umar, Y. M. Adamu, & K. I. Dandago (Eds.), *Issues in youth development in Nigeria: A multidisciplinary perspective* (pp. 69–92). Bayero University.

Shehu, S. (2014a). A study of the Islamic perspective of cognitive development: Implications to education in the Muslim world. *Revelation and Science: Interdisciplinary Journal of Intellectual Revival,* 4(2), 1435.

Shehu, S. (2014b). Religion and adolescent development: An Islamic conceptual model for designing a youth empowerment scheme. *Bayero Sociologist: A Journal of Sociological Studies (SOJOSS), 1*(5).

Shehu, S., & Dantata, F. G. (2020). Islamic perspectives of special education: Theoretical and historical backgrounds. Bayero Journal of Educational Research and Innovation. 1(BAJERI) (1) 1, 29-40.

MUHAMMAD IBN ABDULLAHI

Abdullahi, M. i. (2008). *Human nature, causes of anxiety and counselling process in selected theories: A comparison of conventional and Islamic perspectives.* (Unpublished PhD thesis). Department of Education, Bayero University, Kano, Nigeria.

Abdullahi, M. i. (2017). Human nature in selected counselling theories: A comparison of conventional and Islamic perspectives. *Journal of Educational Psychology and Counselling.* Department of Education, Ahmadu Bello University, Zaria, 2, 2, 203-212.

Abdullahi, M. i. (2018). *Anxiety in selected counselling theories: Islamic perspective.* An unpublished conference paper presented at the National Conference on Counseling Association of Nigeria, Abuja.

Abdullahi, M. i., & Mukhtar, R. H. (2018). *Counselling communities for blood donation: Islamic perspectives.* National Conference of the Nigerian Association of Educational Administration and Planning, NAEAP, Bayero University, Kano.

ABDUL KADIR USMAN ISMA'IL

Isma'il, A. U. (2013a). Athar Itqaan Lugha al-Jism fi al-Tawasulwa al-Ta'atheer ala al-Mad'u: Lugha al-Wajhi Unmuzhajan (The Influence of Mastery of Body Language in Relarting with and Impacting on the Invitee). International Conference on Da'awah and Human Development, University of Malaya, Malaysia.

Isma'il, A. U. (2013b). Ma'alim Tauzeef al-Zhaka'a al-Atifi fi al-Sunnah al-Nabawiyyahwa Aafaq Tahsilihi (Features of Emotional Intelligence in the Sunnah and Perspectives of Attaining it) International Conference on Hadith, Dubai.

SANI MUSA AYAGI

Ayagi, S. M. (2013, April). Ilm al-Nafs min wijhatnazr al-Qur'an al-Kareem (Qur'anic Perspective of Psychology) (Arabic paper). IIIT Monthly Seminar, Bayero University, Kano.

RABIU GARBA IDRIS

Garba, R. I. (2019, August). *Positive Islamic psychology: An emerging trend for achieving fantabulous happiness.* IIIT Monthly Seminar, Bayero University, Kano.

IBRAHIM DOOBA

Dooba, I. (2020), *The social science of Prophet Muhammad (s.a.w): Actionable strategies on how to be happy here and the hereafter.* AMAB Books and Publishing.

MUSTPHA AUWAL

Auwal, M. (2020, November). *Islamic psychology: A psychotherapy for enhancing Muslim mental health.* IIIT Monthly Seminar, Bayero University, Kano.

## Challenges of IP in Nigeria

Modest achievements and developments on IP in Nigeria have been made. However, because of the limited human resources available to Muslims in Nigeria, the accomplishments and progress could have been more substantial than what has been observed. Other challenges have limited these endeavors. One such challenge is the insufficient confidence among many Muslim faculty members in researching an Islamic perspective or a concept of knowledge. The usual notion has been that only Ulama (Islamic scholars) can perform these efforts. That sense of incapability prevents them away from attempting to make efforts in that regard. Many faculty members remain skeptical and consider it unnecessary to study the modern sciences from a religious perspective. This group usually discourages students who intend to conduct research on IP. Another serious challenge is the dearth of references and teaching materials for IP. Many faculty members and postgraduate students want to undertake research on IP, but no materials available in Nigeria.

## Prospects of IP in Nigeria

As daunting as the challenges are, there are prospects that inspire hope and optimism. One such prospect is increasing awareness among the lecturers and students of the need to re-examine, redefine, and recast knowledge in the context of various worldviews, belief systems, and values. Proponents of IP and the entire integration of knowledge undertaking can leverage this increasing awareness and consciousness to further advance this subject in Nigeria's universities, colleges, and polytechnics. Another important prospect is the emergence of a new generation of Muslim intellectuals who are much more learned and well-versed than their current counterparts are in the Qur'an and Hadith, the primary sources of knowledge and law in Islam. These young faculty members are also well acquainted with the modern sciences and are enthusiastic about re-examining and critiquing the dominant system of knowledge through the Qur'anic spectacle. This phenomenon suggests a brighter future for the integration of knowledge generally and the social sciences specifically, including IP.

## Conclusion

Today's world is open, and this reality is engendered by the preponderant influence of information and communication technology and digitalization. Instructively, this condition has presented a paradox. Life has become more competitive while accentuating mutual interdependence, cooperation, and collaboration. Against the backdrop of these phenomena, one recommendation may suffice: the need to cooperate, collaborate, and communicate for the purpose of knowledge and information sharing. Implementing this recommendation should be easy because of the availability of electronic and virtual sources and tools for acquiring and transmitting knowledge. In this regard, the IAIP should assert its presence, bring its global community together, and disseminate its information and intellectual and academic materials and resources to the world through virtual meetings and communication systems, the fastest and easiest means to advance the cause of IP globally.

## References

Al-Faruqi, I. R., & Ashraf, S. A. (Eds.) (1978). *Social and natural sciences: Islamic perspective.* Hodder and Stoughton/King Abdul-Azeez University.

Badri, M. (1979/2016). *The dilemma of Muslim psychologists.* Islamic Book Trust.

Maiwada, D. A. (1982). *The spiritual dimension in the social science.* (Unpublished Seminar Paper). Department of Education, Bayero University, Kano, Nigeria.

Maiwada, D. A. (1994). Therapeutic Effects of Prayer (salat) and Supplication (du'a). *Journal of General Studies, VII* (1).

Maiwada, D. A. (1995). *Parameters and paradigm of Islamic psychology.* Proceedings of the 1995 African Regional Conference of the International Association of Cross-Cultural Psychology, Obafemi Awolowo University (OAU), Ile-Ife, Nigeria.

Maiwada, D. A. (2017). Spirituality in man as a natural dispension: Its consequential and therapeutic effects. In A. Khan (Ed.), *Studies in Application of Psychology and Counseling in Asian Context.*

CHAPTER TEN

# A Journey from Muslim Psychology to Islamic Psychology in Pakistan

TAMKEEN SALEEM
MUHAMMAD TAHIR KHALILY

THE HISTORICAL SEQUENCE of Islamic Psychology (IP) in Pakistan is a transformative journey from Muslim psychology to Islamic psychology. This emergent discipline was taught and practiced in various educational institutions under different names, grounded in Islamic teachings. This chapter focuses on how IP has evolved over time through institutions teaching courses, conferences held, psychological tests developed, major publications and its current status in Pakistan.

## Introduction

Contemporary Islamic psychology (IP) is based on Islamic teachings because many of the epistemological concepts of human nature are found in the Quran and Sunnah of Prophet (PBUH). Historically, in Muslim societies, psychology was known as ilm-ul-Nafs, an Arabic analogue (Deuraseh & Talib, 2005), and was a predominant area of study in the Islamic Golden Era, from the $8^{th}$ century to $14^{th}$ century (Haque, 2004). In addition to the theoretical illustrations, the applied side of mental health was known as "*al-ilaj al nafs*," "*al-tibb al ruhani*," and "*tib-al- qalb*," with a focus on qalb (heart), *ruh* (soul), *aql* (intellect), and *irada* (will) as central features of the self (Haque, 1998, 2004).

The Indian subcontinent with a substantial part of the nation's Muslim population observed *ilm-ul-Nafs* in their practice rooted in the guidance of the great scholars of Islam, for example, Shah Muhammad Ghaus (1703–1759), Shah Waliullah (1703–1762), Maulana Muhammad Ilyas (1884–1944), Allama Muhammad Iqbal (1879–1938), Maulana Ashraf Ali Thanvi (1873–1943), Maulana Syed Abul Ala Maududi (1903–1979), and Maulana Amin Hassan Islahi (1904–1997), as the epitome of Muslim psychology (Shahzad, Khan, & Khalily, 2020; Salma, 2010).

The Sufis in the subcontinent have remained equally influential in shaping the thinking patterns of the population; therefore, mysticism (*Tasawwuf*) expanded substantially in the region. After the emergence of Pakistan in 1947, this action became the hub of religious and spiritual activities and promoted spirituality in the region (Salma, 2014). However, the educational institutions as a British legacy were substantially influenced by Western ideology and the colonization of knowledge. Nevertheless, the majority of workers in these institutions retained their traditional Muslim cultural heritage and practices and subsequently reflected their Muslim identity in the social science disciplines. Psychology was one of the disciplines that had Western influence because of the colonization of knowledge and emerged as an independent discipline in different universities and institutions of Pakistan.

Just after the independence of Pakistan and until the 1960s, psychology was taught as a core subject in the philosophy curriculum. Psychologists in Pakistan continued their struggle for the recognition of psychological experimental studies and the foreign-launched programs, for example, Fulbright and the Ford Foundation helped local psychologists develop their competencies. These psychologists had opportunities for training in well-equipped laboratories in the West, and they brought back modern ideas, enabling them to promote a level of psychology on par with other countries (Haque, 2011).

However, in 1962, an independent psychology department was created at the Government College Lahore (GCL) by Muhammad Ajmal (1919–1994), to indigenously establish a separate psychological construct in the form of Muslim psychology, highlighting Muslim contributions to psychotherapy. Ajmal was inspired by Carl Jung's theory of collective unconsciousness and the teachings of Martin Lings, a spiritual Muslim orientalist. Ajmal (1968) proposed that psychology and spirituality are interlinked, and he published a seminal paper, "An Introduction to Muslim tradition in psychotherapy" (Saeed, 2019). Through this academic work, he invited psychologists fascinated by colonized thinking to think critically and acquaint themselves with the treasures of knowledge and thoughts of their ancestors on psychology. He posited that faith plays a significant role in promoting social values and regularizing human activities that foster positive mental health. His work on Muslim traditions in psychotherapy inspired his student Syed Azhar Ali Rizvi (1936–2004), who established the discipline of Muslim psychology in the GCL in the late 1970s. Rizvi introduced a compulsory paper of Muslim psychology in a syllabus for a Master of Science in psychology in 1978 and founded the Society for Advancement of Muslim Psychology (SAMP), which organizes an annual national conference.

The SAMP was formed with two main goals: proliferation of traditional Islamic knowledge of psychology and integration of Muslim traditions in psychology and modern trends grounded in the scholarly works of Ashraf Ali Thanvi and Shah Waliullah. Rizvi's other landmark work was the development of three indigenous personality tests: Ghazali Personality Inventory, *Shakhsiyat Ka Serukhi Jaiza* (Complete Analysis of Personality), and Dewan's Projective Test for Children. Rizvi later established the Institute of Muslim Psychology in Lahore, a few years before his death. During this time, Shahabuddin Muhammad Mughni established the Department of Psychology at Peshawar University in 1964 and published a paper on the Characteristics of Ummah. He had visited the Imam Muhammad University Riyadh, where he met Malik Badri in 1966.

The Department of Psychology at the University of Peshawar encouraged Syeda Farhana Jehangir, whose works on the role of faith and religion and mental health are noteworthy. She focused on the people of the subcontinent who have been in therapy with non-psychologists to overcome their problems of a psychological nature. These non-psychologists are considered pious, blessed, and endowed with the power to heal. They are known as sheiks or mentors and provide treatment according to their religious order. However, they generally love Allah and have deep religious faith. This system is said to provide a cure and has a long history of treatment. However, no such research had been conducted on this subject. Farhana Jehangir *paved the way* for research and therapy based on a religious framework.

Additionally, Mahnazir Riaz significantly contributed to the integration of Islamic perspectives with contemporary psychology. In 1985, she wrote and presented papers such as Religious Faith and Mental Health and the Islamic Approach to Prevention and Cure of Drug Addiction. Between 1991 and 1994, Mahnazir Riaz made a greater contribution by introducing the subject of Muslim psychology in the curriculum of Peshawar University at the bachelor and master's level. She presented a paper titled "Mental Health: Quranic Perspective" at the 8$^{th}$ International Conference of the Pakistan Psychological Association in 1991, which resulted in appreciation and support for the topic. Examples of her other works are the Attitude of Teachers and Students Towards Religion and the Quranic Theory of Moral Development and its Implications for Human Development. These psychologists made pioneering efforts in introducing Muslim psychology in Pakistan.

## Introduction to Muslim Psychology Course

The first time a paper on Muslim psychology was introduced, only the students enrolled in the University of Peshawarhad access to this course. Subsequently, the Department of Psychology at the University of Peshawar introduced Muslim psychology in its master's curriculum. However, after the restructuring of the University Grants Commission, the Higher Education Commission Pakistan (HEC) was established in 2002 to enhance the quality of higher education. Accordingly, the National Curriculum Revision Committee for Psychology met in Lahore in 2006 to scrutinize the contents, aims, and objectives of this discipline and introduce Muslim psychology as an optional subject for eighth-semester students, in lieu of the availability of a resource person (HEC, 2006). However, in some departments of psychology, it remains compulsory at the master's level, and at International Islamic University Islamabad (IIUI), a core subject for doctoral students during their first semester.

## Muslim Psychology to Islamic Psychology

Since 1991, most of the curriculum for Muslim psychology has been taught at various universities with almost the same content, approved by HEC (2006), in this paper, it is called "the course." The content of the course is based on the historical background of Muslim psychology and contributions of Muslim scholars of psychology with a focus on the works of Al-Kindi, Ibn-e-Sina, Al-Ghazali, Ibn-e-Miskewah, Maulana Ashraf Ali Thanvi, and Shah Waliullah. Thus, the course emphasizes their contributions in the understanding of personality, self-determination, psychometric tools, and treatments and focuses on the psychological implications of *Huqooqul Allah* and *HuqooqulIbad* and the Quranic concepts of the human psyche.

Some psychologists and senior faculty members that have taught this content for years felt that because of recent developments and scientific literature on the subject, revisions were necessary. Some institutes attempted to reformulate the course according to Islamic teachings. To promote this subject as an independent discipline within contemporary psychology, some departments started to teach the current dimensions of IP. In this regard, few important steps have been taken by IIUI in advancing the subject. Because IIUI's primary goal is the Islamization of knowledge, Malik Badri was invited in 2007 to lead the department of psychology in line with the objectives of the university. Accordingly, a three-credit course on Muslim psychology was introduced in the bachelor program as optional and in the Master of Science and doctoral programs as compulsory. Other three-credit courses added IP content, such as some in the department of history and school of psychology, emphasizing contributions of Muslim philosophers in psychology. Positive psychology, including the practical aspects of forgiveness, gratitude, pro-social behavior, spirituality, and religiosity were also introduced. A three-credit course was introduced at the doctoral level in 2014, comprising the themes of the Islamic theory of personality; Quranic concepts related to *Nafs*; the Islamic model of the Ruh (soul); contributions of Muslim scholars in psychology; Prophet Muhammad (S.A.W) as a model for psychologists, traditionalists, and rationalists' approaches; faith healers; and applied work on forgiveness, self-forgiveness and Taubah/Istighfar; and Sabr and Shukar and their significant contribution to the psychological well-being of individuals. These courses also focused on the integration of Muslim beliefs and practices as a healing method in therapy, cognitive behavior therapy, schema-focused therapy in the Islamic perspective, religiously motivated counseling, and importance of spirituality in the treatment of substance abuse.

Although the journey of Muslim psychology commenced from Lahore and was continued by many psychologists at the individual level, their struggle is commendable. A turning point for Muslim psychology that transformed it into IP occurred during a five-day certified course of IP organized by Muhammad Tahir Khalily in January 2019 and offered in collaboration with the International Association of Islamic Psychology (IAIP) on the *Islamic Approaches to Psychology and Psychotherapy.* Psychologists from across Pakistan and a few from the United Kingdom and the Middle East participated and benefited from the five-day modules taught by Rasjid Skinner and Abdallah Rothman on the history and philosophy of Western psychology, defining IP, an Islamic model of the self, diagnosis and treatment from Islamic perspectives, and the useful and the toxic in Western psychotherapy. Consequently, the department considered the major recent developments and latest additions and formed a committee to revise the Muslim psychology course into an IP course. A consensus on the definition of IP must be grounded in Islamic teachings from the Quran and Sunnah. A sectarian perspective may be added later because the sects in Muslim history emerged when they interacted with people under the influence of Roman and Persian empires, where philosophy, math, logic, and other disciplines prevailed. At the time of Prophet Muhammad (PBUH), the people of the Arabian Peninsula were experts in language and literature. There was no philosophical or logical discourse on the common man's agenda of the time. We propose that that reason kept the Quran and teaching of Prophet Muhammad PBUH intact, because they were practiced until the time of the rightly guided caliphs (Khulafa Rashedeen). As for the history and the later arrival of different sects because of the expansion of the Muslim world in non-Arab regions, the problem of interpretation and understanding emerged. Subsequently, the great scholars took responsibility for making the message of Islam easy and comprehensive for non-Arab communities and for filling this gap that emerged in different schools of thought that later converted into sects because of local political involvements.

However, building a comprehensive glossary of IP to provide a repertoire of the epistemology of words is important. For instance, scholars' translations of Arabic to English differ, and the original text loses its essence. For example, Ruh is sometimes known as spirit, which is not appropriate because in some cultures, spirit has negative connotation, and Ruh is from Allah. An appropriate English translation for Ruh is soul and for nafs is self. Fortunately, the authors' university has a Department of Islamic Studies and a Department of Sharia and Law with faculty members and scholars from various countries. They also suggest that the appropriate English word for Ruh is soul and for Nafs is self and that spirituality means Tazkiah. The maladies are not from the Ruh; it is from the Nafs where the lower part interacts with the world and Satan has access to the nafs. IP is an emerging discipline, and in many countries, psychologists have promoted this subject to solve their native problems. In this regard, the subject matter of IP is the profound study of Nafs (self) mentioned in the Islamic teachings, which could be understood in the context of the interaction among the three stages of Nafs.

As aforementioned, the main purpose of the course was to enable the students to distinguish culturally relative factors from universal factors in Western psychology, identify and describe Islamic models of the self, understand the therapeutic relationship from an Islamic perspective, and apply Islamic psychological principles in diagnosis and treatment by using case studies. Initially, the five-day certificate course was for a fixed capacity of 25 participants. Subsequently, due to high demand, the capacity was increased to 62 participants. In the certificate ceremony, the IIUI rector formally announced the establishment of the International Islamic Institute of Clinical Psychology, approved by the academic council and endorsed by the president of IIUI.

Khalily established the Psychological Services Clinic on a male campus in 2013 and on a female campus in 2017. The focus of the clinic was to introduce indigenously adopted psychotherapies grounded in Islamic principles to treat the staff and students who had psychological ailments. Khalily initiated an International Diploma on Mental Health, Law and Human Rights in 2017 with the technical support of the World Health Organization; the emphasis of the diploma was on the Islamic perspective of mental health and Sharia regulations. In addition, in the Department of Psychology at IIUI, Khalily completed two research projects approved by HEC: Indigenously Adapted Cognitive-Behavioral Therapy for Excessive Smartphone Use (IACBT-ESU): A Randomized Controlled Trial, published in the Journal of Psychology of Addictive Behaviors

(APA), and Challenges in Mental Health, Law and Human Rights, published in International Journal of Law and Psychiatry, with blended Islamic perspectives. Khalily also introduced Islamic perspectives in drug addiction treatment and a schema model therapy for a doctoral syllabus. In 2020, an IP scholarship was approved by IIUI for master's and doctoral research.

In 2015, another progress in the course development dimension was the establishment of the Riphah Institute of Clinical and Professional Psychology (RICPP) Lahore, under the leadership of Anis Ahmed, Vice Chancellor, Riphah International University. The objective of RICPP was to develop a wide-ranging educational program for skilled psychologists in Pakistan, to enrich the role of psychologists in managing a wide range of psychosocial problems of individuals and communities. The Centre for Islamic Psychology (Islamabad Campus) was established in collaboration with the IAIP, the Khalil Center (USA), the Ihsan Project (UK), and International Association of Muslim Psychologists (IAMP), Indonesia. In September 2019, the Center of Islamic Psychology and Tarbiyah Department launched a six-month certified course in IP facilitated by G. H. Rassool from the United Kingdom. The course comprised four modules: Introduction to Islamic Psychology, Islamic Sciences, Human Nature and Personality Development, and Psychosocial and Mental Health Problems. Hussain's recently published book on IP blended contemporary psychology and IP. The Centre of Islamic Psychology intends to start a clinical service on the Lahore campus to provide clinical services to help clients manage their mental health. The main aim of the clinical services is to provide Islamic-oriented psychotherapy and counseling services. The center further plans to initiate an advanced diploma in IP and an advanced diploma in Islamic counseling and psychotherapy.

## Articles, books, and conferences

### Peer reviewed journal articles and conference papers:

| | |
|---|---|
| Amjad, N. (1996). Traditional Islamic science of behavior and modern empirical psychology: points of convergence and conflict. *Islamic Thought and Scientific Creativity, 1*, 71–78. Islamabad. | Institute of Applied Psychology (IIAP), University of Punjab |
| Khalily, M. T. (2011). Uncontrolled anger and its management in the light of sunnah. *Journal of Insight, 3*(3), 33–62. | IIUI |
| Khalily, M. T. (2012). Schema perpetuation and schema healing: A case vignette for schema focused therapy in Islamic perspective. *Journal of Islamic Studies, 51*(3), 327–336. | |
| Naz, S., & Khalily, T. M. (2015). Indigenous adoption of Novaco's model of anger management among individuals with psychiatric problems in Pakistan. *Journal of Religion and Health, 54*(2), 439–447. | |
| Khan, M., & Aslam, N. (2016, March 5). *Accentuating profound traditions to experience presence of god during stressful situations.* Oral presentation at International Conference Islamic Tradition in Psychology. Society for Advancement of Muslim Psychology, Lahore School of Management, The University of Lahore, Pakistan. | The University of Lahore |
| Amjad, N. (2016). *Islamic tradition in psychology*. International Positive Psychology/Association, Lahore School of Management, University of Lahore. | Institute of Applied Psychology, University of Punjab |
| Ijaz, S., Khalily, M. T., & Ahmad, I. (2017). Mindfulness in Salah prayer and its association with mental health. *Journal of Religion and Health, 52*(3), 1–11. | IIUI |
| Zadeh, Z. (2018, July 14–15). *Understanding the power of emotions as parents: A theoretical review explaining the role of culture and parenting.* Paper presented at International Conference on Islamic Awakening (ICIA), Islamic University Maldives. | Institute of Professional Psychology (IPU), Bahria University Karachi |
| Farooq, A., & Shareef, N. (2018, July 14–15). *Efficacy of selected Quranic verses along with CBT intervention used to increase gratitude and hopefulness in depressive patients.* Paper presented at International Conference on Islamic Awakening (ICIA), Islamic University Maldives. | IPU, Bahria University Karachi |

| | |
|---|---|
| Khalily, M. T., Bhatti, M. M., Ahmad, I., Saleem, T., Hallahan, B., Ali, S. A.-e-Z., Khan, A. A., & Hussain, B. (2020). Indigenously adapted cognitive behavioral therapy for excessive smartphone use (IACBT-ESU): A randomized controlled trial. | *Psychology of Addictive Behaviors.* Advance online publication. https://doi.org/10.1037/adb0000677 |

## Books

| NO. | BOOK | AUTHOR | YEAR | PUBLISHER |
|---|---|---|---|---|
| 1 | Muslim contributions to psychotherapy and other essays | Muhammad Ajmal | 1986 | National Institute of Psychology, Centre of Excellence, Quaid-i-Azam University |
| 2 | Nabi-Karem-Batoor-Mahir-e-Nafsiat (Holy Prophet as a Psychotherapist) | Syeda Sadia Ghaznavi | 1989 | Zahid Publishers |
| 3 | Muslim Traditions in Psychotherapy and Modern Trends | Azhar Ali Rizvi | 1989 | Institute of Islamic Culture |
| 4 | Muslim psychology and positive psychology | Azhar Ali Rizvi | 1990 | IMP |
| 5 | Qu'ranic Concepts of Human Psyche | Zafar Afaq Ansari | 1992 | Adam Publishers |
| 6 | Traditions, paradigms, and basic concepts of Muslim psychology | Azhar Ali Rizvi | 1994 | IMP |
| 7 | Three chapters in Muslim Nafsiat kay khad-o-Khal (Features of Muslim Psychology). A book in Urdu about Muslim perspective in Psychology | Azhar Ali Rizvi, Naumana Umar and Amjad Tufail | 1997 | Markazi Urdu Board, Lahore |
| 8 | Muslim nafsiat kay khadokhal. (Features of Muslim Psychology) | Azhar Ali Rizvi | 1998 | IMP |
| 9 | Deviant behaviour in the light of Sufi concept of self | Naumana Amjad | 1998 | Al-Adwa, Islamic Centre, University of Punjab Press |
| 10 | Discourse between science and religion: The way out | Naumana Amjad | 1998 | IIIT |
| 11 | Muslim Nafsiat kay Khadokhal | Azhar Ali Rizvi | 1998 | IMP |

| | | | | |
|---|---|---|---|---|
| 12 | Holistic health, healing and spirituality | Latif | 2000 | Psyche Hope, Lahore |
| 13 | Quranic concept of psyche | Azhar Ali Rizvi | 2005 | IMP |
| 14 | Reading therapy | Azhar Ali Rizvi | 2005 | IMP |
| 15 | Taking Faith seriously in therapeutic psychology | Muhammad Tahir Khalily | 2018 | Institute for Research & Dialogue (IRD), Islamabad |
| 16 | Smartphone addiction and evidence-based intervention | Muhammad Tahir Khalily and Mujeeb Masood Bhatti | 2019 | IRD |
| 17 | Hijacked mind benign rage and malignant violence of humanoid. Dialogue, Islamabad Pakistan | Muhammad Tahir Khalily, Mujeeb Masood Bhatti, Tamkeen Saleem | 2020 | Iqbal International Institute of Research & Dialogue, IIUI |
| 18 | Islamic psychology | G. H. Rassool | 2021 | |

## Conferences

In addition to curriculum development, books, and research related to Islamic perspectives in psychology, many conferences were organized that focused on Muslim psychology, which later transpired into IPIP. SAMP was set up in 1974 and has conducted many conferences. The main objective of the conferences organized between 1995 and 2016 was to familiarize the students, professionals, and researchers with Islamic perspectives in psychology and build a skilled workforce of psychologists so that they could develop indigenized models and psychotherapies.

The 2nd International Conference on Mental Health was organized jointly by the Department of Psychology, IIUI, Pakistan the Kulliyah (Faculty) of Islamic Revealed Knowledge and Human Sciences, International Islamic University Malaysia (IIUM), International Institute of Islamic Thought in the U.S. and IAMP based in Indonesia. The conference was held on May 5 and 6, 2015, at IIUM, Kuala Lumpur, Malaysia. The focus of the conference was to integrate modern psychotherapeutic techniques with cultural and religious tools and practices, to make IP more effective and applicable. Another two-day International Conference on Islamic Awakening (ICIA) was held on July 14 and 15, 2018, at the Islamic University Maldives (IUM). At this joint collaborative venture of IUM, Male, Maldives, and the International Institute of Islamic Thought (IIIT) Islamabad where the presentation included 45 oral papers by scholars, academicians, and professors worldwide.

The three-day International Conference on "Islamic Perspectives in Modern Psychology" was held September 24–26, 2019, at the Royal Palm Golf & Country Club, Lahore. This conference was organized by Riphah International University and several pre- and post-conference workshops were conducted, for example, Islamic Model of Parenting and Islam and Psychoanalysis: Same Elements but Different Chemistry. The keynote speeches, for example, Living Islam and Psychology, An Evaluation of a Culturally Adapted Pain Management for Muslim Patients, Tazkia Therapy, Advancement of Islamic-based CBT, Spiritual Wisdom and Mental Illness, and Rediscovering Transpersonal Psychology, were delivered by eminent psychologists from around the world.

A conference held in Malaysia on October 12 and 13, 2019, was called Future of Education: Challenges for Traditional and Modern Approaches. The conference was organized by the Center for Peace and Global Studies Islamabad with the support of IIIT Malaysia and may have contributed to the development of IP. This conference advanced the critical and thoughtful account of the contemporary challenges of tradition and modernity in the overall area of the education and Tarbiyah of the students. However, many psychology professionals and researchers attended and presented their work, indicating that the Islamic perspectives of psychology are gaining interest.

These conferences made significant contributions to the Islamization of psychology in Pakistan and globally in both theory and clinical applications by motivating the participants to develop their practice and projects in line with Islamic teachings and perspectives. Hopefully, in subsequent years, more scholars will contribute evidenced-based approaches and practices, improved curriculums, and effective teaching strategies based on Islamic conceptions. Moreover, because of the growing interest in IP in Pakistan and at IIUI, an increasing number of students is interested in integrating Islamic perspectives with contemporary psychotherapies to obtain empirical evidence by studying various psychological theories and practicums integrated with IP during their master's and doctoral research.

| | CONFERENCE TITLE | ORGANIZATION | YEAR |
|---|---|---|---|
| 1 | 1st Muslim Psychology Conference in Pakistan | Society for Advancement of Muslim Psychology, Government College, Lahore | 19 March 1995 |
| 2 | 2nd Muslim Psychology Conference | Society for Advancement of Muslim Psychology | 1996 |
| 3 | 3rd Muslim Psychology Conference | Society for Advancement of Muslim Psychology, Government College, Lahore | March 1998 |
| 4 | 5th International Muslim Psychology Conference | Society for Advancement of Muslim Psychology, Government College, Lahore | February 16–18, 2001 |
| 5 | 6th International Muslim Psychology Conference | Society for Advancement of Muslim Psychology, Government College, Lahore | February 20–22, 2004 |
| 6 | 7th Muslim Psychological Conference on Advancement of Muslim Psychology | Society for Advancement of Muslim Psychology, Government College, Lahore Fountain House, Lahore | 2005 |
| 7 | 8th Muslim Psychology Conference | Society for Advancement of Muslim Psychology, Government College, Lahore Fountain House, Lahore | December 17–18, 2008 |
| 8 | 10th Muslim Psychology Conference | Society for Advancement of Muslim Psychology, Fountain House, Lahore | May 10–11, 2012 |
| 9 | 11th Muslim Psychological Conference | Society for Advancement of Muslim Psychology, Fountain House, Lahore | May 24–25, 2013 |
| 10 | 12th Muslim Psychology Conference on Muslim Psychology: Theory and Practice | Society for Advancement of Muslim Psychology, Fountain House, Lahore | November 10–11, 2014 |
| 11 | 13th Muslim Psychology Conference | Society for Advancement of Muslim Psychology, Fountain House, Lahore | November 27, 2015 |
| 12 | International Conference on Islamic Tradition in Psychology | Society for Advancement of Muslim Psychology, at Lahore School of Management, the university of Lahore, Pakistan | March 5, 2016 |

| 13 | 2nd International Conference on Mental Health | Department of Psychology, IIUI, Pakistan, the Kulliyah of Islamic Revealed Knowledge and Human Sciences, International Islamic University Malaysia (IIUM), International Institute of Islamic Thought in the U.S. and International Association of Muslim Psychologists based in Indonesia | May 5–6, 2015 |
|---|---|---|---|
| 14 | Two-day International Conference on Islamic Awakening (ICIA) | Islamic University Maldives (IUM), International Institute of Islamic Thought (IIIT), Islamabad Chapter | July 14–15, 2018 |
| 15 | 3-dayInternational Conference on "Islamic Perspectives in Modern Psychology" | Riphah International University | September 24–26, 2019 |
| 16 | International Conference on Future of Education: Challenges for traditional and modern approaches | Center for Peace and Global Studies and International Institute of Islamic Thought Malaysia | October 12–13, 2019 |

## Conclusion

The theoretical developments and therapeutic competencies in IP have been gaining interest in recent years. Historically, IP emerged as a discipline identified with the early contributions of Muslims scholars. Initially, the progress of Muslim psychology was passive because of the resistance to the radicalization of knowledge. Muslim psychologists were hesitant to integrate religion and science. However, after the contributions of Muslims psychologists who worked in environments where Western psychology was considered superior to other forms and Muslim contributions to psychology were labeled as backward and old-fashioned, the persistent efforts of attachment to the roots of Muslims psychology enabled many contemporary psychologists to think critically and innovatively and search for indigenous solutions for their native problems. Notably, we acknowledge the contributions of Western psychology to contemporary knowledge. These contributions are based on the Western experiences, cultures, norms, and values. However, a turning point was when contemporary Muslim psychologists integrated contemporary knowledge and modern techniques in a systematic manner. Consequently, the Muslim psychology became IP, which applies refined modern methodologies to resolve the psychological ailments in Pakistani society.

ACKNOWLEDGMENT: The authors are indebted to Dr. Amber Haque for preparing the initial outline of this chapter and for his efforts in the establishment of the IP scholarship for postgraduate students at IIUI, Pakistan.

## References

Ajmal, M. (1968). An introduction to Muslim tradition in psychotherapy. *Psychology Quarterly, 4*, 28–33.

Ajmal, M. (1986). *Muslim contribution to psychotherapy and other essays*. National Institute of Psychology, Quaid-i-Azam University.

Deuraseh, N., & Talib, M. A. (2005). Mental health in Islamic medical tradition. *The International Medical Journal, 4*(2), 76–79.

Haque, A. (2011, September 20). *Development of psychology in Pakistan* (online edition). Young Sociologist.

Haque, A. (2004). Psychology from Islamic perspective: Contributions of early Muslim scholars and challenges to contemporary Muslim psychologists. *Journal of Religion and Health, 43*(4), 357–377.

Haque, A. (1998). Psychology and religion: Their relationship and integration from an Islamic perspective. *American Journal of Islamic Social Sciences, 15*, 97–116.

Higher Education Commission (HEC). (2006). *Revised curriculum of psychology for BS (Hons) 4 years program and MS (Hons) 2 years program 2006*. Retrieved: https://www.google.com/url?sa=t&source=web&rct=j&url=https://hec.gov.pk/english/services/universities/RevisedCurricula/Documents/2005-2006/City%2520Regional-2006.pdf&ved=2ahUKEwj5krWTj-7uAhXSolwKHZmTCxkQFjABegQIGhAC&usg=AOvVaw1uYMPtJP82fPAveokAUER0

Rizvi, A. A. (1990). *Muslim psychology and positive psychology*. Institute of Muslim Psychology.

Rizvi, A. A. (1989). *Muslim tradition in psychotherapy and modern trends*. Institute of Islamic Culture.

Rizvi, A. A. (1998). *Muslimnafsiat kay khadokhal*. Urdu Science Board.

Rizvi, A.A. (1994). *Traditions, paradigms, and basic concepts of Muslim psychology*. Institute of Muslim Psychology.

Rizvi, A. A. (2005). *Quranic concept of psyche*. Institute of Muslim Psychology.

Rizvi, A. A. (2005). *Reading therapy*. Institute of Muslim Psychology.

Saeed, S. (2019). *Dr Muhammad Ajmal*. http://saadatsaeed.ca/DOC/Dr_Ajmal.htm

Salma, U. (2014). Scholarly and literary thoughts of Shah Mohammad Ghaus. *Journal of Research in Humanities and Social Science, 2*(3), 16–22.

Salma, U. (2010). Sufic vision of Shah Muhammad Ghaus and Shah Waliullah in the light of Quranic studies. *The Dialogue, 5*(3), 270–283.

Shahzad, M.N., Khan, A.Z., & Khalily, M.T. (2020). *An analysis of psychological developments, role and effects of early psychological experimental approaches in Pakistan.* Al-Qalam, 25(1), 277-288. Institute of Islamic Studies, University of the Punjab, Lahore, Pakistan.

CHAPTER ELEVEN

# Islamic Teaching-Informed Psychology and the Somali People: Current Practice and Future Directions

JIBRIL I.M HANDULEH
ABDIKANI ASKAR
ABDILAHI E MOMIN

ISLAM ORIGINATED IN the Arabian Peninsula in the 7th century and introduced in the northern Somali coast shortly after its inception, making Somali one of the earliest Muslim societies in the world. Somalis inhabit the horn of African countries, mainly Somalia, Djibouti, Ethiopia, and Kenya, in a transnational area known as the Somali Peninsula of the horn of Africa. Islamic teaching-informed psychology has a major influence on the lives of Somalis and, in turn, influences their culture. Islamic and other traditional healing methods had been the mainstream care for mental health disorders and psychological conditions for centuries in Somali communities. These traditions are still relevant in current psychological and psychiatry services in the Somali Peninsula, as well as in Somali communities living in other parts of the world, especially in Western and Middle East countries. In IP, practitioners are not healthcare professionals, but mostly clergy based in different private practice settings. IP education, curriculum, and practitioners are not found in Somalia as of now, but given the predominant Muslim population of Somalia, this is a promising clinical practice area for the Somali population.

## Introduction

This chapter on Islamic psychology will discuss the history and practical application of Islamic teachings in treating psychological distress and mental health disorders among Somali peoples. Although the chapter focuses on Somalia, a country in the horn of Africa bordering Djibouti, Ethiopia, and Kenya and south of the Arabian Peninsula, it will also present the state of Islamic psychology in the horn of Africa (Lewis, 1960) in general.

We discuss IP among Somali ethnic groups living in different countries. The Somali people inhabit a sizable portion of the horn of Africa, including present-day Somalia, Djibouti, Ethiopia, and Kenya. Both Ethiopia and Kenya have Somali regions with majority Somali populations. There are also large Somali communities in East Africa (Uganda and Tanzania), Southern and North African nations, and other world regions including Oceania, Europe, and North America. After the collapse of the Somali Republic in 1991, the country went into chaos with one of the longest civil wars in the world (Caverella et al. 2016).

The northern part of the country seceded from the rest of Somalia in May 1991, self-declaring the Republic of Somaliland, which lacks international recognition. On the northeast part of Somalia, Puntland constitutes an autonomous administrative state within the country. Finally, most of south-central Somalia has remained politically unstable for decades and subject to an ongoing civil war (CIA, 2013) in addition to climate change–attributed calamities (flooding, famine, droughts), which has placed an enormous strain on the mental health of Somalis (Somalia Relief, 2020).

Somalia has a particular diverse and rich geographic, social, cultural, and religious country profile. The country has African, Arab, and Muslim identities, which affects the ways mental health conditions are presented among Somalis (Somalia, 2020). Geographically, it is a sub-Saharan African nation, but its religion and psychopathological profiles are more like those in other Arab-Muslim nations. Somalia is a member of the World Health Organization—Eastern Mediterranean region, which is headquartered in Cairo, Egypt (WHO, 2020). Therefore, it has both African and Arabian identities. Most Somalis in the horn of Africa and those in the wider Somali diaspora have been Muslim, with a millennial tradition dating back to the early times of Islam in the Arabian Peninsula; Somalia's official religion is Islam (Handuleh, 2012). Official languages of the country are Somali and Arabic, with many inhabitants able to also speak English, French, and Italian; those living in neighboring countries speak in the official languages of Ethiopia (Amharic) and Kenya (Swahili).

This chapter presents the outcomes of a systematic literature review on IP in Somalia and the author's experience in working in the mental health field in the horn of Africa. Interviews with key informants in the field were not possible as most potential interviewees were not available, and the expert observations of the authors with significant practical work in the mental health field in the country are the sources of the information of this chapter. The authors outline a thorough history of IP and the practical application of IP to the treatment of mentally sick Somalis in the horn of Africa and among the Somali Diasporas. Lastly, the future directions of this discipline in the mental health delivery of Somalis around the world are discussed. The IP practices of Somali people are not well studied, but the current situation in this chapter is the first written on Somalia.

Islam reached the northwestern shores of the Somali coast in the early days of Islam, which dates to the time Prophet Mohamed was in Mecca before he emigrated. This means Islam was in the Somali peninsula before it was in its birthplace in Mecca. The best evidence for this is the landmark historical building in the Zeila town named the Qiblatain (two minaret mosques). This means Somalis have been Muslim for 14 centuries. Islam is part of the Somali society in every aspect of their lives, including perceptions of diseases and management of diseases.

The field of IP as such is not an established field in all Somali regions now part of Djibouti, Somalia, and two Somali dominated regions in Ethiopia and Kenya, but it is possible to soon have IP as an independent specialization. There are several colleagues who have IP qualifications mainly from Sudan. They mostly practice in academia, teaching in both universities and private institutions as a part of Islamic sharia. The IP practice is mainly in private practice where the practitioners are office based with outpatient services. This has been happening over the course of three decades, and almost all practitioners are male colleagues. The authors invited them for in-depth interviews, but they all declined to be contacted. According to Y.A. Abdi (personal communication, Dec. 2020), Mental Health Coordinator at Somaliland Ministry of Health, Hargeisa, Somaliland, the concepts of IP for Somalis are that Islam is the treatment of choice of not only psychological disorders, but also some other medical diseases are supposedly regarded as mediated through psychological distress that subsequently leads to medical illnesses.

Examples including medical conditions such as strokes, hemorrhoids, and some skin manifestations have Islamic psychology connotations that Quran heals heart, mind, and soul holistically based on Quranic teaching.

Many patients seek care in this growing field among Somalis. Islamic psychologists have positively and actively engaged with mental health professionals recently in different parts of the Muslim world, but they are reluctant to collaborate with other mental health professionals, dismissing anything not Islamic oriented as nontraditional and nonconventional for Somali people (Handuleh,

2012). In a careful search of the literature, the authors did not find work done on Islamic psychology that has been published in Somali, English, Arabic, French, or Italian, which are the languages widely spoken in the Somali territories, on Somali people within the horn of Africa and the diaspora.

In academia, IP is a short course that students pursue in their undergraduate medical school, which is a blending of Islamic ethics laws, medical ethics, and Islamic perspectives of both physical and psychological disorders. Amoud University in Borama, Somaliland, offers such courses in undergraduate medical and nursing schools. This has been in place for the last 3 years and became an official course as part of the undergraduate training. In psychiatry and psychology courses, it is not still part of the clinical undergraduate training in mental health, in which the lead author is a lead psychiatry faculty in Somaliland.

According to S. Ali (personal communication, Dec. 2020), Islamic Law lecturer at Amoud University School of Law in Borama, Somaliland, IP psychology is also a course offered for Sharia and Islamic law undergraduate and graduate training in Somaliland, which focus on the aspects of psychology where law, Islamic teaching, and patient care interact, particularly in areas of civil law including marriage, divorce, and child mental health. In a similar study addressing the Somali immigrants in London, United Kingdom, Somalis recognize mental health disorders as a religious problem. The communities trust their religious and community leaders in matters of treatment, particularly Islamic teaching-oriented services (Johnsdotter, et al. 2011).

There are six Islamic psychologists in the wider Somali peninsula practicing private Islamic psychology office work, and there are no conferences, associations, and other think tanks related to Islamic psychology in this part of the horn of Africa. Note that clinical psychologists trained in Western philosophy and Islamic psychologists have no collaboration. Islamic psychologists are isolated in their practice, mainly serving the religiously conservative part of the society.

Both academic and nonacademic practices are also in place. For instance, there are no books written on this subject on Somali diaspora and the Somali residents in East Africa. Therefore, the book chapter will address the direction of Islamic psychology among Somalis, how it will fit into psychological practice, and propose a possible collaboration strategy in the future.

## Islamic Teaching and Mental Health Interpretations among Somali Population

Somalis used to receive advice for their psychological needs from Islamic scholars. It is not only psychological treatment but also every health condition affecting a Somali person that is addressed with an Islamic healing process. Islamic religion plays a role in every aspect of Somali health-seeking behavior. Culture and religion are interconnected in the Somali perception of mental health disorders. Mental health distress and Islamic approaches are studied in the Western countries with Somali refugees. Owing to the civil unrest in Somalia, research on the Islamic interpretation of psychological problems is limited in the country. The bulk of evidence is generated in those high-income countries. Of note, Somali populations have blended their tribal culture with Islamic interpretation. Islamic teaching informs any aspect of mental health presentation of the Somali people. Somali patients first contact their local Sheikh or Imam on issues relating to their psychological well-being. In a study among Somali students in Minnesota, United States, Somali patients have consulted religious coping mechanisms for their mental health disorders such as anxiety and depression (Islam in Somalia, 2020). A study on Somali refugees in Kenya showed that religious leaders are mainly accepted by patients for consultation about mental health services instead of psychologists or psychiatrists (Areba et al., 2018).

All aspects of mental health services are informed with Islamic interpretation in terms of symptoms and presentation. For example, sleep and dissociation is interpreted as being mediated by "Rooxan," which is a culturally bound syndrome among the Somalis where the patient is possessed by either evil eye or ghosts. This is believed due to ghosts of ancestors or implanted by the person's enemy, while "Jinn" possession is when Jinn is supposed to cause a patient's illness. Sheikhs are the main delivery of services of behavioral disorders that are perceived as mediated through devils. This is illustrated in a study among the Somali Swedish community in Malmo; southern Sweden researchers recommend understanding the religious interpretation of Somali patients on their mental ill health, which hinders understanding the psychological distress of Somali patients living in countries where IP is not known (Mutiso et al., 2019). Somali regard mental illness as disorders related to Quran reading and better negotiating with Jinn instead of Western biomedical understanding of the etiology of mental health disorders (Mutiso et al., 2019).

Somali refugees in Rochester, New York, in the United States regarded that prayers and the Islamic teaching are the common modalities for their mental health disorders, which they interpreted as "Jinn" (possession), sadness ("Murugo" in Somali), and "Waali" (mental illness) (Palmer, 2006).

Research within Somali territories is basically nonexistent on the Islamic translations of mental health. In the author's field experiences, Somali patients seek the Islamic way of treatment informed by the Quran reading as well as Sunnah and herbal medication use with Islamic medicine. Mental health treatment is one of the last resorts, which delays visits to psychiatrists, psychologists, or even general practitioners. Psychological supportive therapy sessions are common in Hargeisa and Mogadishu, which are the largest Somali cities where Sheikhs in private service offer mental health services. In the last two decades there is a growing trend of Quran reading sessions, which are conducted in a group therapy and individual therapy, where Sheikhs who are only trained in Quran and Sunnah offer treatment. Islamic teaching healing now excludes the cultural aspects of mental health treatment as previously done with Sufi Sheikhs.

Jinn removal, evil eye, and Sihr (conspiracy by an enemy) are the most common meanings given to ill mental health conditions. The interpretation when done by less-trained Sheikhs leads to human rights violations such as waterboarding patients with water cannons. This is the practice of some Sheikhs who advocate removing jinn via beating, waterboarding, and use of electrical wires, and this is mainly broadcast live or in recorded sessions via social media. Platforms such as Facebook, YouTube, and Western European–based Somali language TV stations are also a source of those Islamic practice-oriented works. There is overall lack of understanding of mental health disorders, which mainly sends many patients to Sheikhs who may not be experts in any form of care including IP.

## Islamic Tradition and Somali Perception of Psychological Issues

Somalis are one of the earliest communities to embrace Islam before the Arabs themselves. The Arab and Persian migrants came in several waves, bringing with them Islam and their respective traditions (Ahmed, 1995). Somali tradition is Muslim oriented, and the Islam religion shapes many aspects of Somali cultural belief and tradition. It is of great note that Somalis consulted their Islamic faith in issues relating to psychological problems. Lewis points out that Saar is a culturally bound syndrome among Somalis in the horn of Africa and the diaspora. At the same time, the Saar has its own informed treatment regimen for mental health disorders. It was one of the traditional ways of presenting mental distress like trance, anxiety disorders, and depression (Lewis, 1998). This culturally bound syndrome has been disappearing among the Somali people in the last three decades because of the philosophical and cultural shift of the Somali people. The change is mainly religious and cultural transformation.

There are two faces of this special issue. There is IP practice before the 1990s, and after the 1990s a new approach was on the horizon. In the earlier days, Somalis had Sufi Islam. Sufi practice has many psychological contributions to Islamic-oriented psychology in which the traditional Sheikh is also a healer for both physical and mental health diseases. This includes the tradition of Saar that involves the boundary between a traditional interpretation of mental health issue and application of Islamic tradition, which has been based on Islamic knowledge via Somali Sufi Islam teaching. Saar spirits are Jinn/devil caused in the eye of Somalis that Sufi scholars used to heal through Quran reading. The reading of the Quran and sacrificing the Jinn with dancing and meat were the traditions. They used dancing and Quran citation as IP modality of patient care.

From 1990 onwards, the conservative radicalized ideology of Wahhabi Islam penetrated Somali culture, which corrupted the understanding of the Somali people of their faith and Islam-oriented treatment infiltrated into Somali society (Kroessin & Mohamed, 2008). This is related to not only traditional aspect of the IP but also every part of the country's population. In Sweden, the conflict of the two classes of elder community—the Sufi way of interpreting of mental health disorder and the conservative Wahhabi teaching—was apparent (Wedal, 2011).

In a comparative study among Somali diaspora in Finland and Somalis in Somaliland, the same trend of understanding the transnational aspects of Islamic interpretation of mental health disorders would be of value to Somali patients with psychological problems. It is understood it is important in the horn of Africa and in the diaspora.

Somalis have difficulty accessing mental health clinics because of differences in religion and culture in the countries that offer them asylum. They reason that this is due to lack of understanding of their religion (Tiilikainen & Kohen 2011, Ellis et al., 2010).

Islamic psychology scholarship in knowledge generation as social scientists, anthropologists, and researchers studied in Western countries does not exist in Somalia and in the diaspora, and Somalis do not contribute to this.

There are no institutions in the Somali inhabited territories that register and license practitioners of the field. The authors also could not locate committees and IP related think tanks in the country. Therefore, ethical principles of practicing among them are not known, or research they produce is not now available.

IP understanding is relevant for many professionals where Somali people live because not understanding the Islamic ways of expressing their condition in places where there is no IP leads them to seek treatment elsewhere. A New Zealand study reveals cultural and religious competence to Somali Muslim patients (Guerin et al., 2004) who were lost to treatment due to lack of understanding. IP practiced in appropriate ways that adjust to the modern needs of the Somali Muslim population is vital.

## Current Practice and Trends of Islamic Psychology in the Region and the Diaspora

Islamic psychologists have private office practice in most of their clinical work as their practice is limited. They meet patients and do Islamic-informed mental health clinical psychotherapy. These are individual psychotherapy sessions and sometimes group therapy. They use techniques such as reading, ruqya/exorcism to expel Jinn, and cupping addressed for Islamic psychology management. There is no formal training for the practitioners, and they claim to base their practice on the Quran and Sunnah teachings. They do not have clinical psychological training. This is not also part of traditional healer practices. They do not integrate cultural, religious, and Western psychology principles. This practice attracts many patients to the horn of Africa, or they go to the Arabian Gulf states where they can get such services. There are instances of Somalis who also practice this in Western countries (Naess,2020; Eneborg, 2013). This practice is popular with both Somalis in East Africa and in the diaspora due to limited number of Somali psychiatrists and psychologists.

Somalis in the West prefer to access their psychological care via some Sheikhs who perform this practice via television in live sessions when they present their conditions to their Sheikh. Examples of such programs are aired in Somali-speaking television stations in the United Kingdom (Al Ruqyah Al-Shariah, 2020).

Within Somalia, there are Sheikhs who are not trained in IP who deliver Islam-informed psychological treatments who use social media such as YouTube and Facebook (Ruqyah Al Shariah, 2020). They are popular among Somalis everywhere. Those practitioners. if not well controlled. have both legal and ethical risks to the Somali people, as they are the gateway to pathways of mental health delivery, but they do not refer those who may need psychiatric or IP treatment on time, which delays their overall prognosis. Authors witnessed many such patients who have been denied proper access to health care by those practitioners.

## Sociocultural Implications of Islamic Teaching for Somalis

Somalis regard anything that happens to them is from God. They regard mental health as something society cannot judge, but Allah can take it away. Some regard losing of mind (psychological disturbance) as a sign of discord with God, as this is observed in both diaspora and at home (Mölsä, Hjelde & Tiilikainen, 2010). Bettmann and his colleagues found that Somali patients in the United States regard Quran as the treatment of choice for psychological needs (Bettmann et al., 2015) rather than IP, which is not known through Somali society.

Many Somali patients suffer from mental health and comorbid substance use disorders. Khat use, which is a stimulant substance prevalent in Southern Arabia and East Africa, is a major cause of mental health disorder among Somalis. Many Somali patients with disorders like Khat use disorders present with psychosis with religious contents, and patients may be referred for shifting delusions. The religious nature of a patient determines the source of treatment as some may not seek clinical care (Kroll, Yusuf, & Fujiwara, 2011).

An Italian researcher reports that herbals are used for psychological treatment and are based on cultural practices and Islamic teaching on herbal medicine (Reggi, 2014). The authors observed that patients use herbal medications that the Islamic scholar gives for psychological relief.

As Islamic psychology is not available in the country, there are Sheikhs who take the role of the Islamic treatment, which has a combination of Quran and herbs. They sometimes employ psychiatrists as the Sheikhs in those facilities offer inpatient service. They combine medical treatment and Quran reading. These centers are known as Cilaaj or Healing Centers (Tiilikainen, 2012). In the Somali regions this is a popular mode of psychological services. This is a growing mental health care trend that IP is a part of, but it has some commercial implications that can put patients at risk due to financial exploitation through the name of religion. They propose Quran teaching but have no "psychological" component of it. The quality of care is quite questionable in those settings where patients are given medications by less trained "mental health practitioners" and Sheikhs who are not psychology trained, whether Islamic or any form of psychological training.

Cilaaj centers tend to be one of the settings where Islamic psychology can be found now, although private office practice also is a player of the field. Because of the Somali region's huge burden of mental health disorders, the services, if they exist, are just the tip of the iceberg in terms of whoever treats patients with psychological problems. These kinds of services are mainly either inpatient or outpatient settings that address treatment and rehabilitation of people with severe mental health disorders. Although this is usually crowded with poor working and living conditions, it remains a big part of psychological practice in the Somali territories and countries in East Africa. However, it is not part cultural or psychiatry/psychological treatment modality. In the meantime, it stands as Islamic teaching–oriented mental health service delivery in this part of the world. This is standing alone in most times, but in the last few years, there is a collaboration between general practitioners who practice mental health and Sheikhs. Sheikhs do religious treatment and general practitioners or nurses who are trained as mental health providers do psychopharmacological treatment. This seems a way that those practitioners work. World Health Organization estimates that one of three Somali has severe mental health disorder (WHO, 2011), which is higher than any other country in low- and middle-income countries. This means any services that are accessible and affordable for Somali people would alleviate the suffering, but many of them are apparently not safe institutions for patients and their families, with many Somali people being just imprisoned in those settings.

Those places are usually crowded with many patients who are mainly suffering from severe mental health disorders. Currently, IP operates in a way that is commercial in addressing mental health in general. This is not Islamic psychology as it is known in the Muslim world or in the West where Muslim psychologists practice, but it is unique to the Somali context with its circumstances, which is shaped by prolonged civil wars and lack of professionally trained practitioners. This is a result of an institutional and human resource–related vacuum, which is the direct consequence of strong training schools and the migration of the country's skilled workforce due to a three-decade-long civil unrest. The aforementioned approach for the religious figures puts many clinically distressed patients at risk when they try to treat patients that would best benefit from pharmacological treatment, which again brings issues of chaining of patients to control them when medications are scarce, and expertise is lacking. Some IP practitioners refer their patients for mental health assessment. Oftentimes, they work independently, which puts many patients at risk and makes the chaining of patients a way to control disturbing patients.

Somalia is part of the Arab world, and it has one of the least developed mental health services in the region. The presentation of mental health disorders fits most to Muslim and Arab understanding of mental health disorders (Okasha, Karam & Okasha, 2012), which is different from other African countries that share borders with the Somali peninsula such as Ethiopia, Eritrea, and Kenya. Mental health psychopathology and understanding of mental health presentations are unique for Somalis. They share mental health perceptions with other Muslim and Arab nations. The symptoms are mainly presented with Muslim views of mental health disorders.

## Islamic Psychology and Psychotherapy

In the Somali society, IP will hold important areas of work in family therapy. Family and marriage discord is an increasing trend in both diaspora and the horn of Africa region. Somalis tend to consult their religious leaders on issues of family importance, which also includes child and adolescent issues. Somalis would not lean to psychotherapy but would seek their Sheikh for psychotherapy sessions. This inspires many of them to have their own programs on television to discuss psychological issues on the air but with no psychology training.

Raising children and prioritizing Islamic education is a promising area where

IP can be of strong value to Somali society. Nowadays, university students question their mental health well-being, and the primary contact is their local mosque or Sheikh with understanding of IP or a motivational speaker.

Among the limited number of IP practitioners, psychotherapy and other potential practitioners such as social workers are areas where they commit to practice, but given the higher number of demands, they have difficulty allocating counseling time for their patients.

Women's mental health is another important area; women with psychological disorders seek clinicians with Western psychology and psychiatry in the Somali region for care. Women with psychiatric disorders, mainly depression, dissociative disorders, and conversion disorder, first seek consultation from IP practitioners and the clinical psychologists or psychiatrists are second and third in line for assistance.

Because of the Islamic understanding of Somali patients, for non-psychotic disorders, they seek Islamic psychology advice for them.

Authors with significant number of years of clinical psychiatry practice in the Somali peninsula rarely meet patients with conversion disorder or dissociative trances in their practice. As dissociation is associated with psychological trauma, those patients with acute stress or post-traumatic stress disorder seek IP advice for their symptoms.

## Islamic Psychology and Psychotic Disorders

Delusional disorders and religious interpretation of any psychotic delusion and hallucination is perceived as mediated through action of Jinn/Sihr. They intend consulting IP colleagues for this condition as Quran is regarded as the treatment from the Somali practice.

In the authors' clinical practice experience, there are many examples where whole families claim that Sihr was used to affect the people and give distress. Somalis do not regard suicidality and aggressive behavior as psychological problems and take this as a sin discouraged by religious teachings.

## Future Directions of Islamic Psychology for the Somali People

It is apparent that Islamic psychology will become a discipline of practice for Somali people. Somalis are predominantly Muslim, and this attracts the attention of the public in seeking care where they prefer this as their point of entry. Somalia is in a state of mental health emergency where many factors affect the mental health situation in the country.

It is a matter of time before IP will organize themselves and set standards for their specialty. This will be from the start in terms of services, organizing themselves, and teaching to the next generation of practitioners. Collaboration between clinical psychology, psychiatry, and social workers will be important to help patients access services both in the horn of Africa and in the diaspora. Strong regulation and licensing are an important area, and the medical council will license the professionals to meet their clinical and ethical responsibilities. National data on IP and its practice are lacking from the Somali peninsula. The studies in Western countries inform service utilization and access to services but do not discuss issue of IP practice for Somalis in the diaspora. It is in the benefit of the Somali population to have qualified, registered, and certified IP professionals work closely with psychiatrists and socialists to address mental health disorders holistically.

IP has a promising place in the mental health industry of the Somali people. Word of mouth is the common way of communication in Somali society.

Learning from IP practices from other countries such as the International Association of Islamic Psychology (IAIP) and making Somali Islamic Psychology Association would be vital to make the profession morally grounded and safe for Somalis. Somali people do not know IP as a practice. IP as a new specialty of contemporary psychology will need to present itself to the public and work closely with nonpracticing Islamic scholars as they have a strong voice in the community. This may include collaborating with other Muslim countries or other institutions that offer Islamic psychology to deliver training in this field and work with psychiatrists who are being currently trained for the country from many countries to establish IP as a psychosocial discipline in the country.

## Pitfalls for Potential Islamic Psychology for Somalis

One pitfall is the lack of professional service foundation where non-IP specialists claim the profession could jeopardize the dignity of such services. There are Sheikhs who are trained as religious scholars and claim via Ruqya Sharia that they are IP specialists, sometimes suggesting dangerous modes of treatment. IP communities will need to keep in mind that such potential malpractices could easily get out of hand. Patients would also need to have support groups to advocate them for services deemed to be of benefit to them. IP specialists would seek to make sure their practice is in consistent with the Islamic psychology practice around the world, the good example being the International Association of Islamic Psychology, which is an authority in this area of practice. In conclusion, collaboration with other mental health professionals and with the ministry of health to set up regulation and code of practice for this practice is needed.

## References


Ahmed, A. J. (Ed.). (1995). *The invention of Somalia*. Lawrenceville, NJ: The Red Sea Press

Al-Ruqiya Sharciya, Universal Somali TV, https://www.youtube.com/watch?v=RKVL_t9-1KU accessed October 14, 2020.

Areba, E. M., Duckett, L., Robertson, C., & Savik, K. (2018). Religious coping, symptoms of depression and anxiety, and well-being among Somali college students. *Journal of Religion and Health*, 57(1), 94-109.

Bettmann, J. E., Penney, D., Clarkson Freeman, P., &Lecy, N. (2015). Somali refugees' perceptions of mental illness. *Social Work in Health Care*, 54(8), 738-757.

Cavallera, V., Reggi, M., Abdi, S., Jinnah, Z., Kivelenge, J., Warsame, A. M., & Ventevogel, P. (2016). Culture, context, and mental health of Somali refugees: A primer for staff working in mental health and psychosocial support programmes. Geneva: United Nations High Commissioner for Refugees.

Central Intelligence Agency. (2013, January 4). *The World Fact book 2012-13*. Central Intelligence Agency.

Ellis, B. H., Lincoln, A. K., Charney, M. E., Ford-Paz, R., Benson, M., & Strunin, L. (2010). Mental health service utilization of Somali adolescents: Religion, community, and school as gateways to healing. *Transcultural Psychiatry*, 47(5), 789-811.

Eneborg, Y. M. (2013). Ruqya Shariya: Observing the rise of a new faith healing tradition amongst Muslims in east London. *Mental Health, Religion and Culture*, *16*(10), 1080-1096.

Guerin, B., Guerin, P. B., Diiriye, R. O., & Yates, S. (2004). Somali conceptions and expectations concerning mental health: Some guidelines for mental health professionals. *New Zealand Journal of Psychology*, 33(2), 59-67.

Handuleh, J. (2012). Experiences of a junior doctor establishing mental health services in Somaliland. *Intervention*, *10*(3), 274-278.

Islam in Somalia, https://en.wikipedia.org/wiki/Religion_in_Somalia accessed on September 28, 2020.

Johnsdotter, S., Ingvarsdotter, K., Östman, M., & Carlbom, A. (2011). Koran reading and negotiation with jinn: Strategies to deal with mental ill health among Swedish Somalis. *Mental Health, Religion and Culture*, 14(8), 741-755.

Kroessin, M. R., & Mohamed, A. S. (2008). Saudi Arabian NGOs in Somalia: 'Wahabi'da'wah or humanitarian aid? In *Development, civil society and faith-based organizations* (pp. 187-213). London: Palgrave Macmillan.

Kroll, J., Yusuf, A. I., & Fujiwara, K. (2011).Psychoses, PTSD, and depression in Somali refugees in Minnesota. *Social Psychiatry and Psychiatric Epidemiology*, *46*(6), 481-493.

Lewis, I. M. (1960). The Somali conquest of the Horn of Africa. *The Journal of African History*, *1*(2), 213-230.

Lewis, I. M. (1998). *Saints and Somalis: Popular Islam in a clan-based society*. Lawrenceville, NJ: The Red Sea Press.

Mölsä, M., Hjelde, K., & Tiilikainen, M. (2010). Changing conceptions of mental distress among Somalis in Finland. *Transcult Psychiatry, 47*(2), 276-300.

Mutiso, V., Warsame, A. H., Bosire, E., Musyimi, C., Musau, A., Isse, M. M., & Ndetei, D. M. (2019). Intrigues of accessing mental health services among urban refugees living in Kenya: The case of Somali refugees living in Eastleigh, Nairobi. *Journal of Immigrant and Refugee Studies, 17*(2), 204-221.

Næss, A. (2020). Migration, gender roles, and mental illness: The case of Somali immigrants in Norway. *International Migration Review, 54*(3), 740-764.

Okasha, A., Karam, E., & Okasha, T. (2012). Mental health services in the Arab world. *World Psychiatry, 11*(1), 52-54.

Palmer, D. (2006). Imperfect prescription: Mental health perceptions, experiences and challenges faced by the Somali community in the London Borough of Camden and service responses to them. *Primary Care Mental Health, 4*(1), 45-56.

Reggi, M. (2014). Il Tempo Lungodella Violenza. Etnografiadella Salute Mentalenella Somalia Contemporanea. [Unpublished]: Università di Milano-Bicocca.

Ruqyah Al Shariah- Mini mosque, https://www.facebook.com/Ruqyah-Al-Shariah-Mini-Mosque-130420060442020/ accessed October 14, 2020.

Somalia, Relief web, https://reliefweb.int/country/som accessed September 28, 2020.

Somalia, https://en.wikipedia.org/wiki/Somalia accessed September 28, 2020.

Tiilikainen, M., & Koehn, P. H. (2011). Transforming the boundaries of health care: Insights from Somali migrants. *Medical Anthropology, 30*(5), 518-544.

Tiilikainen, M. (2012). Somali health care system and post-conflict hybridity [Internet]. Afrikan Sarvi, http://afrikansarvi.fi/issue4/42-artikkeli accessed October 14, 2020.

Wedel, J. (2011). Mental health problems and healing among Somalis in Sweden. *Bildhaan: An International Journal of Somali Studies, 11*, 73-89.

World Health Organization, Eastern Mediterranean regional office, http://www.emro.who.int/countries/somalia/index.html accessed on September 28, 2020.

CHAPTER TWELVE

# Direct and Indirect Developments of Islamic Psychology in South Africa

JURAIDA LATIF
SHAAKIRAH D. BODA

THERE IS GREAT diversity in the ethnic and racial composition of Muslims in South Africa that dates to the 1600s. In South Africa, Muslims are in the minority, and they form distinct subgroups in which attitudes, cultures, and traditions candiffer. These differences have an impact on the Muslim perception of psychology and its therapeutic application. Mainstream psychology in South Africa is a product of Western culture, and this has become a particularly salient issue because this brand of psychology is unable to meet the needs of different religious, racial, and ethnic groups. To address such areas of need, Muslim academics, scholars, professionals, and practitioners began the process of integration by looking at the psychological traditions found in other cultures and more specifically within Islam in relation to different forms of therapy based on the Islamic Prophetic teachings. Locally speaking, this growing interest in the field of Islamically oriented psychology—more popularly referred to as "Islamic Psychology"—has, over the last decade, become increasingly prevalent even though differentially contextualised. Islamic Psychology takes a holistic view of the person as a dynamic balance between the body, inner heart, self, intellect, and spirit.

## Islam and its historical context in South Africa

A befitting start to this chapter is a short discussion of how Islam came to South Africa. The earliest record of Muslim migration to southern Africa dates to the mid-1600s, particularly the Cape of Good Hope (present-day Western Cape located in the southernmost part of Africa). Migrants predominantly comprised slaves and political exiles who were in resistance against Dutch colonisers (Tayob, 1996). This suggests that Islam in South Africa was primarily the result of Dutch interest in the Far East and the corporate ambition of the Dutch East India Company, founded in 1602 by a coterie of Dutch merchants. Apart from the thousands of slaves who arrived at the Cape, princes, emirs, advisors, and imams were banished from the Indonesian archipelago from 1667 to 1793 (Shell, 2006). Among the migrants were religious scholars who played central and decisive roles in laying down spiritual foundations for the emerging Muslim communities in the Cape, who later became symbols of resistance against the ugly faces of oppression.

In the 1800s, Indian plantation workers, merchants, and traders from different cities in India, such as Calcutta, Madras, Bombay, and Gujarat, to name a few, arrived in Natal and Transvaal, which are the northern and eastern parts of South Africa. By the mid-nineteenth century, Islam became attractive to many others who were not migrants, and this translated into a considerable number of locals converting to Islam (Gunther, 2018). The different historical and geographical roots still, to some extent, influence the Muslim minority in South Africa in terms of ethnic, linguistic, cultural, and socioeconomic division and differentiation. Using an external lens, it first appears that these differences did not affect theological and religious practices; however, a closer look reveals that this is not the case.

South Africa is well known for the Apartheid regime. The year 1948 heralded a transition from colonialism to apartheid—the final erosion of black rights in South Africa and a focus solely on white Afrikaner privilege (Gunther, 2018). Cultural and ethnic backgrounds reinforced the "racial demarcation" of the regime. The Group Areas Act, or forced removals, shifted thousands of black South Africans to state-allocated ghettos or Bantustans. Muslims, who were classified "Indian" or "Malay," were not spared. Despite the segregation through racial classification, religious practices were not affected by the apartheid regime (Tayob, 1996).

Different subsets of the Muslim population had different reactions to Apartheid (Quinn & Quinn, 2003). The Muslim community's response to apartheid was either sullen submission or fierce resistance. Many South Africans died in protests, political executions, and state-stirred conflicts. Thousands of South

African Muslims resisted apartheid, joining civic associations, trade unions, and organisations. Muslims in South Africa come from a variety of ethnicities and classes and speak different languages, and because of Apartheid, these divisions run deep (Nadvi, 2008; Vahed, 2007).

Since 1994, the South African community has been strengthened by thousands of refugees, economic migrants, and academics from Africa, the Indian subcontinent, and the Middle East. Unlike recent immigrants in countries such as the United States, Muslims in South Africa are well integrated in terms of language and general culture (Quinn & Quinn, 2003). They are, however, very much in the minority, consisting of approximately 4% of the population.

## Perceptions of psychology and treatment by South African Muslims

Following Apartheid, Muslims in South Africa were faced with redefining their identities along religious as opposed to political lines (Nadvi, 2008; Vahed, 2007). Consequently, Muslims in South Africa formed distinct subgroups within which attitudes and traditions may differ. Psychological research involving Muslims is scarce internationally (Sheridan & North, 2004), and little is known about how Islamic Psychology and therapy is perceived among the various subgroups of South African Muslims.

Islam has a long and complex psychological tradition, one that has not experienced the West's division between religion and psychology (Skinner, 2010). Islam takes a holistic view of the person as a dynamic balance between the body, inner heart, self, intellect, and spirit (Haque, 2004). When an imbalance occurs between these entities, the person experiences illness, either physical or spiritual (Skinner, 2010).

Similarly, treatment may involve an intervention that is physical, spiritual, or both (Ally & Laher, 2008). Faith is considered a powerful healer and essential to recovery (Youssef & Deane, 2006). Lowenthal, Cinnirella, Evdoka, and Murphy (2001) argue that Muslims tend to believe—more than any other religious group—in the efficacy of religious coping mechanisms for mental illness. In Islam, believers often refer to 'the will of Allah' and accept their illness as such and do not turn to professional or any other form of help (Rack, 1982). Perhaps more importantly, illness can be perceived as a symptom of distance from God, which should be treated by restoring faith and drawing closer to God (Haque, 2004). Therefore, amongst many South African Muslims, choosing to see a psychologist may be perceived as both compounding the issue of separation from God and a betrayal of faith (Weatherhead & Daiches, 2010), which is why in the past, and to a lesser extent in the present, many South African Muslims either choose to not seek help or to seek help from sheikhs and imams in their local communities. Another common barrier to seeking psychological assistance, particularly among the South African Indian Muslim male community, is the element of patriarchy and the notion that men do not need help. Furthermore, within that same community there persists a strong view that only crazy people need to see psychologists.

From an academic perspective, in the past, there were a few studies on mental health in Muslim communities (Abu-Raiya & Pargament, 2011), and these few indicate that in Western countries, Muslim populations underuse mental health services (Weatherhead & Daiches, 2010). Even though this has changed somewhat and there are more studies globally, in South Africa, very few studies exist. It is difficult to generalise international results to local Muslims, but it comes as no surprise that a similar reality exists within the South African context, although this would require empirical studies to confirm. Studies conducted in Western countries involve immigrant populations, whereas the South African Muslim population is well integrated into South African society (Quinn & Quinn, 2003). This creates some significant differences between Muslim populations in South Africa and those internationally. As such, the gap in literature is a clear one and perhaps an area that needs further work.

Muslim psychologists, practising in mainstream paradigms in South Africa, have noticed a distinct shift in the South African community regarding the integration of Islam into everyday life. In addition, a Muslim client's interpretation of mental health must have some linkage to or incorporation with their faith. For a mental health treatment plan to be successful, it too would need to be integrated with Islamic tradition (Weatherhead & Daiches, 2010). Without some knowledge of Islam and the ability to integrate its principles into treatment, it is unlikely that a Western practitioner could provide the help that is needed (Cinnirella & Loewenthal, 1999).

It might be beneficial to mention two South African studies that highlight how illnesses are perceived and classified as well as how these perceptions are integrated into therapy by lay counsellors. Before we begin, it is important to define what a volunteer or lay counsellor is in terms of these studies. A lay counsellor and/or volunteer is someone who works for the community primarily because they chose to do so (Kashyap, 2004). Volunteering is something that can be done as part of a non-profit organisation and is often viewed as official volunteering; however, people also choose to volunteer their services in times of crisis on an individual or group basis (Kashyap, 2004). A volunteer receives no monetary or other form of compensation for their services; however, they may be reimbursed for personal money spent for the services rendered (Bond, 1993).

In the first South African study, illness was perceived as having two possible causes, mundane or spiritual. Illnesses with mundane causes were considered to fall within the domain of Western practitioners (Ally & Laher, 2008). For spiritually caused illnesses, treatment from a doctor or psychologist was considered insufficient since it would only mask the symptoms. To cure the illness, a spiritual intervention would be required to remove its source. Islam was an integral part of how the study sample perceived the psychological makeup of a person, the sources of potential illness, and treatment options. However, there was also an emphasis on collaboration with other practitioners.

The second South African study examined lay counsellors/volunteers to determine their understanding of mental illness and to establish the role played by the religion of Islam, if any, on the perceptions of mental illness. In addition, the study explored whether a stigma towards mental illness exists within the community and what effect the stigma may or may not have on the understanding and treatment of mental illness. The study was conducted with a community-based, non-profit organisation that depends largely on the services of volunteers to assist with its telephone-based, one-to-one counselling services (Laher & Moosa, 2007). This organisation operates within the premise that people in the community can work towards alleviating certain mental illnesses. Significantly, as a community-based non-profit, the volunteers understand the people who utilise the services on a deeper level and want to give back to their community (Laher & Moosa, 2007).

It is also said:

> "*The believers, men and women, are Auliya (helpers, supporters, friends, protectors) of one another...*" (Qur'an, 9:71, trans. 2001)

This implies that it is the duty of every Muslim to provide relief and aid to others (Al-Qarni, 2002, trans. 2003).

It is therefore not surprising that several volunteers at this organisation felt that counselling was done for the pleasure of the Almighty (God). Others reported counselling as a way of giving back to the community. They also reported experiencing an internal fulfilment from the work they did and felt that playing a role and having a positive impact on someone's life was worthwhile (Laher & Moosa, 2007). This suggests that their cultural and religious values influence their decision to volunteer (Roberts, 2002).

The findings of this study suggest that one's religious and cultural beliefs play an imperative role in an individual's perception of mental illness. It also implies that the values and beliefs held by a specific community may influence an individual's choice of treatment for a mental illness. Furthermore, it is suggested that the existence of stigma within this community towards people with mental illnesses may also play a role in an individual's perception of mental illness and the route they choose regarding treatment.

No other known studies exist in South Africa involving Muslim lay-people, and rates of uptake of mental health services among Muslims in South Africa are unknown as it stands.

Nell (1990) suggests that mainstream psychology needs to be expanded to include different approaches in specific areas of need. One way to begin this process of integration is to look at psychological traditions found in other cultures. Islam is of particular interest since it has a rich psychological tradition of its own (Haque, 2004), and while Muslims are in the minority in South Africa, Islam nevertheless maintains a significant presence (Vahed, 2007).

## Contributions by South African Muslims in academic and practical spheres

Against this backdrop, this chapter aims to address the work that has been done based on personal communication by Muslims in South Africa in terms of their approach to psychology from an Islamic perspective. This perspective includes the incorporation of other Islamic holistic therapies from the Sunnah, which has been achieved at an academic level as well as at a practical level at various organisations in South Africa.

At the academic level, we begin with the highly recognised and respected Yasien Mohamed, the Emeritus Professor of Arabic Studies and Islamic Philosophy, Department of Foreign Languages, University of the Western Cape, South Africa. He has authored over 100 peer-reviewed articles on classical Islamic philosophy, Islamic Psychology, Qur'anic ethics, and modern Islamic thought. He is a founding member of the International Association of Islamic Psychology (IAIP) and recipient of the international award-winning book, *The Path to Virtue: The Ethical Philosophy of al-Raghib al-Isfahani.* He also authored the well-known book, *Fitrah: The Islamic Concept of Human Nature* (Mohamed, 1996). He currently teaches a postgraduate module in Contemporary Islamic Thought at the International Peace College of South Africa.

On an academic level, there are currently no courses being taught in Islamic Psychology except those previously taught by Professor Mohamed in 2008 at the International Peace College. There, he taught a group of approximately 20 undergraduate students a module on Islamic Psychology. The prescribed textbook was *The Psychology of Personality: Islamic Perspectives* (2008), edited by Amber Haque and Yasien Mohamed. It is the first edited volume of selected papers on human nature and personality from an Islamic perspective. The text clarifies the conceptual confusion that resulted in keeping psychology separate from religion, separate from a soul. The authors have incorporated religious and transcendental concepts that shape human personality based on the Quran and the works of early Muslim scholars.

*The Psychology of Personality* is not a book on psychotherapy; however, its views on human nature are important for the development of an Islamic approach to therapy. The text is timely due to the increased attention being given to Islam's significance in the lives of more than one billion believers, and because modern psychology is demonstrating a new interest in alternative perspectives of psychology. It is hoped that this work will stimulate further research on the psychology of personality based on Islamic assumptions of human nature.

Furthermore, Professor Mohamed has recently published a paper through the Yaqeen Institute titled "Perspectives on Islamic Psychology: al Raghib al Isfahani on the Healing of Emotions in the Quran." The paper deals with the immoderate emotions of fear, anger, and sorrow and how these emotional states can be healed by changing one's perspective.

In terms of practical application in South Africa, the following organisations supplement the social department of the Jamiatul Ulema of South Africa, which was established in 1923 for the purpose of serving the religious needs of Muslims. The registered non-profit organisations include the Islamic Careline in Johannesburg, the Islamic Hopeline in Pretoria, and the Islamic Helpline in Lenasia. Two of these organisations, namely Islamic Careline and Islamic Helpline, are highlighted for purposes of this discussion.

The need for the establishment of the Islamic Careline in Johannesburg was realised in 1992 when three Muslim women who were working in the field identified the need for professional psychosocial services in the community. These services began from a predominately Western lens of psychology. All three women were doing voluntary work at counselling organisations during the late 1980s. The fact that an increasing number of Muslims were seeking these services prompted them to explore the possibility of an Islamic-based counselling service for the local community.

The needs assessment showed a definite gap in this field, and together with the Jamiatul Ulama of South Africa the women recruited, trained, and supervised five volunteers who opened the doors of the Islamic Careline offices on 4 May 1992. Today, Islamic Careline is a registered non-governmental organisation that has grown to include and offer a wide variety of services to the entire community. These services include counselling for marital, drug, and family problems; career counselling; assessments; play therapy; trauma debriefing; reversions to Islam; bereavement counselling; community development programmes; support groups; basic counselling skills training; and poverty reduction programmes.

The staff and volunteers are academically trained and include social workers, psychologists, psychometrists, and other social science professionals. Ongoing in-service training ensures that counselling is done efficiently, and professional standards are always maintained. The foundation for counselling models that are used for all training is based on Rogerian and person-centred therapy. Interestingly, many Muslim scholars (or Moulanas) also attend the basic counselling training.

Islamic Careline has made great strides in achieving a healthy, holistic, and harmonious Muslim society. This project aspires to grow stronger and progress to become an integral psychosocial resource for the Muslim community.

The second organisation, Islamic Helpline, based in Lenasia, southwest of Johannesburg, was founded in 1999 by a group of driven and motivated women ready to serve their community. Islamic Helpline consists of a group of volunteers ranging in age from 24 to 70 years old, committed to serving their community for the pleasure of the Almighty.

The team consists of:

- 1 educational psychologist
- 2 social workers
- 2 occupational therapists
- 4 lawyers
- 23 counsellors
- 30 volunteers who do home visits for the elderly

Over the years, Islamic Helpline has identified the needs of the community and designed programmes accordingly. Counsellors discuss, amongst themselves, the prevailing, current community issues and work closely with a set of ulema (Muslim scholars) on a weekly basis to allow for guidance from an Islamic Shariah, or *fiqh*'s, perspective on related issues. One example of a prevalent community issue would be the high incidence of suicide in the community. In response to this issue, the counsellors would develop a programme to raise awareness and enlist the aid of Muslim scholars to provide an Islamic perspective and ruling on suicide, which would then be added to their programme. Similar to Islamic Careline's model, Helpline's model of counselling and training new counsellors is based on a Western framework but incorporates positive psychology and psychoanalytic theory as well as concepts from life coaching as their foundational approach. There is no evidence to suggest that Helpline incorporates any aspects of Islamic Psychology—namely the key concepts aql, ruh, qalb, and nafs—into their model of counselling. Instead, they offer various types of counselling such as play therapy, teenage and adolescent counselling, pre-marital counselling, anger management, drug counselling, trauma counselling, career counselling and family counselling as well as woman empowerment seminars and senior citizens programmes. The organisation is underpinned by an Islamic ethos, and the counsellors have been trained in various skills development courses to enhance their knowledge of counselling and what to consider when counselling. The organisation aims to grow in terms of service offerings and to evolve as the needs of the community change.

The next and very renowned organisation that will be highlighted is the Ibn Sina Institute of Tibb. Founded by the acclaimed and humble Professor Rashid Bhika, the Tibb journey began in the early 1980s as Professor Bhika participated in the establishment of the Islamic Medical Association of South Africa. In the words of Professor Bhika, "I became aware of the Muslim contribution to the theory and practice of medicine—pioneers such as Ibn Sina, Rhazi, Ibn Nafis, made me realise that not only their contribution to medicine but also within the context of the Quran and Hadith. This has been specifically highlighted in the Medicine of the Prophet books by Ibn Qayyim and As-Suyuti" (personal communication with Dr. Bhika). A paper written by Professor Bhika, "Islamic Medicine - Revisited (2007)," published in the Islamic Medical Association Journal, provides a background of his interest and pursuit of Tibb (medicine) and the establishment of the Ibn Sina Institute of Tibb. The vision of the institute is to promote healthcare locally and internationally through quality, cost-effective, and integrative medicine.

In line with its vision, the institute is committed to

- Facilitating the training and development of Tibb practitioners,
- Introducing the Tibb philosophical principles to healthcare professionals wishing to integrate Tibb into their current practice,
- Integrating the Tibb principles in primary healthcare clinics and at consumer levels, with emphasis on the role of lifestyle in health promotion and illness management, and
- Establishing primary healthcare clinics and holistic wellness centres in underprivileged areas.

According to the founder, in order to promote the training and practice of Tibb (also known as Unani-Tibb) locally, the following three requirements had to be met:

1. Recognition of Tibb with the Department of Health. This was achieved in 2001 when Unani-Tibb was included as the 11th modality under the auspice of the Allied Health Professions Council of South Africa (which includes other modalities such as Homeopathy, Chinese medicine, Phytotherapy, Ayurveda, Naturopathy, etc.).
2. Arrangements for the registration and availability of Unani-Tibb medication with the South African Health Products Regulatory

Authority (SAHPRA), previously known as the Medicine Control Council. This was achieved in 2002 when Unani-Tibb medication was included as one of the disciplines of medication in Complementary Medicine under SAHPRA.

3. Training Unani-Tibb doctors at the University of the Western Cape [UWC] (discussed below).

The training of Unani-Tibb commenced at the School of Natural Medicine (SoNM) at UWC in 2003 to achieve both a one-year postgraduate diploma for medical doctors and clinical healthcare primary nurses as well as a five-year double bachelor's qualification for undergraduate students that included disciplines of Unani-Tibb, Chinese Medicine, Neurotherapy, and Phytotherapy. The first degree is a BSc, a complementary science degree for all four disciplines, followed by a two-year specialisation degree in the four disciplines, known as a Bachelor of Unani Medicine. Both Unani-Tibb programmes were designed and implemented for SoNM and UWC by the institute. In fact, Professor Bhika's completed PhD dissertation is titled, "African Renaissance in Health Education: Developing an Integrative Programme of Unani-Tibb Training for Healthcare Professionals in Southern Africa." The academic support for the training was obtained from Hamdard University, Pakistan, and Jamia Hamdard University and Aligarh Muslim University, both in India. In November 2002, before the programme commenced, the institute undertook a Curriculum Review Workshop, which included experts from the above-mentioned universities.

To date, the number of undergraduates from UWC has been less than 40, mainly because the lack of medical aid reimbursement compromised the viability of practising Tibb. For the last 3–4 years, only an average of 2–4 undergraduate students have qualified. To make matters worse, since the 2019 academic year, UWC made the decision to review the viability of all programmes at SoNM, and no new students have been admitted for the past two years.

UWC's decision, according to Professor Bhika, brought him to a realisation that the future of Tibb in South Africa is not promising at this stage. The institute has therefore developed a new strategy to promote the practice of Tibb—both locally but more so internationally—by developing an online consumer course with the main outcomes of Health Promotion and Illness Management. This online course is said to become available in the next few months and will be followed by an online course to help health and wellness practitioners integrate the Tibb principles into their current practice in terms of all disciplines related to the medical and health promotion fields. It was noted, however, that since this will be a short introductory course, the participants will not be able to refer themselves as Tibb doctors.

This shift could be a resource to practising Muslim psychologists and counsellors who would like to learn more about Tibb, particularly aspects relating to Tibb-an-Nabawi and Islamically related teachings surrounding health and wellness. An important consideration taken to establish the online consumer course was the successful training of the Tibb Lifestyle Advisors programme, initiated in 2010. This programme was well received by the city of Johannesburg's Health Department to the extent that the Tibb institute trained 220 clinic health promoters and more than 4,000 ward-based outreach teams affiliated with the city's clinics.

From a research perspective, the institute has published a few books over the years aimed at both consumers and academics, all of which are available for download on their website. When asked about the specific connection with Islamic Psychology, Professor Bhika highlighted that the Tibb concept of temperament is a key aspect in diagnosis and an important approach in treatment when it comes to physiological as well as mental health and is therefore relevant to both the fraternity and field practitioners.

One issue faced by psychologists in the world today is the need to adapt to multicultural societies (Haque & Kamil, 2012). Mainstream psychology is a product of Western culture and, as such, is not always equipped to serve the needs of non-Western communities. This is a particularly salient issue in South Africa, where psychology has been accused of being irrelevant to the needs of most of its population (Nell, 1990). The next organisation under discussion, The South African Institute of Islamically Integrated Wellness (SAIIIW), aims to address this very issue in terms of its Muslim population.

SAIIIW is a recently registered private company in Johannesburg (www.saiiiw.co.za) whose mission is to advance the adoption, education, and practice of Islamically integrated counselling and overall wellness and incorporate Quranic and Sunnah/Prophetic-based methods and applications within the Republic of South Africa (RSA). SAIIIW is a spiritual wellness organisation pioneering the application of traditional spiritual Islamic healing methods as the backdrop of the therapeutic setting, whether in the form of counselling or otherwise. The organisation aims to offer a holistic integrative approach to therapy, and their service offerings incorporate all varieties of counselling and cover anxiety, personality disorders, addiction-adjustment problems, marital conflict, premarital interventions, family conflict, social phobias, PTSD, obsessive-compulsive disorder, trauma, loss, grief, anger management, personal/spiritual growth, work/life balance, and spiritual affliction. The company also focuses on organisational development initiatives, organisational diagnosis, and related interventions. Furthermore, they offer religious consultations by religious practitioners and are designed to offer religious awareness, education, and religious rulings (*fatwas*) regarding individuals with mental health or family concerns. At times, people with mental health concerns have religious dispensations, rights or privileges, which are consequential to their mental health. In addition, the company offers integrated wellness services that include Hijaamah (sunnah cupping), Tibb, Ruqyah-ash-Shariah, and Sunnah sports. The directors of SAIIIW and the authors of this chapter are organisational psychologists registered with The Health Professions Council of South Africa and are practitioners certified by the IAIP, trained in Istanbul and Cambridge (UK) by the esteemed and universally recognised pioneers in the field of Islamic Psychology, Malik Badri, Abdallah Rothman, and Rasjid Skinner. Both directors and authors were clinically supervised by Sheikh Saeed Nasser in the UK.

The authors of this chapter have also been utilising learnt approaches in their private practices based both in the north and south of Johannesburg. Furthermore, they have successfully developed and facilitated the first known marriage workshop in the country based on integrating Islamic Psychology concepts and principles and incorporating them into their training with participants. It was well received, and there is a huge request for more such workshops.

SAIIIW also collaborated with IAIP to further develop the organisation's mission in relation to its Islamic Psychology practice component in the RSA, based on IAIP's knowledge, experience, and expertise. The organisation has also been recognised as the only existing body in RSA to develop and market IAIP courses and to present other courses in South Africa based on Islamically integrated approaches to counselling and wellness interventions.

## Foundations for the future: Recommendations and potential ways forward

It is suggested that religious beliefs often provide a sense of order and help an individual to understand what may otherwise seem overwhelming and unpredictable (Carone & Barone, 2001). Muslims, for example, are taught that all misgivings, calamities, hardships, and illnesses, to name a few, occur due to the "Will of Allah (God)" (Al-Qarni, 2002, trans. 2003).

> "Nothing shall ever happen to us except what Allah has ordained for us." (Qur'an, 9:51, trans. 2001)

It is important to also consider how culture shapes the way in which mental illness is expressed and, consequently, how an individual will manifest and express his/her psychological ailments according to what is appropriate and allowed in their culture (Hayward, 1999). Thus, the understanding of mental illness is not universal, and the way certain conditions are labelled in different settings and how they are expressed in different cultures needs to be taken into consideration (Swartz, 2002). The beliefs of people suffering from mental illnesses are key factors in determining the most effective treatment and may influence their clinical outcome (Taylor, 2003).

With this is mind, the South African Muslim community is made up of many diverse cultures, and understanding these rich diversities will undoubtedly enable Islamic Psychology practitioners and psychotherapists to improve their service in terms of diagnosis and treatment. The phenomenal effect of globalisation on cultures should also be kept in mind, as cultures are constantly integrating with other values and beliefs to which they are exposed. Therefore, it would be valuable to have consistent Muslim cross-cultural research regarding perceptions of mental illness in order to stay constantly updated with the shifts that occur with each new generation and the cultural values and beliefs that impact them.

In addition, there are many gaps in society's knowledge and understanding of social exclusion and stigmatisation towards those suffering with mental illness. It is imperative that we understand the discrimination that exists against those with mental illness and help to create more reliable methods of educating communities to reduce the stigma related to mental health. Even though efforts are being made in South Africa and globally, there is more that we as Islamic Psychology practitioners and psychologists can do to assist in this process. We can raise awareness through campaigns, utilise social media platforms, and use the platform in local mosques to propagate and advance the importance and benefit of Islamic Psychology, guiding the community to seek help and directing them towards Islamic counselling as opposed to secular-based counselling from non-Muslim therapists.

Hence, Islamic Psychology practices should allow the provision of advice and guidance, therapy, counselling, and spiritual interventions, keeping within the Islamic lens. It is well known, and not only a South African concern but a global one, that Western or mainstream counselling as it stands is problematic in its ability to apply culturally and/or religiously appropriate services to Muslim clients. In addition, there still exists a great need and a growing demand among the Muslim community of South Africa for more Islamically integrated mental health therapies and interventions to become available and, more importantly, accessible and affordable.

With this in mind, particularly within the South African context, there appears to be a twofold challenge. The first is the desperate need for more trained Islamic Psychology practitioners, and the second is tied to the training programmes or courses that will allow for such training to occur. An additional contextual challenge that may be of further concern regards the regulation (or lack thereof) in terms of practising from this paradigm. Considering that multicultural or faith-based counselling is not a "recognised category" per the mainstream regulatory bodies in South Africa, the regulation of what constitutes "true" Islamic psychology-based interventions/therapy/counselling may remain a grey area and allows room for loose usage of the term as a marketing strategy; and it certainly keeps doors ajar for some level of exploitation. A way forward in this regard would perhaps be for the Islamic Psychology fraternity or more specifically the IAIP to establish a regulatory department/segment and investigate placing satellite branches across continents and countries to allow for some level of regulation and standard when it comes to the practice of Islamic Psychology as a growing and needed category of practice, not only in South Africa but across the globe.

## Conclusion

In conclusion, and as noted above, there has been some noteworthy and active efforts in terms of the informal and formal development of Islamic Psychology, particularly from a scholarly or academic point of view in the South African context. In terms of application and implementation, however, the Islamic Psychology community in South Africa is still in its infancy stages; and there is a need for more research by South African Muslim practitioners in terms of exploring Islamically integrated psychotherapies. This is needed and will have significant implications and benefits for the Muslim community in terms of mental health and wellness in South Africa.

## References

Abu-Raiya, H., & Pargament, K. I. (2011). Empirically based psychology of Islam: Summary and critique of the literature. *Mental Health, Religion and Culture, 14*(2), 93-115.

Ally, Y., & Laher, S. (2008). South African Muslim faith healers' perceptions of mental illness: Understanding, aetiology and treatment. *Journal of Religion and Health, 47*(1), 45-56.

Al-Qarni, A. i. A. (2002). (Translated by: Shafeeq, F. i. M). (2003). *Don't Be Sad.* Riyadh, Saudi Arabia: International Islamic Publishing House.

Bhikha, R. (2007). Islamic medicine revisited. *Journal of Islamic Medical Association,* 1-7.

Bond, T. (1993). *Standards and Ethics for Counselling in Action.* London: Sage Publications.

Carone, Jr., D. A., & Barone, D. F. (2001). A social cognitive perspective on religious beliefs: their functions and impact on coping and psychotherapy. *Clinical Psychology Review, 21*(7), 989-1003.

Cinnirella, M., & Loewenthal, K. M. (1999). Religious and ethnic group influences on beliefs about mental illness: A qualitative interview study. *British Journal of Medical Psychology, 72*(4), 505-524.

Gunther, U. (2018). Islam in South Africa. Muslims contribution to the South African transition process and the challenges of contextual readings of Islam. Al Mesbar Studies and Research Center.

Haque, A. (2004). Psychology from Islamic perspective: Contributions of early Muslim scholars and challenges to contemporary Muslim psychologists. *Journal of Religion and Health, 43*(4), 357-377.

Haque, A. Kamil, N. (2012). Islam, Muslims and Mental Health. In S. Ahmed and M. M. Amer (Eds.) Counseling Muslims: Handbook of Mental Health issues and Interventions (pp. 3-14).

Haque, A., & Yasien, M. (2008). *Psychology of personality, Islamic perspectives.* Cengage Learning Asia.

Hayward, P. (1999). Culture and mental illness: A client centered approach. *British Journal of Psychology, 38*, 103-105.

Kashyap, L. (2004). Introduction to lay counseling. *International Journal of Advancement of Counselling, 26*(4).

Laher, S., & Moosa, A. (2007). Volunteer care: Innovations in practice. *Islamic Quarterly, 51*, 237-256.

Lowenthal, K. M., Cinnirella, M., Evdoka, G., & Murphy P. (2001). Faith Conquers All? Beliefs about the roles of religious factors in coping with depression among different cultural-religious groups in the U.K. *British Journal of Medical Psychology, 74*(3), 293-303.

Mohamed, Y. (1996). Fitrah: The Islamic Concept of Human Nature. Taha Publishers.

Nadvi, L. (2008). South African Muslims and political engagement in a globalising context. *South African Historical Journal, 60*(4), 618-636.

Nell, V. (1990). One world, one psychology: "Relevance" and ethnopsychology. *South African Journal of Psychology, 20*(3), 129-140.

Quinn, C. A., & Quinn, F. (2003). *Pride, Faith, and Fear: Islam in Sub-Saharan Africa.* New York: Oxford University Press.

Rack, P. (1982). *Race, Culture and Mental Disorders.* London: Tavistock Publications Ltd.

Roberts, L. W. (2002). Informed consent and the capacity for volunteerism. *American Journal of Psychiatry, 159*, 705-712.

Shell, R. (Ed.). (2006-2007). From diaspora to diorama: The slave lodge in Cape Town, Cape Town. *Ancestory, 24*, 451.

Sheridan, L., & North, A. (2004). Perspective: Representations of Islam and Muslims in psychological publications. *The International Journal for the Psychology of Religion, 14*(3), 149-159.

Skinner, R. (2010). An Islamic approach to psychology and mental health. *Mental Health, Religion and Culture, 13*(6), 547-551.

Swartz, L. (2002). *Culture and Mental Health: A Southern African View.* Oxford: Oxford University Press.

Taylor, S. (2003). Mental disorders. In S. Taylor & D. Field (Eds.), *Sociology of Health & Health Care* (3rd ed., pp. 137-154). Oxford: Blackwell Publishing.

Tayob, A. (1996). Islam in South Africa, Encyclopaedia of Islam. *London,* (9), 730-731.

Vahed, G. (2007). Islam in the public sphere in post-apartheid South Africa: Prospects and challenges. *Journal for Islamic Studies, 27,* 116-149.

Weatherhead, S., & Daiches, A. (2010). Muslim views on mental health and psychotherapy. *Psychology and Psychotherapy: Theory, Research and Practice, 83*(1), 75-89.

Youssef, J., & Deane, F. P. (2006). Factors influencing mental-health help-seeking in Arabic-speaking communities in Sydney, Australia. *Mental Health, Religion and Culture, 9*(1), 43-66.

CHAPTER THIRTEEN

# Development and Characteristics of Islamic Psychology in Sudan

AHMED MOHAMMED AL-HASSAN AL-AWAD SHENNAN

THE EMERGENCE AND development of Islamic psychology in Sudan over the years has been influenced by the works of several Sudanese researchers and their practice of psychological professions which have brought forth general characteristics of IP in Sudan. However, it is the highly influential impact of the writings and lectures of Malik Badri in particular that has shaped Islamic psychology in Sudan. The history of psychology and its establishment in Sudanese universities in terms of university programs, graduate studies, and scientific activity in general, and the practice of counselling and psychotherapy played a major contributing factor to the current state of the discipline, its development and characteristics.

## Introduction

Psychology is a relatively modern science in Sudan. It started in Sudanese universities in the departments of philosophy and sociology, until the establishment of the first department of applied psychology at the Faculty of Education, University of Khartoum in 1976. This was followed by the department of psychology at the Faculty of Arts in 1977, marking it as a major specialization in the bachelor's degree from the University of Khartoum. Soon after, a new Psychology department opened in Ahfad University for Girls, and other Sudanese universities followed suit. However, a few psychologists who graduated from Arab universities, especially the Egyptian universities and the American University of Beirut, carried the banner of the profession in Sudan (e.g., Malik Badri and others). Their specialization was either in psychotherapy or teaching at universities or social affairs departments in the government and social reform institutions, public schools, and research centers (Shennan & Khalifa, 2004).

## The emergence of IP and its development in Sudanese universities

The beginning of IP in Sudan can be dated to Malik Badri's return from his studies in Great Britain and from Arab Universities (where he worked for some time) back to his home country of Sudan. He joined as a professor at the Faculty of Education, the University of Khartoum, in early 1977 to join the first department of psychology, where he started working with his friend Mahmoud Abdullah Pratt. Badri was undoubtedly known for his scientific prowess and influence at the national, regional, and international levels. Badri started teaching his students (the current author was one of them) psychology courses such as general psychology, the psychology of personality and individual differences, mental health, abnormal psychology, etc. He used to conclude any course with critical views of Western theories and their different schools from an Islamic perspective. When the students reached the last year in the bachelor's program, they were taught a course called 'Islam and psychology' as their program's conclusion. In that course, students reviewed all previous courses from an Islamic perspective. They had to submit a research paper and present a seminar on any subject of their choice so that they focus on Islamic psychological understanding and its applications.

This approach, which Badri had uniquely followed, was unfamiliar to students at the University of Khartoum at the time. Nevertheless, it was an attractive approach, especially since Badri was popular in his fun and easy-going teaching style. This approach has had a clear impact on psychology students' intellectual and academic development, opening their sights to the treasures of knowledge inherent in the Islamic heritage. The department of psychology continued to work along this path, which Badri had initiated. Badri's influence was not limited to the psychology department and his students, but he passed it on to other students in the Faculty of Education and the university at large. As he continued to give public lectures and participate in seminars, cultural and intellectual sessions in 1981, he raised the awareness of students and the entire academic community about the importance of psychology and Islamic social sciences. Thus, from those mentioned above scientific and professional initiatives of Badri, we can say that he was the true founder of IP in Sudan.

## The terminology Issue (Islamic psychology)

Through his book 'Modern Psychology from an Islamic Perspective' (1987), we can say that Badri has resolved the long-running debate in the scientific field about the most appropriate term that should be used in psychology: Is it Islamization of psychology, Islamic interpretation of behavior, Islamic guidance of psychology, Islamic authenticity *(Taaseel)* of psychology, or Islamic psychology. Badri adopted the term IP and described the methodology to be followed in laying down its foundations. Al-Subayh (1422AH) pointed out that Badri perhaps is one of the most prominent critics of Western psychology, and in doing so, he described two criteria:

> Firstly, *"The more we take from Western psychology is dependent on empirical field research, the more acceptable and consistent it is with Islamic thought." (p. 1146).*
>
> Secondly, *"The more modern psychological sciences study a limited aspect of behavior, such as the study of sensory perception, reaction time, intelligence, or the effect of therapeutic drugs on behavior, the more accepted in Islamic terms. In contrast, the more they are concerned with general human behavior, the more distant they are from the Islamic umbrella" (p. 1146).*

The following section addresses some examples from Badri's scientific writings while he was in Sudan only and citing evidence from other researchers' reports to set the stage for IP in Sudan.

## The Dilemma of Muslim Psychologists (Badri, 1979)

Badri wrote this book during the time he taught at the Faculty of Education, University of Khartoum. The book was based on his previous articles, such as "Muslim psychologists in the Lizard's Hole," where he provided harsh criticism to the Western schools in their theoretical origins and applied practices, indicating their inconsistency with human nature (*Fitrah*) and the fallacy of their claims. Badri described Muslim psychologists in their blind following of their Western masters and Western theories' general tradition by entering into Lizard's Hole. Fortunately, Badri had not left them in that Lizard's Hole but provided a road map to free those Muslim psychologists and researchers from Western psychological and intellectual slavery. In this endeavour, he described three stages: the phase of infatuation, the phase of reconciliation, and the phase of emancipation.

## Modern Psychology from an Islamic perspective (Badri, 1987)

This booklet was based on his study presented to the Fourth World Congress of the International Institute of Islamic Thought held in Khartoum, Sudan, in

1987. In explaining his comprehensive critical vision of Western psychology, he set a standard for the accepted and rejected aspects of psychology and built its standard on the fact that:

*"Psychology is an experimental science, philosophy, and art. There is no pure evil in such theories" (p. 1149),* and *"Psychology as art or fine craft requires practical training and long experience in conducting activities such as the arts of psychotherapy and the application of IQ tests and teaching, there is nothing wrong if we learn and benefit from them unless their methods and purposes contradict our Islamic thinking."* (p. 1149, IIIT Behavioral Sciences and Methodology, Part 2).

## The AIDS Crisis: An Islamic Sociocultural perspective (Badri, 1998)

This book represents one of Badri's best contributions to the international scientific arena in psychology and social sciences. This book received the award of best contribution in Islamic Medicine for the year 2000 by the Islamic Medical Association of South Africa. Badri argued that AIDS is a natural result of the sexual revolution founded on the doctrine of modernity and secularism, which grew up in the Western cognitive pattern, and that it represents a manifestation of the psychological, social, and philosophical aspects of Western civilization. Badri demonstrated comprehensive vision and encyclopedic knowledge in dealing with the AIDS crisis. Equipped with deep Islamic insights, he eloquently described the root causes of the problem rendering it as the natural progeny of the Western sexual revolution.

## Contemplation: An Islamic Psychospiritual Study (Badri, 2000)

This book is a study of contemplation in its psychological, cognitive, and emotional dimensions from an Islamic perspective as a religious rite. The study illustrates the importance of contemplation and meditation in the formation of one's mental and emotional makeup and the influence they have on behavior and motives. It demonstrates the importance of the treatment of disorders and the richness of one's psychological and spiritual life. The study also showed the Quran's methods in urging the Muslims to contemplate on God's creation as free worshiping that transcends the spirit and promotes the sense of being a faithful slave to Allah. Badri also discussed the nature of contemplation and its stages from the early Muslim scholars such as Al-Ghazali and ibn al-Qayyim Al Jawziyyah, comparing it to modern psychology.

## Psychology in the Arab-Islamic Heritage (Taha,1995)

The theme of this book is to identify the treasures of psychological knowledge transmitted in the writings of Islamic scholars such as Ibn Sina, Ibn al-Qayyim, Ibn al-Haytham. The book tries to draw parallels with contemporary psychology, such as identifying the mental processes and their neural mechanisms as described by Ibn Sina. The author has also identified the concept of intelligence in Ibn al-Qayyim's writings and cognitive growth and its stages in the story of *Hay Bin Yaqzan,* narrated by Ibn Tufayl. The author urges contemporary Muslim scholars to learn from the psychology inherent in Islamic heritage. He concludes that what we get from the Islamic heritage is real psychology as an integrated discipline with its theoretical framework and rigorous methodology that distinguishes it from other branches of Islamic knowledge like Fiqh, Hadith, law, or Education. This book's importance stems from the fact that it went directly to the Islamic source of psychological knowledge to illuminate perspectives on learning, intelligence, personality, human growth, psychopathology, and psychotherapy.

## Experimental Psychology in the Arab-Islamic Heritage (Khalifa, 2001)

This book is primarily concerned with tracking psychological knowledge embedded in the experimental works of early Muslim scholars. The author addressed the scientific value of Hassan Ibn al-Haytham's contributions in psychological measurement, psychology, visual deception, and ibn Tufayl's contributions to cognitive development. Besides, the analysis has included the experiments of Razi, Ibn Sina, and another Muslim scholar. The author tried to highlight experimental psychology's scientific merits in Arab-Islamic heritage, particularly in physiological psychology, perception, and psychopathology.

## Introduction to Psychology (Khatib and Shennan, 2003)

Like others, this text book starts by introducing psychology to new students, but it differs remarkably from other similar textbooks in other ways. It represents an important stage in the development of IP teaching in Sudanese universities as, in addition to the usual scientific materials in psychology textbooks, this book includes content on Islamic psychology. For example, chapter one introduces the history, aims, and subject matter of psychology. Then, modern psychology is addressed and compared to psychology in the Islamic heritage in terms of history, goals, and the source of knowledge. The concept of *Fitrah* is addressed while shedding light on the unity of the soul in Islam with its three conditions: The nafs Al ammara (bad)- the nafs Al lawwama (hesitating)-and the nafs Al mutmainah (reassuring). The relationship between heart, mind, and soul was also explained.

The book follows this approach in the rest of the chapters. It provides the Islamic perspective of personality, human growth, perception and attention, mental health and psychotherapy, and psychological measurement. This approach proved to be successful in raising students' awareness of IP at an earlier stage of their study. The book represents a paradigm shift in teaching psychology at Sudanese universities. Reports from universities indicate the attractiveness of this book and its popularity among students.

FIVE STAGES COULD BE IDENTIFIED AS FOLLOWS:

1. The stage of revolution against western psychology, as in the article (Muslim psychologists in the Lizards hole) and The Dilemma of Muslim Psychologists.
2. The stage of drawing methodology and milestones for the Islamization process (Modern Psychology from an Islamic perspective).
3. The stage of scrutinizing the Arab-Islamic heritage to identify and classify scattered psychological knowledge and presenting it in contemporary scientific jargon (Taha and Shennan, 1992; Taha,1995; Khalifa, 2001).
4. Original scientific production of Islamic psychological literature directly from the Quran and Sunnah as in (*al Tafakkurmin al mushahadahila al shuhud*),
5. Expanding the teaching of IP in Sudanese universities, which gains popularity and attractiveness among students and marks good progress in writing university textbooks.

## Content of Syllabus taught in Sudanese Universities

The course title is generally known in academic institutions as Islamic Psychology and sometimes known as Authentication –(*Taseel*) of psychology, while other courses only include some contents of IP without referring to the name.

An overview of the major universities shows that they largely agree on the following contents:

1. Definition of IP/and Arab Islamic heritage
2. The importance of IP with a focus on the contributions of Islamic heritage scholars such as Ghazali and Ibn Sina.
3. Efforts of current scholars in IP and criticism of Western psychology, for example (Badri-Najati-Shargawi).
4. IP compared with modern psychology in terms of the history of psychology and its subject-matter and the source of knowledge,
5. The nature of man and the concept of *Fitrah*
6. The concepts of heart, mind, and soul (Nafs).
7. The unity of the soul in Islam and its three conditions
8. The importance of the spiritual aspect as an essential factor in forming human behavior is generally overlooked in contemporary psychology.
9. Self and social adjustment, mental health, and psychotherapy, learning and perception from an Islamic perspective
10. Identifying the theoretical foundation of IP and methods of research about it
11. The role of IP in enriching the various branches of modern psychology.

**Masters and Ph.D. thesis submitted to Sudanese universities**

| | UNIVERSITY | THE ATTRACTIVENESS OF IP TO POSTGRADUATE STUDENTS | DATE | NUMBER OF THESES | THE ATTRACTIVENESS OF IP TO UNDERGRADUATE STUDENTS |
|---|---|---|---|---|---|
| 1 | University of Khartoum | 80% | 2017 | 80 | medium |
| 2 | Islamic University of Omdurman | 70 | 2016 | 56 | high |
| 3 | International University of Africa | 55 | 2018 | 24 | high |

| | | | | | |
|---|---|---|---|---|---|
| 4 | University of Gezira | 50 | 2016 | 25 | high |
| 5 | Al Neelain University | 60 | 2017 | 33 | medium |
| 6 | Sudan University for Science and Technology | 40 | 2015 | 22 | medium |

*Source: Ministry of Higher Education and Scientific Research*

From the above table, we can observe that Psychology theses submitted to and approved by Sudanese universities have reached 240 till 2017. It is also noted that the subjects of IP were highly attractive to graduate students. Simultaneously, according to the universities' psychology departments mentioned above, its attractiveness ranged from medium to high for undergraduate students. It is worth noting that the author looked into the titles and topics of these theses and found that they were based on a sound and authentic understanding of IP and reflected a clear development of its motion in Sudan. Here are some selected examples of theses:

- The effect of the Quran in the treatment of pathological anxiety by Iman Mohammed Zaki (2001).
- The psychological wisdom inherent in the sexual legal controls in Islam by Omiema Hassan al-Mahdi (2007).
- Islamic psychotherapy and its success in treating patients whom modern psychotherapy has failed to cure by Elham Mustafa El Siddiq (2010).
- Environmental and hereditary effect on children's cognitive development in Islamic legacy compared to modern psychology by Asra Mfarah (2005).
- Construction of an intelligence test for adults based on Islamic legacy of Ibn Hazam book about Intelligence by Nagda M Abdelrahim (2005).

## Examples of research published between 2015-2020

1. The psychological dimensions of facial expression in the Qur'an. Al-Rashed Library. Saudi Arabia. (2017). Sir Ahmed Suleiman.
2. Criteria for indigenizing the psychology of technological talent: Khartoum school of psychology as a model. University of Sudan for Science and Technology Scientific Research Skills Conference, Ashria.
3. The Effectiveness of Qur'anic Stories in Behavioral Education for Chil-

dren (The Story of Ibrahim (Peace Be upon Him as a Model), Arab Journal of Psychology, Tunisia, 2017 Mohamed Osman Al-Mehaisy.

4. Khartoum School of Psychology: Milestones in the Way of Enlightenment and Spiritual Energy Therapy, Conference on Enlargement and Spiritual Energy Therapy, Salalah - Oman 2019, Ahmed M. El-Hassan Shennan.
5. Psychological aspects associated with walking in the Quran. Sports Psychology Conference at Hafr Al Batin University in Saudi Arabia in 2019. Sir Ahmed Suleiman

The contents of the research mentioned above examples may reflect the latest development stage in the production of Sudanese researchers, which have been characterized by original research topics motivated directly by their commitment to IP stage perhaps represents the intellectual maturity of young researchers who followed their pioneer masters.

Scrutinizing the research examples cited above and the topics of the Ph.D. theses submitted to the Sudanese universities, we might draw a preliminary profile that characterizes Sudanese researchers in IP. Perhaps the Sudanese researchers' acquaintance with the Islamic epistemological system has enabled them to see the differences compared to systems in other cultures. This is very important because the interaction between cultures may result in a mutual impact or sometimes a dominant effect unilaterally. Both cases require the researcher to be aware of the differences in the sources of knowledge, methodology, and the values of utilizing its substance. For instance, the Islamic epistemological system expresses monotheism which manifests itself in studying man's behavior and relatedness with the total universe.To illustrate this idea, let us take an example of the behavioral sciences, including psychology; we recognize their features in the Western epistemological system compared to the Islamic paradigm. There are apparent paradoxes in the sources of science where modern behavioral sciences are based mainly on the paradigm of logical positivism, which valued the sensory experience in obtaining knowledge solely, i.e., they limited science to the perceptible experience only (Al-Amin and Sherif, 2004). As for the origin of man, modern behavioral sciences have based their knowledge on the principles of the philosophy of evolution, while the sources of the correct understanding of the soul in the Islamic epistemological system stems from the fact that man is created in a dignified manner (Badri, 1979: Taha & Shennan, 1992: Khatib & Shennan, 2003: Shennan, 2007).

Modern behavioral sciences, in their general purposes, are based on the materialistic aspects inherent in logical positivism. In contrast, Islamic behavioral sciences are distinguished in their general objectives, whereas exploring the *nafs (soul)* is driven by aspiring to truly knowing Allah, the Creator of the Universe. These concepts remain active in IP and vividly reflected in behavioral investigations (Taha, 1995).

Another critical factor in the formation of the Sudanese scholar is perhaps the extent of his or her religious commitment and sense of belonging to Islam's doctrine, strengthening one's feeling of Islamic belonging. He or she will subsequently be active and responsible in national issues as sincere worship to his Creator.

## Scientific Conferences in Sudan

### 1 4TH CONFERENCE ON METHODOLOGY AND BEHAVIOURAL SCIENCES (1987)

The Department of Psychology at the Faculty of Arts, University of Khartoum, organized this conference in collaboration with the International Institute of Islamic Thought (IIIT) held in Khartoum and attended by scholars from all Islamic countries. Participants from Sudanese psychologists were Malik Badri, who presented his famous paper, Modern Psychology from an Islamic perspective, and Elzubair Taha& Ahmed Shennan, who presented their research paper, The Origins of Psychological Concepts in Islamic Heritage.

### 2 THE SUDANESE PSYCHOLOGICAL SOCIETY CONFERENCES

Although it was officially registered in the 1980s, the Sudanese Psychological Society was formed several years earlier, and the first President was Professor Malik Badri, followed by Professor Elzubair Bashir Taha. The society organized its first conference at Khartoum and Gezira Universities in 2003 (Professor Omar Haroun Khalifa was instrumental in this success). In this conference, IP research papers accounted for 8% of the total research presented.

### 3 THE INTERNATIONAL ASSOCIATION OF MUSLIM PSYCHOLOGISTS

This association was founded in 1997 and elected Malik Badri as its first President. Firstly, it was based in Malaysia and later moved its headquarters to Khartoum in 2003 and then elected Elzubair Bashir Taha as its President. Sudanese researchers' participation in the conferences and scientific activities organized by this association was significant, as they participated in all successive conferences held at Khartoum, Sharjah, Kuala Lumpur, and Indonesia and presented a total of ninety research papers.

## Sudanese Scientific Journals

Besides the main *Journal of Psychological Studies,* which is published biannually by the Sudanese Psychological Society, several other scientific journals published psychology research, such as *the Gezira Journal of Humanities and Edu-*

*cational Sciences,* a major file of psychology. Also, *Tafakkur* is published by the Institute of Islamization of Knowledge, University of Gezira, and the Journal of *Taaseel,* published by the Ministry of Higher Education and Scientific Research. Both latter journals focus on the topics of Islamic social sciences.

## Islamic Counseling and Psychotherapy

Although applied psychology's earlier practices were limited to educational psychology, exceptional counseling and psychotherapy services were achieved by three great scientists of their time: Al-Tajani Al-Mahi, the first African psychiatrist (al-Mahi, 2006), Taha Bashar, and Malik Badri. This generation has been interested in establishing the profession through free practice and conscious application of counseling and psychotherapy theories with the view of adapting them to the cultural and social atmosphere in Sudan (Al-Mahi, 2006). Taha Bashar went on in the same direction, deepening his professional practices by emphasizing Sudanese Islamic wisdom and faith (Bashar, 1972). Furthermore, Bashar developed robust connections with traditional treatment centers because he believed that there was a vital link in counseling and psychotherapy between traditional and modern. He became famous as a psychiatrist and psychotherapist in Sudan for this success (Shennan & Khalifa, 2004).

The third symbol in this generation was Badri, who practiced psychotherapy in different hospitals in London, Morocco, Riyadh, and Malaysia. In addition to his native country Sudan, Badri adopted a method that recognizes social and cultural realities and their role in psychotherapy but added a new dimension by focusing primarily on the Islamic approach to mental health in general. Based on this approach, Badri skillfully developed unique and innovative psychotherapeutic techniques depending on the psycho-spiritual dimension of the Muslim personality. Badri's innovations in cognitive behavior therapy and Islamic psychotherapy are well documented in his international publication (Badri, 1966;1972; 1978; 1989;1996; 2015; Meyer, 1971; Lynn,1981).

The second generation included Sir Doleep, Elzubair Bashir Taha, Shamsaddin Zain al-Abidin, and other members of their generation in the 1970s – and in the early 1980s. They practiced counseling and psychotherapy in hospitals and centers of guidance and are apprenticed by these large number of psychologists and university professors who fill the field these days in Sudan. This generation has been greatly influenced by the thesis of the pioneer generation in their practice of psychotherapy, taking the concept of authenticity and contemporary stance as a slogan (see: Taha, 1989; Khalifa, 2001; Shennan, 2007).

The third generation is represented by students of the second-generation (e.g., Ahmed Shennan, Mohammed Salah Khalil, Mohammed Mahjoub Haroun Salah Al-Jili, Mohammed Abdul Majid, Abderhman Osman, Fathia Omar,

Ilham Mustafa, Omar Haroun Khalifa) who are now professionally involved in universities, psychotherapy centers, and social institutions.

It can be said from this history that the practice and success of counseling and psychotherapy in Sudan were linked to the personality of the great professors, like Malik Badri, and the scientific and professional foundations they established based on IP or putting psychology in its faith-based pattern. Belief in God's divinity and his lordship to existence, including the hidden, unseen and the foreseeable universe, God Almighty as the source of creation, and man as created from a fist of clay and a whiff of His spirit integrating the body and the soul in one unity.

This conception continues to influence practices of counselling and psychotherapy in Sudan and can be summarized as follows:

1. The assumption that the basis of Islamic counseling and psychotherapy is rooted in the religious dimension of the human personality.
2. Sudanese researcher's contributions stem from the comprehensive monotheistic pattern of the Muslim individual's personality; this monotheistic psychology is manifested in the practice of psychological counseling. The use of the Qur'anic guidance methods that promote spiritual, psychological energy is documented in many works, such as:
   - The Healing Power of Faith (Bashar; Badri).
   - Treatment and psychological guidance based on spiritual energy (Badri in Islam & Alcoholism–the case of the Moroccan girl who was cured through innovative Islamic cognitive behavior therapy - and Islamic perspective in dealing with the AIDS crisis).
   - Qur'anic guidance Techniques - Repentance (tawba) - tolerance - compassion - cooperation - righteousness - charity - honesty - (Elzubair Taha in his practice in the psychiatric clinic of the University of Khartoum).

All these efforts might represent an asset for developing and promoting Islamic psychotherapy and counseling techniques in Sudan and elsewhere.

## Conceptual Issues

### COUNSELING, PSYCHOTHERAPY, AND PROFESSIONAL NEUTRALITY:

In their paper, 'Towards an Ethical Charter for Practicing Counselling in Arab Countries' which was presented at the Counselling Arabia Conference held in Dubai. Shennan & Khalifa (2004) discussed that some codes of ethics originated in America and the rest of the West stand in sharp contrast to other Eastern cultures, particularly the Islamic culture. This is typical when the Muslim counselor tries to implement the code of professional neutrality as it poses that the practicing counselor should not interfere with the client's intellectual or religious beliefs. So, does one follow this, or should he adhere to his Islamic commitment? When we look at successful professional practices in Sudan, we can see how this dilemma is resolved. For example, Badri believed that successful psychotherapy considers the individual's psychological, spiritual, cultural and social context (1987). When the spiritual and psychological dimensions are used in treatment, it brings about a positive change in cognitive, emotional, and behavioral aspects. In this respect, Badri cited experimental evidence from his own experience (the Moroccan girl as an example). Badri (1996) mentioned that recent developments in psychology reveal Islam's wisdom in treating many social problems such as the prevalence of alcoholism, drugs, and criminality. Badri (1996a) emphasized that psychological studies show remarkable results every day, confirming the value of faith and personal meaning in one's life, protecting oneself from stress, anxiety, existential emptiness, and fortifying from the psychological and somatic disorders. Moreover, Badri (1998) urged more explicitly Muslim doctors and psychologists to take away from themselves the robe of neutrality, the term that western professionalism gives to itself.

## THE QUESTION OF INDIGENIZING PSYCHOLOGY

Most of the ethical charters that we have come across are influenced by the American Psychological Association's ethical charter (APA). Is this influence exerted by Western psychology safe from the criticism of those psychologists who call for indigenizing psychology embodied in the book "Indigenous Psychologies: Research and Experience in Cultural context (Kim & Berry,1993)? This idea posed by psychologists Kim and Berry has also appeared in several international journals of Psychology that encourage and advocate the importance of the rise of indigenous theorizing and psychology practices worldwide (see, e.g., *The International Journal of Psychology, 2001&2002*). This trend has been active in Southeast Asia, Canada, Mexico, Venezuela, Greece, and Poland (Khalifa, 2009). For example, researchers in Korea have provided evidence of Western psychology's inappropriateness in Korean culture as Western curricula have been rejected and replaced by developing holistic and qualitative curricula in national psychology. This approach urges the adaptation and reconstruction of Western psychology in the national culture to find the air and soil suitable for growth in the new (national) cultural environment (Khalifa, 2009). It is interesting to see these ideas put forward in the psychology global scene have already found their way since the 1970s and 1980s in the thesis and practices of Sudanese psychologists.

## Studies in Psychological Measurement

1. Psychologist Omar Khalifa studied Al-Hassan bin al-Haytham's experiments of visual deception. The study proved that Al-Hassan bin al-Haytham is the true pioneer of this science. He was the first to introduce the concept of *itibar,* i.e., measurement, and that his experiments and contributions still retain their scientific vitality in the psychological literature (Khalifa, 2001).
2. Najda Abdul Rahim has attempted to construct an intelligence test after performing an in-depth analysis of Ibn al-Jawzi's book on intelligence. The new derived intelligence test consists of 60 items distributed over six axes, proved to have good evidence of validity and reliability (Abdul Rahim, 2005).
3. The Islamic Religious Characteristic Scale: Development and Psychometric Properties. A preliminary study in a Sudanese Sample (Shennan, 2002). This study reports the development and preliminary analysis of the psychometric properties of the Islamic Religious Observance Scale "IROS." The IROS measures the concept of religiosity from an Islamic perspective. The IROS was found to have satisfactory test-retest reliability, good internal consistency, and good construct validity. The author believes that the IROS might have utility for screening and research purposes, not only as an assessment and outcome measure but also for testing hypotheses about connections between religion and mental health in Sudan and other Islamic countries.

## Prospects for the future

The initiatives taken by the prominent pioneers of IP and their students are solid contributions to the establishment and development of the discipline in Sudan. These efforts may continue to create ideas and techniques which take advantage of the Muslim individuals' spiritual potentials to improve their life quality. Yet, there is still far to go. For instance, psychology programs in Sudanese universities should design Islamic studies modules as a prerequisite for IP specialization. The Islamic theory of knowledge, methodology of science, and specific chapters from the Qur'an should be taught thoroughly. IP can soundly contribute to Sudan's public life, such as social reconciliation, conflict resolution, social cohesion, and reinforcing the spirit of cooperation among the community. It can also contribute to social and economic development by maximizing production and respect for work and purity in political activities as psychological traits that characterize the Islamic personality.

Psychometrics is a field in which the Muslim psychologist needs to implement his tools and experience to design and develop psychometric measures that address the cognitive, emotional, and psychological dimensions of the Muslim individual. These instruments might be implemented in measuring the mental and personal abilities, psychological treatment, and psychological prevention based on the Islamic understanding of the human soul recognizing the balance of its worldly and spiritual needs. Sudanese universities might benefit from this scientific legacy in designing a master's-level teaching program that devotes all its credited hours to in-depth study and expanding IP.

## Conclusion

IP in Sudan is indebted to Malik Badri as a prime founder of its legacy, development, and attractiveness in Sudanese universities, inspiring students, and young scholars to proceed in this field confidently. Badri not only adopted the term IP but also described the methodology to be followed in laying down its foundations. Perhaps, the Sudanese researchers' acquaintance with the Islamic epistemological system has helped them be aware of the distinct sources of knowledge, methodology, and values of IP utility as a science.

Sudanese researchers' successful contributions in Islamic counselling and psychotherapy might have stemmed from their conviction that the basis of this practice is rooted in the religious dimension of the human personality. The use of the Qur'anic guidance methods that promote spiritual, psychological energy is manifested in Sudanese counsellors' many works. Such belief has helped them overcome the tension and paradoxes that often arise from confronting conceptual issues such as professional neutrality and indigenizing psychology.

The general characteristics of IP appear in its integrity as a discipline to deal with human behavior in its totality composed of the biological, environmental, and psycho-spiritual aspects. It has also implemented methods of research and experimentation. Although IP is inspired by the dictates of revelation (*Wahy*), it has been the sum of human efforts that help it take its shape and identity. One of the most important characteristics of IP may be its focus on studying the behavioral phenomenon in its human field based on observations and experiences in human behavior rather than animals. Moreover, IP is characterized by its general purposes, for as behind the exploration of the soul lay another purpose which is seeking to know Allah, the Almighty. This understanding continues to influence various psychological investigations and theoretical manifestation.

The prospects of IP might point to possible contributions in public life in Sudan, such as social reconciliation, conflict resolution, social cohesion, and reinforcing the spirit of cooperation among the community. It can also soundly contribute to social and economic development by maximizing production, respect for work, and purity in political activities as psychological traits that characterize the Islamic personality. Indeed, Sudanese psychologists may need to deepen their understanding of the Quran and Islamic literature to have more insights to deal with the psychological phenomena that often recur in Sudanese society. Finally, Sudanese psychologists might think about a comprehensive research project in which all theoretical and applied IP branches are integrated.

## References

Abdul Rahim, N. M. (2005). *Construction of an intelligence test based on Ibnal-Jawzi's book on intelligence.* Unpublished Ph.D. Thesis, University of Khartoum.

Al-Amin, Abdalla, M., & El- Sherif, J., Abdelaziz (2004). Sources of Knowledge. The Open University of Sudan Publications.

Al-Mahi, S. A. (2006). Al-Tajani Al-Mahi is the first African to specialize in psychiatry. *Sudanese Journal of Medical Sciences. Vol. (1),* No.(2).

Al-Mehaisy, M. O. (2017). Effectiveness of Quranic stories in educating sons (Prophet Ibrahim's story as a Model). *The Arab Journal of the Psyche.* Tunisia.

Al-Subayh, A. N. (1422). Islamic Authentication *(Taaseel)* of Psychology *Journal of Imam Mohammed Bin Saud Islamic University,* Issue No. 22, Year 22, pp. 469-506.

Ashria, Ikhlas, H. (2017). Criteria for indigenizing the psychology of technological talent: Khartoum school of psychology as a model. University of Sudan for Science and Technology Scientific Research Skills Conference.

Bashar, T. (1972). The Healing Power of Faith. *World Health Organization Publications.*

Badri, M. B. (1966). A new technique in systematic desensitization of pervasive anxiety and phobic reactions. *Journal of Psychology,* USA.

Badri, M. B. (1972). Customs, Traditions, and Psychopathology. *Sudan Medical Journal, Vol. 10,* No., 3

Badri, M. B. (1978). Muslim Psychologists in the Lizard's Hole. *Journal of Muslim Social* Scientists, USA.

Badri, M. B. (1979). *The Dilemma of Muslim Psychologists.* MWH. London.

Badri, M. B. (1987). *Modern Psychology from an Islamic perspective.* Publications of the International Institute of Islamic Thought, Washington.

Badri, M. B. (1989). The essentials of mental health for the Muslim child. *The Journal of Child rearing in Islam, University of Emirates,* pp. 98-135.

Badri, M. B. (1996 a). al Tafakkurmin al mushahadahila al shuhud: dirasahnafsiyah Islamiyah

Badri, M. B. (1996 b). Counseling and Psychotherapy from an Islamic Perspective. *Al- Shajarah, Journal of ISTAC, Vol. 1,* No., 1& 2.

Badri, M. B. (1998). *The Aids Crisis: An Islamic sociocultural perspective.* ISTAC, Kuala Lumpur.

Badri, M. B. (2000). *Contemplation: An Islamic Psychospiritual Study*. Publications of the International Institute of Islamic Thought, Washington.

Badri, M. B. (2015). *Cyber –Counselling for Muslim Clients*. The Other Press Kuala Lumpur.

Khatib, M. Al Amin & Shennan, Ahmed M. (2003). *Introduction to Psychology*. The Open University of Sudan Publications.

Kim, U.& Berry, W. (Eds.) (1993). *Indigenous Psychologies: Research and Experience in Cultural context*. APA PsyNet.

Khalifa, O. H. (2009). *Indigenization of psychology in the Arab World*. Dar Al Fikr, Amman, Jordan.

Khalifa, O. H. (2001). *Experimental Psychology in Arab-Islamic Heritage*. Arab Foundation for Studies and Publishing, Beirut.

Lynn, R. (1981). *Behavior Therapy for Depression*. The Academic Press.

Meyer (1971). *Behavior Therapy in Cultural Psychology*. Penguin Books

Shennan A. M.H. (2002). The Islamic Religious Characteristic Scale: Development and Psychometric Properties. A preliminary study in a Sudanese Sample. *Tafkur, Vol.,4,* No.1.

Shennan, A. & Khalifa, W. (2004). *Towards a Code of Ethics for the practice of psychological professions in Sudan*. Paper presented at the Conference of Counselling Arabia held in Dubai UAE.

Shennan A. M.H. (2007). Characteristics of the Muslim Researcher in Psychological Sciences. *Sudanese Journal of Medical Sciences, Vol.* 2, No.(1).

Shennan A. M.H. (2012). The Impact of Religion on Childhood Behaviour problems as perceived by Sudanese Parents and Teachers. *The Sudanese Journal of Medical Sciences, Vol.7*, No, 4.

Shennan A. M.H. (2019). *Khartoum School of Psychology: Milestones on the way of Enlightenment and Spiritual Energy Therapy*. Enlightenment and Spiritual Energy Therapy Conference, Salalah, Sultanate of Oman.

Suleiman, A. (2017). *The psychological dimensions of facial expression in the Qur'an*. Al-Rashud Library, Saudi Arabia.

Suleiman, A. (2019). *Psychological and cognitive aspects associated with walking sport in the Qur'an*. Sports Psychology Conference at Hafr Al-Batin University in Saudi Arabia.

Taha, Z. B. (1989*). Quranic Technique in Cognitive Behavioural Therapy*. World Religious Conference, New Jersey.

Taha, Z. B. & Shennan, A. (1992).*The Origins of Psychological Concepts in Islamic Heritage*. The International Institute of Islamic Thought Publications Washington.

Taha, Z. B. (1995). *Psychology in Arab-Islamic Heritage*. University of Khartoum Publishing House, Sudan. The International Institute of Islamic Thought (III) (1992). *Behavioral Sciences and* Methodology, Part 2, Washington.

CHAPTER FOURTEEN

# Studies on Islamic Psychology in Turkey: Present Situation, Possibilities, and Challenges

SÜLEYMAN DERIN

TAHA BURAK TOPRAK

THE INTEREST IN Islamic psychology (IP) in Turkey is increasing. The history of IP dates back to the last century of the Ottoman State (1865–1923). After the transformation of the Ottomans into a secular Turkey, this movement ended abruptly. However, after the 2000s, there was a renewed interest among mental health professionals and clinicians, and theologians eager to develop Islamically oriented psychology at both the clinical and theoretical level. This chapter attempts to review the researchers, universities, institutions, foundations, and centers that use the Islamic legacy in promoting IP in Turkey.

## Introduction

Turkey has great potential to advance the field of Islamic psychology (IP). However, since the fall of Ottoman rule, in the newly established secular Turkey in 1923, the use of Islamic values in the field of psychology has been ignored. Intellectuals in the last period of the Ottoman State (1860–1923) studied Western psychology, translated some of the works they studied, wrote books on the subject, and emphasized the differences and similarities between the Islamic and Western psychology. The pace of these developments in IP sharply decreased with the establishment of the secular state and its secular institutions, and the religion's influence shifted to outside the public sphere, not only in psychology but also in aspects of intellectual life.

After the 2000s, Muslim intellectuals and mental health professionals started to contribute to the field, especially from the perspective of the Sufi tradition of Islam. During this time, Islamic heritage, including its rich resources, has been studied to produce material for the field of psychology and psychotherapy at the theoretical and practical levels.

This chapter outlines the study of psychology in the early period of the Turkish Republic, and its difference from the late Ottoman period. The intellectuals and mental health professionals who devolved new paradigms of therapy based on Islamic heritage are the focus of the chapter. The chapter also discusses programs at the universities, institutions, foundations, and centers that use the Islamic legacy as a basis of research and practice in the fields of IP and psychotherapy. The foundational books on IP by Turkish scholars are introduced, and their contributions to IP are outlined. Television and radio programs dedicated to IP are also introduced.

## Historical Process

### PSYCHOLOGY STUDIES IN THE LATE OTTOMAN PERIOD

Hoca Tahsin (d.1881), a Darul Fünun Scholar, is the father of psychology in Turkey. His work, Psychology or Ilm-iruh is considered the first Western psychology textbook in Turkey. In 1878, Yusuf Kemal's work titled Gayetü'l-beyan fi hakikat'ül-İnsan or İlm-I Ahval-iRuh was published. The beginning of psychology in the Ottoman era dates back to1869, when a conference entitled Emzâc ü Ekâlim was held by Aziz Efendi in Daru'l Fünun (Istanbul University). Notably, despite the translated works in the late Ottoman period, efforts have been made to provide a unique name for the field of psychology (Şirin, 2019).

In this context, notable scholars such as Fillibeli Ahmet Hilmi (Sehbenderzade Filibeli, 2019), Babanzade Ahmet Naim and İsmail Hakkıİzmirli, of the late Ottoman intellectuals, have built a close relationship between Islamic thought and modern psychology, which was developing at that time both through written and translated works, successfully discussing the concepts and propositions of this new science within the intellectual framework of Ottoman civilization (Kızılgeçit, 2013).Ottoman scholars translated the new concepts of the new science without any semantic losses and conducted discussions on psychology in the context of fiqh, kalam, and Sufism, the foundation of Islamic cultural heritage. (Sehbenderzade Fillibeli, 2019; Kızılgeçit, 2013; Naim, 2018).

## Republican Period of Turkey

In 1923, the Ottoman government system became a republic. The modern Turkish Republic made many reforms, limited the Ottoman cultural heritage and language, and removed the Islamic intellectual tradition's authority and its ability to be an active agent in explaining the essence of human beings, the universe, and society. In this period, the early exchange between psychology and the Islamic tradition evolved into transferring and accepting knowledge from the West (Gülerce, 2006). This policy, which severed the relationship between Islamic culture and intellectual life continued for decades, systematically preventing attempts to link psychology with the Islamic tradition (Kızılgeçit, 2013).

The encounters between the Islamic tradition and psychology in the late Ottoman era re-started after 2000. Despite these difficulties and interruptions, because of Turkey's strong Islamic heritage, the academic and clinical professionals with an Islamic worldview regained their enthusiasm for this field. Today, the interest in IP is increasing, and research is being conducted.

### RECENT STUDIES ON ISLAM AND PSYCHOLOGY

Especially after the 2000s, the arguments that primarily started in the field of Sufism and psychology gradually initiated discussions on other fields of Islamic intellectual tradition and modern psychology and debates on integrating the study of psychology and psychotherapy fields with the rich heritage of Islamic thought, such as the thoughts on medicine, philosophy, theology, and Sufism (Toprak, 2021a).

## Current Scenario: IP and Psychotherapy

### PIONEERS IN THE CLINICAL FIELD

This section presents studies that benefited from the knowledge and experience of the Sufi tradition in their attempts to overcome the limitations in clinical intervention, defining the nature of humans, and the theory and practice of modern psychotherapy.

#### *Mustafa Merter*

Merter formally studied psychiatry and psychotherapy in Switzerland in the 1990s and then returned to Turkey. Since the early phases of his professional life, he believed that Western psychology was insufficient to understand the essence of human beings and attempted to develop a method that would compensate for those inadequacies by including Sufi intellectual heritage. He wrote books, such as "Nine Hundred Layer of a Human" (Merter, 2016) and "Nafs Psychology" (Merter, 2014),that offered a new theoretical and practical framework for the field. He developed a psychotherapy model by combining Islamic mysticism with the universally accepted aspects of modern psychology and psychotherapy theories and practices. He also provided psychotherapy services to many people within the framework of the "Nafs Psychology" school (Merter, 2014), in which the interpretation of dreams constituted the core of Merter's theory and practice.

To develop this field in Turkey, Merter trained many students of psychology and defended the strengths of Islamic thought and the limitations of Western psychology. He defended that the Quran and hadiths of the Prophet should guide all aspects of psychology, to understand and explain humans and intervene in their problems. Recently, he has begun writing a Quranic exegesis from a psychological perspective (Merter, 2021).

In the studies of the Sufi tradition, the hermeneutic method is generally used to generate knowledge, and the theory and practice are validated through phenomenological experience. Notably, the number of studies of Islam and psychology has increased, especially in specific fields within the Islamic tradition, for example, medicine, philosophy, fiqh, kalam, and Sufism, in which they are studied separately and sometimes with synthetic approaches (Toprak,2021b). A different and crucial dimension of this movement to explore the relationship between the Islamic tradition and modern psychology and psychotherapy is the discourse and studies that emphasize the need to apply the scientific method, namely, working with the evidence-based findings and methods of empirical psychology Toprak, 2021c; Yanık, 2021; Yavuz, 2021).

*Medaim Yanık*

Since the early 2000s, Psychiatrist Medaim Yanık, a psychiatry professor, has developed projects primarily for the formation of reading groups and research teams, with an emphasis on the idea that the study of IP is possible through the approach of systematic studies (Yanık, 2021). The first reading group open to professionals on the relationship between Islamic thought and psychology was held in 2006 by Medaim Yanık and neurologist Lütfi Hanoğlu under the name of İlm>s *Nefs* readings; however, the group stopped meeting. Subsequently, the Psychology Department of İbn Haldun University, founded under his chairmanship, systematically included research and discussions on Islam and psychology in seminars of its academic staff and students. The most notable of these discussions was between the Rector of İbn-i-Haldun University, sociologist Recep Şentürk, and Medaim Yanık, debating the key topics of this field for seven weeks: one side defended Islamic thought, and the other side defended the modern psychology paradigm (İbn-i-Haldun Üniversitesi, 2018). This debate was followed by Yanık's newspaper articles for seven weeks on the possibilities of cooperation in this field and the problems that require attention.

*Mustafa Ulusoy*

Ulusoy is a psychiatrist who maintains the relationship between IP and psychotherapy, especially in his professional work and his psychological novels. These texts especially focus on how acceptance and commitment therapies and existential psychotherapies can be used within the framework of the Quran. In this context, based on the works of Said Nursi, Ulusoy wrote academic articles discussing the effect of a Quranic ontology on psychotherapy. In these studies, he discussed how the principles of Aqidah (e.g., believing in an afterlife and angels) affect individuals' emotions (e.g., hatred and destructiveness) and create a difference in the consciousness established with existence. He is currently working on a novel on the construction of human psychology from a Quranic perspective.

*Taha Burak Toprak*

Clinical Psychologist Taha Burak Toprak has been researching this subject for more than 10 years. Along with studies on the historical value of classical İlmu'n *Nafs* texts and the human models of these texts, in 2015, he transformed the 4T model[1] that he developed with inspiration from Said Nursi's *Vesvese Risalesi* into practice and research on patients with obsessive compulsive disorder (OCD) with an empirical method and presented it at the World OCD Congress (Toprak, 2016). Toprak has concentrated his work on the areas where modern psychotherapy, especially cognitive behavioral therapy, is limited. For example, although cognitive therapy cognition is explained by two concepts and without hierarchy as "image" and "thought," Nursi explained it as "images," "definition-design," "thought," and "belief-faith." These four concepts have hierarchical differences and define cognitive functioning in terms of non-voluntariness and proximity to action. Additionally, in modern cognitive behavioral therapies, there is a gap: no clarity is provided on the areas of values and cognitive process. By contrast, Nursi's writings distinguish between "dimağ," "kalp" and "nefs." Thus, an opportunity is created to understand and create psychoeducation for thought action fusion (Toprak, 2018).

Toprak has deep interests in such areas where models such as "4T" could be an alternative approach to filling the gap and has been working on developing similar models. He also has focused on the theoretical and practical contributions

1 The 4T model is a psycho-education of normalizing "intrusive thoughts" of a patient with OCD, by using ranks of cognition, which are the four Ts:Tahayyül-imagination-, Tasavvur-conception-, Taakkul-reasoning-, and Tasdik-confirmation-. The focal point of this model is that the patient receives psycho-education on the following: there is no responsibility of the cognitive process in his/her mind until he/she reaches the "Tasdik" confirmation layer.

of Islamic thought on the limitations of modern psychotherapy. He presented his psycho-ontological models and empirical work on international platforms such as the World Psychotherapy Congress (Toprak, 2018) and World Congress of Behavioural and Cognitive Therapies 2019 (Toprak, 2019). During this period, he gave seminars on how fiqh (Islamic jurisprudence) and Sufi traditions explain modern psychopathologies (Toprak, 2018), and he organized presentations and workshops on how to apply models that can be developed from Islamic fiqh, kalam, and Sufism in contemporary clinical practice (Toprak, 2017, 2018).

Toprak is continuing his works on comprehending the differences in psychology understandings that arise as a result of ontology and epistemology discussions of different traditions of Islamic thought, creating models from the classical texts of Islamic thought that suggest solutions to the problems in modern psychotherapy, in addition to understanding the debates on the relationship between psychology, Islamic thought, and the philosophy of modern science. The Psychology in Islamic Thought Platform, which he established with a group of his colleagues as being the first platform established in the country, is still holding general seminars, specialized reading groups, and symposiums (İslam Düşüncesinde Psikoloji, 2020).

*Hooman Keshavarzi*

Keshavarzi is a psychologist from the United States and founder of Khalil Center, a psychological treatment and training center focused on teaching and providing Islamically oriented mental health services. Keshavarzi joined Ibn Haldun University (IHU). He is collaborating with the university and its faculty, to advance the novel study and practice of Islamically integrated mental health care. Hence, IHU has rapidly become a beacon of the momentum for the further development of an Islamic orientation or school of psychology in Turkey, by collaborating with the Khalil Center among other partners. Additionally, IHU operates a mental health clinic (IPAM)that is also a training center for IHU's clinical graduate students.

In the fall of 2018, Keshavarzi began teaching in Turkey a model of care he founded and used at Khalil Center, called "Traditional Islamically Integrated Psychotherapy" (TIIP). He now supervises student theses, helping to reinforce a program for the training of IP at IHU. Students in this program receive course instructions in Islamically integrated psychotherapy and clinical supervision by IHU's faculty. These students use the teaching clinic (i.e., IPAM) to conduct clinical research on the viability and clinical efficacy of Islamically integrated interventions, one of the streams of research at IHU. Furthermore, to further advance Islamic psychologies, IHU plans to offer certificate-based training in the TIIP model of care to mental health professionals.

*Malik Badri (d.2021)*

The leading role of Badri, the pioneer of this field, in these studies is well-known worldwide. Badri moved to Turkey in 2017 and started teaching in the Psychology Department of Sabahattin Zaim University. He also participated in many organizations and programs in the field of psychology and Islam in Turkey. His presence in Turkey has contributed to the introduction of international researchers of psychology into Turkish academics. Badri was influential in establishing the International Association of Islamic Psychology in Istanbul, Turkey, and hosted at his university many notable scholars such as Abdallah Rothman and Rasjid Skinner.

## THEORETICAL CONTRIBUTIONS FROM OUTSIDE THE CLINICAL FIELD

*Recep Şentürk*

Şentürk, the Rector of IHU, is a scholar who endeavors to form the theoretical background of IP. Furthermore, to practice the ideas against modern psychology's reductionist approach, he attempts to strengthen the psychology department by hosting pioneers in IP. The best examples of these attempts are the addition of Hooman Keshavarzi as a lecturer at IHU and opening a clinic that uses IP models. In this sense, Şentürk endeavors to make his university unique.

*Turgay Şirin*

Şirin is a pioneer in the field of spiritual counseling and the head of the Department of the Spiritual Counseling and Guidance in Turkey. He has endeavored to use religious data in psychotherapies and developed a therapy with religious elements called the "İHSAN Model." He recently established an association of spiritual counseling and guidance (Manevi Danışmanlıkve Rehberlik Derneği, n.d.)

## LEADING ASSOCIATIONS AND CENTERS AND THEIR LATEST WORKS

*Transpersonal Psychology Association*

The studies in this field have been periodically included in curricula of different associations and organizations' reading groups. However, systematic lectures were not held until the establishment of the Transpersonal Psychology Association. The first lecture was given by Merter in 2007.The association became a center providing theoretical and practical training in this field. Subsequently, Merter continued his training outside the association and in private. Although the association no longer exists, the activities continue around Merter's courses and lectures, mostly online.

*Psychology in Islamic Thought Platform*

The intellectual pursuit and the academic interests of this field have long sought an arena where they can flourish. In 2020, the Psychology in Islamic Thought Platform was established and became a venue where academic clinicians and those who are interested can exchange ideas, for example, mental health professionals and academicians in Islamic studies, to collaboratively conduct research. On the Psychology in Islamic Thought Platform, there are two structures: psychology in Islamic thought, where theoretical discussions are held in the context of modern science and psychology, and psychotherapy in the Islamic tradition, where discussions on the use of knowledge and concepts of Islamic thought in psychotherapy practices (İslam Düşüncesinde Psikoloji, 2020) are held. The activities on the platform are, for example, seminars on Islamic thought, psychology, and psychotherapy and opportunities to participate in reading groups, research teams, publications, and symposiums.

*IHU - the Psychology Department*

For the first time, in 2018, an Islamic-based psychology course was opened as an elective course in the Doctoral Program of Clinical Psychology at Ibn-i-Haldun University and taught for two semesters by Hooman Keshavarzi (İbn Haldun Üniversitesi, 2018).

*Khalil Center Türkiye*

Khalil Center is establishing a Family Wellness Center in Istanbul. This center is in response to the need for Islamically oriented marital and family services in Istanbul, Turkey. Khalil Center will follow its teaching clinic model by setting up a practice for the development of Islamically integrated models of family and marital well-being both for professionals and the community. The services offered to clients will include marital and family therapy and preventative community education such as seminars and workshops. The center will conduct research on Islamic models of marital and family therapy and provide a training program for student clinicians to learn and apply these modalities under the supervision of Medaim Yanık and Hooman Keshavarzi, among other distinguished faculty members.

MISCELLANEOUS IMPORTANT ACTIVITIES

*Spiritual Psychology Symposiums*

In this symposium series, efforts are made to discuss the relationship between Islam and psychology in various fields by bringing local and foreign scholars who are collaborating on this subject. The series was started in 2014 by Mustafa Atak and has continued in different provinces of Turkey through 2020. The studies have been transformed into scientific publications and five published books, a series called "Spiritual Psychology," where the sixth of the same series is being published.

*International Islamic Psychology Conference*

This historical event, hosted by Sabahattin Zaim University, was held for the first time in Istanbul in 2018, bringing the pioneers of this field from worldwide and Turkey together. It was again at İZU that training was led by Malik Badri and Abdallah Rothman on applying IP, providing courses such as "The Islamic Model of the Self," "How to Work with Clients within an Islamic Psychology Framework," "Understanding the Muslim Client," "Assessment of Muslim Clients- General Guidelines," and "The Fiqh and Ethics of Counseling." *Ilmu'n Nafs* and Modern Psychology Dialogues

In 2018, the Rector of IHU Prof. Dr. Recep Şentürk and Prof. Dr. Medaim Yanık discussed the key topics of this field for seven weeks, one side defending the Islamic thought, the other defending the modern psychology paradigm (İbn Haldun Üniversitesi, 2018).

*Psychology in Islamic Thought, Psychotherapy in Islamic Tradition Seminars*

The most systematic series of seminars in this regard were conducted by pioneers of psychology and psychiatry and Islamic studies fields of the "Psychology in Islamic Thought Platform," on the relationship of psychology and psychotherapy with medicine, philosophy, and Sufi traditions within the tradition of Islamic thought. Seminars were held under two categories: *"Psychology in Islamic Thought" "Psychotherapy in the Islamic Tradition."* Additionally, interviews were held with the seminar lecturers on the future of the relationship between Islamic thought and psychology and psychotherapy (Toprak, 2021a) [2].

---

2 İDP - 1 Taha Burak TOPRAK - Basic Questions, Basic Concepts, Basic Discussions, İGP 1 – Taha Burak TOPRAK – A case sample of an implementation, İDP 2 - Ömer TÜRKER - Psychology in Medicine and Philosophy of Islamic Traditions, İGP 2 - Medaim YANIK - Opportunities and Difficulties of Creating a Psychotherapy Model from Medicine and Philosophy of Islamic Traditions, İDP 3 - Ekrem DEMİRLİ - Psychology in the Islamic Sufi Tradition, İGP 3 - Mustafa MERTER - The Opportunities and Difficulties of Creating a Psychotherapy Model from the Islamic Sufi Tradition, İDP 4 - Zuhal AĞILKAYA ŞAHİN - Religion in Psychology and Psychotherapy, İGP 4 - Fatih YAVUZ - Our Relationship with Psychology and Psychotherapy, İDP 5 - Malik BEDRI - Islam and Psychology: Past, Present, Future, İGP 5 - Hooman KESHAVARZİ - Application of Islamic Thought to Clinical Practice: Introduction to Islamically integrated psychotherapy. These seminars were published as a book in the new period and organized the 1st Symposium on Psychology-Psychotherapy in Islamic Thought (Toprak, 2021).

### *Symposium on Psychology and Psychotherapy in Islamic Thought*

The Symposium of Psychology and Psychotherapy in Islamic Thought was held with participants who were motivated during the general seminars of the "Psychology in Islamic Thought" platform, to transform their interests into academic research. The symposium was shaped by presentations under general topics such as the relationship between Islamic thought and modern psychology and psychotherapy, the history of psychology, developmental psychology, psychopathology, and psychotherapy. The symposium has also contributed to identifying research themes and exchanging knowledge and experience, to create a base for further studies.

## RADIO AND TV PROGRAMS

### *Sufism and Human Psychology*

The Sufism and Human Psychology program was prepared and presented by Süleyman Derin, a professor in the field of Sufism. In this program, the leading names in IP and local and foreign intellectuals and academicians eager to establish a relationship between the rich knowledge of the Islamic heritage and psychology, such as Malik Badri, Mustafa Merter, Abdallah Rothman, Faik Özdengül, and Turgay Şirinve Ali Rıza Bayzan, are being hosted. In this program, some works such as İhya'uulumiddin of al-Ghazali, Mathnawi of Jalaladdin Rumi, and Masâlihu'l-Abdanwal'anfus of Balkhi are being studied again with a psychological perspective, in addition to various psychotherapy models and works of Western psychologists that are being discussed from an Islamic perspective.

The program is developing a theoretical background based on ideas rather than practical therapy. These weekly presented radio programs have been aired since 2018 and can be accessed athttps://www.erkamradyo.com/tasavvuf-ve-insan-psikolojisi.html (Derin, 2018). Derin has also presented many papers on Sufis and their possible contribution to psychology, such as "Spiritual Psychology of al-Ghazali, Rumi and Psychology" and "Positive Psychology and Sufism."[3]

### *Fîhi Mâ Fîh*

On TRT Avaz, one of the Turkish State's television channels, a medical doctor, Faik Özdengül, presented programs on Sufi psychology based on the works of Jalaladdin Rumi, called Fihi Ma Fih. The main theme of the programs was

3 Derin, Süleyman, Mevlânâ'nın Mesnevi'sinde Psikolojik Yaklaşımlar, Uluslararası Mevlânâ Sempozyumu Bildirileri = International Mevlânâ Symposium Papers, 2010, cilt: I, s. 345-358; Spiritual Psychology and Ghazali, 900. Vefat Yılında İmam Gazzali : Milletlerarası Tartışmalıİlmi Toplantı 07-09 Ekim 2011 İstanbul, 2012, s. 787-798; Rumi's approach to Happiness, 2nd Eurasian Congress of Positive Psychology, 2017

"Rumi and transcendental therapy." Dr. Ozdengul has authored books that mostly study Rumi's contribution to psychology.

### BOOKS

The books written in this field in Turkey can be divided into two categories. The first category comprises books that present a critical approach to the materialist ground of modern psychology and psychotherapy. They emphasize the contribution of religious and idealistic philosophies to psychology and, at times, refer to Islamic tradition.

Among these books are *Does Life Have a Meaning?* by psychiatrist Erol Göka (2013); "Labyrinths of the Spirit" and "Resistance of the Heart" by Psychiatrist Kemal Sayar (2003, 2006), and the "Language of Emotions" and "Beautiful Human Model" by Psychiatrist Nevzat Tarhan (2006, 2014).

The second category of books comprises the studies that directly emphasize the relationship between the Islamic tradition and psychology and psychotherapy, limiting the focus of the discussion to these two areas. The most important published book among these books is "900 layers of human being" written by Psychiatrist Mustafa Merter (2016), because it was the first systematic work in this field in Turkey and a best seller for a long time. Subsequently, Merter's work titled Nafs Psychology and the Language of Dreams was published (Merter, 2014).

Tarhan's "The Conscience of the time: Bediuzzaman" (Tarhan, 2012a) and "The Journey from the Mind to the Heart"(Tarhan,2012b) are considered to be psycho-biography essays on an important Muslim scholar, inspiring studies on how modern science and psychology can relate to the works of this scholar. In addition, Tarhan has other works titled "Mathnawi Therapy" (Tarhan, 2012c) and "Yunus Therapy" (Tarhan, 2013), on the effects of the works of Sufis on psychological well-being.

Another book that studies the relationship between Sufism and psychology is Kemal Sayar's (2009) work "Sufi Psychology", in which Sayar compiled relevant articles by the leading names in the field on the relationship between Sufi thought and psychotherapy.

Another work in this field is Prof. Ekşi's edited work, titled "The Spiritual Counseling and Psychotherapy," analyzing both historical and contemporary Islamic scholars and thinkers in the context of psychotherapy and spiritual counseling (Ekşi & Kaya, 2016).

Another important work is Ağılkaya Şahin's (2020) book. This book is especially crucial for Turkish readers because it compiles all the discussions worldwide and presents information on the studies conducted in Turkey that are related to the subject.

Another important contribution to the field is a book that comprises 10 seminars, systematically conducted by the Psychology in Islamic Thought Platform on the methodology of IP. This work is the first of its type in the field because it explains in detail the methodology discussions of Taha Burak Toprak, Medaim Yanık, Fatih Kasım Yavuz, and Hooman Keshevarzi and the application of the models of Taha Burak Toprak, Mustafa Merter, and Hooman Keshevarzi in psychotherapy (Toprak, 2021a).

## Discussion

The relationship between Islam and psychology in Turkey, especially in the Ottoman era, was conducted in a combined manner with Islamic philosophical tradition and the current psychological debates of their times. However, with the newly established republic (1923), the country conducted a strict secular modernization process. The state removed religion, including the Islamic tradition, which guided nearly all fields of life for centuries, from its operations. As a result, there were consequences like loss of practical language tools, a language revolution, and the removal of religion from the operations of the government.

Therefore, IP and psychotherapy studies, especially in the practical clinical field were not possible until the 2000s. The return to the Islamic civilization's resources, which also started in the academic fields as well after the 1990s, have facilitated the intellectual process of "being yourself," where a reflection on the studies of Islam, psychology and psychotherapy is evident.

The contributions to this field can be categorized as contributions from the clinical and non-clinical fields. Clinical contributions started in the field of Sufism and then proceeded with the studies of re-establishing a relationship with all the rich scientific traditions of Islamic civilization such as theology, philosophy, and fiqh and the production of knowledge on psychology and psychotherapy within this context. The theoretical contributions in the clinical field are based on the Sufi tradition and the works of classical Muslim scholars, such as those of Said Nursi. Since the beginning of 2000, theoretical studies have been criticized as being insufficient because empirical studies are necessary to establish IP as a science. Notably, this criticism is valid because very few empirical studies have been conducted.

However, important names in IP have found parties in Turkey who are interested in their models. In addition to clinical contributions, the number of theoretical and practical television and radio programs is increasing, showing a deep interest among the public. A few universities, for example, IHU and Sabahattin Zaim University, are open to adding IP to their curricula. Furthermore, the civil society activities that started with the Transpersonal Psychology Association in the 2000s continued with the works of the Psychology in Islamic Thought

Organization on Islam, psychology, and psychotherapy http://islamvepsikoloji.com). As for the books, the contributions in the context of Sufism, theology, fiqh, the philosophy of Islam, psychology, and psychotherapy were predominantly on the theoretical aspects. The theoretical richness of IP is not supported by empirical evidence, except for that in the work of the Psychology in Islamic Thought Platform titled "*Islam, Psychology – Psychotherapy - Solid Fundamentals and New Horizons.*"

## Conclusion

In conclusion, the pioneering names and institutions of IP in the Turkish context have debated the philosophical background of modern psychology and Islamic thought and recognized the necessity of conducting research that applies empirical methods to establish IP. When all these aspects are considered, Turkey is a promising country in terms of Islam, psychology, and psychotherapy.

ACKNOWLEDGMENT: This article was translated by Sena Akbay Safi.

## References

Ağılkaya Şahin, Z. (2020). *Psikoloji ve psikoterapide din [Religion in psychology and psychotherapy]*. Çamlıca Yayınları.

Derin, S. (2018). *Tasavvuf ve insan psikolojisi [Sufism and human psychology]* [Radiobroadcast]. Erkam Radyo. https://www.erkamradyo.com/tasavvuf-ve-insan-psikolojisi.html

Ekşi, H. & Kaya, Ç. (2016). *Manevi yönelimli psikoterapi ve psikolojik danışma [Spiritually oriented psychotherapy and psychological counseling]* (1st ed.). Kaknüs Yayınları.

Göka, E. (2013). *Hayatın anlamı var mı?[Does life have a meaning?]*. Timaş Yayınları.

Gülerce, A. (2006). History of psychology in Turkey as a sign of diverse modernization and global psychologization. In A. C. Brock (Ed.), *Internationalizing the History of Psychology* (pp. 75–93). New York University Press.

İbn Haldun Üniversitesi. (2018, March 21). *İlm-inefsve modern psikoloji diyaloğu [a dialogue between ilmun Nafs and Modern Psychology]* [Video]. YouTube. https://www.youtube.com/watch?v=6fUPgIjGZc&list=PLw60El9Uz6M2L-LuBdYaNuPFzySmfKrLxf

İslam Düşüncesinde Psikoloji Platformu. (2020, February). *Biz kimiz? [Who are we?]* Retrieved from http://islamvepsikoloji.com

Kızılgeçit, M. (2013). The history of modern psychology in "İlmü>n-Nefs" written by İzmirli İsmail Hakkı. *Dinbilimleri Akademik Araştırma Dergisi, 13*(1), 157–173.

Manevi Danışmanlıkve Rehberlik Derneği. (n.d.). *MDR nedir? [What is SC?]* Retrieved from https://mdr.org.tr/mdr-nedir/

Merter, M. (2014). Psikolojinin üçüncü boyutu nefs psikolojisi ve rüyaların dili [The third dimension of psychology, the psychology of Nafs and the language of dreams] (1st ed.). Kaknüs Yayınları.

Merter, M. (2016). Dokuz yüz katlı insan: Tasavvuf ve benötesi psikolojisi (Transpersonal psikoloji) [Nine Hundred Layer of a Human; Sufiism and transpersonal psychology] (15th ed.). Kaknüs Yayınları.

Merter, M. (2021). İslam tasavvuf geleneğinden bir psikoterapi modelleri oluşturmanın imkan ve zorlukları [the Opportunities and the difficulties of creating psychotherapy models from the Islamic Sufi tradition]. In T. B. Toprak(Ed.). İslam *düşüncesinde psikoloji ve psikoterapi: Sağlam temeller ve yeni ufuklar içinde [Psychology and Psychotherapy in Islamic thought: Solid Fundamentals and New Horizons]."* (pp. 231–251). Turkuvaz Yayınları.

Naim, B. A. (2018). İlmü>nnefs tercümesi felsefe açısından psikoloji meseleleri. [Translation of Psychology: psychology issues from the point of view of philosophy] R. Alpyağıl & F. Yıldız (Eds.), İz Yayıncılık. (Original work published 1332.)

Sayar, K. (2003). Ruhun labirentleri [Labyrinths of the spirit]. Ufuk Kitapları.

Sayar, K. (2006). *Kalbin direnişi [Resistance of the heart]*. Karakalem Yayınları.

Sayar, K. (2009). *Sufi psikolojisi [Sufi psychology]*. Timaş Yayınları.

Şehbenderzade Fillibeli, A. H. (2019). *Ruh hallerinin ilmi ilm-i ahvalir'r-ruh [Knowledge on the states of the soul] (Psikoloji)* (1st ed.) (H. Osta, Çev.). Büyüyenay Yayınları. (Original work published 1911.)

Şirin, T. (2019). *Modern Psikoloji Tarihinde Osmanlı'nın Yeri [The Place of the Ottoman Empire in the History of Modern Psychology]*. Book of Abstracts of the Symposium on the History of Civilization Sciences in Islam (pp. 22-23). Istanbul: Ibn Haldun University

Tarhan, N. (2006). *Duyguların dili [Language of emotions]*. Timaş Yayınları.

Tarhan, N. (2012a). *Akıldan kalbe yolculuk: Bediüzzaman modeli [The conscience of the time: Bediuzzaman]* (13th ed.). Nesil Yayınları.

Tarhan, N. (2012b). *Çağın vicdanı Bediüzzaman [The journey from the mind to the heart]*. Nesil Yayınları.

Tarhan, N. (2012c). *Mesnevi terapi [Mathnawi therapy]*. Timaş Yayınları.

Tarhan, N. (2013). *Yunus terapi [Yunus therapy]*. Timaş Yayınları.

Tarhan, N. (2014). *Güzel insan modeli [Beautiful Human Model]*. Timaş Yayınları.

Toprak,T. B. (2016, August). Çağdaş *OKB teorilerinde tıkanma ve 'dimağdaki meratib-iilim' bilgisi* üzerine *[a work on the contemporary theories of OCD and the ranks of knowledge in the dimağ (brain)]* [Video]. Periscope.https://www.pscp.tv/karakalemdergsi/1BdGYdqlRaAKX

Toprak, T.B. (2017, September 29–October 1). İlmün *nefse göre insanın yapısı ve işleyiş [the structure and the functioning of humans according to ilmun Nafs].* [Conference presentation].I. Ulusal Bütüncül Psikoterapi Kongresi "Psikoterapileri Bütünleştirme", Darıca, Kocaeli, Türkiye.

Toprak, T.B. (2018, June 7–9) *An attempt for alternative approach for the structure of human and its applications: Ilm'unafs.* [Conference presentation]. 22nd World Congress of Psychotherapy, Amsterdam.

Toprak, T.B. (2018). Dini obsesyon ve kompulsiyonların psikoterapisinde kuramlar, imkanlar, sınırlılıklar [Theories, opportunities and limitations of the psychotherapy on religious obsessions and compulsions]. *Bütüncül Psikoterapi Dergisi, 1*(1), 123–141.

Toprak, T.B. (2019, June 17–20). *An integrative model for religious OCD.* [Conference presentation]. 9[th]World Congress of Behavioral and Cognitive Therapies, Berlin.

Toprak, T. B. (Ed.). (2021a). İslam *düşüncesinde psikoloji ve psikoterapi: Sağlam temeller ve yeni ufuklar [Psychology and Psychotherapy in Islamic thought: Solid Fundamentals and New Horizons].*Turkuvaz Yayınları.

Toprak, T. B. (2021b). İslam vepsikoloji: Temelsorular, temelkavramlar, temeltartışmalar [Islam

and Psychology: Basic Questions, Basic Concepts, Basic Discussions]. T. B. Toprak (Ed.). İslam *düşüncesinde psikoloji ve psikoterapi: Sağlam temeller ve yeni ufuklar içinde [Psychology and Psychotherapy in Islamic thought: Solid Fundamentals and New Horizons].*(pp. 5–38). Turkuvaz Yayınları.

Toprak, T. B. (2021c). İslam ve psikoterapi: Bir model ve uygulama örneği. [Islam and Psychotherapy: A case sample of an implementation]. T. B. Toprak (Ed.). İslam *düşüncesinde psikoloji ve psikoterapi: Sağlam temeller ve yeni ufuklar içinde [Psychology and Psychotherapy in Islamic thought: Solid Fundamentals and New Horizons].*(pp. 98–146). Turkuvaz Yayınları.

Yanık, M. (2021). İslam tıpvefelsefegeleneklerindenbirpsikoterapimodelioluşturmanınimkanvezorlukları [Opportunities and Difficulties of Creating a Psychotherapy Model from Medicine and Philosophy of Islamic Traditions]. In T. B. Toprak (Ed.), İslam *düşüncesinde psikoloji ve psikoterapi: Sağlam temeller ve yeni ufuklar içinde [Psychology and Psychotherapy in Islamic thought: Solid Fundamentals and New Horizons].* (pp. 205–231). Turkuvaz Yayınları.

Yavuz, K. F. (2021). Psikolojivepsikoterapiyleilişkimiz [Our relationship with psychology and psychotherapy]. In T. B. Toprak (Ed.), İslam *düşüncesinde psikoloji ve psikoterapi: Sağlam temeller ve yeni ufuklar içinde [Psychology and Psychotherapy in Islamic thought: Solid Fundamentals and New Horizons].* (pp. 251–279). Turkuvaz Yayınlar

CHAPTER FIFTEEN

# Islamic Psychology in the United Kingdom: Development in Theory and Application

RASJID SKINNER

ON FIRST SITTING DOWN to write this chapter, the author realised it would be better written by someone else—someone with knowledge in the field, but not so intimately involved with its history. As the writer was intimately involved, probably from around the time of inception of Islamic psychology (IP) in the UK, he realised his account would inevitably lack objectivity. As far as he was able, the writer has sought and included other perspectives, and he apologises to all those whose contributions to the IP movement in the UK is missing or has not been given its full due.

## The early years: the gestation of a concept

In the main, the story of IP in the UK begins with individual clinicians (working largely in their own silos) who found "Western" psychology inadequate for explaining their own personal experiences, and for understanding and treating the needs of their clients (especially, but not exclusively, Muslim clients). As such, they then sought something more appropriate from Islamic sources.

The growth of the IP movement in the UK slowly gathered momentum when these clinicians found each other and began to collaborate. It has often come to the writer's mind that, in this gathering, he was witnessing (first nationally, and then internationally) the formation of a diamond, with its growing number of facets, each reflecting a different nuance of the one light.

Starting in the late 1970s, there would seem, on reflection, to have been three major vectors that have pushed the writer to develop his thoughts on the concept of IP. The primary one (as with many others attracted to the field) was the recognition that mainstream "Western" clinical psychology theories and derived therapies offended a sense of fitrah, and were inadequate for explaining personal and clinical experiences. For example "true" dreams that healed as well as illuminated; "true" but counterintuitive intuition; out-of-reality states of ecstasy which differed from manic states of psychoses; and the way the body could take command of the Self at times of critical danger and, otherwise, override both reasoning and biological instinct.

The author was aware that such phenomena were recognised in the marginal "Western" psychologies of Carl Jung and George Groddeck, (see Jung, 2009; Groddeck, 1923), but was not fully satisfied by their explanatory models—although he has maintained the view that Jung's psychology is the closest "Western" tradition to IP– a view which has found favour with others.

In 1977, the writer said the Shahadah (Muslim profession of faith) at the London Central Mosque. This gave him access to some outstanding Islamic scholars. Over the next few years, the writer was able to benefit from discussions with, notably, Mukhtar Holland, Hasan le Guy Eaton, and Shaykh Zahran Ibrahim.

These scholars generously gave the writer hours of their time, explaining the various meanings and nuances of key concepts, such as nafs, qalb, aql, fuad, fitrah, and their use by classical Islamic scholars, particularly Hamid Al-Ghazali. From this information the writer was able to select meanings that made sense of personal and clinical experiences, and to sketch out (with the help of Hakim Salim Khan see below), a conceptual framework of the Self as an aid to clinical formulation. In addition, Shaykh Zahran (one of the Al-Azhari trained imams at the London Central Mosque), gave the writer an understanding of the principles of Fiqh and its therapeutic value when applied correctly.

Having an Islamically based conceptual framework for understanding the Self and its "mental" diseases did not, however, by itself lead the writer to the concept of an IP as is generally understood today, that is, a psychology rooted in Islamic paradigms and distinct from the psychology that has evolved from Western paradigms. The term "Islamic psychology" was certainly in use by the early 1980s, and probably before then (and, in the UK, there was an interest around Islam and psychology connected with the Islamicisation movement).

Generally, however, the term applied to the fitting of Quranic terms into Western psychological concepts. An "online" search by Paul Kaplick (Kaplick & Skinner, 2017) failed to find any use of IP in its generally accepted current sense prior to 1989. This is not to say others had not conceived of an Islamic paradigmatic psychology prior to this date. Malik Badri was certainly thinking in these terms in the 1970s, as they told the writer when they first met in the early 1990s (see the introduction to the second edition of *The Dilemma* (Badri, 2016)). But for the writer, conceiving of a psychology entirely identified by its Islamic paradigm itself involved something of a paradigm shift in thinking. For this shift the vectors came principally from Malik Badri, Hakim Salim Khan, and the anthropologist Akbar S. Ahmed, who was in London in the late 1970s and early 1980s.

Akbar S. Ahmed, already an established anthropologist, was then developing his proposition of an "Islamic anthropology" (see Ahmed, 1984, 1986); that is, an anthropology based on Islamic sources exemplified by classical Muslim social scientists, and which provided a basis for critiquing Western anthropology. Interestingly, Akbar S. Ahmed's proposition attracted much debate within the Royal Anthropological Institute, one edition of the institute's journal being entirely devoted to it. By contrast, the British Psychological Society has maintained a stolid indifference to the emerging IP movement in the UK.

Malik Badri's (1979) book *The Dilemma of Muslim Psychologists* was given to the writer in the early 1980s by Samir, owner of the Dar ul Taqwa bookshop near the London Central Mosque, with words to the effect, "You need to read this." For the writer, as with others, this book had a decisive impact. Though the writer thought the book had not gone far enough in conceptualising an IP, it was the first work he had read that clearly started from an Islamic basis in critiquing Western psychology, rather than from that of Western psychology, and mostly of the American variety, and which tended to assimilate Islamic concepts (see Kaplick & Skinner, 2017). Furthermore, it was refreshingly written by someone who was a clinician and not only a scholar. *The Dilemma* encouraged the writer by making him realise that others, from outside his own silo, saw the need to develop an Islamically grounded clinical psychology.

The third person to seed the writer with a concept of "Islamic psychology" was Hakim Salim Khan. The writer met Hakim Salim in the early 1980s, when he was already becoming known as an expert on Unani Tibb. Hakim Salim introduced the writer to a tradition of Islamic medicine that was rooted in classical Islamic thought and which extended into psychology. Hakim Salim was then working on his influential book *Islamic Medicine*, which included a section on psychology (Khan, 1986). He later established the Mohsin Clinic and has on occasion taught courses on Islamic counselling from a Tibb perspective.

In 1989, the International Institute of Islamic Thought invited the writer to speak at a workshop on Islam and psychology. The resulting paper was entitled "Traditions, paradigms and basic concepts in Islamic psychology" (the paper was accessibly published in 2018 (Skinner, 2018), but without the original diagram). The paper argued from Kuhn's thesis (Kuhn, 1964) that all science precedes from culturally influenced paradigms of thoughts, and that it was therefore legitimate to speak of Islamic Architecture, Islamic Medicine, and so on, when these were based on Islamic paradigms. It thus defined IP as a psychology based on Islamic paradigms, that included concepts (such as Qalb, Aql, Fitrah) used in the Quran with respect to the human self. But the paper proposed that account should also be made of the understanding and use made of such concepts by classical Muslim scholars, such as Al-Ghazali.

It argued that one of the paradigms of IP was that, unlike most Western schools, it encompassed the spiritual component of the Self (at its heart), and the body. It mentioned that there were ways of treating mental illness that were distinctly Islamic (such as traditions of music therapy, "Tibb", and therapeutic architecture) but that treatments evolving from every tradition could be used, provided they fitted with an Islamic conception of the Self and used with an Islamic understanding of mental health.

The three levels of the Self mentioned in the Quran were mentioned as a guide to defining mental health and ill health, and the fundamental dynamic within the Self with which the therapist could work. Levels of the Self higher than that of Nafs Mutmaina, as described in some Sufi traditions, were not mentioned, partly to avoid unnecessary controversy, but also due to the view whereby a patient who desires help to progress beyond "Nafs Mutmaina" would be ill advised to seek it through the average psychotherapist.

FIGURE 1 (FROM THE 1989 PAPER)

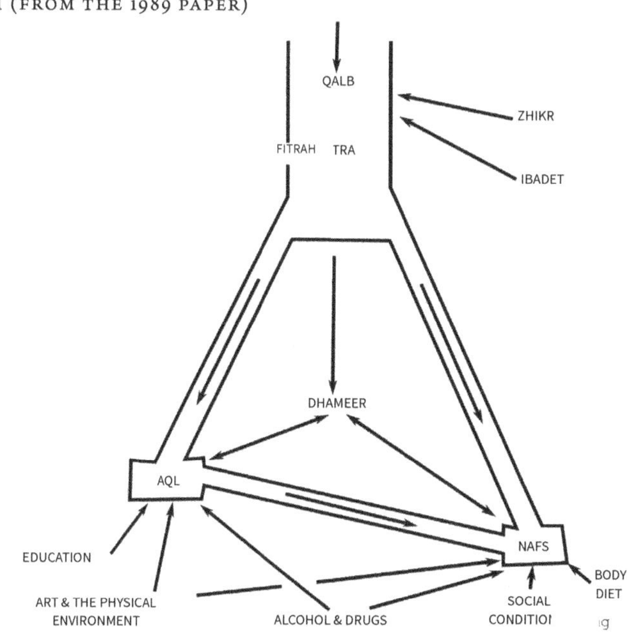

A simple diagram of the Self was presented with the paper (see Figure 1). This diagram had been sketched out with Hakim Salim Khan, as an aid to help the working clinician diagnose and treat holistically from an Islamic perspective. The diagram was based largely (from the discussions with Mukhtar Holland) on Al-Ghazali's general use of terms, particularly in the Ihya llum al Din. It was stressed that the terms used (such as Qalb, Aql, Fitrah) had subtleties and depths of meaning that were open to different translations into English, but that the simple meanings given in the model were sound, and sufficient for clinical purposes. It was stressed that other authentic models could be derived from Quranic concepts. By and large, the model of the Self presented in the 1989 paper has been used to the present day in the UK in clinical practice and in teaching, but with some modifications.

The "Conscience" (Dhameer) was included in the original diagram because, at the time, there was a tendency to equate Islamic terms with Freudian vocabulary. "Dhameer" was thus included in the diagram to make clear this was formed from the Qalb as well as external forces and was therefore different from Freud's Superego. As the tendency to "Freudianise" Islamic terms declined over time, "Dhameer" was dropped from the diagram as an unnecessary complication.

A later diagram included "Sirr" as an inner part of the Qalb, and "Mithal" to indicate a faculty within the Qalb for translating spiritual realities into understandable symbolic imagery, and which invited comparison with Jung's understanding of "archetypes". Both terms were later dropped from the diagram, again because experience indicated they were unnecessary complications for clinical practice. Over time, some additions to the model were made. Following discussions with Samir Mahmoud on Ibn Arabi's understanding of the body, more emphasis was given to the connection between Qalb and body, and a connecting line drawn between them on the diagram.

Following discussions with Abdal Hakim Winter (and with reference to Gionotti, 2001) two other changes were made. Firstly, a section of Aql was located within the Qalb, described, following Al-Ghazali, as the "fifth level of Aql", to indicate that there is an aspect of Aql directly connected to the Qalb, which receives, articulates, understands, and transmits true inspiration (gnosis). The other four levels of Aql (memory, deduction, etc.) essentially operate from input from the outer world. Secondly, the term "Nafs", to denote the animal drives or energies within the Self, was replaced by Al-Ghazali's preferred term "Hawa". From a lengthy conversation with Mukhtar Holland on the meaning of the term Nafs, the writer's recollection is that he was told there were at least eleven different uses of the term in the Quran, from a basic root sense that could perhaps be translated as "vital force" with a derivative sense of "state of being". In the original 1989 diagram, Nafs was used in its common colloquial sense of collective psychological drives or appetites. Those forces contained therein being in themselves morally neutral, or, more positively, in Ibn Arabi's understanding, with a disposition to aid the human being as their master.

However, it became increasingly apparent that the multiple senses of "Nafs" was a cause of confusion. In particular, confusion occurred between the sense of "Nafs" as psycho-biological drives and "Nafs" as in "Nafs amara bi su"—a state of the Self when under the control of unruly "animal" forces.

"Hawa", the term in the model used to replace "Nafs", can be loosely translated (Abdal Hakim Winter, personal communication) as "animal self". However, a better term, perhaps, is "appetitive self"—that is, the "vis appetita" of Thomas Aquinas. Idris Watts has suggested a further useful modification, adding the term "Shawah" with "Hawa" to indicate the two possible states of the appetites/drives; that is, either being in a state of harmony with the qalb or in an unruly state.

The diagram of the Self in current use is illustrated in Figure 2, and the current diagram illustrating the different levels of the Self in Figure 3 (from Skinner, 2019).

FIGURE 2 (SKINNER, 2019)

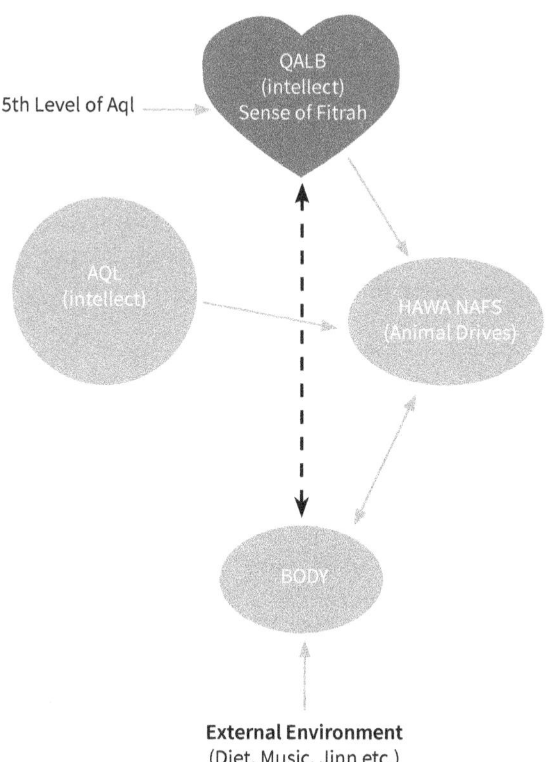

FIGURE 3 (SKINNER, 2019)

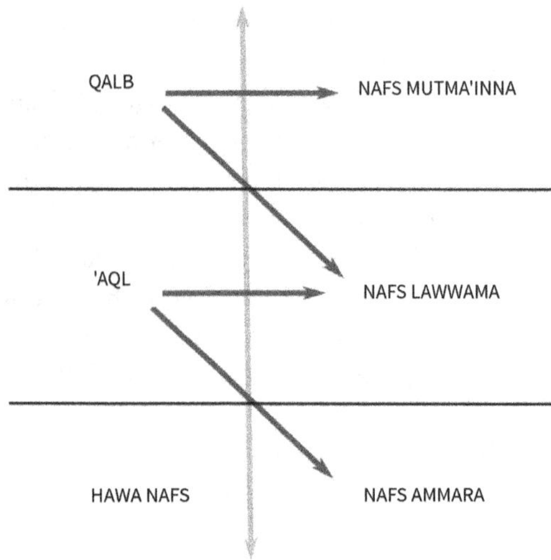


The model of the Self and its diagrammatic representation, as described above, have in substance been widely used in clinical practice and teaching since 1989, so an ijma can be said to exist regarding its usefulness and authenticity. In 2018, when attending the first international conference of the IAIP in Istanbul, the writer was agreeably surprised to discover that the Sudanese clinical psychologist, Elham Abubakr Elsiddig, had produced an almost identical model, also based on Al-Ghazali's work. This, of course, is not to say that there could not be other models equally as useful, or more so.

## Putting into practice: teaching and organising

Initially, the writer's motive to devise an Islamically based psychology was to aid his own understanding of the Self and to improve his therapeutic practice, which was almost entirely with non-Muslim clients. IP was seen as, in reality, a universal psychology, and there has been recurrent debate, in the UK as well as elsewhere, about whether it should therefore be labelled as "Islamic", with the implication that it is culturally specific. It is certainly the writer's view that as Aquinas conceived "Christian" psychology would look much the same. He has been informed that a "Jewish" psychology has been developed at the University of Jerusalem for use with Haredi (Orthodox) communities, which has points of similarity with Islamic models, and with Islamic therapeutic principles. The writer has not been able to confirm this.

It was, however, apparent by the late 1970s that there was a need to put into practice specifically Islam-compatible psychological therapies for the benefit of the Muslim community, in particular, therapies that would accommodate Islamic spiritual belief and experience. At that time, there were very few Muslim psychological therapists in the UK (the writer knew only one apart from himself). There were, however, several Muslim psychiatrists who had become aware of mental health problems in the Muslim community and who were not being adequately treated within the National Health Service. One such psychiatrist was Dr. Ahmed Khan, a consultant at an east London hospital.

Ahmed Khan conducted a survey of Muslim mental health in the early 1980s (the first of which that the writer was aware). He was one of several Muslim health professionals involved at the time with an organisation called the Transcultural Psychiatry Society (not to be confused with the transcultural special interest group of the Royal College of Psychiatry). This organisation was involved with a community mental health centre for ethnic minorities in London. Khan and others were concerned that this centre and the Transcultural Psychiatry Association were side-lining Muslim interests.

Matters came to a head in the early 1980s at a conference on ethnic minority mental health needs. The organisers wanted participants to break into "geographic groups" (e.g., Mediterranean, Asian, etc.) to discuss their views. The Muslims present, about twenty, argued that their needs were the same irrespective of geographical origin. The chairman, a well-known "transcultural" psychiatrist, was not happy and argued against the proposal. A heated debate ensued. Eventually, the Muslims got their way, and all but one joined the Muslim group. When the conference proceedings were published, however, the deliberations of the Muslim group were conspicuously excluded. Clearly not welcome were identities based on religious affiliation, nor demands for mental health services that accommodated religious beliefs. The writer's application to join the TPS was, unsurprisingly, refused, without any cogent explanation.

Ahmed Khan continued to be an active supporter of the IP movement, and, as a visiting professor at the University of Karachi, initiated a conference on IP, at the University, in 2006.

In the late 1970s, Jafar Kareem, a psychoanalyst at the Tavistock clinic—the citadel of Freudian therapy in the UK—established an out-centre in North London called "Nafsiyat". It was intended to cater for the mental health needs of ethnic minorities (initially, it seemed, mainly Muslim). The writer visited Nafsiyat shortly after it opened and spoke to the staff. The impression he gained was that, despite its name, the Nafsiyat clinic was making no real attempt to accommodate therapies to Islamic beliefs and was, essentially, only offering culturally adjusted psychoanalytic therapy. Later, the writer met Jafar Kareem and found him unsympathetic to the view that Islam had anything to offer by way of understanding or treating mental illness. (Khalida Khan, see below, told me that in the 1980s she also visited the Nafsiyat clinic and took a similarly dim view of it.)

In 1984, the writer assumed a post at Lynfield Mount Hospital in Bradford, the hospital which boasted the first "Transcultural" psychiatry unit in the UK. The unit presented itself nationally as an authority in the field. Almost all its clients were Muslims. The writer was requested to join the unit, because of his qualifications, but received a distinctly unfriendly reception at his first team meeting. Later, he discovered the reason. Almost all the members of the team were connected with a Christian mission in Peshawar, and seemed to view Islam as psychologically dysfunctional, and practised therapy (in Urdu, Pushtu, and Bengali) to weaken the hold of Islamic culture. (Therapy, for example, was conducted in mixed gender groups to eliminate "dysfunctional" views of gender; also, reportedly, Muslim women patients were taken to "mixed" swimming lessons for the same reason.) There was clearly the need to advocate an Islamically rooted psychology and therapeutic services that saw Islam as part of the cure, not as part of the problem. Others too were aware of the need. Two sisters Khalida and Humera Khan were the first people the writer came across who attempted to meet the need in an organised way.

Khalida and Humera can perhaps best, though still inadequately, be described as politically savvy community activists, sometimes operating at governmental level, who have been instigators of numerous Muslim projects over the years. In 1985, they established in London the An Nisa Society to promote the welfare of, in particular, Muslim women and children. They were aware that the Euro-centric forms of psychological therapy being offered to Muslim clients by mainstream services were at best lacking in efficacy, and at worst were damaging. As such, they began to seek the resources required to set up an Islamically compatible counselling service, but at that time were unable to find either a theoretical model or available practitioners.

Within a year or two of the publication of the 1989 paper, the writer met with Aliya Haeri, an American-trained psychotherapist and wife of Shaykh Fadhlalla Haeri, a Shia Shaykh of Tariqa and writer on psychology from a Sufi perspective. Aliya, who had an expert knowledge of Jungian psychology and had written at least one (unpublished) article on its relationship to Islam, had liked the ideas in the 1989 paper and, the writer believes, published the diagrammatic model of the Self it contained—–at least for circulation within the Tariqa. She also, as the writer remembers, asked the husband-and-wife team of Abdullah Maynard and Sabnum Dharamsi to teach courses on Islam and counselling. These started, the writer believes, in the mid-1990s.

By the mid-1990s, An Nisa had become aware of the 1989 paper and had sought opinions from the known practitioners of Islamically based therapy. They then succeeded in acquiring funding to seed an Islamically compatible "person-centred" counselling course, succeeded in getting it accredited by one of the national counselling bodies, and asked the Maynards to teach it. The first course started in 1997.After a couple of years, the Maynards ran the course independently of An Nisa and have done so ever since.

It has been difficult to obtain full details about the Maynard's Islamic counselling course, but their website (islamiccounselling.info) refers to the Sufi inspiration of their teaching approach, which is incorporated within the framework of the Rogerian Person-Centred model. The writer has never been aware of any conflict between the Maynards' approach to IP and what is taught on the IAIP-approved five-day course, and with what is put into practice in the Ihsaan network (see below). Over the years, Abdullah and Sabnum's course has generated many people trained in "person-centred" counselling from an Islamic perspective.

In 2002, An Nisa held a watershed two-day conference, "Healing the Self", in London. This conference highlighted the issues around mental illness in the Muslim community, something of a taboo subject then. It brought together most of the people working with Islamic psychology at the time, including Hakim Salim Khan, Abdullah Maynard, Sabnum Dharamsi, and Rabia Malik, whom the writer met for the first time. Rabia Malik presented her research on Pakistani women's understanding of depression (Malik, 2000). As far as the writer was aware, this was the first demonstration that Muslims had a distinctive way, even at a folk level, of understanding mental illness, that related to Islamic traditions of thought; thus, ipso facto, there was a need for psychological therapies that related to those traditions.

Like other pioneers in the field of IP, Rabia had experienced a dissonance between her own personal and clinical experience that drove her to conceptualise a psychology based on Islamic metaphysics, which did not split body, mind, and spirit in its understanding of illness and treatment. Rabia undertook a course on Unani Tibb with Hakim Salim Khan and planned to develop her understanding of IP under the guidance of Halima Krausen and Shayh Iman Mehdi Rizvi. Rabia worked as a Systemic Family Therapist at the prestigious Marlborough Cultural Therapy Centre, until it was closed, where she was able to develop therapies consistent with Islamic culture. She has continued to do so; in particular, developing therapies based on the Ninety-nine names, and on Quranic narratives.

Shortly after the "Healing the Self" conference, An Nisa brought together a number of people in the field, including Rabia Malik, Abdullah Maynard,

Sabnum Dharamsi, Hakim Salim Khan, Hanif Bobat, Alijan Haider (an NHS Health Commissioner), Halima Krausen, and the writer, in an attempt to form an Institute for Islamic Counselling and Psychotherapy. By that time, there was a considerable number of Muslims trained as therapists, and one need was to have an accreditation system to distinguish those who were working from an Islamic paradigm, from those who were simply following "Western models". The attempt failed, mainly because of the inability to attract the funding to support a secretariat.

An Nisa continued to put on events on Islam and mental health. This writer continued to give conference papers and lectures on IP, or referred to it within papers on culture and clinical psychology, including papers to a Royal College of Psychiatry conference, the British Psychological Society "race and culture" conference, a series of talks around the UK regions as part of a BPS Clinical Division "race and culture" roadshow (which met with a decidedly mixed response), and the first of three broadcasts on BBC Radio 4 in 2009 (*Beyond Belief*, 2009, 2017, 2019). In 2010, the writer was asked to submit a paper on Islam and psychology to a mainstream journal (Skinner, 2010). Rabia Malik was also giving talks and publishing (Malik, 2018; Malik & Mandin, 2012; Malik et al., 2007). Abdullah Maynard submitted a report to the Home Office on Muslim mental health (Maynard, 2008), which described the way different Muslim therapists were putting IP into practice. Malik Badri's (2000) book, *Contemplation*, as well as *The Dilemma*, were widely circulated.

All these activities publicised the concept of IP, and attracted the attention of Hanif Bobat and Abul Hussain, who were connected with the UK members of IAMP (the International Association of Muslim Psychologists). Hanif and Abul had been running popular conferences on culture and mental health, under the title of EHI (Ethnic Health Initiative) from the late 1990s, capitalising on a growing interest from "mainstream" mental health professionals aware of the inadequacy of "Western" therapies in treating "ethnic minorities". In 2001, Abul published an article on Islamic belief and mental health in a widely read mainstream journal (Hussain, 2001).

From about 2008 the EHI conferences always included a specifically "Islamic psychology" content. In addition to UK speakers, Hanif and Abul invited speakers from abroad. Malik Badri accepted the invitation, and later Hanan Dover from Australia and Carrie York from the US, who produced an elegant and influential research paper on the effective use of Quranic Rukiya to heal non-Muslims with mental disorders (see Al-Karam, 2015). The EHI conferences sadly ended in 2015, due largely to cutbacks in NHS training budgets. However, when these conferences had been up and running, they attracted a large number of Muslim practitioners, including those from the UK branch of

IAMP, and created networks and an appetite for more involvement with IP.

One person who attended an EHI course was Nasima Khanom. Nasima, a systemic family therapist, went on to attend one of the five-day courses in IP (see below) and then, in 2015, established IPPA (Islamic Psychology Professionals Association). IPPA has proved immensely important in the development of the movement. It has run monthly seminars in London on IP topics, which attract those curious about IP, as well as the converted. It has started supervision groups from an IP basis and set up the first "online" network, which has proved vital in connecting those with an interest in IP, and for distributing news of events. It would be fair to say that almost everybody with an interest in IP in the UK is now connected with IPPA.

In 2008, four clinical psychologists in Bradford met to design a short syllabus on the principles of IP. Initially the intention was to produce a course for local imams, but shifted to a course for psychological therapists, with the objective of helping them out of "the lizard's hole". The group included Dr. Ruksana Arshad, and the writer, and was led by Dr Abul Wali Wardak. Abul Wali initially studied Islamic sciences at Mecca University under Muhammed Al Ghazali, and after graduation switched to psychology, studied with Charles Figley and Terence Keene in the US, studied for a British doctorate on trauma reactions in Afghanistan, was the UN/WHO representative for trauma work in Kuwait and Bosnia, and then qualified as a British clinical psychologist. During nearly a year's course of seminars, we were able to examine, with Abdul Wali, the Quranic terms used to describe psychological processes and the use of these by early Muslims. The "Al-Ghazali" model provided in the 1989 paper was revisited and we were able to arrive at a perspective about the most important elements of knowledge to impart in a short intensive course.

The outcome was the five-day course "Approaches to Islamic psychology and psychotherapy". The course involved components on the cultural niche of Western clinical psychology and psychiatry, the Islamic paradigm, key Islamic concepts, an Al-Ghazali-based model of the Self, key Islamic diagnostic principles (such as consideration of primary as well as secondary causation), the relationships between Fiqh and therapy, the importance of the therapist's state as a variable in successful therapy, a critique of Buddhist-derived and the main Western schools of therapy, and an examination of belief in occult influences on mental health, with several case studies and discussions.

Around 2010, the writer was asked to provide some training to a group of psychological therapists committed to operating a service within a south London community organisation. The writer taught the five-day course for the first time, and it was favourably received. Meanwhile, the Cambridge Muslim College (CMC) had been brought together by Abdal Hakim Winter in 2009 and quickly became a hub for Islamic scholarship in the UK. In 2011, it began its one-year diploma course and Sabnum Dharamsi was asked to organise a counselling module. She arranged for Rabia Malik and the writer to teach part of the module. The following year, the writer was allowed to run the five-day course at CMC. Members of staff attended and gave the course the imprimatur of the college.

CMC has been of immense value in the development of IP in the UK. Its accreditation of the five-day course has given a confidence that this teaching is theologically sound. The college's secretariat and the teaching facilities have made the courses easy to organise (the course has run once or twice a year since 2012) and its social network has advertised the course and the concepts behind it—both in the UK and abroad. Nevertheless, most importantly, the college has facilitated a fertile interaction between its resident and visiting scholars and course participants.

It was through CMC that the writer met Samir Mahmoud, then a post-doctoral fellow, and was introduced to Ibn Arabi's understanding of the body and movement, which made much sense of some otherwise mystifying clinical phenomena.

Another post-doctoral scholar, Samir Dajani, introduced the course to the fiqh of As Sayuti and his school—an approach to fiqh that seemed particularly apt for the complex issues that arise in therapy—whilst avoiding the dangers of modern itjihaad.

The five-day course has largely been taught by the writer, but with specialist scholars giving seminars. Samir Dajani has provided seminars on relevant fiqh. Other regular contributors to the course teaching have been Abdal Hakim Winter, who explains in depth some of the basic conceptual building blocks of IP; Rabia Malik, who gives seminars on specifically Islamically based therapy; and Hakim Salim Khan, on the relationship of Unani Tibb to psychology. Shahnawaz Haque and Saeed Nasser, both experienced psychotherapists and imams, have also more recently been making regular contributions to the course teaching. Both had independently been working on Islamically based approaches to their therapy but joined the wider network when they attended the course as students. Shahnawaz has been developing an Islamic understanding of psychodynamics, and Saeed Nasser has been developing the ethical framework for IP.

Abdallah Rothman attended the course in 2016 and liked it. After he and Malik Badri established the International Association of Islamic Psychology (IAIP) in 2017, the five-day course was accredited as the Level 1 course of the IAIP's route to accreditation as an Islamic therapist. The course was thereafter taught in Istanbul with the addition of Malik Badri and Abdallah Rothman for two summers in a row, in 2018 and 2019.

In 2016, Hakim Salim Khan, Rabia Malik, Shahnawaz Haque, and the writer made a second attempt to establish a UK association for IP. The impetus again came from the public confusion that was occurring between a Muslim psychotherapist and someone practising psychotherapy from an Islamic paradigm, and this confusion renewed the need to define and register the latter. This attempt to forge a national organisation did not progress, largely because of the inabiity to find people with the time and competence to form an administration.

## Putting into practice: Clinical Services

Individuals have been practising Islamically based psychotherapy in the UK since at least the 1980s, with numbers growing appreciably once the An Nisa/ Maynards' counselling course started in 1997. However, to the writer's best knowledge, the first comprehensive clinical service based on Islamic principles started in Bradford in 2012. At that time, a group of seven clinical psychologists, psychotherapists, and counsellors, plus one Tibb practitioner, formed "Ihsaan" (see ihsaan.org.uk). The name was chosen after two members dreamt of it. The team was later joined by a Raqi (one who performs ruqiyah - the use of Quranic recitation to rid a person of evil spirits) and two more therapists. All the team members work for Ihsaan in their spare time, providing their services at reduced or no fees. The team has attended the five-day course and uses the diagnostic model taught on the course. The varying clinical skills of the team enable comprehensive treatment programmes in alignment with the model. For example, Islamic dream analysis, Quranic ruqiyah (following Carrie York's work), Tibb-based dietary advice and herbal treatments to, for example, help with emotional processing, and techniques to bring body movement in alignment with Dhikr can be added to Islamically adjusted CBT and psychodynamic therapies. Two of the team are reasonably well trained if Fiqh and the team has access to experts in this area for particularly tricky issues.

Shortly after Ihsaan was established, the writer was asked to provide training to a group of therapists in Lancashire, brought together by Yasser Ali, an experienced psychotherapist. This group, in 2015, formed a similar service to Ihsaan called "Inayat" (inayat.co.uk) and has developed its own area of expertise in community arbitration.

More recently, hubs of clinicians, who have attended the five-day course, have formed in the Midlands (under Saeed Nasser) and Manchester (under Georgina Cardo), with the intention of starting Ihsaan-like services in those locations. Ihsaan, Inayat, and the two embryonic services in the Midlands and Manchester all form part of the "Ihsaan network" and collaborate, along with IPPA and Inspirited Minds (see below). There is also a strong interest in starting an Ihsaan-type service in Glasgow, but progress has been delayed due to COVID-19 restrictions. There is, in addition, at least one other clinical service operating in London, led by (mainly Shia) therapists trained on Abdullah Maynard and Sabnum Dharamsi's course and the five-day IAIP Level 1 course.

In 2016, Talaat Baig established "Inspirited Minds". This is a consortium of therapists and others who provide highly regarded online articles on Islam and mental health, and direct people seeking help to a network of mostly online counsellors who work on Islamic principles. Talaat works closely with the Ihsaan consortium.

Ihsaan Bradford has sufficient qualified clinical supervisors to take on student therapists ("interns" in the American system) and all the teams in the Ihsaan consortium provide IP clinical supervision. Furthermore, IPPA has started operating a clinical supervision group.

## Plans for the future

The establishment, by Malik Badri, of the International Association of Islamic Psychology, (IAIP) with Abdallah Rothman as its executive director, has made it easier to further develop IP in the UK. There are more IAIP members in the UK than in any other country. Recently, several of us met to form a UK association for IP, under the chairmanship of Saeed Nasser, to be affiliated with the IAIP. As the IAIP is able to accredit courses and qualifications and keeps a register of UK members, this leaves the UK associates free from an oppressive administrative burden. One of our intentions is to run a series of study days around the country. Some are intended to be "masterclasses", using experts in particular fields, such as family therapy and "somatic" therapies. Other day events will be organised as symposia to explore difficult topics on which none of us feel we have confident expertise, such as the Islamic approach to understanding and dealing with psychoses, and Islamic understandings of psychodynamics.

The IAIP-accredited five-day Level 1 course has continued to run despite COVID-19 restrictions, and further courses are planned once the restrictions have been lifted. A five-day Level 2 IAIP course was successfully run at CMC last year. Those of us involved with the Level 1 teaching, however, have suggested a revised syllabus with more clinical topics. This has been approved by the IAIP and it is hoped that this course will start running as soon as possible, since there is strong demand both within the UK and internationally.

In 2017, the online Al Balagh Academy was established by Dr Rafaqat Rashid, a medical doctor and Islamic scholar in the Deobandi tradition. The Academy specialises in high-grade courses around Fiqh and medicine and has a large international following. Rafaqat has been an ardent supporter of the Ihsaan service from its inception and invited it to design a webinar course on IP. These started in 2019 and have proved one of the most popular of the Al Balagh courses. Though the target audience is "the interested lay person" and is made clear it is not a course of professional training, it nonetheless attracts professional psychological therapists from around the world who would have difficulty accessing any other courses on IP.

Ihsaan is now designing, with Al Balagh, a second course around "being the good friend" (khalil). Again, it will be geared towards the layperson, but particularly those who people turn to for help at times of difficulty. It is expected to include sessions on such things as "community conflict resolution," "loss of Iman", and conditions that need referral for professional help. It is hoped that this course will be ready by the Autumn of 2021, and it will be open to those who have completed the first course.

It is expected that clinical services on the Ihsaan model will continue to increase around the UK once the COVID-19 restrictions are over, providing not only Islamic concordant therapies, but also clinical supervision and student training. This will enable those who have completed the Level 1 and Level 2 courses to proceed to accreditation under IAIP criteria.

The collective experience at Ihsaan is that working from Islamic paradigms, especially in a multi-disciplinary team, has much better than normal clinical outcomes, both in terms of the depth of healing and the speed (even complex cases, often involving childhood trauma, rarely take more than 10 sessions). A small study on Ihsaan clients' experience of its therapies (contrasting experiences with "mainstream" services) has been done from Bradford University. It is hoped this will reach publication this year (2021). More research would be very useful for the movement.

Market conditions in the UK make it difficult for the Ihsaan model of service to develop into the full-time clinics that the Khalil centres have achieved in the US. This is because, though there is high demand and need for Islamically concordant formulations and therapies, the existence of the National Health Service means that very few people have private medical insurance, and often the neediest are the least able to pay for treatment. Also, unlike the Khalil centres, Ihsaan has been unable to interest any Zakat organisation in helping the mentally unwell. For the foreseeable future, therefore, we would expect the Ihsaan clinical services to operate as now—with clinicians putting in their spare time at low or no fees, and using facilities provided by friendly mosques and community charities.

For some years, the aspiration in the UK has been to have an independent post-graduate course in IP and therapy, leading to its own qualification to practice, thus reducing the risk of therapists falling into "the lizard's hole" in the first place. The professional environment in the UK makes this a more feasible option than is the case in, say, the US. In the UK, although clinical psychologists, counselling psychologists, and some other therapy professions, have protected titles, the same does not apply to the terms "counsellor" or "psychotherapist". In other words, anybody can use their titles, provided they are not fraudulent. There is some government regulation of people offering therapy services to the public, but no equivalent of the US "state license". Currently, a semantic distinction is commonly made between psychotherapists (psycho-dynamically trained), counsellors (trained specifically in the Rogerian "person-centred" model), and CBT therapists, but the trend is to train in "integrative therapy", which involves all three. It is, however, not uncommon for someone to train and practise in one very specific therapy, such as CAT (Cognitive Analytic Therapy) or NLP (Neuro Linguistic Programming), with a qualification awarded by a commercial training organisation. It is thus quite feasible for, say, the IAIP to set up and accredit its own bespoke designed course in "integrative" IP and therapy, without having to fit it into the culturally niched mould of any "Western" school.

Since the formation of the IAIP, it has attempted to set up such a course with an Islamic university abroad that would afford easy access to UK students. So far, these attempts have not been successful. However, with the recent appointment of Abdallah Rothman as Principal of CMC, there is a glimmer of hope as such a course is now being established in the UK.

## Conclusion

This has been written in the deep shadow of Malik Badri's passing. It is impossible to imagine how IP in the UK could have developed in the way it has without Badri's pioneering work and inspiration. The UK movement, strengthened by the support of the IAIP—which Badri established to further his work—is now poised to move ahead with extending its theoretical basis, training system, and clinical services, and an accreditation process for IP therapists. We hope, with the help of Allah (SWT), that these objectives will be met and extended into the foreseeable future as a fitting legacy for a remarkable man and dear friend to so many of us.

## References

Ahmed, A. S. (1984), Al Beruni: The first Anthropologist. *RAIN, 60*, 9–10.
Ahmed, A. S. (1986). Toward Islamic Anthropology. *American Journal of Islamic Social Sciences,3*(2).https://doi.org/10.35632/ajis.v3i2.2893
Al-Karam, C. Y. (2015). Complementary and alternative medicine. In C. Y. Al-Karam & A. Haque (Eds.), *Mental health and psychological practice in the U.A.E.* Palgrave MacMillan. Pp. 169-178.
Badri, M. (1979). *The dilemma of Muslim psychologists.* MWP.
Badri, M. (2000). *Contemplation: An Islamic psychospiritual study.* IIIT.
Badri, M. (2016). *The dilemma of Muslim psychologists* (2nd ed.). Islamic Book Trust.
Beyond Belief, BBC Radio 4. 16.6.2009 Alzheimer's disease. 6.3.2017 Mental Health. 22.7.2019 Free Will.
Gianotti, T.J. (2001). *Al Ghazali's unspeakable doctrine of the Soul: Unveiling the esoteric psychology and eschatology of the Ihya.* E.J. Brill.
Groddeck, G. (1923). *The book of the It* (1976 edition). International Universities Press.
Hussain, A. (2001). Islamic belief and mental health. *Mental Health Nursing, 21*(2), 6–7.
Jung, C. (2009). *The red book.* W. W. Norton.
Kaplick, P.M., & Skinner, R. (2017). The evolving Islam and psychology movement. *European Psychologist, 22*(3), 198–204.
Khan, S. (1986). *Islamic medicine.* Routledge & Kegan Paul.
Kuhn, T.S. (1964). *The structure of scientific revolutions.* University of Chicago Press.
Malik, R. (2000). Culture and emotions. In C. Squire (Ed.), *Culture and psychology.* Routledge. Pp. 147-162.
Malik, R., Shaikh, A., & Suleyman, M. (2007). *Providing faith and culturally sensitive support services to young British Muslims* (Research Report). National Youth Agency and Muslim Youth Helpline.
Malik, R., & Mandin, P. (2012). Engaging within and across culture. In I.-B. Krause (Ed.), *Culture and reflexivity in systemic psychotherapy.* Karnac. Pp. 201-221.
Malik, R. (2018). Family therapy and the use of Quranic stories. In C.Y. Al-Karam (Ed.), *Islamically integrated psychotherapy* (pp. 152–174). Templeton Press.
Maynard, S. (2008). *Muslim mental health.* Report to Home Office.
Skinner, R. (2010). An Islamic approach to psychology and mental health. *Mental Health, Religion and Culture,13*(6), 547–551.
Skinner, R. (2018). Traditions, paradigms, and basic concepts in Islamic psychology. *Journal pf Religion and Health, 58*(4), 1087–1094.
Skinner, R. (2019). A beginner's guide to the concept of Islamic psychology. *Journal of the British Islamic Medical Association, 3*(1), 22-26.

CHAPTER SIXTEEN

# Islamic Psychology in the United States: Past, Present, and Future Trajectory

CARRIE YORK AL-KARAM

ISLAMIC PSYCHOLOGY HAS been re-emerging globally since at least the 1970s, but it has only started to emerge into a recognizable distinct field in the United States in the past few years (York Al-Karam, 2020a). However, what we today call psychology is by no means new to the Islamic intellectual tradition (for example, see Awaad et al, 2019; Awaad et al, 2020). In an attempt to harness the current momentum the field is experiencing, the objective of this chapter is to present some of the earlier and present contexts in which IP has been developing and to chart where the field currently stands in terms of institutions, initiatives, conferences, courses, publications, and other areas that are illuminating the US landscape

## Islamic Psychology Early Beginnings and US Contexts

It is nearly impossible to pinpoint exactly when Islamic Psychology (IP) began in the United States because it was not a one-time event where the field simply "arrived". Scholarly fields never arrive, they are a phenomenon of constant becoming from within a dynamic context that is constantly emerging. To that end, in this section some of the various contexts in which IP has been emerging in the United States will be described as well as some noteworthy incidences that happened that relate to IP specifically. This account is based on some of the author's previous writings on this topic (Al-Karam, 2018a; 2018b; 2020a) as well as discussions conducted specifically for the purpose of this publication with well-known IP figures including Malik Badri, Amber Haque, Abdallah Rothman, and Laleh Bakhtiar.

## BEHAVIORISM, CONSCIOUSNESS STUDIES, AND THEIR INTERSECTION WITH PSYCHOLOGY

Psychology in the 1960s and 1970s was leaving behind psychoanalysis and questions related to consciousness and was becoming increasingly behavioristic in orientation. To demonstrate this, consider the story of Amber Haque and his meeting with BF Skinner, the father of modern behaviorism and one of the most influential figures in modern psychology.

Haque, a graduate student from India enrolled in a clinical psychology master's program in Michigan in 1983, was given an opportunity to interview Skinner the night before a conference they were both attending in Milwaukee. Haque recounts (personal communication, A. Haque and C. York Al-Karam, 2020) that he spoke about many things with Skinner, including a question as to whether he had ever read the Quran. Skinner's position was that religion had not done anything good for humanity and pointed to the Iran-Iraq war as a case in point. He also said he raised his own daughter as an atheist and that she was a highly moral person. The following day, Skinner delivered the keynote address and, in total mocking fashion, came to it dressed like a Catholic priest. Today, this might be akin to wearing black-face, but this highlights certain attitudes towards religion that existed in psychology during that time as well as what was socially acceptable.

However, this is in stark contrast to what was going on in other areas of psychology. The socio-political context of the 1960s and 1970s leading up to Haque's meeting with Skinner included the Civil Rights Movement, Women's Liberation Movement, and the Vietnam War. These movements had produced a hippie counter-culture where people started to "look East" for spirituality, and that included psychologists. Perhaps the most noteworthy example can be seen in the case of Harvard psychologists Timothy Leary and Richard Alpert and their experimentation with mystical and peak experiences and psychedelic drugs. Richard Alpert eventually became the spiritual teacher known as Ram Dass and the author of the famous book *Be Here Now* (1971) amongst many other books. But this is not the only example. This era also witnessed the emergence of such movements as transpersonal psychology, humanistic psychology (for example the work of Abraham Maslow. For more on this see Grogan, 2013), parapsychology and consciousness studies, existential psychology, and Buddhist psychology. These movements materialized into actual institutions like the California Institute of Integral Studies (1968), Naropa University (1974), and the Institute of

Transpersonal Psychology (1975) to name a few. As this trend in psychology relates to IP specifically, consider an experience of Malik Badri, who many consider to be the father of modern IP. Badri, a Sudanese born, British trained clinical psychologist who heartbreakingly passed away at age 89 in the final stage of this book project (February 2021), delivered a seminal paper in 1976 at a conference in Indianapolis in which he discussed the "lizard's hole" that Muslim psychologists were in and the fact that Western psychology was not in alignment with Islam. He recounts that the non-Muslim American psychologists who were in the audience were very understanding and supportive of the idea of an Islamic psychology (although he did not use that term at the time.). Cross-cultural psychology was on the rise so it made sense to them to have a psychology that was tailored to the Muslim worldview. This was in stark contrast to Skinner's keynote address where he mockingly dressed like a priest as well as the attitude of Badri's Arab Muslim psychologist colleagues who he accused of being "more royal than the king" (Badri, 2009, p.16) – of trying to be more secular than the Western psychology they imported! He recounts that they would say things like "Islam is a religion and psychology is a science. Do we need to have a *fasiq* botany, or *kafir* physics? Then why do we need an Islamic psychology?" (p.15). His talk in Indianapolis later turned into his landmark publication *The Dilemma of Muslim Psychologists* (1979). If there ever was a point in time where IP in the US began, some have suggested that this talk was it.

## THE EMERGENCE OF ISLAM AND THE ISLAMIZATION OF KNOWLEDGE MOVEMENT

Although Islam has been in America for centuries, it starts to finally take root in the twentieth century in two important ways. First, there was a sharp rise in the number of Muslims coming into the country as a result of the Immigration and Nationality Act of 1965. Many of these immigrants were skilled workers and have been instrumental in the establishment of flourishing Muslim communities throughout the country. Second, and preceding this, is the emergence of the Nation of Islam within the African American community. Both of these influenced Islam's development in the US. As they relate to IP specifically, consider the following.

An extremely significant but not publicly well-known connection between the rise of Islam in the US and IP specifically can be seen in a very close relationship between IP's founder Malik Badri and one of the most influential Muslims in American history – Malcolm X. Malcolm visited Badri in Sudan in 1959 and the two subsequently kept in regular contact. Badri played an important role in Malcolm's decision to leave the Nation of Islam. In an extremely moving account (Malik Badri, 2020), Badri details how Malcolm, after completing Hajj in 1964, flew directly to Beirut specifically to see Badri and to reveal to him his new name – el-Hajj Malik el-Shabazz. For those unaware of the significance of this relationship, as previously mentioned, Black Muslims play an extremely important role in the development of Islam in the US. Malcolm leaving the Nation of Islam for Sunni Islam was a major event that impacted that trajectory. The modern founder of IP (amongst others) had an important connection to the unfolding of this history, thereby linking the trajectory of Islam's development in the US with that of IP via this relationship.

The Islamization of Knowledge (IOK) movement has also facilitated the emergence of IP. Key figures in this field include Ismail Faruqi, Fazlur Rahman, Seyyed Naquib Al-Attas, and Seyyed Hossein Nasr, although his ideas about what constituted Islamization were somewhat distinct. The influence of this movement, which emerged primarily from Malaysia, can be seen in the US via the establishment of the International Institute of Islamic Thought (IIIT - 1981) and the American Association of Muslim Social Scientists (AAMSS, 1972). An AAMSS publication, the *American Journal of Islamic Social Sciences,* and in collaboration with IIIT and the International Islamic University Malaysia, published an important special edition of the journal in 1998 (Vol. 15, No 4) on Islamic perspectives in psychology. According to Haque, this was probably the first publication in the US on IP.

### SUFI MOVEMENTS

In tandem with Islam's development in the US and also overlapping with what was happening in the "looking East" trend, the rise of Sufism in the US is also a context that is connected to IP's emergence. It is important to acknowledge that Sufism is vast, with many different forms of it. Some versions are universalist and consider themselves only peripherally connected to Islam. Other versions profess to be squarely within Islam's orthodoxy. Looking to this latter strain, it has been argued that the science of spirituality (*tasawwuf*) and purification of the self/soul (*tazkiyat al-nafs*) are Islam's version of psychology/psychotherapy (York Al-Karam, 2018a; 2018b; 2020a). Like psychology, these sciences also aim to improve the human condition via a transformation of the mind/self/soul and behavior, albeit within a different framework. Many of the teachings and techniques found within this domain are also examined in IP. For example, Islamic/Sufi notions of ontology such as the nafs, ruh, aql, and qalb, practices such as dhikr, muraqaba and muhasaba, and even exploring "disorders" like anger or gossip (York Al-Karam, 2020).

An important contribution coming from this context can be seen in the works of Laleh Bakhtiar. In a recent interview the author conducted with her in July 2020 three months before her unexpected passing, she discussed her experience of working mostly in isolation in the 1990s. Although not working within an explicitly IP framework, she produced many books on what today could be considered IP such as the Sufi enneagram and other topics (for example see Bakhtiar, 2013; 2019). Also noteworthy is the work of clinical psychologist Saloumeh Bozorgzadeh and her establishment of the Sufi Psychology Association. Examples of other Sufi psychology work, some of which is also core to IP, can be seen in the work of Robert Frager, Lynn Wilcox, and others. Moreover, American-based Sufi practitioners who incorporate psychological concepts into their teachings and writings that have popularized Sufi psychology include Inayat Khan, Vilayat Khan, Bawa Muhaiyaddeen, Llewellyn Vaughan-Lee, and others.

In terms of bringing orthodox Sufism into the purview of IP, there are endless possibilities, especially when one considers work being done at Sufi and spiritual psychology institutions that deal with psychology relevant themes like meditation and the transformation and stages of the soul. What remains somewhat unclear is how the *fields* of Sufi and Islamic psychology see themselves in conversation today. There is no doubt much overlap between them, but also important distinctions, especially depending on the type of Sufism.

## The Evolution of Mainstream Psychology

Like all scholarly disciplines, psychology is constantly evolving. As behaviorism took hold of the field in the second half of the twentieth century, there always remained peripheral elements that explored beyond behavior. Consider Division 36 of the American Psychological Association – the Society for the Psychology of Religion and Spirituality. Established in 1976, it actually began in 1946 as the American Catholic Psychological Association and whose initial aims were to bring psychology to Catholics and to bring a Catholic viewpoint to psychology (Reuder, 1999). This entity reorganized in 1970 and became Psychologists Interested in Religious Issues (PIRI). It reorganized once again in 1976 to become Division 36 (for a full history of this see https://www.apadivisions.org/division-36/about/history.pdf).

Today, there are diverse perspectives as to what this subfield of psychology is about. Some consider it a purely scientific/empirical approach to understanding *psychological* aspects of religious belief and behavior or as some would say, to "explain away" religion and spirituality (Sisemore and Knabb, 2020) as mere psychological (biological and other) phenomenon. On the other hand, there has been the emergence of the spiritually integrated psychotherapy domain beginning in the late 1990s where psychologists, sometimes ones with strong confessional ties to religion, sought to explore the role that religion and spirituality might play in the psychotherapeutic encounter. This domain also includes the investigation of religion-related themes such as coping, stress management, and even spiritual struggles. A number of psychologists like P. Scott Richards, Allen Bergin, Ken Pargament, and Thomas Plante, as well as psychiatrist Harold Koenig amongst others, were early advancers of this type of inquiry. Since then, there have been a large number of books published on this topic, many by the American Psychological Association itself, including its peer-reviewed journal *Spirituality in Clinical Practice,* founded in 2014, that focuses on this explicitly (this author serves as Associate Editor for this journal and the editors of this book – Abdallah Rothman and Amber Haque – are regular reviewers). There is also a Division 36 taskforce that has been exploring the development and implementation of graduate training mandates on religious and spiritual diversity in psychology.

In the United States, these developments are couched within a broader trend in psychology in the United States to become more diverse and inclusive. Such sentiments are a direct by-product of various movements, such as the emergence of post-modernist thinking and its pushback on medical models and claims of universalist truths; the indigenization and decolonization of psychology that embrace minority perspectives; and social movements of the day like Black Lives Matter and more. It could be argued that psychology might be experiencing its "Fifth Force" and it might be described as "Diversity and Inclusion" or "Unity through Diversity", where there is room for religion and spirituality in some capacity, although there is still certainly much room for growth especially as it relates to philosophical pluralism.

## MUSLIM MENTAL HEALTH

It is in these aforementioned contexts and in a post 9/11 world where we see the field of psychology begin to make inroads into the Muslim American community. This can be seen in the emergence of the field of Muslim mental health (MMH). MMH can be said to have emerged primarily as a result of the 9/11 attacks and the subsequent rise of Islamophobia and its impact on the mental health of Muslim Americans. Other issues, such as war and forced migration, domestic violence, divorce, and addiction and substance abuse have also been important themes. Muslim mental health professionals responded to this need and their answers can be seen in the establishment of important MMH infrastructure. For example, the Institute of Muslim Mental Health and its peer-reviewed journal, the *Journal of Muslim Mental Health,* were both established in 2006 by psychiatrist Hamada Hamid Altalib. There is also a related annual conference – the Muslim Mental Health Conference – headed by Hamid's colleague – psychiatrist Farha Abbasi. The conference will have its 13th annual meeting in 2021. Other noteworthy infrastructure also appeared. Examples include the Family and Youth Institute established in 2006 by psychologist Sameera Ahmed; Khalil Center established in 2010 by Hooman Keshavarzi; the Muslim Wellness Foundation established in 2011 by Kameelah Mu'min Rashad; and the Muslims and Mental Health Lab at Stanford University established in 2014 by psychiatrist Rania Awaad. It is also important to highlight an important publication that emerged from this period – the edited volume *Counseling Muslims* (2012) by Sameera Ahmed and Mona Amer. This is just some of the earlier infrastructure. In the past few years so much more has exploded onto the scene and is simply too numerous to list here.

Many have argued that the MMH field is distinct from IP in that MMH is about the mental health needs of Muslims whereas IP is about developing frameworks of psychology rooted in Islam, with potential application on anyone, not just Muslims. However, these fields overlap primarily in the domain of spiritually/Islamically integrated psychotherapy. Not only is Islamically integrated psychotherapy one of the many ways that IP is conceptualized today (for a review of other conceptualizations, see York Al-Karam, 2018b; 2020a), it has emerged in part within the MMH domain and in response to a great need in the Muslim community for mental health care that is informed by an Islamic worldview.

Another example that demonstrates the field of MMH facilitating the emergence of IP in the US is the 12th annual Muslim Mental Health Conference held in July 2020. This conference is sponsored annually by Michigan State University and the Institute of Muslim Mental Health. In 2020 however, there was a special IP track that provided an opportunity for scholars to present on distinctly IP topics. The range of presentations included the contributions of early Muslim scholars to the field of psychology, topics in Islamically integrated psychotherapy, and much more. To facilitate this track, the conference was co-sponsored by the International Association of Islamic Psychology and Khalil Center.

It is also worth mentioning that MMH has also given rise to other psychology-related developments within the American Muslim community. Examples include the emergence of Islamic / Muslim chaplaincy (including programs at Bayan Claremont, Hartford Seminary, the Islamic Seminary of America, and the American Islamic College) as well as the ongoing trend of mental health literacy amongst Imams and other "first responders". Within these broader trends, there has also been the establishment of a whole host of initiatives that address mental health and related issues that Muslim Americans face, including anxiety, depression, substance misuse, pornography addiction, domestic violence, and parenting (for examples, see the Peaceful Families Project, SEEMA, Purify Your Gaze, and Positive Parenting to name a few).

## IP IN THE UNITED STATES TODAY

The previous section examined some of the contexts and ways in which IP has been emerging in the US. In this section, some of the current landscape, including institutions, conferences, publications, initiatives, scholars, and more will be reviewed. As one reviews this landscape, it is important to keep in mind a few important points. First, IP is a multidisciplinary field. However, this chapter is a review of initiatives primarily in the field of *psychology* and does not include work that could be considered IP but is being done in other fields like religious studies, theology, Islamic sciences, or others that might go by a different name. IP is only now starting to emerge into a field that is using this term explicitly and most of us are psychologists, so this is the landscape that is being covered in this chapter, although some of what is recounted here is work that might not always use the term IP either. That said, it could be argued that IP work is being done in other domains and this scholarship has been around for a while; but because it does not use the term IP, it is likely not in conversation with the field that is being called IP today. A review of such scholarship is therefore not included in this section because it would be difficult to capture.

## KHALIL CENTER

Khalil Center (KC) began in 2010 in Chicago as the private psychotherapy clinic of Hooman Keshavarzi, a licensed professional counselor. By 2014, it had transformed into a non-profit organization that describes itself as being "a psychological and spiritual community wellness center advancing the professional practice of psychology rooted in Islamic principles". According to KC, it is the largest provider of Muslim mental healthcare in the United States and now has numerous clinics throughout the country including the states of Illinois, California, and New York as well as Toronto, Canada. KC provides direct MMH and Islamically integrated psychotherapeutic services and makes significant scholarly contributions.

For example, Keshavarzi and KC colleagues Fahad Khan, Bilal Ali Ansari, Rania Awaad, and others, have made important contributions to the IP literature. Their most recent edited volume *Applying Islamic Principles to Clinical Mental Health Care: Introducing Traditional Islamically Integrated Psychotherapy* (Keshavarzi et al., 2020), describes in detail the Islamically integrated approach used at KC which they call Traditionally Islamically Integrated Psychotherapy (TIIP). It also delves into the broader Islamic intellectual tradition in which this approach is positioned. Moreover, the TIIP approach was the only Islamic psychotherapeutic modality studied as part of the Bridges Research Project. Bridges is the largest study to date on spiritually integrated psychotherapy and it explored processes and outcomes of 21 different modalities. It was supported with a $3.5 million dollar grant from the John Templeton Foundation and Brigham Young University. KC collaborated with the Alkaram Institute on this study and a published report of their findings is expected in 2022.

KC also established the Khalil School for Islamic Psychology and Research in 2020 which serves as a home for research and publications, provides clinical training for psychology interns wanting to learn their method, and mental health first aid training for Muslim community members, amongst other things.

## MUSLIMS AND MENTAL HEALTH LAB AT STANFORD UNIVERSITY

The Muslims and Mental Health Lab at Stanford University was founded by psychiatrist and Islamic scholar Rania Awaad in 2014. Her formal training in both the Islamic and psychiatric and psychological sciences laid the foundation for the current interdisciplinary nature of the lab's work. The lab's mission is to serve as the academic home for the study of mental health as it relates to the Islamic faith and Muslim populations by providing intellectual resources to clinicians, researchers, trainees, educators, and community and religious leaders working with or studying Muslims. So far, the lab has produced important publications on the contributions of early Muslim scholars to the field of what today is called psychology. A noteworthy example can be found in two publications (Awaad and Ali, 2014; 2015) that demonstrated how 9thcentury scholar Abu Zayd al-Balkhi's classification of OCD and phobias from over one thousand years ago is nearly identical to today's DSM-5. Such findings dispel the myth that Muslims did not concern themselves with the study of psychology or that great advances in the field only started with 19th century European psychologists. Rather, such work highlights the importance Islam placed on understanding the psyche as well as the fact that what today is being called IP is simply a re-emergence of the field.

The Muslims and Mental Health lab also offers research internships in its 14 lines of research, including lines on historical understandings of IP and IP frameworks of mental health, for graduate students from varying disciplines. The lab provides a platform from which interns can publish their work, take part in active research projects or books the lab is working on, partner with other institutions, seek out expert advice, and benefit from peer-level feedback on their work. In 2019, Awaad also created and taught the first permanent course on IP in the US at Stanford University entitled *Islamic Psychology: PSYC 244.*

## THE INTERNATIONAL ASSOCIATION OF ISLAMIC PSYCHOLOGY

The International Association of Islamic Psychology (IAIP) was established in 2017 in the state of Washington. Conceptually, however, it had existed for over a decade. The mission of the IAIP is to "advance the development and application of Islamic psychology to enhance the understanding of human psychology and promote health and wellbeing for all people". For the past few years the association has offered quite a number of IP certification courses and conferences – all of which have taken place outside of the US. Overall, it promotes the work of its global fellows. In addition to certifying individual practitioners in IP and psychotherapy clinical practice, the IAIP also certifies academic institutions and clinics. Khalil Center is currently the only clinic certified by the IAIP in the US. The IAIP also established the *Journal of Islamic Psychology* with plans of publishing its first volume within the coming few years.

IAIP's founder and founding president was Malik Badri. He established the association to advance the field, which he envisioned as setting professional standards in IP globally. The Executive Director of the IAIP is Abdallah Rothman and although he is the only founding member who is American, he said he, and especially Badri, both see the organization as being an integral part of the US landscape. According to Badri, one reason IAIP was established in the US is because America was receptive to the idea of an IP. Recall his seminal talk in 1976 and the stark contrast between how American psychologists received his ideas as opposed to his Arab Muslim colleagues. Given this and the fact that much of the Arab and Islamic world look to America to import so much, his hope was that if IP developed and took root in the US, perhaps it would eventually make its way to the Islamic world via importation! Given his experience, one can understand his logic. However, it should be noted that much has changed since the 1960s and 1970s. Today, much IP scholarship is being advanced in the Islamic world and some of that landscape is described in other chapters in this edited volume.

### THE ALKARAM INSTITUTE

The Alkaram Institute was founded in 2018 by Carrie York Al-Karam and like the IAIP, conceptually it had been around for over a decade. The institute's mission is to "advance the field of Islamic Psychology through research and education" and its longer-term vision is to become the first Muslim graduate school of psychology in the United States.

Building upon intellectual infrastructure laid by York Al-Karam prior to the institute's establishment (see section on other initiatives), to date the institute has initiated a number of projects. Most recently (2019) is the establishment of an Islamic Psychology Research Fellowship which is for graduate students anywhere in the world doing their MA thesis or doctoral dissertation on an IP topic but whose home institution does not have faculty to support such scholarship. The institute provides this expertise, including ongoing IP lab meetings where fellows present their work to the group, which consists of other fellows and senior scholars, for feedback and guidance. The fellowships advance the IP field and build bridges with existing institutions of higher education as they are home institutions for fellows and faculty, which in turn elevates the profile of IP. Examples of institutions that fellows are from include Harvard University, Columbia University, Hamad bin Khalifa University, International Islamic University Islamabad, University of Wisconsin, and more.

The institute also collaborated with Khalil Center on the Bridges Research Project on spiritually integrated psychotherapy previously mentioned. It also published a children's character development book called *Maya and the Seven Limbs* (2020b) and has other book publications in the works including an IP textbook. Future initiatives include a global IP conference and various IP courses.

### THE H.O.M.E INSTITUTE

The H.O.M.E Institute (Heart Over Mind and Ego) was founded in 2019 by Marwa Assar, a psychologist who did her doctoral work on IP (Assar, 2017) and who also has a background in the traditional Islamic sciences. The institute offers "holistic psycho-spiritual education that prioritizes the transformation of the heart and is taught through an Islamic Psychological lens". Examples of courses HOME offers include "The God and Me Program," "Anxiety and Piety," "Psychology of Worship," "Sacred Self Love," "Unmasking the Heart," as well as various psycho-spiritual retreats, some of which she holds in collaboration with scholars of Islamic sciences.

### OTHER INITIATIVES, PUBLICATIONS, CONFERENCES, AND COURSES.

There are other happenings related to IP's development in the United States that need to be mentioned. In (somewhat) chronological order, they are as follows:

First is what was called the WIP (work in progress/process) – a research group that held monthly meetings from roughly 2014-2015. This was started by Carrie York Al-Karam with the intention to advance the IP field through the creation of a book and an IP course. In addition to York Al-Karam, the group was comprised of Hamada Hamid, Hooman Keshavarzi, Khalid Elzamzamy, Rania Awaad, Paul Kaplick, and a few non-regular attendees. Various collaborations came from this group but it eventually dissolved. The book project and course did emerge though and are described next.

Carrie York Al-Karam subsequently established the Al-Karam Lab for Islamic Psychology at the University of Iowa (2017-2018) from which three noteworthy IP projects emerged. First, was the development of the first and only course on Islamic Psychology to be offered in an American university called *Introduction to Islamic Psychology RELS 2570*(York Al-Karam, 2017)) which was taught in Fall 2017. Second, was the article *Islamic Psychology: Towards a 21st*

*Century Definition and Conceptual Framework* where a definition of IP and a theoretical framework for the field were offered. Third, was the publication of the book *Islamically Integrated Psychotherapy: Uniting Faith and Professional Practice* (Templeton Press, 2018) and included chapters by other known IP contributors including Hooman Keshavarzi and Abdallah Rothman, amongst others. This lab eventually morphed into the Alkaram Institute.

Another IP initiative is the Center for Muslim Mental and Islamic Psychology (CMMHP) at the University of Southern California founded by psychologist Heather Laird-Jackson. CMMHIP presents itself as a clinic, offering direct services to Muslims in southern California and Maryland. Of relevance was a "working conference" the center hosted in 2018 and 2019 that explored various facets of the IP field primarily with the objective of treating Muslim clients.

In terms of presentations, it is impossible to provide a list of all that have ever been given in the US on a topic that could be considered IP. However, the following are two that were recently given at the annual convention of the American Psychological Association:

- *Emerging Spiritually Integrative Psychologies: Indian Psychology and Islamic Psychology*. August 2016. Carrie York Al-Karam
- *Islamic Psychology: Science and Practice*. August 2018. Carrie York Al-Karam, Hooman Keshavarzi, Rania Awaad, and Bilal Ali Ansari.

In terms of publications, it is difficult to present an exhaustive list. However, the following are some noteworthy contributions by US-based IP scholars:

**Books:**

- *Developing a Model of Islamic Psychology and Psychotherapy: Islamic Theology and Contemporary Understandings of Psychology* by Abdallah Rothman. London: Routledge. 2021.
- *Applying Islamic Principles to Clinical Mental Health Care: Introducing Traditional Islamically Integrated Psychotherapy* by Hooman Keshavarzi, Fahad Khan, Bilal Ali Ansari, and Rania Awaad. London: Routledge, 2020. Edited volume with chapters by IP scholars such as Abdallah Rothman, Khalid Elzamzamy, and others.
- *Quranic Psychology of the Self: A Textbook on Islamic Moral Psychology* by Laleh Bakhtiar. Chicago: Kazi Publications. 2019.
- *Islamically Integrated Psychotherapy: Uniting Faith and Professional Practice* by Carrie York Al-Karam PA: Templeton Press, 2018. Edited volume with chapters by IP scholars such as Hooman Keshavarzi, Fahad Khan, Abdallah Rothman, Fyeqa Sheikh, and others.
- *Principles of Islamic Psychology* (2017) by Farid Younos.

**Select Articles and Book Chapters:**


- York Al-Karam, C. (2020). Islamic psychology: Expanding beyond the clinic. *Journal of Islamic Faith and Practice,* 3(1), 111–120.
- Rothman, A. & Coyle, A. (2020). Conceptualizing an Islamic psychotherapy: A grounded theory study. *Spirituality in Clinical Practice,* 7(3), 197–213. http://dx.doi.org/10.1037/scp0000219
- Awaad, R., Elsayed, D., Ali, S., & Abid, A. (2020). Islamic Psychology: A Portrait of its Historical Origins and Contributions. In H. Keshavarzi, F. Khan, S. Ali, & R. Awaad (Eds.), *Applying Islamic principles to clinical mental health care: Introducing traditional Islamically integrated psychotherapy*. Routledge.
- Pasha-Zaidi, N. (2019). Indigenizing an Islamic Psychology. *Psychology of Religion and Spirituality*. https://doi.org/10.1037/rel0000265
- Awaad R., Mohammad, A., Elzamzamy, K., Fereydooni, S., & Gamar, M. (2019). Mental Health in the Islamic Golden Era: The Historical Roots of Modern Psychiatry. In H. S. Moffic, J. Peteet, A. Hankir, & R. Awaad (Eds.), *Islamophobia and psychiatry: Recognition, prevention and treatment.* Springer International Publishing Switzerland.
- York Al-Karam, C. (2018). *Islamic Psychology: Towards a 21st century definition and conceptual framework.* Brill Publications.
- Rothman, A., & Coyle, A. (2018). Toward a framework for Islamic psychology and psychotherapy: An Islamic model of the soul. *Journal of Religion and Health* 57(50), 1731–1744.
- York Al-Karam, C. (2018c). Islamic perspective of mental illness. In L. Lambert, & N. Pasha-Zaidi (Eds.), *An introduction to psychology for the Middle East (and beyond)* (p. 287). Cambridge Scholars Publishing.
- Haque, A., Khan, F., Keshavarzi, H., & Rothman, A. E. (2016). Integrating Islamic Traditions in modern psychology: Research trends in last ten years. *Journal of Muslim Mental Health, 10*(1).https://doi.org/10.3998/jmmh.10381607.0010.107
- Awaad, R., & Ali, S. (2015). A modern conceptualization of phobia in al-Balkhi's 9th century treatise: Sustenance of the body and soul. *Journal of Anxiety Disorders,* 37, 89–93. https://doi.org/10.1016/j.janxdis.2015.11.003
- Awaad, R., & Ali, S. (2014). Obsessional disorders in al-Balkhi's 9th century treatise: Sustenance of the body and soul. *Journal of Affective Disorders, 180*, 185–189. https://doi.org/10.1016/j.jad.2015.03.003
- Haque, A. & Keshavarzi, H. (2013). Outlining a psychotherapy model for enhancing Muslim mental health within an Islamic context. *The International Journal for the Psychology of Religion,* 23, 230–249.

- Abu-Raiya, H. (2012). Towards a systematic Qur'anic theory of personality. *Mental Health, Religion & Culture, 15*(3), 217–233.
- Haque, A. (2006). Psychotherapy and soul-searching: Responses to the spirituality roundtable. *Psychoanalytic Perspectives: A Journal of Integration and Innovation, 4*(2), 49–58.
- Haque, A. (2004). Religion and mental health: The case of American Muslims, *Journal of Religion and Health, 43*(1), 45–58.

## THE FUTURE OF IP AND CONCLUSION

This chapter attempts to describe some of the context from which the field of IP in the US has emerged. It has also provided a brief overview of some of its landscape today. Although it is by no means exhaustive, it should demonstrate the most prominent scholars, institutions, publications, courses, and initiatives illuminating the field today.

In terms of the future of IP, there are many challenges the field faces in the US and the author has written about many of them in other publications (York Al-Karam, 2018b; 2020a). Briefly, some include the pervasive lack of clarity as to what IP is and the existence of a field that uses this term specifically; that Islam is a minority perspective in the US; the disjointed nature of the Western academy that separates science and religion; the need for more scholars from diverse disciplines to advance the field; the need to articulate the potential relevance and benefit of IP to anyone, especially given the non-Muslim American context; to have more Muslim psychologists in general and that they serve in positions of leadership; the need for a Muslim graduate school of psychology; the need for a peer-reviewed journal; and the need for funding. This is where some of the aforementioned scholars and institutions can have an impact as they are addressing many of these challenges in a variety of ways.

Despite challenges, there are also many opportunities, some of which include: the raising of IP's profile globally; trends in society and beyond towards diversity and inclusion; trends in psychology and science opening to spirituality; and Muslims having a more active voice in all spheres of American life than ever before to name a few.

Good work is being done by many and it is exciting to see where the field will go. As to the future of IP in the US, or anywhere for that matter, it is essential to keep in mind that the unfolding of this field is not only linked to who does what but, like all things, has an element of Divine destiny. However, it is meant to unfold, it will; and however it is not, it will not. This leaves those of us attempting to advance the field doing our part, or "tying our camels" as the saying goes, but also surrendering to the continual state of becoming of this important and necessary field.

## References

Abu-Raiya, H. (2012). Towards a systematic Qur'anic theory of personality. *Mental Health, Religion & Culture, 15*(3), 217–233.

Ahmed, S., & Amer, M. (Eds.) (2012). *Counseling Muslims: Handbook of Mental Health Issues and Interventions*. Routledge.

Assar, M. (2017). *An Islamic psychological approach to psychotherapy* (Doctoral dissertation). Chicago School of Professional Psychology.

Awaad, R., & Ali, S. (2014). Obsessional disorders in al-Balkhi's 9th century treatise: Sustenance of the body and soul. *Journal of Affective Disorders, 180*, 185–189. https://doi.org/10.1016/j.jad.2015.03.003

Awaad, R., & Ali, S. (2015). A modern conceptualization of phobia in al-Balkhi's 9th century treatise: Sustenance of the body and soul. *Journal of Anxiety Disorders, 37*, 89–93. https://doi.org/10.1016/j.janxdis.2015.11.003

Awaad, R., Elsayed, D., Ali, S., & Abid, A. (2020). *Islamic psychology: A portrait of its historical origins and contributions.* In H. Keshavarzi, F. Khan, S. Ali, & R. Awaad (Eds.), *Applying Islamic principles to clinical mental health care*. Routledge.

Awaad, R., Mohammad, A., Elzamzamy, K., Fereydooni, S., &Gamar, M. (2019). Mental health in the Islamic golden era: The historical roots of modern psychiatry. In H. S. Moffic, J. Peteet, A. Hankir, & R. Awaad (Eds.), *Islamophobia and psychiatry: Recognition, prevention and treatment.* Springer International Publishing Switzerland.

Badri, M. (1979). *The dilemma of Muslim psychologists*. MWH London.

Badri, M. (2009). The Islamization of psychology: Its "why", its "what", its "how" and its "who." In N. Noor (Ed.), *Psychology from an Islamic perspective* (pp. 13–41). IIUM Press (First delivered as a keynote speech circa 2002).

Bakhtiar, L. (2013). *The sufi enneagram: The secrets of the symbol unveiled.* Kazi Publications.

Bakhtiar, L. (2019). *Quranic psychology of the self: A textbook on Islamic moral psychology.* Chicago: Kazi Publications.

Dass, R. (1971). *Be here now*. RHUS.

Grogan, J. (2013). *Encountering America: Humanistic psychology, sixties culture, and the shaping of the modern self.* Harper Perennial.

Keshavarzi, H., & Khan, F. (2018). Outlining a case illustration of traditional Islamically integrated psychotherapy. In C. York Al-Karam (Ed.), *Islamically integrated psychotherapy: Uniting faith and professional practice*. Templeton Press.

Keshavarzi, H., Khan, F., Ali, B., & Awaad, R. (Eds.). (2020). *Applying Islamic principles to clinical mental health care: Introducing traditional Islamically integrated psychotherapy.* Routledge.

Malik, A.-R., & Badri, M. (2020). *The Fifth Pillar: Hajj Stories: Malcolm X*. https://

www.youtube.com/watch?app=desktop&v=lr7z4L_DTZk&ab_channel=-CambridgeMuslimCollege

Reuder, M. (1999). *A history of division 36 (psychology of religion)*. In D. A. Dewsbury (Ed.), *Unification through division: Histories of the divisions of the American Psychological Association* (Vol. 4, pp. 91–108). American Psychological Association.

Rothman, A. (2018). An Islamic theoretical orientation to psychotherapy. In C. York Al-Karam (Ed.), *Islamically integrated psychotherapy: Uniting faith and professional practice*. Templeton Press.

Rothman, A., & Coyle, A. (2018). Toward a framework for Islamic psychology and psychotherapy: An Islamic model of the soul. *Journal of Religion and Health* 57(50), 1731–1744.

Rothman, A., & Coyle, A. (2020). Conceptualizing and Islamic psychotherapy: A grounded theory study. *Spirituality in Clinical Practice*. https://doi.apa.org/doiLanding?doi=10.1037%2Fscp0000219

Sisemore, T. & Knabb, J. (Eds.). (2020). *The psychology of world religions and spiritualities*. Templeton Press.

York Al-Karam, C. (2017). *Introduction to Islamic psychology course RELS 2570 at University of Iowa*. https://myui.uiowa.edu/my-ui/courses/details.page?id=851872&ci=170950

York Al-Karam, C. (Ed.) (2018a). *Islamically integrated psychotherapy: Uniting faith and professional practice*. Templeton Press.

York Al-Karam, C. (2018b). Islamic psychology: Towards a 21st century definition and conceptual framework. Brill Publications.

York Al-Karam, C. (2018c). *Islamic perspective of mental illness*. In L. Lambert, & N. Pasha-Zaidi (Eds.), *An introduction to psychology for the Middle East (and beyond)*(p. 287). Cambridge Scholars Publishing.

York Al-Karam, C. (2020a). Islamic psychology: Expanding beyond the clinic. *Journal of Islamic Faith and Practice*, 3, 111–120.

York Al-Karam, C. (2020b). *Maya and the seven limbs*. Alkaram Institute.

CHAPTER SEVENTEEN

# Islamic Psychology in Western Continental Europe: A Top-down Approach

PAUL M. KAPLICK
AMIN LOUCIF
IBRAHIM RÜSCHOFF

WHILE MUSLIM MENTAL health has received some attention in Germany throughout the last 35 years or so, discussions on Islamic Psychology (IP) have only sparked interest among health care professionals and occurred in academic literature during the last 10–15 years. In recent years, a new generation of Muslim psychologists has revived activities in IP, by investigating religious, spiritual, and existential resources in the therapy of practicing Muslim patients. The primary objective of this work is to construct a top-down Islamically integrated psychotherapy (IIP) uniquely fitted for German regulatory, scientific, and professional standards. The main assumption of IP that has emerged in Germany so far is that Islamic elements can be integrated into scientifically validated and insurance-covered psychotherapy schools, without the need to construct an entirely new school. Most of our colleagues presumably agree that bottom-up approaches that attempt to construct a school of psychology and psychotherapy based on the indigenous Islamic intellectual tradition are neither feasible, as they would obscure well-established scientific standards in the psychology of religion in Germany, nor are they required even for the most efficient psychotherapeutic treatment of Muslim patients. In effect, various spiritual and religious treatment methods can be employed, but in a scientifically sound manner.

Current discussions around IP among German Muslim psychologists will pave the way for a unique top-down IIP that can find its home in the regulatory and scientific standards of academia and psychotherapeutic practice in Germany.

## Introduction

Religion and spirituality (R/S) have been increasingly perceived as resources in psychiatry and psychotherapy in recent decades. Especially in the United States, religion and spirituality have always had a stronger place in the social public than in Europe, due to social and structural differences, and psychotherapists have integrated these elements into their professional work relatively without difficulty. In Europe, however, psychiatrists and psychotherapists may have had considerable reservations about considering existential, religious, and spiritual needs of patients in therapy. This skepticism has stemmed primarily from concerns about a violation of scientific standards such as objectivity (Utsch & Frick, 2015). This climate has naturally influenced the attitudes of Muslim psychologists toward R/S, who, as we see it, have often seemed more concerned about mixing theological and psychological levels of work than our fellow colleagues in the UK or the United States (Rüschoff & Kaplick, 2020).

The situation, however, is changing noticeably in Europe (at least at the Western continental side), so that R/S are no longer seen only as obstacles to be removed but also as potentially useful therapeutic factors that can positively modulate treatment outcomes particularly for Muslim patients (Kizilhan, 2015). This view is also reflected in professional political statements by therapeutic professional associations (e.g., Utsch et al., 2017).

Throughout the last few years, we have been in touch with Muslim psychologists across Europe. Our experience has been that many Muslim psychologists in Continental Europe have an interest in Muslim mental health and thus recognize the importance of treating Muslim patients in a religiously and spiritually sensitive manner (e.g., via value-free recognition of religious norms). However, we have found less enthusiasm for the therapeutic use of resources and competences from the religious and spiritual tradition of Muslim patients or even a complete rejection of it.

In Germany, there are a growing number of Muslim psychiatrists, psychotherapists, psychology students, and counselors who are not categorically rejecting the professional adoption of Islamic integrated psychotherapies (IIPs), but rather support their development and integration into the health care system in the interest of their patients and clients.

## PSYCHOSOCIAL CARE IN GERMANY

For understanding and assessing not only the lines of development and possible applications of IP and IIP but also the practical limitations of a putative IIP in Germany, it is useful to know the basic architecture of the psychosocial care system in the country.

### *Outpatient and inpatient medical and psychotherapeutic care*

In Germany, almost all of the residents are covered by health insurance. For treatment, patients must first consult an outpatient doctor or psychotherapist, who will then refer them to a hospital if necessary. The payment of the outpatient therapists by the health insurance companies ensures that they have a considerable influence on therapy methods, content, and proof of therapeutic success, so that therapy is strongly regulated by framework agreements that also set narrow limits to the development of new therapy methods such as IIP. Only 12% of all patients have private insurance and can therefore visit private practices that do not have these restrictions and could therefore also offer IIP. However, therapy would have to be paid for by the patients themselves, which is only possible for very few of them.

In-patient psychiatric and psychotherapeutic treatment is mostly provided in clinics run by various institutions, in particular the Christian churches. However, the treatment itself is paid for by the statutory or private health insurance companies. In in-patient treatment there are far fewer restrictions on therapy methods, as these are integrated into the overall concept of the clinic (music therapy, work therapy, sports therapy, etc.). Although it would theoretically be possible to open a private clinic under Muslim sponsorship, which also offers IIP, the organizational and financial hurdles are currently practically insurmountable.

### *Differentiation of therapy and counseling*

There is a strict legal distinction between therapy and counseling: Only state-examined and licensed physicians, psychologists, and pedagogues who have completed a state-approved training course can treat patients and thus become psychiatric or psychotherapeutic professionals. These strict conditions do not apply to consultations in counseling centers, as those seeking advice do not suffer from an illness but are in a crisis (marital crisis, crisis of upbringing, etc.) for which the counselor is supposed to help them.

### *Financing of therapy and counseling*

Therapy is financed by health insurance companies while counseling centers are funded by their providers (churches, welfare associations, etc.) in addition to government grants or income from foundations. The dependence on financial resources restricts the ability of the individual counselors to shape their own activities in different ways and thus also limits the development and use of an IIP.

As the previous remarks make clear, institutional preconditions have a considerable influence on the discourse and development of IP and IIP (Rüschoff & Kaplick, 2020). Islamically integrated psychotherapy, especially if it meets the scientific standards of psychotherapy, can probably only be developed, tested, and applied in the foreseeable future by independent, licensed psychotherapists and counselors working in their own practices or institutions under Muslim sponsorship. The existing institutions for psychosocial care in Germany continue to set narrow limits for religiously-sensitive therapy and counseling, especially for practicing Muslims, despite some efforts to open up to multiculturalism. At present, there are no significant opportunities to remove these institutional barriers other than by establishing local, Muslim-run counseling services.

## ISLAMIC PSYCHOLOGY (IP) AND ISLAMICALLY INTEGRATED PSYCHOTHERAPY (IIP)

The discussion around IP and IIP often lacks a sufficient differentiation of the research goal and sharp distinction between psychology and psychotherapy (Kaplick & Rüschoff, 2018b). This leads to different expectations and possible misunderstandings.

The development of IP is an extensive undertaking because academic psychology is both basic and applied science. In the canon of its neighboring sciences, psychology strives to describe and explain patterns of thinking, feeling, and acting that are common to all humans and is thus inevitably interdisciplinary (Fetchenhauer, 2012). It is this idea of universal functions that qualifies general psychology (Müsseler & Rieger, 2017) and provides reasons to deal critically with bottom-up approaches that aim at deducing the methods and content of human psychology from Islamic sources.

IIP, on the other hand, can be much more narrowly defined. Psychotherapy is oriented toward the therapeutic outcome, which consists primarily in the reduction of symptoms and the regaining of disease-related, restricted degrees of freedom (Rüschoff & Kaplick, 2018b). The goal is a result-oriented practice, which should be theoretically and scientifically sound, but which does not have to deal systematically with the breadth and scope of human experience and behavior, as psychology as a basic science does.

## REMARKS ON THIS CHAPTER

In general, the group of state-licensed Muslim psychotherapists and those in private practice in Germany as well as those publishing and speaking on the topic of IP and IIP, though constantly growing, is still rather small. As such, the discourse around IP and IIP in Germany has not yet produced a variety of opinions, and we have attempted to differentiate those views in this chapter that are ours and those that we assume to be general. Unfortunately, IP and IIP are not established enough and professionals are not sufficiently connected to provide opinions that we can claim to represent a majority in the country, nor can we generally exemplify the differences in streams of thought as a whole. We put forward that this point in and of itself may also illustrate how careful Muslim psychologists in Germany seem to articulate their opinion regarding IP and IIP.

The chapter is structured as follows: First, some of the historical literature and activities as well as contemporary work on Islamic psychology (IP) in Germany are presented. Second, we introduce the German conceptual discourse on IP and provide insight on essential differences to the United States and the UK. Third, we illustrate how a scientifically sound IIP, as preliminarily conceptualized by several German authors, shapes differences in opinion regarding treatment options and outcome explanations of IIP therapeutic interventions compared to British and American streams of work. To this end, we argue that an exemplary CBT explanation of IIP interventions is based on less complex theoretical assumptions and is therefore a simpler and scientifically preferable explanation than one based on religious truth claims (e.g., existence of God, divine intervention in a mechanistic physical world, metaphysical effects of spiritual and other interventions that can heal clinical phenomena).

## Islamic psychology literature and events

### HISTORICAL PRECURSORS

A few publications have appeared in the German Orientalist literature before the 1990s elaborating on topics that would nowadays touch upon the subject matter of IP. As early as 1868, the German orientalist Friedrich Dieterici wrote on the psychology of Arabs in the 10th century. Following Taeschner's work on the psychology of Qazwini (Taeschner, 1912), Gätje (1971) studied the roots of Aristotelian psychology in Islam. Only by 1967, the psychiatrist E. Bay wrote on Islamic psychiatric hospitals in the Middle Ages. This publication began to spark interest in Islam in disciplines other than Oriental studies.

#### *Phase 1: The 1990s*

The interest in psychological thought of polymaths in the Muslim world such as Ibn Sina (Babai, 1999) and Abu Zayd al-Balkhi (Özkan-Rashed, 2019) was taken up by Muslim psychologists and psychiatrists and reframed in a psychological context in the 1990s (Al-Manssour, 1998). The 1990s literature uniquely targeted the importance of appreciating the religious identities of Muslim patients in both psychotherapy and psychiatry. To this end, Rüschoff (1988, 1992) argued that assessing the individual Muslim patient's understanding of Islam in his everyday life is important to therapeutic success. Furthermore, Özelsel (1995) examined some of the therapeutic elements that may take effect in Sufi practices. Thus, publications in the 1990s focused on the religious identity of Muslim patients and the Islamic imprint of scholarly literature.

These academic efforts were accompanied by a number of events that shaped the interest in IP. Perhaps most importantly was the foundation of the Islamic Association of Social and Educational Professions (IASE, Islamische Arbeitsgemeinschaftfür Sozial- und Erziehungsberufe) in 1988. Following its establishment, 11 conferences gathered psychologists, psychiatrists, pedagogists, and nursery schoolteachers from across Germany, Austria, and Switzerland almost on a yearly basis (see Table 1). These conferences provided a platform to discuss culturally and religiously sensitive psychotherapy and counseling of Muslim patients and families as well as initial ideas on IP. For instance, the scholar and philosopher Abdoljavad Falaturi proposed a framework for defining the healthy, distorted, and diseased human soul by investigating to what extent the soul is capable of realizing and balancing its God-given abilities, strengths, and weaknesses.

*Phase 2: The 2000s and 2010s*

Phase 2 of publications and activities on IP still showed some overlap with MMH content. However, the investigation of psychological concepts in early Muslim scholarly literature was intensified and the IP label was explicitly assigned to a growing body of literature that began to investigate religious and spiritual resources in the therapy of Muslim patients, designating this body of work in most part for Muslim authors but also a non-Muslim readership.

**Table 1. Conferences organized by IASE**

| DATE | TOPICS AND SPEAKERS | LOCATION | ATTENDEES |
|---|---|---|---|
| **PHASE 1** | | | |
| Nov '88 | Basic ideas in Islamic psychology (A. Falaturi)<br><br>Islamic families in Germany (A. Al-Mrayati) | BFMF,[1] Cologne | 13 |
| Mar '89 | Psychological approaches in Quran and Sunna (A. Al-Mrayati)<br><br>The psychosomatic medicine of al-Balkhi (Z. Özkan) | BFMF Cologne | 10 |
| Nov '89 | Working in women's shelter (A. Erades Peterhoff)<br><br>Health and disease in the Islamic conception of the human (A. Falaturi)<br><br>Islamic women's shelter: Practical perspectives (A. M. Peterhoff) | BFMF Cologne | 8 |
| Apr '91 | Islamic education—Perspectives from Quran and Sunna (N. Elyas)<br><br>Everyday problems of Muslim pupils (A. Köhler) | Cologne | 19 |
| May '92 | Sufism—Psychotherapeutic core of Islam? (M. Özelsel)<br><br>Psychotherapeutic approaches in Ghazali's works (A. Al- Mrayati) | Cologne | 17 |
| Nov '94 | How do we treat our children? (E. El Shabassy)<br><br>Health and migration (M. Özelsel) | Cologne | 20 |
| May '95 | Islam and psychotherapy (A. Butollo)<br><br>Psychotherapy and Islam (I. Lützen) | Cologne | 22 |
| Apr '96 | A curriculum for qualifying professions working with Muslim clients (several speakers) | Cologne | 6 |

1 Muslim Women's Centre for Encounter and Further Education

| | | | |
|---|---|---|---|
| Nov '98 | Theory and practice of Islamic psychosocial support (T. Beg, M. Douallal, A. Köhler, I. Rüschoff, M. Zepter) | BFMF Cologne | 14 |
| Nov '99 | Violence in Muslim families I (N. Yardim, M. Zepter, M. Douallal) | BFMF Cologne | 34 |
| May '00 | Violence in Muslim families II (K. Gössinger, B. El-Toukhi, C. Özcan, M. Tosun) | BFMF Cologne | 19 |
| **PHASE 2** | | | |
| Feb '15 | Challenges of the psychosocial support of Muslims—Islamic perspectives (several speakers and workshops) | Frankfurt | 95 |
| Dec '15 | Violence prevention and intervention in the psychosocial support of Muslims (G. Mazarweh; E. Tule) | Frankfurt | 68 |
| Oct '16 | Arabic-Islamic dream interpretation (A. Reidegeld) | Freiburg | 45 |
| Apr '19 | Islam and psychology—Current ideas in theory and practice (P. Kaplick, M. Kellner, I. Rüschoff) | Frankfurt | 67 |

The *International Journal for the Psychology of Religion* published an insightful discussion between the German psychoanalyst and religious studies scholar Sebastian Murken and the Pakistani psychologist Ashiq Shah in 2002. The article elucidates some misunderstandings that occur when Western and non-Western epistemologies and ontologies interact. The privileged status of religion and its impact on how science is understood among a vast majority of Muslim psychologists is still more topical than ever as we see a rise of controversial IP interventions and outcome explanations in recent years. The article by Murken and Shah (2002) is thus a fantastic read and can help one understand the way scientific psychology is applied in Germany and how its methodological assumptions may stand in opposition to classical IP assumptions.

**Table 2. Exemplary publications on IP by German-speaking psychologists and psychiatrists**

| TITLE | YEAR | PUBLISHER | **Authors** |
|---|---|---|---|
| Naturalistic and Islamic Approaches to Psychology, Psychotherapy, and Religion: Metaphysical Assumptions and Methodology—A Discussion | 2002 | *The International Journal for the Psychology of Religion* | Sebastian Murken, Ashiq A. Shah |
| *Medicine, Psychology, and Counselling in Islam: Historical, Depth Psychological, and Systemic Approaches* [German book] | 2007 | Helmer | Ulrike Elsdörfer |
| *Psychology, Psychotherapy, and Islam: Initial Stages of Building an IP Theory* [German book] | 2008 | VDM | Shiva Khalili |
| *Islam and Psychology: Current Concepts in Theory and Practice* [German book] | 2018 | Waxmann | Ibrahim Rüschoff, Paul Kaplick |

Khalili (2008) provided an analysis of the psychological thought of early Muslim scholars and Elsdörfer (2007) published a book describing some counseling-like practices in Sufism and their importance for intercultural counseling settings. Furthermore, Rüschoff and Kaplick (2018b) used 17 key texts on IP from the last 40 years, translated from English into German, to show the development of the discussion and synthesized which of the approaches developed would be useful for adoption in Germany.

Alongside these publications, German Islamic theologians have also written on the topic of the soul and translated relevant texts (Elleisy, 2013; Ibn Qayyim al-Gawziyya, 2020) and increasingly recognize their responsibility to improve the accessibility of Islamic primary and secondary texts and to facilitate formulating Muslim notions of health and disease of the soul in psychological contexts (Kellner, 2020).

Apart from these publications, not many activities could be observed from the turn of the century until the mid-2010s. Only by 2015, specifically, a new generation of Muslim psychologists has started to revive activities and interest in IP, mainly by reviewing and critically reflecting upon the English and German IP literature and organizing conferences to network and to exchange ideas with fellow colleagues (Kaplick, 2017a). This new generation of young professionals and those in training has often felt uneasy with the secularized psychotherapy training programs in the country.

A key activity was the foundation of the "Islam and Psychology" research group within IASE. The activities of this group comprise (1) translation and synthesis of IP publications from languages other than German (Rüschoff & Kaplick, 2018b), (2) theory development (specifically a top-down IIP uniquely fitted for Germany; Kaplick & Skinner, 2017; Rüschoff, 2017; Rüschoff & Kaplick, 2018b; Öz & Kaplick, 2018), (3) networking for Muslim psychologists and Islamic theologians at the national and international level (Kaplick, 2017b; Kaplick & Rüschoff, 2018b), and (4) development of a literature database for IP publications.

Figure 1. Timeline of events by the Islamic Association of Social and Educational Professions (IASE, www.iase-ev.de, a translation link can be found at the bottom of the page) that have shaped the interest in IP.

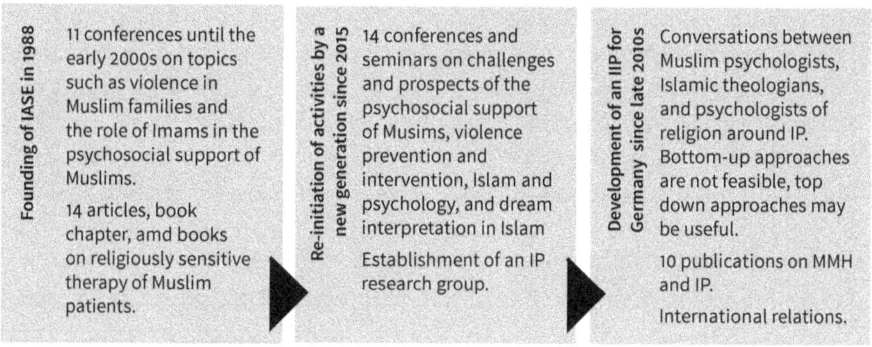

Founding of IASE in 1988

11 conferences until the early 2000s on topics such as violence in Muslim families and the role of Imams in the psychosocial support of Muslims.

14 articles, book chapter, amd books on religiously sensitive therapy of Muslim patients.

Re-initiation of activities by a new generation since 2015

14 conferences and seminars on challenges and prospects of the psychosocial support of Musims, violence prevention and intervention, Islam and psychology, and dream interpretation in Islam

Establishment of an IP research group.

Development of an IIP for Germany since late 2010s

Conversations between Muslim psychologists, Islamic theologians, and psychologists of religion around IP. Bottom-up approaches are not feasible, top down approaches may be useful.

10 publications on MMH and IP.

International relations.

## Conceptual discussions in Germany

Having described historical and contemporary efforts to develop IP in Germany, the following section will introduce concepts and definitions of IP that have been discussed so far. Current challenges and prospects of the conceptual IP development will be synthesized and will help unearth some of the fundamental differences to the conceptual discussions in the UK and the United States.

### WHO IS SPEAKING?

Broadly, there are three interest groups shaping IP in Germany.

#### *Muslim psychologists and psychotherapists*

The above-mentioned new generation of Muslim psychologists and psychotherapists is increasingly organizing itself. This group consists mainly of fresh psychology graduates who undergo training in psychotherapy or have recently finished their training. Additionally, there are more than 600 individuals from various health care professions who receive information via the internal mailing list of IASE. However, as we have indicated earlier, the number of professionals running their own practice is rather small. About 250+ psychology students, psychologists, counselors, and therapists follow regular discussions about IP in a Telegram group and the IASE blog (which has 190+ followers).

In general, the experiences with our Telegram Group are positive: Owing to the high training standards in Germany (therapists are required to study psychology for at least 5 years and have another 3–5 years of therapy training; also, there are strict professional distinctions between psychotherapy, counseling, and pastoral care/chaplaincy), popular topics of IP discussions such as the role of Jinn in mental illness are dealt with the appropriate professionalism. Many of the conflicts that have arisen between psychologists and Imams, for instance, in Britain are non-existent in Germany, presumably because of the rigorous entry requirements for psychology and psychotherapy and because, in our experience, psychologists and theologians are of the opinion that each profession should stick to its own level of work (e.g., questions of clinical treatment modalities may not belong into the area of expertise of theologians and questions of spirituality require theologians to provide content, though opinions on the necessary room for gray area or crossover may vary across therapists).

*Islamic theologians and Imams*

Islamic theologians as well as Imams have recognized the urgency for specialized psychotherapeutic services for some of their community members. Conversations between psychologists and theologians are open and unproblematic, although various attitudes toward the growing IP work in Germany can be observed. While some theologians welcome the formulation of Islamic models of the soul (e.g., via qalb, aql, nafs, ruh, etc.) and related concepts, others argue passionately against the ideological influences of modern Islamic thought on the emergence of IP and maintain the theological illegitimacy of bottom-up approaches. By bottom-up approaches we refer to a set of views that argue that an understanding of human psychology can be informed by the Islamic primary sources (Rothman, 2018).

*Psychologists of religion/spiritual care professionals*

German psychologists of religion are following current ideas and debates on IP with much interest, at times even contributing to the literature themselves (e.g., Murken & Shah, 2002). This third group exerts a strong influence on theory building, in that Muslim psychologists are urged to strictly adhere to scientific standards if they want to be recognized in academic circles. Here, tensions occur particularly at the level of basic psychology because psychologists of religion investigate R/S as the explanandum and reject religious and spiritual truth claims in the explanans. Otherwise, it is argued, scientific objectivism would be obscured, and the doors would be opened for all sorts of "truths" whether these are religious or political in nature. However, at the level of applied and practical psychology, tensions may appear less strong as German Muslim psychologists favor top-down Islamically integrated approaches that build on scientifically established therapy schools.

## WHAT DOES THE IP DISCOURSE LOOK LIKE?

The main assumption regarding IP that has emerged in Germany is that Islamic elements can be integrated into scientifically validated psychotherapies like CBT, psychodynamic therapy, or psychoanalysis without the need to construct an entirely new therapy school. "Islamic elements" are defined broadly and primarily encompass the unique therapeutic relationship between a Muslim therapist and a Muslim patient and the underlying conception of humans employed by the therapist, the religious identity of the therapist, specific therapy goals, but also more explicit elements such as the inclusion of Qur'anic verses and religious practices such as dhikr (litany) or tafakkur (contemplation). Islamic elements are understood here to be those resources that are religious, spiritual, or existential in nature, are inherent to the indigenous intellectual tradition of Islam in the broadest sense, and have the potential to have a meaningful psychological impact within the framework of the factors that determine the effectiveness of psychotherapy. We believe that most Muslim psychologists in Germany agree that a bottom-up approach that attempts to construct a comprehensive school of psychology and psychotherapy based on the indigenous Islamic intellectual tradition is neither feasible, as it would obscure well-established scientific standards in the psychology of religion and regulatory standards of psychotherapy in Germany, nor is it required even for the most efficient psychotherapeutic treatment of Muslim patients. This crucial assumption is the result of recent conversations between Muslim psychologists (in particular, the authors of this chapter and other colleagues involved in IASE), Islamic theologians (predominantly from the University of Osnabrück), and psychologists of religion (primarily those professionals and academics represented in the Religion and Spirituality sections of large professional bodies such as the DGPPN/German Association for Psychiatry, Psychotherapy and Psychosomatics) in Germany. Furthermore, top-down approaches have received support from most attendees at the 2019 conference on Islam and Psychology (see Table 1) and is the basis for most chapters in an upcoming German book on Islamically integrated psychotherapy (see Table 3; Rüschoff & Kaplick, 2021).

Many authors explain their reasons for the inclusion of Islamic elements into therapy with the argument that it significantly increases therapy motivation and compliance of (practicing) Muslim patients (Rüschoff & Kaplick, 2021). This also explains why many authors believe that the religious identity of the therapist is the key characteristic of a top-down Islamically integrated psychotherapy and that there is no need for explicit "Islamic" therapeutic interventions and techniques. The integration of Islamic elements and teachings should hence result purposefully from the religiousness and spirituality offered by the patient.

The existing ideas and concepts for the application of Islamic elements in therapy in Germany are not scientifically validated and do not represent therapy manuals. They are intended to serve as inspirations for future empirical studies on the development of an Islamically integrated psychotherapy for a German-speaking context based on the criteria of scientific psychology and Islamic theology, and to prepare an empirical examination of the need for an Islamic-influenced therapeutic orientation and its effectiveness and mechanisms of action.

*The Muslim therapist*

The therapeutic relationship determines 30% of the effectiveness of psychotherapy (40% non-therapeutic factors, 15% therapeutic techniques, and 15% expectations, hopes, "placebo") (Lambert, 2013; Norcross & Lambert, 2011), and thus it offers a particularly important basis for an Islamically inspired therapeutic approach, which is primarily reflected in the therapist's view of humanity. In addition to the aforementioned aspects, the view of man regards the patient as the son of Adam, who was honored in his function as a vicegerent on earth and is not a mere product of biological evolution (Rüschoff, 2021). The human being is grasped as a fundamentally problematic one (Kellner, 2021), who has inherent destructive as well as positive-transforming potential, and who, although marked by weaknesses such as forgetting, is also characterized by its sociability (Kellner, 2020). This observation prepares a spiritual horizon of meaning and significance that, in practicing Muslims, extends to the examination of creation—in everyday life at work and with family and friends—as well as with the Creator. Every action is put into the service of the soul and its positive development (Rüschoff, 2017).

A Muslim therapist is almost indispensable for a therapeutic approach that is influenced by Islam, as they offer a common wavelength regarding the religious horizon (Utsch, Bonelli, & Pfeifer, 2018). This is reflected in various areas such as the use of language and the examples used. Furthermore, Muslim therapists can—within the scope of their possibilities—provide spiritual competencies in a very natural way (Laabdallaoui, 2021) and consider, for example, religiously frowned upon views and convictions also against the cultural background of the individual patient (Loucif, 2021). In addition, the therapeutic relationship is shaped by the therapist's self-understanding as *rizq* (care) of God. Consequently, the therapist also has a very special responsibility for the care of his own spirituality, because he acts as an instrument of God (Qur'an 26:80; Rüschoff, 2021). The role of mosque-based care structures gains special significance in this respect (Alkan-Härtwig, 2021).

*Therapy goals*

Closely related to the therapeutic relationship is the Islamic orientation of the therapeutic goals. The basic goals are the elimination of symptoms and the regaining of illness-related limited freedom, which has left the patients at the mercy of depressions, fears, drive disorders, etc. and thus also restricted their religious practice: The therapy should enable the patient to lead a conflict-free religious life and a development toward a state of nafs al-mutmainnah (the calmed soul; Rüschoff, 2021).

*Therapeutic interventions and techniques*

Therapeutic techniques explain 15% of the success of therapy (Lambert, 2013; Norcross & Lambert, 2011). Correspondingly, Islamically integrated interventions, even when used in a highly efficient manner, are of a rather subordinate nature but nevertheless represent the majority of current efforts in Islamically integrated psychotherapy (York Al-Karam, 2018). Often, Islamically integrated therapeutic interventions are developed based on soul models conceived by Muslim scholarship with different instances, such as traditional Islamically integrated psychotherapy (TIIP) that proposes cognitive (*'aql*) and emotional (*ihsaas*) instances, behavioral impulses (*nafs*), and spiritual (*ruh*) soul parts. Psychopathologies are a result of the imbalance of these entities, and Islamically integrated interventions can be aimed at identifying and correcting such imbalance (Keshavarzi et al., 2020). In Germany, the development of Islamic elements in interventions occurs primarily in cognitive behavioral therapy and thus also manifests itself in the inclusion of Quranic verses (Karim, 2021) or overriding rules of Islamic legal doctrine (*qawaid ul-fiqhiyyah*, Loucif, 2021). Prophet stories are also used in school social work (Fuchs-El Bahnasawy, 2021).

Some practitioners in the environment of IASE have recently attempted to formulate their own practice of Islamically integrated psychotherapy or professional counseling, and we have referenced some of the content in the previous paragraphs. We are currently editing a volume on how some of these Muslim therapists and professional counselors integrate Islamic elements into therapy and counseling of religious Muslim patients and clients (Rüschoff & Kaplick,

2021, in preparation). Table 3 shows those chapters that describe different kinds of Islamic elements and their integration into therapy, giving an impression of the current state of IIP ideas in Germany.

**Table 3. Exemplary ideas on IIP interventions in Germany**

| THEME | ISLAMIC ELEMENTS/ INTERVENTIONS | AUTHOR |
|---|---|---|
| The religious-spiritual anamnesis SPIR in the psychotherapy of Muslim patients | Religious anamnesis | M. Laabdallaoui |
| Islamic expectations and depth psychological approaches in child and youth psychotherapy—Expectations of parents and loyalty conflicts of children and youth | *Amana* as therapeutic principle | H. Hassan-Michl |
| Islamic elements in CBT/neuropsychotherapy | Quranic verses and ahadith | A. A. Karim |
| Counselling and therapy of Muslim couples—Integrating clarification-oriented psychotherapy and Islamic concepts | *Qawaaid ul-fiqhiyyah* | A. Loucif |
| Religion and spirituality in the counseling practice of the Muslim spiritual care hotline | Several counseling practices | I. Saghir |
| Using the 99 Names of God (*asmaa-ul-husnā*) in Psychodynamic Psychotherapy with Muslim Patients | Connection between image of God and image of parents | I. Rüschoff |
| Social pedagogy in Muslim schools—Counseling, accompanying, empowering, and promoting | several | S. Fuchs |
| Using spirituality in the social work with young men | several | A. Borno |
| Mindfulness-like practices in Islamic texts and their implementation into relaxation techniques | several | Z. Elibol |
| Psychiatric counseling in mosques | Mosques | E. Alkan-Härtwig |
| Islamic elements in the social work and counseling of an Imam (interview) | several | I. Rüschoff/ M. Doukali |

## The unique stance of German thought in IP

In the following, we illustrate how the multifaceted IP discourse in Germany with its stakeholders and interest groups has led to several opinions regarding treatment options and outcome explanations of IIP psychotherapeutic interventions. To this end, we have taken material from a recent chapter on traditional Islamically integrated psychotherapy (TIIP).

### CASE STUDY

The case describes a 30-year-old unmarried man who presented with a pornography use accompanied by masturbation. He understood his porn consumption as immoral, but it seemed "to be 'all he had to look forward to.'" He described depressive feelings, low motivation, hopelessness, fatigue, and other related phenomena. During the diagnosis, problems related to his spiritual functioning (spiritual depletion, sense of purposelessness, hopelessness) were unveiled and contextualized in relation to other psychic entities (cognition, behavioral impulses, feelings). A major depressive disorder was diagnosed. The cycle and nature of spiritual depletion and its link with his routine animalistic behaviors (secondary gain to cope with a lack of purpose in life) were identified in therapy. Spiritual exercises (e.g., contemplative reflection) were used to generate motivation to change and a renewed sense of purpose. The primary spiritual intervention used was *tawbah* (ablution, *nafilah* prayer, recital of the *Sayyid al-Istighfar*), which is supposed to "remove the effects of darkness, [increase] light, and transform the behavioral impulses to a spiritual inclination to do good." Other prayers and spiritual litanies were recommended to enhance spiritual connection and to indirectly attenuate unhealthy sexual drives. Porn use and depressive symptoms decreased, and the patient showed an increased spiritual connection with God (Keshavarzi et al., 2020, pp. 285–287).

### SIMPLER EXPLANATIONS ARE (SOMETIMES) BETTER EXPLANATIONS

The principle known as "Ockham's razor" states that when developing explanatory theories and concepts for a given subject, the simpler and less complex one is always preferable (Audi, 1999). This is especially true for the development of a result-oriented theory like TIIP, which is based on religious claims of truth (e.g., existence of God and divine interventions in a mechanistic physical world). Here, simpler concepts such as CBT or other scientifically established therapy schools are helpful in several respects, as they are easier to communicate to the patient regarding therapy motivation and compliance ("Practice makes perfect!") and can be better evaluated with regard to effects and side effects. However, for the description of the therapeutic relationship and the therapist's image of the human being, which in any case have a far greater share in the therapeutic outcome than the method (Hubble, Duncan, & Miller, 2001) but especially for complex concepts such as an epistemologically founded and comprehensive IP, simple models are not suitable because of the complexity of the facts.

*Schematheory and clarification-oriented psychotherapy*

Klärungsorientierte Psychotherapie (KOP)/clarification-oriented psychotherapy is a cognitive behavioral psychotherapy model of the third wave (Sachse et al., 2016). The main proposition of this model is based on the importance of innate motives and desires (e.g., the need of having importance, autonomy, soundness/reliability, solidarity, respected boundaries, and being defined with positive values) and the learned schemas toward them. The main goal in KOP is to restore or construct a functional self-regulation by means of self-awareness (here, KOP and TIIP converge and can inform each other usefully) and learning about one's own functional and dysfunctional schemas, to work on the dysfunctional schemas, and how to fulfill the innate motives and desires. According to KOP, dysfunctional schemas strongly influence an individual's information processing and cause misinterpretation of information, and only through the knowledge of the dysfunctional schemas significant changes in psychopathology can occur. For instance, a dysfunctional schema can motivate a pupil to work hard to receive positive feedback from peers or teachers. This conflicts with the innate motive of humans to not achieve value through performance but through being themselves, ultimately leading to maladaptive behaviors because the innate motive is not satisfied appropriately.

Figure 2. Situations and their influence of schemas on information processing.

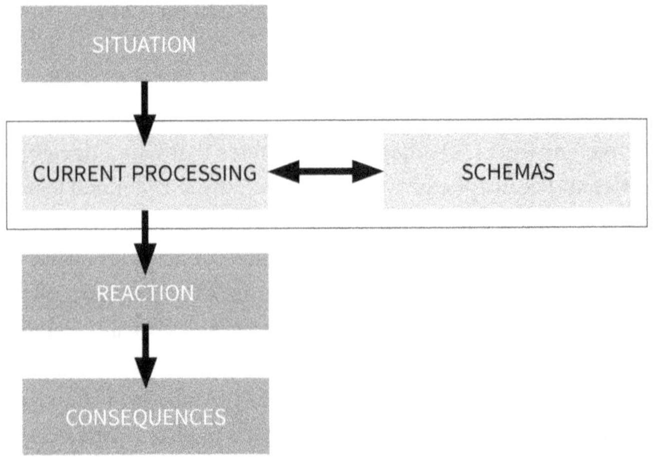

A schema is a mental structure that describes a pattern of thoughts or behaviors that organizes categories of information and their mutual relationships (Young, Klosko, & Weishaar, 2003). Schemas result from experiences and their interpretations and conclusions drawn from these experiences. Schemas are activated ("triggered") by activating stimuli ("bottom up") and then control ("top down") the person's information processing. Schemas exert an influence if normally "neutral" information is experienced as highly dangerous or good for our well-being (Sachse & Langens, 2014). For example, receiving feedback on a test in school is, normally, just a chunk of information. However, through our schemas (e.g., through a repeated childhood experience that getting criticized leads to valueless in the eye of others), it could be interpreted as an attack. Schemas can thus influence all types of information processing: situation interpretation, interpretation of the degree of personal relevance, coping abilities, etc.; and can greatly influence the genesis of emotions (Sachse & Langens, 2014). This process is depicted in Figure 2.

*What do spiritual litanies do to clinical symptoms?*

The cognitive behavioral take on the application of spiritual litanies in the above case is that these may facilitate building a distance to dysfunctional trigger activation of the schema. This enhances resilience against negative effects on the spiritual domain, and it may lead to different outcomes: First, a construction and continuous reinforcement of a functional schema is achieved through new and positive experiences and renders a dysfunctional schema activation less likely. Another possible outcome is to masquerade the symptoms and their negative outcome through avoidance and suppression of maladaptive thoughts and behaviors, without resolving the source itself. This can be illustrated borrowing from the Mpemba effect: This effect describes a phenomenon where, under certain circumstances, an initially hot body of water freezes at a faster rate than an identical body of initially cold water. While this remains a disputed phenomenon, one of several possible explanations is based on considering differences in bonding between water molecules in the hot and cold bodies of water. These differences in bonding provide more favorable conditions for the nucleation process that leads to the formation of ice (Tao, Zou, Jia, Li, & Cremer, 2016). We can use this analogy for better understanding resilience against negative effects on the spiritual domain, in that spiritual exercises can help us to stay in a "less oscillatory" position. Ideally, schema-activation and proximity to triggers are avoided or a certain distance is maintained—similar to exposure and response prevention intervention—until the association between situation and negative feelings is weakened and reframed. As a result, dysfunctional mental processes and behaviors require more activation and more negative energy to be triggered.

There are some similarities and differences concerning the acceptance and commitment therapy (ACT). By using spiritual litanies, the client is enabled to accept his/her limited emotional and cognitive resources to solve the problem by himself or herself. The client would be able to accept that everything happens in the will of Allah. The client may learn that he/she can be in control of his/her own reactions, thoughts, and emotions, especially through the methods and the help of Allah. Also, he/she can give himself or herself time for problem solving. These are no direct effects of spiritual exercises, but they must be geared by a qualified psychotherapist. As such, we must recognize that there is a risk to use spiritually based interventions in an unreflected manner. Instead of putting more cold water into the boiler or to cool down the water, we should analyze from where the heat originates and change the source. This, of course, may occur only over the course of several months of psychotherapy with an increased frequency in therapy sessions and psychospiritual education.

More specifically, addictions and sexual preference disorders are difficult to treat, and the long-term outcome of the delivered spiritual remedies should be evaluated with extreme caution! Even months into a professional rehabilitation, many patients report that they feel like being nearly cured but experience backfalls rapidly after returning into their usual environment (Körkel, 2013). One explanation of this is that addictions are chronic diseases that require lifelong awareness and treatment and standard rehabilitation centers still lack the respective addictive and other common stress triggers for the individual patient. Symptom-free patients in trigger-free environments can be mistaken with actual symptom reduction. One way to circumvent this problem is via confrontation with triggers toward the later stages of the rehabilitation program when the patient is sufficiently stabilized. One of the chief problems is that the root cause of the addictive behavior is not addressed, whether it be child abuse history, misguided stress regulation, or a lack of impulse control. As such, spiritually based interventions in the aforementioned case study should be understood as a purely additional treatment, unless possible risks and unintended side effects are systematically investigated. This restriction applies even more to deep-seated personality developments or changes that *necessitate* a referral to the appropriate treatment modality, such as psychoanalysis or derived psychodynamic therapies and cognitive behavioral therapy (CBT). Just as there is not the one and only established therapeutic school of thought that is appropriate for every patient and every dysfunction, it is equally applicable that spiritually integrated psychotherapy has to be aware of its own potential and limitations (Rüschoff & Kaplick, 2018a).

## Current challenges and prospects

Unlike the natural sciences, psychology as the science of man is always closely related to his cultural environment and language, which structure and reflect the realities of human life. This is all the truer for psychotherapy, which is even more strongly embedded in the respective cultural and religious norms and ideas of right and wrong, especially because of its claim to cure illnesses, and is influenced in terms of therapeutic goals.

Islam does not exist in a vacuum but manifests itself in the life of people with their social and individual characteristics. Here, psychology proves to be much stronger than religion; unfortunately, one would like to say, because otherwise we would undoubtedly be better people. For this reason, Islam is ultimately as diverse on the micro-level of individuals as the psychology of human beings, even if they largely share common views of right behavior and belief and practice their religion in this sense.

Apart from cultural conditions, economic and social circumstances in individual nations also have an influence on the development of IP and IIP. For example, Muslims have only been living in Germany in significant numbers since the 1960s, and there were virtually no practicing Muslim psychiatrists and psychotherapists at that time. The local professionals were more concerned with a cultural opening; Muslims were not perceived and treated as Muslims but as migrants, and psychiatric and psychotherapeutic care was provided within the general health care system. Psychosocial counseling was provided by compatriots in special counseling centers, particularly because of language problems, where religion played no role in the sense of what was understood as "neutrality." For this reason, issues of Muslim mental health have been in the foreground in Germany in the past decades. Only in the last 10 years or so has the focus shifted toward IP and IIP, also because of a new generation of Muslim psychiatrists and psychotherapists.

To have a chance for a therapeutic application of IP at all, the focus of the present investigation was directed on a top-down solution and CBT was illustrated for its usability in the context of an IIP. Based on the results of health care research, that 30% of the therapeutic outcome can be attributed to the therapeutic relationship and only 15% to the therapeutic method (Utsch, Bonelli, & Pfeifer, 2018), we investigate the possibilities of a top-down approach and use proven therapeutic methods as different, partly disorder-specific "maps" for orientation in the "human landscape" and its current symptomatology. We have described this approach in various places (e.g., Rüschoff & Kaplick, 2018b).

In addition to describing the situation of IP and IIP in Germany, a central concern of this work was to show, using a short case study from TIIP, that a top-down approach allows a meaningful and result-oriented therapeutic approach to the patient's symptoms. In doing so, we understand the TIIP's statements on the concepts of nafs, 'aql, ruh, and qalb and their relationship to each other not as a methodological approach but as an important statement about the patient's nature and an indispensable element of a Muslim therapist's view of man, which has a direct and not to be underestimated influence on the therapeutic relationship as the most important agent of healing. This would be a crucial adaptation of TIIP that would allow an employment of its spiritual and religious treatment methods in a manner palatable to a German audience.

In the following years, we intend systematically developing the experiences made so far and describing the current situation of IIP in Germany in a book that is currently in print and will be published next spring (Rüschoff & Kaplick, 2021).

## References

Alkan-Härtwig, E. (2021) Als die Psychiatrie in die Moschee kam: Ein Erfahrungsbericht zur beraterischen Arbeit des SPIRA-Projekts in den muslimischen Gemeinden in Berlin (When psychiatry entered the mosque: A report on the counseling work oft he SPIRA-project in Muslim communities in Berlin). In Rüschoff, I., & Kaplick, P. M. (Eds.), *Islamintegrierte Psychotherapie und Beratung. Professionelle Zugänge zur Arbeit mit Menschen muslimischen Glaubens (Islamically-integrated psychotherapy and counseling. Professional approaches for working with people of Muslim faith)*, Gießen, Germany: Psychosozial Verlag (in press).

Al-Manssour, I. (1998). Zum Wissenschaftserbe der Islamisch-Arabischen Zivilisation — Ein Beitrag zur Geschichte der Internationalen Pädagogik und Psychologie (The scientific heritage of the Islamic-Arabic Civilization – A contribution tot he history of Internal Pedagogy and Psychology). In R. Golz, R. W. Keck, & W. Mayrhofer (Eds.), *Humanisierung der Bildung [Humanising of Education]* (pp. 155-173). Bern, Switzerland: Peter Lang Europäischer Verlag der Wissenschaften.

Audi, R. (1999). *The Cambridge dictionary of philosophy.* Cambridge: Cambridge University Press.

Babai, A. (1999). *Zur Psychologie und Psychotherapie Ibn Sinas [On the psychology and psychotherapy of Ibn Sina]*. Glienicke, Berlin, Germany: Galda + Wilch.

Bay, E. (1967). *Islamische Krankenhäuser im Mittelalter unter besonderer Berücksichtigung der Psychiatrie* (Dissertation). Düsseldorf, Germany.

Borno, A. (2021). Schöpfergedanke und Spiritualität im sozialpädagogischen Beratungsprozess junger Männer (Spirituality in the socio-pedagogical counseling process with young men). In Rüschoff, I., & Kaplick, P. M. (Eds.),

*Islamintegrierte Psychotherapie und Beratung. Professionelle Zugänge zur Arbeit mit Menschen muslimischen Glaubens (Islamically-integrated psychotherapy and counseling. Professional approaches for working with people of Muslim faith),* Gießen, Germany: Psychosozial Verlag (in press).

Dieterici, F. (1868). *Die Logik und Psychologie der Araber im zehnten Jahrhundert n.Chr.* (Logic and psychology of the Arabs in the 10th century AD). Leipzig, Germany: J. C. Hinrichs'sche Buchhandlung.

Doukali, M. (2021). Zwischen Fatwa und psychosozialer Beratung – Imame im Spannungsfeld von Theologie, Beratung und Seelsorge (Fatwa and psychosocial counseling – Imams between theology, counseling, and pastoral care). In Rüschoff, I., & Kaplick, P. M. (Eds.), *Islamintegrierte Psychotherapie und Beratung. Professionelle Zugänge zur Arbeit mit Menschen muslimischen Glaubens (Islamically-integrated psychotherapy and counseling. Professional approaches for working with people of Muslim faith),* Gießen: Psychosozial Verlag (in press).

Elleisy, M. (2013). Die Seeleim Islam: Zwischen Theologie und Philosophie (The soul in Islamic: Between Theology and Philosophy). Hamburg, Germany: Disserta Verlag.

Elibol, X. (2021). Von Beratern und Sufimeistern – Islamischinspirierte Achtsamkeitsübungen und ihre Implementierung in die hypnosystemische Beratungals Entspannung (Counselors and Sufi masters – Islamically inspired mindfulness practices and their implementation in hypnosystemic counseling). In Rüschoff, I., & Kaplick, P. M. (Eds.), *Islamintegrierte Psychotherapie und Beratung. Professionelle Zugänge zur Arbeit mit Menschen muslimischen Glaubens (Islamically-integrated psychotherapy and counseling. Professional approaches for working with people of Muslim faith),* Gießen, Germany: Psychosozial Verlag (in press).

Elsdörfer, U. (2007). *Medizin, Psychologie und Beratung im Islam: Historische, tiefenpsychologische und systemische Annäherungen (Medicine, psychology and counseling in Islam: Historical, depth psychological and systemic approaches).* Königstein, Germany: Helmer.

Fetchenhauer, D. (2012). *Psychologie.* München, Germany: Vahlen.

Fuchs-El Bahnasawy, S. (2021) Sozialpädagogik an muslimischen Schulen – Begleiten, Stärken und Fördern in der Adoleszenz. In Rüschoff, I., & Kaplick, P. M. (Eds.), *Islamintegrierte Psychotherapie und Beratung. Professionelle Zugänge zur Arbeit mit Menschen muslimischen Glaubens (Islamically-integrated psychotherapy and counseling. Professional approaches for working with people of Muslim faith),* Gießen, Germany: Psychosozial Verlag (in press).

Gätje, H. (1971). *Studien zur Überlieferung der aristotelischen Psychologie im Islam (Studies on the Aristotelian psychological tradition in Islam).* Heidelberg, Germany: C. Winter.

Hassan-Michl, H. (2021). Aspekte tiefenpsychologischer Psychotherapie mit muslimischen Kindern und Jugendlichen: Zwischen Erwartungen der Eltern und

Loyalitätskonflikten der Kinder und Jugendlichen (Aspects of depth psychological psychotherapy with Muslim kids and adolescents: Between expectations of parents and loyalty conflicts of kids and adolescents). In Rüschoff, I., & Kaplick, P. M. (Eds.), *Islamintegrierte Psychotherapie und Beratung. Professionelle Zugänge zur Arbeit mit Menschen muslimischen Glaubens (Islamically-integrated psychotherapy and counseling. Professional approaches for working with people of Muslim faith)*, Gießen, Germany: Psychosozial Verlag (in press).

Hubble M. A., Duncan, B. L., & Miller, S. D. (2001). *So wirkt Psychotherapie. Empirische Ergebnisse und praktische Folgen (Effects of psychotherapy: Empirical evidence and practical consequences)*. Dortmund, Germany: Verlag Modernes Lernen.

Ibn Qayyim al-Gawziyya. (2020). *Die Menschliche Seele: Kitab ar-Ruh (Book on the Soul)* (A. Soytürk, Trans.). Independently published.

Kaplick, P. M., & Skinner, R. (2017). The evolving *Islam and Psychology* Movement. *European Psychologist, 22*(4), 198-204.

Kaplick, P. M. (2017a). Conference Report: The Islamic Association of Social and Educational Professions in Germany. *The American Journal of Islamic Social Sciences, 34*(3), 149-151.

Kaplick, P. M. (2017b). Zum Stand der islamischen Psychologie in Indien (On the State of Islamic Psychology in India). *Spiritual Care, 7*(1), 101-103.

Kaplick, P. M., & Rüschoff, I. (2018a). Islam und Psychologie in Großbritannien, den Vereinigten Staaten und Deutschland: Gegenwart und Zukunft von institutionellen Strukturen muslimischer Psychologen (Islam and Psychology in the United Kingdom, the United States, and Germany: Current and Future Institutional Structures for Muslim Psychologists). *Wege zum Menschen, 70*(1), 78-88.

Kaplick, P. M., & Rüschoff, I. (2018b). Islam und Psychologie—Gegenstand und Historie (Islam and Psychology – History and Subject Matter). In I. Rüschoff & P. M. Kaplick (Eds.), *Islam und Psychologie—Beiträge zu aktuellen Konzepten in Theorie und Praxis*. Münster, Germany: Waxmann.

Karim, A.A. (2021), Methoden zur Integration islamischer Elemente in die kognitive Verhaltenstherapie [Methods for integrating islamic elements into cognitive behavioral therapy]. In Rüschoff, I., & Kaplick, P. M. (Eds.), *Islamintegrierte Psychotherapie und Beratung. Professionelle Zugänge zur Arbeit mit Menschen muslimischen Glaubens (Islamically-integrated psychotherapy and counseling. Professional approaches for working with people of Muslim faith)*, Gießen, Germany: Psychosozial Verlag (in press).

Kellner, M. M. (2020). Psychische Krankheit/Gesundheit und Glaube im Islam—Koranische Konzepte seelischer Zustände und deren Kontextualisierungen [Psychological illness/health and creed in Islamic – Koranic Concepts of states of the soul and their contextualizations]. In N. Mönter, A. Heinz, & M. Utsch (Eds.), *Religionssensible Psychotherapie und Psychiatrie: Basiswissen und Praxis-Erfahrungen (Religiously-sensitive Psychotherapy and Psychiatry: Basic knowledge and practical experiences)* (pp. 102-109). Stuttgart, Germany: Kohlhammer.

Kellner, M.M. (2021). Psychische Entitäten bei Koranexegeten – Ansätze zum islamischen Verständnis der Seele [Psychological entities amongst exegetes – Approaches tot he Islamic understanding of the soul]. In Rüschoff, I., & Kaplick, P. M. (Eds.), *Islamintegrierte Psychotherapie und Beratung. Professionelle Zugänge zur Arbeit mit Menschen muslimischen Glaubens (Islamically-integrated psychotherapy and counseling. Professional approaches for working with people of Muslim faith)*, Gießen, Germany: Psychosozial Verlag (in press).

Keshavarzi, H., Yusuf, A., Kaplick, P. M., Ahmadi, T., & Loucif, A. (2020). Spiritually (Ruhani) Focused Psychotherapy. In H. Keshavarzi, F. Khan, B. Ali, & R. Awaad (Eds.), *Applying Islamic Principles to Clinical Mental Health Care: Introducing Traditional Islamically Integrated Psychotherapy*. New York: Routledge. 266-290.

Khalili, S. (2008). *Psychologie, Psychotherapie und Islam—Erste Entstehungsphasen einer Theorie aus islamischer Psychologie*. Saarbrücken, Germany: VDM Verlag.

Kizilhan, J. I. (2015). Religion, Kultur und Psychotherapie bei muslimischen Migranten. *Psychotherapeut, 60*, 426-432.

Körkel, J. (2013). *Kontrolliertes Trinken - So reduzieren Sie Ihren Alkoholkonsum.* Stuttgart, Germany: Trias.

Laabdallaoui, M. (2021). Die religiös-spirituelle Anamnese SPIR in der Psychotherapie muslimischer Patienten [Anamnesis of religion and spirituality in psychotherapy with Muslim patients]. In Rüschoff, I., & Kaplick, P. M. (Eds.), *Islamintegrierte Psychotherapie und Beratung. Professionelle Zugänge zur Arbeit mit Menschen muslimischen Glaubens (Islamically-integrated psychotherapy and counseling. Professional approaches for working with people of Muslim faith)*, Gießen, Germany: Psychosozial Verlag (in press).

Lambert, M.J. (2013). Outcome in Psychotherapy: The Past and Important Advances, Psychotherapy, 50(1), 42-51.

Loucif, A. (2021). Beratung und Therapie muslimischer Paare – Zur Integration klärungsorientierter und islamischer Konzepte (Counseling and therapy of Muslim couples – Integrating clarification-oriented psychotherapeutic and Islamic concepts). In Rüschoff, I., & Kaplick, P. M. (Eds.), *Islamintegrierte Psychotherapie und Beratung. Professionelle Zugänge zur Arbeit mit Menschen muslimischen Glaubens (Islamically-integrated psychotherapy and counseling. Professional approaches for working with people of Muslim faith)*, Gießen, Germany: Psychosozial Verlag (in press).

Murken, S., & Shah, A. A. (2002). Naturalistic and Islamic approaches to psychology, psychotherapy, and religion: Metaphysical assumptions and methodology—a discussion. *The International Journal for the Psychology of Religion, 12*(4), 239–254.

Müsseler, J., & Rieger, M. (2017), *Allgemeine Psychologie.* Berlin, Heidelberg, Germany: Springer.

Norcross, J.C. & Lambert, M.J. (2011). Psychotherapy relationships that work II. *Psychotherapy, 48*(1), 4-8.

Öz, T., & Kaplick, P. M. (2018). Grundbegriffe eines islamischen Persönlichkeitsmodells: Linguistische, exegetisch-theologische und psychologische Perspektiven (Basic concepts of an Islamic personality model. Linguistic, exegetic-theological, and psychological perspectives). In M. Khorchide & A. M. Karimi (Eds.), *Jahrbuch für islamische Theologie und Religionspädagogik - Religion und Reform*. Münster, Germany: Kalam Verlag. 111-146.

Özelsel, M. M. (1995). Therapeutische Aspekte des Sufitums—Schamanisches und Islamisches (Therapeutic aspects of Sufim – Schamanic and Islamic approaches). *Ethnopsychologische Mitteilungen*, 4(2), 128-150.

Özkan-Rashed, Z. (2019). *Die Psychosomatische Medizin bei Abū Zaid al-Balhī* (gest. 934 A.D.). Düren, Germany: Shaker.

Rothman, A. (2018). An Islamic theoretical orientation to psychotherapy. In C. York Al-Karam (Ed.), *Islamically integrated psychotherapy: Uniting faith and professional practice* (pp. 25-56). West Conshohocken, PA: Templeton Press.

Rüschoff, I. (1988). Islamische Aspekte der Biographie. *Daseinsanalyse. Phänomenologische Anthropologie und Psychotherapie, 5*, 96-103.

Rüschoff, I. (1992). Zur Bedeutung des islamischen Religionsverständnisses für die psychiatrische Praxis. *Psychiatrische Praxis, 19*(2), 39-42.

Rüschoff, I. (2017). Religiöse Ressourcen in der Psychotherapie muslimischer Patienten (Religious resources in the psychotherapy of Muslim patients). *Spiritual Care, 6*(1), 103-110. doi:10.1515/spircare-2016-0206

Rüschoff, I., & Kaplick, P. M. (2018a). *Islam und Psychologie: Beiträge zu aktuellen Konzepten in Theorie und Praxis*. Münster, Germany: Waxmann.

Rüschoff, I., & Kaplick, P. M. (2018b). Integrating Islamic spirituality into psychodynamic therapy with Muslim patients. In C. York Al-Karam (Ed.), *Islamically integrated psychotherapy: Uniting faith and professional practice* (pp. 127-151). West Conshohocken, PA: Templeton Press.

Rüschoff, I., & Kaplick, P. M. (2020). Muslim mental health in Germany. In R. Awaad & H. Hamid (Eds.), *Muslim Mental Health*.

Rüschoff, I., & Kaplick, P. M. (2021). *Islamintegrierte Psychotherapie und Beratung. Professionelle Zugänge zur Arbeit mit Menschen muslimischen Glaubens (Islamically-integrated psychotherapy and counseling. Professional approaches for working with people of Muslim faith)*, Gießen: Psychosozial Verlag. Gießen, Germany: Psychosozial Verlag (in press).

Rüschoff, I. (2021). Zur Integration islamischer Spiritualität in die tiefenpsychologisch fundierte Psychotherapie mit muslimischen Patienten (Integrating Islamic spirituality into depth psychological psychotherapy with Muslim patients). In Rüschoff, I., & Kaplick, P. M. (Eds.), *Islamintegrierte Psychothera-*

*pie und Beratung. Professionelle Zugänge zur Arbeit mit Menschen muslimischen Glaubens (Islamically-integrated psychotherapy and counseling. Professional approaches for working with people of Muslim faith),* Gießen: Psychosozial Verlag (in press).

Sachse, R., Sachse, M. & Fasbender, J. (2016). *Grundlagen Klärungsorientierter Psychotherapie* (1. Auflage). Göttingen, Germany: Hogrefe.

Sachse, R., & Langens, T. (2014). Emotionen und Affekte in der Psychotherapie (Emotions and affects in psychotherapy). Göttingen, Germany: Hogrefe.

Saghir, I. M. (2021). Religion und Spiritualität in der Beratungspraxis des Muslimischen Seelsorgetelefons [Religion and Spirituality in the counseling work of the Muslimische Seelsorgetelefon]. In Rüschoff, I., & Kaplick, P. M. (Eds.), *Islamintegrierte Psychotherapie und Beratung. Professionelle Zugänge zur Arbeit mit Menschen muslimischen Glaubens (Islamically-integrated psychotherapy and counseling. Professional approaches for working with people of Muslim faith),* Gießen, Germany: Psychosozial Verlag (in press).

Taeschner, F. (1912). *Die Psychologie Qazwînis.* Tübingen, Germany: Druck von G. Schnürlen.

Tao, Y., Zou, W., Jia, J., Li, W., & Cremer, D. (2016). Different ways of hydrogen bonding in water - Why does warm water freeze faster than cold water? *Journal of Chemical Theory and Computation, 13*(1), 55-76. doi:10.1021/acs.jctc.6b00735

Utsch, M., & Frick, E. (2015). Religiosität und Spiritualität in der Psychotherapie. *Psychotherapeut,60*, 451–466. doi: 10.1007/s00278-015-0052-5.

Utsch, M., Anderssen-Reuster, U., Frick, E., Gross, W., Murken, S., Schouler-Ocak, M., & Stotz-Ingenlath, G. (2017). Empfehlungen zum Umgang mit Religiosität und Spiritualität in Psychiatrie und Psychotherapie. *Spiritual Care, 6*(1), 141-146. doi:10.1515/spircare-2016-0220.

Utsch, M., Bonelli, R., & Pfeifer, S. (2018), *Psychotherapie und Spiritualität.Mit existenziellen Konflikten und Transzendenzfragen professionell umgehen.* Berlin, Germany: Springer.

York Al-Karam, C (Ed.), (2018). *Islamically integrated psychotherapy: Uniting faith and professional practice* (pp. 127-151). West Conshohocken, PA: Templeton Press.

Young, J., Klosko, J., & Weishaar, M. (2003). *Schema therapy: A practitioner's guide.* New
York: Guilford Press.

# Notes on Contributors

**Abdallah Rothman** is the Principal of Cambridge Muslim College, founder of Shifaa Integrative Counseling, co-founder and Executive Director of the International Association of Islamic Psychology, and visiting professor of psychology at Zaim University Istanbul, International Islamic University Islamabad, and Al-Neelain University Khartoum. He holds an MA and a Ph.D. in psychology and is a Licensed Professional Counselor (LPC) and a Board-Certified Registered Art Therapist (ATR-BC), licensed in the United States and currently living in the UK. Dr. Abdallah is a student of Professor Malik Badri in Islamic psychology. Besides his academic training, he has studied privately with several traditional Islamic scholars throughout the Muslim world. His clinical practice and academic research focus on approaching counseling from within an Islamic paradigm and establishing an indigenous Islamic theoretical orientation to human psychology grounded in the knowledge of the soul from the Islamic tradition.

**Abdur Rasjid Skinner** took Double Honours in Anthropology and Psychology from Durham University and then trained in Clinical Psychology at the Queen's University Belfast while also undertaking Jungian training analysis. He qualified as a clinical psychologist from QUB in 1976 and mainly worked at the consultant level in the NHS until 2015. He was a Clinical Supervisor for the Leed's University Clin. Psych. Doctoral course and lectured on both the Leeds and Sheffield University courses. He began working on Islamic Psychology in the 1970s and was a co-founder of 'Ihsaan' - an IP-based psychological therapy service. He teaches at the Cambridge Muslim College and is Visiting Professor at Karachi University and IIU Islamabad. He is a Director of the IAIP and a Fellow of the Royal Anthropological Institute.

**Ahmed Shennan** is a member of staff at Azza University College for Girls, Khartoum. Formerly, he was professor of psychology, dean of faculty of education – and head of the educational sector, vice-dean of students' affairs at the University of Gezira in Sudan. He is the founder of the Department of Applied Psychology and the Council of Counseling and Guidance at the same university. He also was Executive Director of the International Association of Muslim Psychologists (2003-2007), Head of Gezira regional division of the Sudanese Psychological Society (2005-2010), and member of the Gezira council for mental health. Ahmed was a professor of psychology at Um-al-Qura in Mecca and Bisha Universities in Saudi Arabia. He was also co-founder and Editor-in-chief of the Gezira Journal of Educational and Humanities sciences. Dr. Ahmed holds an MA (Khartoum) and a Ph.D. in psychology (Southampton) and is a student and a close friend of Professor Malik Badri. He published several articles in local, regional, and international Journals of psychology. His academic research focuses on culturally sensitive and Islamic paradigm approaches highlighting indigenous and Islamic themes contributing to human psychology.

**Aid Smajić** is an Associate Professor at the Chair of Religious Pedagogy and Religious Psychology at the Faculty of Islamic Studies (University of Sarajevo) with a bachelor's degree in psychology and Islamic Studies, an MA in Islamic Civilization, and a Doctorate in Psychology. Prof. Malik Badri supervised his MA thesis on "Behavioral Therapy in the Works of Selected Early Muslim Scholars" (2003) at the International Institute of Islamic Thought and Civilization (ISTAC). He is also a Hafiz of the Qur'an, having committed the entire Qur'an to memory. He is the author of a book on *Religiosity and Ethnic Tolerance in Bosnia and Herzegovina.* He has published research studies dealing with Muslim contributions to psychology and psychotherapy, Muslim religiosity, (inter) group dynamics and tolerance, youth value orientations, religion and research policy, work stress among Bosnian *imams*, the religious encounter with modern psychology, and Islam in Bosnia. He has supervised thesis and dissertations on topics including "Psycho-social Dimensions of Qur'anic Concept of Conflict Resolution in Selected Chapters of the Qur'an" (2017), Muslim Chaplaincy and Spiritual Counseling in Bosnian Prisons: Case Study of Tuzla Muftiluk (2019), and "The Concept of Personality in the Works of Abu Hamid al-Ghazali" (2020).

**Akbar Husain** is a Professor at the Department of Psychology, Faculty of Social Sciences, Aligarh Muslim University, Aligarh (India). Professor Husain earned the D.Litt. Degree in Psychology in 2015 for his work on *Explorations and Applications of Spirituality in Psychology*. He has over 40 years of teaching and research experience, authored five, and edited one book. Dr. Husain has published 26 research papers, theoretical articles, and book chapters in National and International Journals and Books. In recent years he has been involved in researching the standardization of the *Taqwa Scale,* Fitrah *Scale, and Idyllic Personality Inventory in* Islamic Psychology.

**Alizi Alias** is a consultant organizational psychologist with more than 20 years of working experience in academia and about two years of working experience in the industry. He had published 13 journal articles and book chapters, presented 25 conference papers, and a regular speaker/trainer in organizational psychology, positive psychology, and Islamic psychology. Alizi Alias graduated from International Islamic University Malaysia (IIUM) with a B.IRKH (Hons) and a B.HSc (Psychology) (Hons). He obtained an MSc in Applied Psychology from the University of Surrey, United Kingdom, and a Ph.D. in Industrial/Organizational Psychology from Universiti Kebangsaan Malaysia (UKM). He has taught at IIUM from 1997 to 2018 and spent nine months at the University of Gloucestershire, the UK as an academic visitor. Apart from IIUM, he had lectured on a part-time basis at UKM, Open University Malaysia, and Alif Institute, London. Besides his consultancy work, he is also currently a part-time lecturer at the University Malaysia of Computer Science and Engineering (UniMy) and Universiti Teknologi Malaysia (UTM).

**Amber Haque** is a Professor of Clinical Psychology at the Doha Institute for Graduate Studies. Previously, he was a Professor of Clinical Psychology at the UAE University in Al Ain, UAE, and earlier an Associate Professor and Head of the Department of Psychology at the International Islamic University Malaysia. Dr. Haque earned his Ph.D. in Psychology from Western Michigan University and Master's in Clinical Psychology from Eastern Michigan University. He also taught part-time at the National University of Malaysia and International University of Sarajevo, Bosnia, served as Visiting Scholar at Cornell University, Ithaca and the University of Pennsylvania in the US. He worked as a psychologist for various mental health institutions in Michigan for over 12 years, published in mental health and Islamic psychology, edited seven books, served as a board member for four, and reviewer for almost 40 international journals.

**Amin Loucif** studied psychology and is a psychotherapist with German-Algerian roots, specialized in culturally sensitive and religiously integrated techniques. Next to his classic psychological career, he is currently studying Islamic sciences. A primary goal for him is to integrate cognitive behavioral therapy with schema therapy and Islam using guidelines based on Quran, Sunna, and Al-qawaaidul-fiqhiyyah. Besides his private practice with almost exclusively Muslim clients, he initiated several information channels to remove taboos about therapy in the Muslim community. He gives lectures to educate the community and its multiplicators. With the Psychosoziales Zentrumfür Muslime (www.pzm.center), he founded a sadaqa-zakat project in 2020 to organize a professional structure for a European and mainly German-speaking audience.

**Bagus Riyono** began interested in Islamic Psychology in 1984, during his undergraduate study at Gadjah Mada University. After finishing his master's degree from Hofstra University, New York, he worked on his dissertation at UGM-Indonesia, which resulted in his work on Anchor theory, a meta-theory of motivation that put meanings and faith into perspective as motivational forces. He served as vice president of the Indonesian Islamic Psychology Association until 2015 and then the president of IAMP from 2016 until today. He runs a regular class on Islamic Psychology in the Campus Masjid called INSANI. Since 2017, he is involved in Mahad Maqasid-Indonesia, in supporting IAMP for producing Islamic-based knowledge. He has shared his theory with interested audiences in Indonesia, Japan, Germany, Netherlands, Moscow, India, Pakistan, and Sydney. In the service for IAMP, MOU was developed with many universities committed to the integration of Islam and science.

**Carrie York Al-Karam** is president of the Alkaram Institute, a nonprofit research and educational institution dedicated to advancing Islamic psychology to benefit society and improve lives. Its vision is to become the first Muslim graduate school of psychology in the United States. She is also an associate editor for APA's peer-reviewed journal *Spirituality in Clinical Practice.* Her areas of interest include Islamic psychology, spiritually integrated psychotherapy, Islamic spirituality, and virtue/character development. In addition to numerous book chapters and journal articles, her edited books are *Mental Health and Psychological Practice in the United Arab Emirates* (2015), *Islamically Integrated Psychotherapy: Uniting Faith and Professional Practice* (2018), and a children's character development book called *Maya and the Seven Limbs* (2020).

**Diana Setiyawati** is the general secretary of the International Association of Muslim Psychologists (IAMP) and the Director of Centre for Public Mental Health, Faculty of Psychology, Universitas Gadjah Mada (UGM). She began to know Islamic Psychology when she was in undergraduate level at The Faculty of Psychology UGM. She was involved in the Student's Association for Islamic Psychology. It motivated her to continue studying at the International Islamic University Malaysia to directly study from Professor Malik Badri. In her professional career, she focused on public mental health, reflected on her Ph.D. thesis at The University of Melbourne. She believes that comprehensive mental health can be achieved by strengthening family, school-based mental health systems, and primary mental health care. Developing psychotherapy that incorporates belief and culture and investigating help-seeking behavior in Muslim mental health is among her research interests.

**Hamid Rafiei-Honar** is Assistant Professor of the *Islamic Sciences and Culture Academy*, Former Vice President of the *Islamic Psychology Association* (*IPA*) in Iran. He graduated from *Hawzah Elmiyyeh of Qom* (Islamic Theological Seminary in Qom, Iran) in the fields of *Fiqh* & *Usul* of *Fiqh* (Methodology of *Ijtihad*), BA in Psychology and Islamic Studies, MA in Clinical Psychology, PhD. in General Psychology from *Imam Khomeini Education and Research Institute (IKERI)*, Iran. He has authored three books and 30 articles in Islamic Psychology, Psychotherapy, & Psychometrics. He has also supervised 40 treatises on developing Islamic scales and psych-education interventions, especially in self-control and self-regulation.

**Hanan Dover** is an accomplished Clinical and Forensic Psychologist who had established one of the most successful psychology clinics that serve the culturally and linguistic communities of Western Sydney, Psychcentral. She is the Vice-President of the International Association of Muslim Psychologists, a Full Member of the Australian Psychological Society (APS), and the College of Clinical and Forensic Psychologists within the APS. Hanan is also an Executive Member of the Psychology from an Islamic Perspective Interest Group of the APS and Convener of the Muslim Mental Health Professionals Network in Sydney. Hanan has established herself as one of the most energetic and resourceful leaders of the Australian Muslim community. Driven by her passion for social justice and community-based empowerment with a deep sense of responsibility, Hanan has worked tirelessly to advocate the position of Australian Muslims. She is in the process of completing a unique self-help book designed for readers interested in the integration of strategies that incorporate modern psychological sciences and Islamic worldviews.

**Ibrahim Rüschoff** studied education and medicine and is a psychiatrist and psychotherapist. After a long clinical career as a senior psychiatric physician, he has been running his practice with almost exclusively Muslim patients since 2007, working with psychoanalytic concepts. His publication list includes books and papers on Muslim Mental Health and, in recent years, writings on IP. With a working group of German Muslim psychotherapists, he strives to integrate Islamic principles into psychotherapy for Muslims and develop the conception of the human being and the therapeutic relationship as the most critical elements of successful therapy from an Islamic perspective. The aim is to implement Islamically-integrated psychotherapy in the care system in Germany.

**Jibril I. M Handuleh** is a psychiatry resident at Saint Paul's Hospital Millennium Medical College in Addis Ababa, Ethiopia, and a former faculty member in public mental health at Amoud University school of Medicine Borama, Somalia. He has an academic interest in transcultural psychiatry, studying the interplay between culture, mental health, and spirituality, focusing on Islamic psychological interventions among Somali people. He has an interest in both Somalis in East Africa and the wider diaspora. He is active with the transcultural group at the Royal College of Psychiatrists and the Society of Study of psychiatry and North American culture.

**Juraida Latif** holds a master's degree in Organisational Psychology from the University of the Witwatersrand. She is the director of The South African Institute of Islamically Integrated Wellness, an organization created to advance the adoption, education, and practice of Islamic Psychology Counselling and overall wellness adopting Quranic and Prophetic based applications such as Tibb, Hijama, Ruqya-Ash-Shariah. Juraida has over 12 years of consulting and counseling experience working with primarily Muslim clients on a wide range of issues and incorporates Ruqya-ash-Shariah and Sunnah interventions into therapeutic practice. Juraida also works as a lecturer and supervisor at the Northwest University (SA) for nine years.

**Khalid Elzamzamy** is currently serving as a Fellow in Child and Adolescent Psychiatry at Hamad Medical Corporation, Qatar. He holds a master's degree in Islamic Studies from Hamad Bin Khalifa University, Qatar. He serves as a Researcher with the Khalil School of Islamic Psychology & Research, USA, and the Family and Youth Institute, USA. His research interests include the contemporary exploration of the Muslim intellectual, psychological heritage, Islamic ethics in clinical practice, psychiatric education, and the intersection between suicide, mental health, and religion.

**Masood Azarbayejani is a** Professor of the *Research Institute of HAWZAH and UNIVERSITY (RIHU)*, Former President of the *Islamic Psychology Association (IPA)* in Iran. He graduated from *Hawzah Elmiyyeh of Qom* in *Fiqh, Tafsir*, Philosophy, and Mysticism. MA in Islamic Theology, MA in Clinical Psychology, & PhD. in Philosophy of Religion from *RIHU*, Iran. He has authored 15 books and 50 articles in Psychology of Religion and Spirituality, Islamic Psychology, Philosophy of Psychology, and Islamic Ethics and Education. He has also supervised 50 master's and doctoral dissertations and has contributed to developing three educational programs in psychology and Islam.

**Mohamed El Mahdi** is Professor of Psychiatry and Ex-President of the Psychiatry Department, Al-Azhar University.

**Muhammad Tahir Khalily** is Professor of Psychology and Vice President Academics in International Islamic University Islamabad (IIUI), Pakistan. He has more than thirty years of national and international teaching, research, clinical, supervisory, academic, administrative, and service development experience. He did Masters in Drug Addiction and Alcohol Treatment Policy from the addiction study center, Trinity College Dublin, and a post-doctoral research fellowship from the University of Edinburgh, UK. His special interest is the rediscovering of religious perspective in therapeutic approaches and their integration in line with the Quran and Sunnah's teaching. He is the principal author of three books and a study report. He also teaches Muslim/Islamic psychology to master's and Ph.D. students at IIUI and has successfully supervised many research projects published in international journals.

**Paul Kaplick** has a B.Sc. in clinical psychology and M.Sc. in cognitive neuroscience. He is currently training as a clinical neuropsychologist in a neurological rehabilitation facility in Germany's Rhine-Main area. He has co-authored various papers on preclinical models of stress-related disorders. He enjoys blending cognitive psychology and neuroscience with concepts, theories, and methods that have emerged in cultural and intellectual traditions other than the West. He is executive chairman of the Islamic Association of Social and Educational Professions (IASE), the leading Muslim Mental Health organization in Germany, and heads its Islam and Psychology research group. He consults for several institutions such as the Alkaram Institute, the Stanford Muslims and Mental Health Laboratory, the Islamic Psychology Professionals Association (IPPA) London, and the journal Spiritual Care. When off work, Paul loves walking the Rheingau hillsides with his wife and son.

**Roaa Moustafa Ahmed** completed her BA in Psychology from Qatar University. Her graduation project was on the Diagnostic compatibility of projective tests on a sample of children in the Qatari community. She is interested in clinical psychology and has completed several postgraduate training courses in Qatar, Saudi Arabia, and Egypt. Roaa has extensive experience working with children and teenagers at various community organizations and primary and secondary international schools in Doha, including Al Jazeera Academy. Recently, she has developed an interest in the emerging field of Islamic psychology (IP).

**Saleh Ibrahim Al Sanie** is a Professor of Psychology at Islamic University, KSA. He has published eight books and 25 research papers in scientific journals, seminars, and conferences and supervised many master's and doctoral dissertations in Saudi and Islamic universities. He was actively involved in the ruling on many promotions of professors from Saudi and Arab universities and many research and studies for Saudi and Arab university journals. He holds membership in several international, Arab, and local psychological societies.

**Salisu Shehu** is a Professor of Educational Psychology in the Department of Education, Bayero University, Kano, Nigeria. He was the Dean of the School of Continuing Education for eight years and a University Senate and Governing

Council member. Presently he is Director of the Centre of Islamic Civilization and Interfaith Dialogue in the University and the National Coordinator of the Nigerian Office of the IIIT in Kano-Nigeria. He has published several books and papers and presented lectures on education, religion, society, social justice, leadership, and governance from Islamic Perspective. He is presently a member of two different Planning and Implementation Committees for establishing two Islamic Universities in Nigeria and involved in various religious activities at organizational and institutional levels at State and National levels. He is also Deputy Secretary-General of the Nigerian Supreme Council for Islamic Affairs, a member of the Board of Trustees of the International Islamic Relief Organization (Nigeria Office), Executive Secretary, Islamic Forum of Nigeria, Deputy Chairman, Board of Trustees, Alhassan Ibrahim Dawanau College of Health Sciences and Technology, Kano. At the community level also, he is a member of the Board of Trustees of various schools, Islamic colleges, and institutions.

**Selvira Draganovic** is an Associate Professor of Psychology at the International University of Sarajevo, Bosnia, and Herzegovina. She teaches psychopathology, trauma psychology, health psychology, clinical psychopathology, and positive psychology. She is a psychology graduate of the International Islamic University of Malaysia with a minor in Islamic Revealed Knowledge and Heritage. Selvira is also Europe accredited EMDR therapist practicing therapy for over a decade. While working with Muslim clients, she is sensitive to their spirituality and religious needs and applies the Islamic psychology approach and principles in the treatment process. She is interested in researching the role of religious practices in mental health and wellbeing.

**Shaakirah Dockrat Boda** holds a master's degree from the University of the Witwatersrand and is the Director of The South African Institute of Islamically Integrated Wellness, and is also the founder of Nahwa Consulting and Counselling. She is a qualified and registered Industrial Psychologist with the (HPCSA) and a practicing Islamic Psychology Practitioner, having completed courses in Istanbul (Turkey) and Cambridge (UK). She is registered as an Associate Fellow with the International Association of Islamic Psychology (IAIP). She has organizational development experience in the pharmaceutical, legal, healthcare, and mining sectors in South Africa. She has over 12 years of experience working with Muslim clients on a wide range of therapeutic issues and has co-developed manuals and co-presents pre-and post-marital workshops from an Islamic Psychology perspective.

**Suleyman Derin** is a professor in the Department of Sufism at the Marmara University, Istanbul. He teaches Ghazali, Rumi, and other Sufis from a psychological perspective and in an interdisciplinary way. He also has a weekly radio program where he hosts academicians, psychologists, and psychiatrists from Turkey and abroad to supply psychology with spiritual content. He has participated in many international symposiums, presenting papers on individual Sufis and their understanding of the human psyche.

**Tamkeen Saleem** is an Assistant Professor of Psychology at International Islamic University Islamabad (IIUI), Pakistan. She developed the IP syllabus for basic and advanced level IP courses for IIUI and served as conference organizer and secretary for several international IP-related conferences. Her research interests include mental health, religiosity, and Islamic psychology. Her research interest is in integrating Islamic principles in forgiveness therapy, anger, depression, stress, and anxiety. She has supervised research projects in areas including, Comparison of the Diagnostic Criteria of Depression in DSM-5 with Assertions of Abu Zayd Al Balkhi, Religiosity and Death Anxiety in Muslim Dars Attendees, Religiously Integrated Enright Model of Forgiveness Therapy, and Islamic Integrated Art Therapy. She has also presented papers on "Surah Al-Rahman Reduces Cortisol Level: A Biomarker of Stress in Medical Students" and Efficacy of Religiously Integrated Forgiveness Therapy among Individuals with Musculoskeletal Pain in Pakistan.

**Taha Burak Toprak** is a lecturer at the Ibn Haldun and Hasan Kalyoncu University. He is a diplomate cognitive psychotherapist from the Academy of Cognitive and Behavioral Therapy and one of the founders and the director of Psychology in Islamic Thought Platform (Turkey). He lectures on the History of Psychology with an emphasis on Islamic heritage and developed a new cognitive psychoeducation model with Islamic heritage on cognition. He transformed his work into practice and research in OCD patients with an empirical method and presented it at the World OCD Congress and has concentrated on the theoretical and practical contributions of Islamic thought on the limitations of modern psychotherapy. He has presented his model and empirical works on international platforms and gave seminars on how fiqh (Islamic jurisprudence) and Sufi traditions explain modern psychopathologies. Toprak and his colleagues compiled the discussions in the field into a book on Islam, Psychology, and Psychotherapy and working on a new psycho-ontological model of Islamic heritage.

**Walid Hassan** is a consultant and lecturer of psychiatry at Ain Shams University in Egypt and a psychiatrist at the Ministry of Health Oman. He completed his MSc degree at the Institute of Psychiatry, Ain Shams University. Dr. Hassan joined advanced training on substance abuse treatment and education at Hubert Humphrey Fellowship at Virginia Commonwealth University, completed his Ph.D. / MD at Ain Shams University in 2015. As faculty/lecturer in Ain

Shams University, trainer at Egyptian National Mental health consortium, and a faculty Oman Medical Specialty Board, he has been teaching mental health and behavioral change management to diverse groups, including psychiatrists and physicians, nurses, psychologists, and social workers.

www.ingramcontent.com/pod-product-compliance
Lightning Source LLC
Chambersburg PA
CBHW020240030426
42336CB00010B/549

* 9 7 8 1 7 3 7 2 8 1 6 0 3 *